Louise Porter lectures in the School of Special Education and Disability Studies at Flinders University in South Australia and is the author of *Young Children's Behaviour* and *Student Behaviour*. She is a child and clinical psychologist with teacher training and a Masters degree in gifted education as well as many years' experience working with children.

Gifted young children

A guide for teachers and parents

Louise Porter

OPEN UNIVERSITY PRESS

Buckingham

Open University Press
Celtic Court
22 Ballmoor
Buckingham
MK18 1XW

Email: enquiries@openup.co.uk
World wide web: http://www.openup.co.uk

First published 1999

A catalogue of this book is available from the British Library.

ISBN 0 335 20552 6

Printed and bound in Singapore.

*For my readers: may this book be a step on your journey
of acknowledging your own talents.*

*For the children in our care: may their journey be a little
easier as a result of our understanding.*

And for Murray (1931–1998)
*who did not recognise his own special talents
as a cherished friend and father.*

CONTENTS

CONTENTS

Figures

TABLES

ACKNOWLEDGMENTS

I am grateful to Maria McCann, who guided my tour of the literature on gifted education; to Dr Phillip Slee, who generously supplied me with comprehensive references on stress in children and assisted in my exploration of that vast literature; and to Jacqui Davenport, librarian, for her willing and reliable assistance with obtaining reference material from near and far.

1

A RATIONALE FOR
GIFTED EDUCATION

Some educationalists have included able pupils in the category of newly disadvantaged groups. Reasons for this include the lack of legislation concerning the needs and rights of able pupils, the lack of government guidance on effective provision for able pupils at a time when guidance in other areas is extensive, and the lack of nominated funding for staff training or school-based development work.

Eyre (1997: 1)

KEY POINTS

- There are two rationales for the provision of special education to gifted children. The first, the 'national resources' rationale, favours special provisions for gifted children so that they can grow up to contribute in significant ways to society. Young gifted children receive little attention under this rationale because, at an early age, it is not certain which of them will grow up to contribute exceptionally to society.
- The second is the 'special education' rationale, which focuses on gifted children's personal needs in the present. Even here, gifted young children are often neglected in the erroneous belief that they are too young to need any special provisions.
- In light of criticisms of segregated gifted education programs and the fact that these are almost non-existent in the early childhood years, a case for mainstreamed gifted education is suggested and briefly described.

ADVOCATES FOR GIFTED EDUCATION

Given that gifted children are seen by many to have already a huge learning advantage, it is often assumed that there is no need for a special focus on gifted learners within the education system. Some of the reluctance to focus on gifted learners may be driven by a distrust of intellectuals. Whether writers are talking of American (Gallagher 1991b), British (Eyre 1997), Australian (Bailey 1998; Wilson 1996) or New Zealand (Fraser 1996) cultures, the message is the same: we value the products of high achievers but denigrate 'bookishness'. Perhaps the pioneer history of most of these countries is the cause, where brawn—not brains—was necessary to carve out a new civilisation in a foreign land (Wilson 1996). Added to that, Australia's penal history generated a suspicion of authority and the intellectuals who made and carried out official policies (Wilson 1996). This history means that Australians use words such as 'intellectual' or 'precocious' as terms of derision (Christie 1995) and, although willing to allocate extra money for elite sports training programs, there is an unwillingness to give it for elite intellectual training (Gross 1993a).

Within this pervasive cultural scepticism, advocates for gifted education offer two main rationales for providing special services to gifted children: the national resources and the special education rationale (Harrison 1995).

The national resources rationale

According to the national resources rationale, the main goal of gifted education is to ensure that gifted children realise their potential so that ultimately they will contribute to society in some exceptional way. The argument goes that the community should invest in gifted education so that society benefits from gifted individuals' achievements as adults.

This sounds fine, as far as it goes. However, some advocates of gifted education make inflated claims for gifted individuals' contribution to society and, in their hyperbole, do their cause a disservice. One such claim is that gifted children will become leaders in their chosen disciplines. Research and common sense tell us otherwise. This is because, as discussed in chapter 3, it takes more than ability alone to be successful: success requires a fortuitous blend of ability, hard work, good chance, and advantageous social circumstances (Freeman 1998a; Pendarvis & Howley 1996; Winner 1996). This commonsense appreciation is confirmed by both Terman's longitudinal study of gifted children (which has followed gifted children from 1920 until the present) and the Hunter College Elementary School sample: rather than becoming world leaders,

2

participants in these studies tended to become well-rounded and well-adjusted professional adults (Bailey 1998; Feldman 1984; Freeman 1995a, 1998a; Gallagher 1996; Hastorf 1997; Sears 1977; Subotnik et al. 1989; Winner 1996).

A second claim is that gifted children's advanced problem-solving abilities enable them to solve moral dilemmas and, in turn, to become moral guardians of society. This assertion leads to a call for moral education for gifted children, which in my opinion, is dangerously close to the concept of Galton and others a century ago that equated intellectual 'superiority' with moral superiority (see Pendarvis & Howley 1996). I believe that moral education (in the sense of learning *how* to think rather than *what* to think) is a requirement for all children—not just those whose development is advanced.

The special education rationale

The special education approach (Harrison 1995) is less utilitarian than the national resources rationale: the view is that if for any reason children are at risk of not profiting optimally from the education system, then the system needs to make some adjustments so that their needs are more adequately met (Pendarvis & Howley 1996). Advocates of this view believe the following.

- There are individuals whose learning capacity and confidence differ from the average.
- Children with atypical learning patterns will have additional needs to children whose development is typical for their age.
- There is no debate that we must identify—and identify early—children whose learning capacities fall significantly below the average, so that we are able to plan a curriculum that is more likely to meet their atypical needs. The same can be said, then, for children whose skills are significantly above the average—that is, those whom we call 'gifted'.
- Although gifted children are advantaged in that they can learn more easily than most, they are still children and need to be taught how to learn (Braggett 1994). As Webb et al. (1991: 10) observe: 'Although gifted students possess exceptional capabilities, most cannot excel without assistance.'
- Early childhood professionals require a thorough knowledge of child development, in order to be able to recognise departures from the norm—not just in intellectual terms, but socially and emotionally as well.
- Having identified children whose needs are not being met, we must set about providing a program that more routinely provides what

they require. This is true for all children, whatever the need, not just for those whom we recognise as having advanced development.

- We should meet these needs for the children's own sake, not just to ensure that they ultimately contribute to society (Corrigan 1994). The end result might be that better-adjusted individuals contribute more to society, but this is a secondary aim (Renzulli 1986). Therefore, the special education approach treasures children for being themselves rather than for what they can do (Corrigan 1994).

Those who hold the special education view contend that gifted children have as much right to have their needs met as other children, but are no *more* deserving than anyone else (Peterson 1993). Thus, advocacy for gifted education becomes advocacy for individualised education for all children, not for better treatment of the gifted. Eyre (1997) is clear about this: 'It is the duty of every school to ensure that no child's needs are overlooked because of the needs of others' (p. 90) and 'time for the most able should not be achieved at the expense of other pupils' (p. 91). In short, many children have particular needs, and gifted children are just one group about whom we need to be aware.

BUT IS IT NECESSARY TO START SO YOUNG?

Special provisions for gifted children are seldom available prior to the middle primary (elementary) school years (Gillman & Hansen 1987). Despite ample evidence of the efficacy of early provisions for educationally disadvantaged children, with the implication that this can apply to gifted children as well, these children are still disadvantaged, because they are both young *and* gifted: a case of double jeopardy.

There is a particular reluctance to label young children in any way, and the gifted label is no exception (at any age). As Fraser (1996) sees it, our reluctance is caused by more than just concerns about the effects of labelling on young children (an issue which I address in chapter 13)— it is also a remnant of our Victorian heritage, with its attitude that children should be seen and not heard. This heritage means that we do not value children in general and 'tall poppies' in particular, and so it discourages children from being articulate and independent thinkers. Even the word 'precocious'—which simply means 'advanced for age'—is used pejoratively and is regarded as undesirable.

Some people fear that early identification will make gifted children conceited or pompous, or will isolate them from peers (Gross 1993a; Mares 1991). However, as Mares (1991: 12) observes: 'This is sheer nonsense. The child is gifted, whether she is identified or not.'

Another source of our reluctance to label young children arises from a deep concern for their welfare. Many are reluctant to see children who have been identified as gifted 'hot-housed' to the point where they lose interest in their special talent, are withdrawn from social and playful contact with other children, and come to define themselves as valuable only because of their talent (Mares 1991). This, however, is not a fault with identification but with misusing assessment information.

Finally, young children can be disadvantaged because, even if the needs of gifted children within the school system are acknowledged, there is a myth that 'little people have little feelings' (Fields & Boesser 1998) and, therefore, that young children are too young to experience any ill-effects from being different from their peers.

RATIONALE FOR A FOCUS ON YOUNG CHILDREN

The concerns listed above lead to an underservicing of young gifted children compared with their older counterparts (Karnes et al. 1985). Although these issues certainly imply that we must be careful when serving gifted young children, they do not negate the need for special provisions for them. The following points are justifications for a focus on gifted children during their early years.

- High-quality early childhood programs have crucial benefits for children's development and for their attitudes to learning and to themselves as learners (Clark 1997; Field 1991; Gallagher 1988; Phillips & Howes 1987; Sylva 1994). The brain is most malleable in the first five years, and so early childhood is a critical period for facilitating children's development (Clark 1997; Smutny et al. 1989).
- There are few studies of the effectiveness of early enrichment for gifted learners (Karnes & Johnson 1991). However, one study (Fowler et al. 1995) offered early language-enrichment training to parents of children aged 3 to 24 months. The researchers found that, whereas 4.8% of children whose parents were university-educated could be expected to be gifted, a massive 68% of these children who also received early enrichment were later identified to be gifted. Even more astonishing is the finding that, whereas only 0.001% of children could be expected to be gifted when their parents did not complete high school, 31% of those children (many from minority cultures) who received early enrichment training were later defined as gifted. Another, meta-analytic study concluded that school-based enrichment programs make most difference to children's achievement in their first few years of school (Vaughn et al. 1991). Together with our knowledge of the benefits of early intervention with children who have disabilities, such studies indicate that early

5

enrichment can promote the development of young children's learning capacities.

- Gifted children are aware from as early as 2 years of age that they are different from their age mates. They need an explanation for this so that they do not assume that there is something wrong with them.
- Compared with their older counterparts, gifted young children have access to a restricted age range of peers and so are likely to be lonelier during their early childhood years than later in life (Whitmore 1980).
- Underachievement can be identified in the earliest years of school, in which case it seems obvious that prevention of underachievement should begin prior to this—namely, in the preschool years, when children's attitudes to learning are most malleable (Karnes & Johnson 1991; Karnes et al. 1985; Wolfle 1990).
- Early childhood is the time when parents are most likely to encounter for the first time the notion that their child has exceptional needs (Smutny et al. 1997). In these early years, parents may need some additional information to maintain confidence in their own ability to satisfy these needs (Creel & Karnes 1988) (see chapter 13). Parents' confidence and subsequent behaviour is likely, in turn, to enhance their children's confidence in themselves as learners (Windecker-Nelson et al. 1997).

A focus on giftedness during children's earliest years does *not* mean hot-housing children such that they are force-fed information in advance of their interests. As Smutny et al. (1989) observe, pumping children full of information is *not* the same as encouraging them to develop their own special gifts and abilities. Hot-housing promotes adults' ambitions; gifted education seeks to foster the skills and interests of the children themselves.

THE DETRACTORS

A number of objections to gifted education have been raised. These merit some close scrutiny as the resulting debate can help us to clarify our reasons for selecting certain courses of action for gifted young children.

The 'everyone is gifted' contention

One objection to gifted education is that all children are gifted and so they all require or deserve special provisions. While few would disagree that all children are special and all have individual strengths, it cannot be true that all are 'above average' in their speed of development: to claim so is arithmetically absurd (Gross 1993a).

This claim arises from politics rather than psychology, driven by a distaste for the higher status that is given to academic giftedness (although many Western cultures simultaneously discourage individual high achievement, as already discussed). The psychological view accepts that giftedness is a reality in that there *are* individual differences in ability (Gallagher 1996; Pyryt 1996); the politics arises when we choose to regard these differences as significant and of differing worth (Sapon-Shevin 1994, 1996b). The tension between the psychological and political aspects of the label 'gifted' can be overcome when we acknowledge that people have differing abilities, while accepting that they have equal worth.

Priorities and resource allocation

Another source of opposition to gifted education comes from those who acknowledge that gifted children have particular needs, but claim that these needs are not as pressing as those of children with learning difficulties. This argument states that society's scarce resources have to be allocated to the most needy, and that gifted children do not qualify.

Sapon-Shevin (1994) contends that the resources used for gifted education are inequitable and represent favouritism. However, US reports tell us that gifted education receives 2 cents out of every $100 that is spent on education—that is, 0.02% of the education budget (Sternberg 1996) or just $1 per gifted child per year (Ford et al. 1993). In Australia, $6.60 was allocated for each gifted child for each of the three years between 1993 and 1995, which compares with the almost $600 each that is allocated to Olympic divers (Wilson 1996). Ford and colleagues thus conclude that Sapon-Shevin is right to argue that the resources used for gifted education are inequitable, but contend that they represent neglect, not favouritism.

Segregated gifted programs

Segregated programs for gifted children in early childhood are rare indeed (Hall 1993; Kitano 1982; Wolfle 1990). Even in the school sector, segregated programs are uncommon especially outside the US; yet our mainly US-based gifted education literature often uses the term 'gifted education' synonymously with segregated programs.

This is unfortunate as it is almost asking for the criticisms which I am about to summarise. The first of these criticisms is that segregated programs give extra status and privileges to children who are already advantaged and for whom educational failure would not be tolerated

(Sapon-Shevin 1996a). This claim is supported by the well-known under-representation of children from minority cultures in segregated gifted programs and rests on the notion of democracy, which demands that everyone be given equal opportunities (Price 1970, in Gross 1993a). However, the notion of democracy is also invoked in defence of gifted education: 'the equal right to develop . . . should not be confused with a right to equal development' (Price 1970, in Gross 1993a: 30). Although children have an equal right to access *appropriate* educational experiences, justice does not demand that these experiences be the *same* for all children (Benbow 1992; Strike 1983).

A second philosophical objection is that the class and school 'community' is disrupted when children are singled out for particular treatment and, in a more practical vein, that teachers and children who remain in the regular classroom must alter their program so that the absent children do not miss anything significant (Sapon-Shevin 1990, 1994, 1996a, 1996b). These are legitimate concerns which, while not yet adequately researched, are nevertheless not easily dismissed (Belcastro 1987; Borland, 1996a, 1996b).

A third criticism is that segregated gifted education perpetuates a special educational approach in which students with additional needs are regarded as deviants and are withdrawn from the mainstream, thus impeding reform of the school conditions that bring about these children's lack of success in regular classes (Pugach 1988; Sapon-Shevin 1996b). A related claim is that regular teachers are de-skilled by the implication that they cannot adequately cater for atypical learners (Delisle 1994c; Sapon-Shevin 1994, 1996b). Some counter this with the claim that teachers cannot be expected to have expertise in all of the specialised techniques that are needed to teach all atypical children (Gallagher 1996; Stephens 1988); without minimising the challenges of providing for all children in the one setting, Sapon-Shevin (1996a) claims that this segregationist view suffers from a lack of vision.

Just as critics decry gifted education's segregating methods, so too do some of its advocates. Even the advocates recognise that segregated programs are subjected to insufficient scrutiny or evaluation, with the result that many are mediocre and ill-serve the children whom they are designed to help: many involve trivial or irrelevant activities which lack a clear rationale and are not coordinated with the regular curriculum (Belcastro 1987; Davis & Rimm 1998; Ford et al. 1993; Irvine 1991; Vaughn et al. 1991). Still other criticisms come from parents, who want more continuous enrichment (Taplin & White 1998) because 'their children are gifted all of the time, not just during pull-out time' (Vestal 1993: 10).

A PROPOSED RESOLUTION

There are two possible resolutions to the above objections. The first is based on a recognition that segregated programs do indeed neglect already disadvantaged children. Despite this realisation, gifted education advocates claim that this neglect does not imply that we should cease doing what we do well: it would be unfair to deny gifted children an appropriate and meaningful education on the grounds that not everyone who is eligible receives it (Borland 1996b; Borland & Wright 1994; Braggett 1992; Gallagher 1996; Pendarvis & Howley 1996). Furthermore, if gifted provisions were withdrawn, wealthy parents could secure enriching experiences privately, while poorer children who were gifted would receive even less than they do now (Borland 1996b). Instead of disbanding segregated programs therefore, advocates contend that we should get better at what we do. Sapon-Shevin (1996a: 196) dismisses this suggestion with the scornful retort of Calvin Coolidge: 'There is no right way to do the wrong thing.'

The alternative and, to my mind, the only possible resolution is based on the fact that only a small minority of advanced school-aged learners are ever selected for gifted programs (where these exist at all); the majority remain in mainstream settings (Archambault et al. 1993; Delisle 1994c; Moltzen 1998; Westberg et al. 1997). This reality is even more apparent through the early childhood years and into middle primary (elementary) school. The conclusion, then, is that since most gifted children are already in mainstream settings, this is where we must direct our efforts: to improving those settings so that they more adequately meet the needs of all children.

I am not alone in holding this view (see Delisle 1994c; Moltzen 1998) and I realise that it is easier to defend for children in their early years rather than later in their schooling, for a number of reasons. First, proportionally there is a narrower range of ability levels in a group of very young children compared with older children. When 4-year-olds are learning 50% faster than usual, they are still functioning only two years ahead of their actual age; but the gap between actual and mental age widens as children get older, creating a greater disparity in the developmental levels within a group of older children. Second, there simply is nowhere else to place gifted young children: they cannot yet go to school (even local authorities that allow early entry to school still have a lower age limit) and there are virtually no early childhood gifted programs.

Third, early childhood centres are inherently child-focused and have a strong history of inclusion of children with atypical development. This is assisted by the fundamental belief that the environment makes a difference to children's achievement levels, which is consistent with more recent notions of giftedness—namely, that it unfolds in response to environmental stimulation. (This is not to deny the role of heredity in shaping a person's intellectual potential but to assert that both heredity and environment contribute to a child's ultimate development. Tannenbaum [1992, in Wilson 1996] says that the relationship is like the sound of two hands clapping: it is hard to tell which hand is making the louder sound.)

For these reasons, gifted education for the very young has and will continue to be—and I believe *should* be—conducted within their regular setting, albeit not always with age peers but for some of the time alongside intellectual peers. (See the discussion in chapter 10 on acceleration.)

EARLY CHILDHOOD GIFTED EDUCATION

Two features make mainstreamed gifted programming a natural extension of early years care and education. The first is early childhood's assessment practices. Whereas in the school sector, standardised testing is a key instrument for assessment (particularly in the US), early childhood testing is less commonly used (Barbour 1992), partly because it is known to be less reliable at younger ages. The early childhood sector thus has a sound history of relying on more authentic and naturalistic assessment (Barbour & Shaklee 1998). This lends itself readily to the practice of assessing not by contrived measures but by providing curricula that allow children's abilities and interests to emerge (Vialle 1997).

Naturalistic assessment means that identification will not be the first task of gifted early childhood education, whereby a select few children are singled out to receive an enriching program. Instead, all children will be exposed to open-ended activities in a wide range of content domains and will engage with the curriculum at their own level. Subsequent programming can respond to their level of participation in order to develop the talents that emerge (Braggett 1992). In this way all children will extend their skills (although only some of them will come to function at significantly advanced levels and so could be said to be gifted).

This naturalistic approach to programming is empowering for caregivers and teachers because they already know how to design developmentally appropriate programs: the same principles will apply for gifted children, although the program content may differ at times, according to the children's readiness.

CONCLUSION

Rather than being a preparation for 'serious' education, early childhood centres and the first years of school provide an education in themselves (Gillman & Hansen 1987). Early childhood centres are not just a downward extension of the school system: they are uniquely equipped to cater for children with a broad range of developmental levels and thus to offer gifted children appropriate programming in a naturalistic setting.

But this is not to say that caregivers and teachers can meet young gifted children's needs naturally. If we are going to charge them with this responsibility, we must equip and support them to do so through some additional training (Christie 1995; Feldhusen 1985, 1997; Hansen & Feldhusen 1994; Moltzen 1998; Reis & Purcell 1993; Reis & Westberg 1994; Van Tassel-Baska 1995).

Early childhood teachers will also need to come to grips with a dilemma of the 1990s—namely, that the children who enter preschools today are not the same as they were a generation ago. In Australia, around half of the population's under 5-year-olds attend child care (Butterworth 1991), with many attending full-time. Some children spend as long as 12 000 hours in child-care centres, which is only 500 hours less than they will spend in their thirteen years of primary (elementary) and secondary schooling (National Childcare Accreditation Council 1993).

Similar trends towards centre-based care are occurring in other countries. This fact makes child care the main educational setting for many young children and so charges caregivers with the responsibility to educate as well as to care; it also means that entrants to preschools nowadays have often 'been there and done that': they have already experienced many of the preschool activities on offer, either in centre-based care or at home as a result of the availability of affordable, commercially-produced educational toys and activities. At the same time, early childhood professionals' detailed knowledge of child development, which is an asset in most respects, can set a ceiling on our expectations of children's abilities as dictated by their ages. Thus, it is probably safe to conclude that some children may not find preschool sufficiently challenging; it is almost certain that children whose development is advanced may already have learned most of what is on offer, especially when they come to preschool having profited from extensive prior learning opportunities.

Research tells us that when centres and schools expand their provisions for their more able children, overall provisions improve (Eyre 1997). The challenge is how to advance children's skills beyond entry level without imposing on such young children the structured teaching that is employed with older children.

SUGGESTED FURTHER READING

For a succinct overview of the key issues pertaining to gifted education, I recommend Freeman, J. 1998 *Educating the very able: current international research* Office for Standards in Education, London.

DISCUSSION QUESTIONS

1. Is there a difference between searching for gifted children and identifying children's needs as they surface during children's engagement with the curriculum? If so, what does this imply for practice?

2. What is your response to the series of statements which I put forward on pp. 5–6 as a rationale for early years gifted education?

3. Can you see any disadvantages of educating gifted young children in mainstream settings? If so, what can be done to overcome these difficulties?

THE MEANING OF GIFTEDNESS

If the gates to excellence are opened and closed only as a function of the abilities typically considered, we run the risk of . . . closing these gates on some of the most able children, who will be blocked from making the contributions that they potentially could make.

Sternberg & Clinkenbeard (1995: 255–6)

KEY POINTS

- Many definitions of giftedness have been proposed. They vary according to whether they are conservative or liberal; are single- or multi-dimensional; and focus on potential or performances.
- Part of the reason for the variation in definitions is that their advocates are searching for one 'true' definition when manifestations of giftedness will differ across time and cultures.
- Thus, it is unlikely that a single definition of giftedness will receive unanimous endorsement. Nevertheless, the breadth of definitions can contribute to a comprehensive view of giftedness and suggest avenues for future research.

DEFINITIONS OF GIFTEDNESS

As Davis and Rimm (1998: 17) observe: 'Defining *gifted* and *talented* is both an important and complicated matter.' Our definition has implications for whom we identify as being gifted, and for our programming or curricular decisions. The resulting label we apply to children can have both positive and negative effects on their self-esteem, self-expectations and family and peer relationships (Davis & Rimm 1998).

Yet the literature on giftedness yields some contradictory definitions. This lack of clarity means that the concept of giftedness is difficult to defend because it is 'defined too loosely while being measured too restrictively' (Gagné 1995: 104). This is perhaps inevitable because the skills that are regarded as most valuable will differ across time and between societies (McAlpine 1996). Therefore, our definition must be sensitive to and will depend on these contexts (Borland 1990).

Reflecting on the diversity of definitions, McAlpine (1996) points out that definitions differ according to whether they are conservative or liberal, are single- or multi-dimensional, and focus on potential or performance.

Conservative versus liberal. Conservative definitions tend to restrict the areas included in the gifted category or how many people will be regarded as gifted (Renzulli 1986)—say, the top 5% on a given ability measure. These definitions use a single criterion, such as high intelligence (as measured by an IQ test), to define giftedness. Liberal definitions, in contrast, observe that there are no discernible differences in productivity between the top 3–5% and the 10–15% who fall just below that IQ level, and so include up to 15–20% of the population in the gifted category (Reis & Renzulli 1982; Renzulli 1982).

Single- versus multi-dimensional. Some definitions focus on achievements within the academic domain only, while others include achievements in a number of domains. The more dimensions a definition embraces, the more liberal the definition is likely to be. The push for an inclusive definition reflects a valid desire to avoid excluding individuals who truly are gifted. At the same time there is a recognition that, although the notion of giftedness needs to be broadened, it cannot become so broad that everyone is regarded as gifted—that is, exceptional—as exceptionality would then *be* the norm (Runco 1993).

Potential versus performance. Some definitions require evidence of ability; others include underachieving children within the gifted category, despite the fact that they are not demonstrating remarkable abilities in everyday situations.

Ultimately, as Sternberg and Davidson (1986: 3) observe: 'Giftedness is something we invent, not something we discover: it is what one society or another wants it to be.' We construct the category of 'giftedness' statistically by choosing where to place the demarcation between 'giftedness' and average abilities. This decision is entirely arbitrary (Birch

1984), and probably has as much to do with how many resources are available for addressing advanced learners as it has to do with any characteristics that distinguish gifted from average learners. In other words, our definition is political as well as psychological (Sapon-Shevin 1994). Therefore, we must temper our judgments about children's abilities and needs with an awareness of the limitations of the constructs and tools that guide our practice.

THE CONCEPT OF INTELLIGENCE

Given that education is mainly concerned with imparting academic skills, the field of gifted education has focused largely on intellectual giftedness. Inevitably, then, this emphasis leads to an elucidation of the concept of intelligence. Spearman (1927, in Cohen et al. 1988: 193–4) observes that: 'Intelligence has become . . . a word with so many meanings that finally it has none.' For practical uses, this clearly is an unsatisfactory state of affairs. In theoretical terms, however, Cohen and colleagues defend the ambiguity on the grounds that most constructs have vague definitions with no sharp boundary between them and related concepts. Defining 'health', for instance, would be difficult, and there is no clear demarcation between being in perfect health and being ill. Cancer, for example, is unhealthy, but good health encompasses more than lacking cancer. Nevertheless, it is important for practitioners to have a clear understanding of a concept such as intelligence, given that application of the concept has important ramifications in the lives of the children for whom we are making decisions (Renzulli 1986).

In chapter 5, I explore the uses of IQ tests in identifying young gifted children. Here it is worth observing that early attempts to measure intelligence occurred in the absence of any scientific understanding of human intelligence (Khatena 1992; Kline 1991). The early definitions reflected a mechanistic view—namely, that intelligence resides within the individual and is largely, although not exclusively, hereditary (Khatena 1992; Kline 1991). For instance, Alfred Binet (1909, in Terman 1919: 45)—the author of the first individual intelligence test and whose fourth edition is still in use today—defined intelligence as:

> [The] tendency to take and maintain a definite direction; (2) the capacity to make adaptations for the purpose of attaining a desired end; and (3) the power of auto-criticism.

David Wechsler, whose tests also continue to be widely used, believed that intelligence is global and has to do with making satisfactory adjustments to one's environment. He defined intelligence as (Wechsler 1958: 7):

> The aggregate or global capacity of the individual to act purposefully, to think rationally, and to deal effectively with his [or her] environment.

Like Binet, Wechsler believed that personality or 'non-intellective' factors played a part in intelligence (Cohen et al. 1988). This is an idea that still has a great deal of currency in the field of gifted education.

In contrast, current views of intelligence are more multi-dimensional and holistic, with a belief that intelligence results from children's interaction with their environments (Rowe 1991). This holistic view regards intelligence as a construct—that is, an abstract idea that has been invented to explain outward behaviours—whose definition will differ across cultures and which is not so much a characteristic of the individual as a result of experience or learning (Khatena 1992).

This view renders irrelevant the debates about apparent differences in intellectual capacities between racial groups (Kaufman 1994): when children have the same opportunities to learn, a child who has learned more will have done so because of more efficient learning ability. But when children have had differing opportunities, then any differences in their achievement is *definitely* environmental and only *possibly* genetic as well.

Contemporary thinking concludes that it is likely that genetic make-up interacts with the environment to produce not an either/or influence on the person's eventual capacities but an interactive effect, whereby the environment alters the expression of the person's genetic make-up, and the genetic make-up alters how the environment is shaped around the person (Clark 1997; Matthews 1980; Plomin 1997; Renzulli 1986; Sattler 1988). Clark (1997) attests to this by reporting that enriching an infant's early environment can increase his/her brain's size and weight and enhance its chemical and electrical functioning.

This is not merely a theoretical debate. As Clark (1997: 49) states: 'What we believe about how people become intelligent will influence the way we plan for their educational development.' If we believe that intelligence is static, then early environmental enrichment is unnecessary; if, however, we believe that intelligence develops dynamically, then we will attempt to provide an enriching environment which supports and challenges children's developing intellect (Clark 1997).

Nevertheless, the debate about the nature of intelligence has most relevance to academic giftedness. Although this is often the domain that is of most interest to educators, most writers in the gifted field acknowledge that there are other ways in which children can be talented. If one accepts this view, the focus broadens from the notion of intelligence alone. This brings us to an examination of the various definitions of giftedness.

DEFINITION 1: A SINGLE CAPACITY

This class of definitions is based on the concept that a single capacity underlies all cognitive processes and that possession of more or less of that capacity distinguishes levels of giftedness (Grinder 1985).

The high-IQ definition

This first definition equates giftedness with high intelligence. In turn, intelligence is thought to be a global, stable, unchangeable trait—which has been termed 'general intelligence', or *g*. In this definition *g* is identifiable by a psychometric test (Morelock 1996). (To understand the term *psychometric*, you can break it into two parts: *psycho* meaning to do with the brain, and *metric* meaning measurement. Therefore, psychometric means measuring an aspect of brain functioning.) The high-IQ definition accepts that the most reliable psychometric test is the intelligence test. This instrument yields a figure called an 'intelligence quotient', which is abbreviated to IQ.

Like many human characteristics, intelligence is thought to be 'normally' distributed, except that there are more people in the highly gifted range than would be expected, and more with very low abilities caused by extreme prematurity or early traumas and injuries (Montgomery 1996). A 'normal' distribution means that the mode (the most common measurement) is also the average, and that half of the population falls above and half below the average. However, while half of the population has above-average abilities, we do not classify these people as gifted until their skills are 'significantly' advanced. The point at which we determine that their advance is significant is both arbitrary and historical. Traditionally, we have defined this point as being around an IQ of 130 points (when the average IQ is 100 and the standard deviation is 15—this statistic is explained in Appendix II). Another way of expressing this same information is to say that the gifted comprise the top 3–5% of the population, if one takes a conservative stance, or up to 15–20%, if one takes a liberal stance (Renzulli 1982). Unlike the IQ score, this second figure has the advantage of being applicable to any domain of giftedness, rather than academic ability alone.

Although the longest-standing definition of giftedness (Ramos-Ford & Gardner 1997), the high-IQ definition has many detractors. Most criticisms arise from its uni-dimensional view that giftedness and high intelligence (or even a high IQ) are one and the same thing. This leads to another oversimplification—namely, that all children with similar IQs are alike (Birch 1984). In turn, this implies that one program will suit all gifted children equally well.

In practical terms, criticisms of the high-IQ definition are that it ignores or underidentifies:

- talents in fields other than academic;
- processing skills other than analysis (Borland 1986; Sternberg 1997);
- metacognitive skills (Carr et al. 1995);
- creativity (Fuchs-Beauchamp et al. 1993; Renzulli 1986);
- the dynamic nature of human development (Horowitz 1987; Treffinger & Renzulli 1986);
- children from minority cultures or disadvantaged backgrounds (Borland 1996b; Braggett 1998a; Davis & Rimm 1998; Gallagher & Gallagher 1994; McKenzie 1986; Maker 1996; Richert 1987, 1997; Scott et al. 1996; Tannenbaum 1983).

Nevertheless, Jackson and Butterfield (1986) contend that doing well on IQ tests is *a* form of giftedness, just not the *only* form. This is a conclusion with which even the most ardent supporters and detractors of IQ testing are likely to agree.

Clark's integrated functioning

Without emphasising a general intelligence factor as such, Clark (1997) posits that advanced and accelerated intellectual functioning in four areas underpins all superior performances. These areas comprise the cognitive, affective (emotional), physical and intuitive domains (see figure 2.1). This brain functioning develops as a result of an interaction between heredity and the environment, and is integrated—that is, all areas are interdependent. Clark argues that the notion of separate intelligences misses the point that all four brain processes must function together in harmony in order for an individual to excel.

Two issues arise from Clark's model. The first is that gifted individuals are known for their internal dissonance—that is, differences in developmental rates—between these four functions. The second issue is that Clark's model has not been tested by research (Gelbrich 1998) and is thus hypothetical at this stage.

DEFINITION 2: MULTIPLE CAPACITIES

Two separate schools have debated the nature of intelligence since the beginning of this century (Gardner 1983; Laycock 1979). On one side of the Atlantic, the British community of scholars under Charles Spearman (1927) believed that the intellect is structured as a hierarchy, in which an overall intellectual force (termed 'general ability') commands

Figure 2.1 Clark's universe of intelligence based on areas of brain function

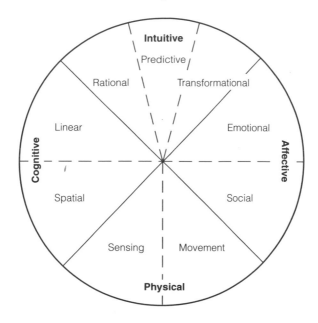

Source: Clark (1997: 30).

and guides lesser subskills or specific abilities. This view is reflected in the high-IQ definition.

On the other side of the Atlantic, the American view under Thurstone (1938) held that intelligence comprises a small set of distinct mental skills that are relatively independent of each other and which come into play in different tasks. This view has spawned a range of multi-dimensional models that are gaining ascendancy. Even adherents of the hierarchical view accept that it is worth examining subskills (in addition to g) in order to avoid failing to identify children whose talents lie in non-conventional areas.

Gould (1981) contends that the difference between these two views is a product of the statistical tests that the researchers use. He argues that any factor analysis of correlated scores will *always* identify a single factor that accounts for most of the variance, but the maths does not determine what that factor is. Each researcher names that factor, depending on his or her professional orientation and interpretation of other supporting evidence: g could be said to reflect individuals' comfort with taking tests, familiarity with pen-and-paper tasks (Gardner 1983), parents' socioeconomic status (Bowles & Gintis 1976), or simply the choices the researcher made about how to conduct the factor analysis

(Gould 1981). In other words, the competing conclusions of these two views can be equally right and equally wrong, depending on the way the statistical analysis and subsequent interpretation are carried out (Gould 1981).

A second argument is posed by Sternberg and colleagues (1996). They contend that the general ability factor might come about because the tests tap a narrow range of abilities; if the tests were broadened to measure other dimensions of intelligence, then multiple factors could emerge.

Thurstone's model

Thurstone (1938) was one of the early American theorists to contend that, rather than a single global capacity, intelligence comprised seven separate abilities: verbal comprehension, word fluency, numerical fluency, spatial visualisation, associative memory, perceptual speed, and reasoning (Gardner 1983: 17). Thurstone originally thought that these 'primary factors' were independent of each other, although he later conceded that their apparent independence had been a result of how his statistical analysis had been carried out and that there probably was a general ability underlying them all (Grinder 1985; McNemar 1964).

Guilford's structure-of-intellect model

Guilford (1959) proposed a structure-of-intellect model, in which five separate intellectual operations could be applied to four content areas to produce six types of product. This 5 x 4 x 6 configuration yields 120 separate functions (see figure 2.2). (This has since been increased to 150 factors by breaking figural content into visual and auditory skills: Khatena 1992.) Although Guilford's model raises the possibility of many types of giftedness, McNemar (1964) claims that it fragments ability into more and more factors of less and less importance, ultimately rendering the model trivial and educationally useless. By this he means that it is not practical to test for each factor and, even if it were, differential scores in the subtests still cannot predict achievement any better than can a single IQ score (McNemar 1964). Furthermore, the various factors correlate so highly with each other that a general ability factor appears to underpin them all (Clarizio & Mehrens 1985; Grinder 1985; McNemar 1964).

Gardner's multiple intelligences

Gardner (1983) suggests that, while neither the global *g* nor the multiple-abilities schools has been able to prove its case because of the limitations of statistics, his review of evidence from psychology and other disciplines

Figure 2.2 Guilford's structure-of-intellect model

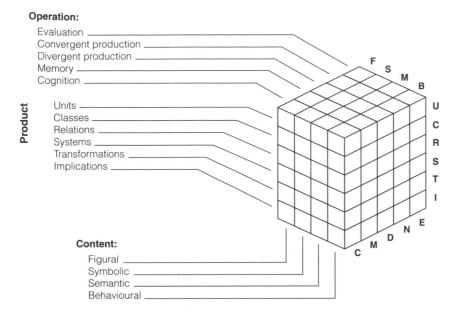

Source: Guilford (1959: 470).

indicates the existence of several relatively autonomous 'multiple intelligences' which can be combined in many adaptive ways by individuals and cultures. He lists these intelligences as (Gardner 1983; Vialle 1997):

- linguistic—involving the use of language in spoken, written or signed forms;
- logical-mathematical—entailing analytic and systematic thinking and 'the ability to recognise and work with patterns or categories through the manipulation of objects or symbols' (Vialle 1997: 33);
- spatial—involving being able to interpret information in two or three dimensions, such as when appreciating art, reading maps or completing jigsaw puzzles;
- musical—involving discriminating sounds and being able to express or gain meaning from ideas or emotions in music;
- bodily-kinaesthetic—entailing physical coordination and accurate use and interpretation of body language;
- interpersonal—involving accurate reading of social cues and enacting this social knowledge and awareness in the form of effective social behaviour (Kelly & Moon 1998);
- intrapersonal—entailing understanding yourself and being aware of your own needs, strengths and weaknesses. Expanding on this, Kelly

and Moon (1998) say that intrapersonal intelligence comprises emotional perceptiveness, being able to use emotions to inform thinking, understanding emotions, and regulating emotions to promote personal growth.

Gardner describes these intelligences as biological and psychological potentials (Gardner 1995) and sees individuals' potential as being unevenly distributed across the different skill areas, each with its own characteristic cognitive style (Morgan 1996; Smerechansky-Metzger 1995). Mostly, however, the intelligences work in harmony, and so 'their autonomy may be invisible' (Gardner 1983: 9).

Gardner has waxed and waned about the appropriateness of the title 'intelligence' in his multiple intelligence theory (see Gardner 1995; Ramos-Ford & Gardner 1991, 1997; Matthews 1980). Others regard intelligence as a *behaviour* (an act or a thought) that is well-adapted to the demands of the task or environment (Haensly & Reynolds 1989). In other words, intelligence is a product or *outcome* of intellectual *processes* and yet Gardner uses the term to denote neither intellectual processing skills nor intelligent outcomes. Thus, for clarity, I and others (Anderson 1992; Morgan 1996) believe that the title 'intelligences' should be abandoned.

Despite this disagreement about nomenclature, Gardner's theory has made a valuable contribution to broadening our view of human abilities and in offering greater educational diversity to all children. A particular strength of the theory is its inclusion of the final two 'personal intelligences' which relate to children's social and emotional wellbeing but which are largely neglected within education (Stedtnitz 1995).

Taylor's multiple-talent totem pole

Taylor (1978) has suggested that each child in a group will display strengths in any of nine areas (see figure 2.3). His original model comprised content areas (such as academic skills, human relations and communicating); intellectual processing abilities (such as decision making, forecasting and planning); as well as performance abilities (including implementation). He has subsequently added productive thinking and discerning opportunities (see Davis & Rimm 1998). This multi-dimensional model assumes that general academic ability helps children to learn information in a variety of domains, while the talents assist them to apply their knowledge to real-life problems (Schlichter 1981). Training in the use of their broader talents or thinking processes will enhance the children's achievement and self-esteem (Maker & Nielson 1995; Schlichter 1981).

To my mind, this model confuses gifts or talents with individual

Figure 2.3 Taylor's multiple talent totem pole

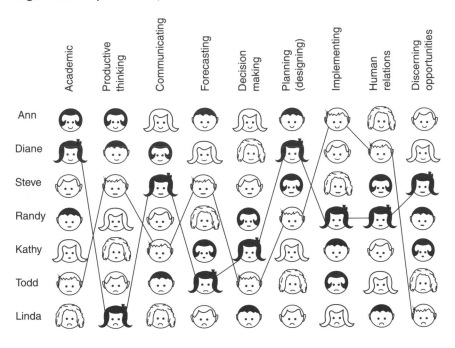

Source: Davis & Rimm (1998: 21).

differences (Runco 1997). While it is true that each child will have individual strengths, these abilities will not necessarily fall so far above the average that the children will need special programming in those domains (Braggett 1992; Gagné 1997; Gross 1993a; Runco 1997). Not only would it be difficult for teachers to cope with so many children for whom to make special provisions (McAlpine 1996), but also it would use resources which could otherwise be directed at children whose abilities *were* extreme (above or below the average) (Maker & Nielson 1995).

Taylor's model might help identify the few children who excel in only one domain—in contrast with the more easily identifiable children who excel in many domains—as well as children from non-dominant social groups (Schlichter 1981). However, the added accuracy of identification comes at the cost of efficiency. This may or may not be tolerable, depending on how many resources (funds and time) are available. Nevertheless, like the other multi-dimensional models, Taylor's totem pole does alert us to the fact that children can be talented in a range of ways, and that we need to broaden our conception of giftedness to include more than academic skills alone (Maker & Nielson 1995).

Sternberg's triarchic model

Sternberg (1997) criticises the definition of intellectual giftedness for focusing on a single ability, contending instead that giftedness comprises three abilities: *analytic* skills, *synthetic* skills and the application of one's thinking skills to *practical* problems. He states that 'an important part of giftedness lies in being able to coordinate these three aspects of abilities, and in knowing when to use each one' (1997: 44). He contends that IQ tests tap analytic skills reasonably well but omit the other two forms. The result is an underidentification of people who are gifted synthetically, who Sternberg says are independent thinkers and who, therefore, might be more successful than conventional, analytic thinkers. (In this statement, we see the national resources rationale for gifted education in play.)

The second part of Sternberg's model describes a range of intellectual processing skills that underpin the three types of intelligence. They involve the abilities to learn new information and to solve problems. These processing skills are supported by information processing research to such an extent that they form a separate theory (see below).

The various multi-dimensional models outlined above show some inconsistencies. While Gardner's multiple 'intelligences' are content areas or domains in which one can excel, Thurstone's and Sternberg's models focus on the intellectual *processes* that are required to produce an intelligent response (with the exception of Sternberg's practical intelligence, which appears to be a domain), while Taylor's model comprises both domains and processing skills. This inconsistency makes for confusion, which I attempt to resolve later in this chapter.

DEFINITION 3: INFORMATION PROCESSING THEORY

The information processing theorists (e.g. Anderson 1992; Borkowski & Peck 1986; Shore & Dover 1987; Sternberg 1997) examine the specific intellectual skills that distinguish advanced from average learners. This class of theory is sometimes referred to as an explicit theory, because it is based on the measurement of intellectual abilities (Sternberg & Zhang 1995). Various studies have focused on the superiority of gifted children's:

- knowledge base and ability to retrieve stored information from their memory;
- use of skills and strategies to solve problems;

- metacognitive skills, which regulate, control or oversee the use of these problem-solving strategies (Borkowski & Peck 1986).

Gifted children might learn more quickly because they use metacognitive skills earlier (Manning et al. 1996). They might have learned these skills by copying their parents (Alexander et al., in Manning et al. 1996), who might be modelling these skills because they have observed that their children are ready to learn them earlier than normal (Borkowski & Peck 1986). This early readiness in turn is likely to be due to the children's advanced language abilities (Moss 1990, 1992). Conversely, impoverished metacognitive skills might account for the underachievement of some gifted children (Manning et al. 1996; Risemberg & Zimmerman 1992) and perhaps for some types of specific learning disabilities (Rabinowitz & Glaser 1985).

These theories contribute to our concept of giftedness through their detailed understanding of gifted learners' sophisticated information processing ability. However, information processing theory does not take into account the wider social and environmental factors that contribute to talent (Feldman & Benjamin 1986). The result is a conception of giftedness that examines in minute detail only one small, albeit significant, aspect of giftedness and its translation into talented performances.

DEFINITION 4: QUALITATIVE DIFFERENCES

Rather than focusing on quantitative differences between advanced and average learners—that is, how much or how quickly they can learn—the qualitative definition regards giftedness as a difference in *how* gifted individuals function neurologically. Some authors highlight the information processing differences, while others—such as the Columbus group—suggest that gifted individuals are different emotionally.

Information processing differences

Eysenck (1986) reports that, owing to efficient transmission between brain cells, gifted individuals process information very accurately—that is, with few errors. As a result, they learn quickly. Error rate controls mental speed and it is their speed that makes gifted individuals efficient learners. This and similar findings suggest that speed of information processing is not only *related* to advanced abilities, but may actually be their *cause* (Borkowski & Peck 1986).

Another biological study by Jausovec (1997) showed two things. First, gifted subjects had higher cortical arousal at rest. This could mean that gifted people are more ready to deal with intellectual demands that arise. Second, gifted subjects showed greater arousal while structuring the problem than they did while solving it. Jausovec interpreted this as meaning that gifted individuals are better able than average learners to structure a problem and thus reduce its complexity. In turn, this makes their problem solving more successful (Shore & Kanevsky 1993).

Despite such findings about differences in gifted children's cognitive and metacognitive skills, Laycock (1979) asserts that talented performances come from 'awesome combinations' of otherwise ordinary mental powers—that is, that the difference between gifted and average achievers is a quantitative, not a qualitative one (Feldman 1984; Pendarvis & Howley 1996). This contention is supported by Jackson and Butterfield (1986), who report that gifted children's information processing skills are similar to older, average learners' skills. This suggests a quantitative difference: which is to say that gifted children use the same strategies as everyone else but simply become more proficient in their strategy use at younger ages (Jackson & Butterfield 1986).

Gallagher (1996) offers a dissenting conclusion, using this analogy: changes in temperature (a *quantitative* measure) can produce *qualitatively* different outcomes when water turns to ice or steam. So it is, he claims, for gifted children: they can combine their advanced skills in exceptional ways to produce qualitatively different thinking.

Emotional sensitivity

The Columbus group believes that gifted individuals' highly attuned nervous system (their brain) contributes both to advanced learning and to an increase in their emotional sensitivity, intensity and responsiveness (Miller, Silverman & Falk 1994; Piechowski 1997; Morelock 1996). The Columbus group's working definition (1991, in Silverman 1993a: 3) is:

> Giftedness is *asynchronous development* in which advanced cognitive abilities and heightened intensity combine to create inner experiences and awareness that are qualitatively different from the norm.

Morelock (1996) argues that the high-IQ definition of giftedness does not encapsulate these qualitative differences between gifted children and individuals of average ability. In turn, this results in a loss of important information about the emotional needs of gifted children (Porath 1996).

Four points need to be made about this qualitative definition. First, evidence about gifted individuals' heightened emotionality is weak. (This issue is debated in chapter 6.) Second, if a child has advanced cognitive development but not heightened sensitivity, does this mean that he or she is not gifted (Gagné 1997)? Third, the definition arises from the Columbus group's interest in the exceptionally gifted, who comprise

1:3000 of the gifted population; their description may not apply to all gifted children (Gagné 1997). Fourth, even if high ability and heightened emotionality are found to characterise gifted children, then it is still by no means certain that these children are *qualitatively* different from average learners (Gagné 1997). It might be simply that they think and feel *more* (a quantitative term) than others.

In chapter 6, I examine the evidence for qualitative differences in gifted children's emotions and conclude that there is very little proof so far of emotional differences between gifted and average learners. In terms of their intellectual skills, it is clear that advanced learners can produce high-quality *products* (Sternberg & Grigorenko 1993), although it is possible to achieve a higher-quality product while simply using *more* of a relevant skill than someone else. Yet the information in chapter 4 about gifted learners' thinking skills suggests that they can manipulate and juxtapose ideas in such sophisticated ways that it is probably safe to conclude that their thinking is both quantitatively and qualitatively distinguishable from that of average learners.

DEFINITION 5: CREATIVITY DEFINITIONS

The adherents of a multi-dimensional view of intelligence believe that beyond a certain threshold of intellectual ability there is an additional skill called *creativity* (Khatena 1992; Moore & Sawyers 1987; Taylor 1978). These researchers believe that creativity is the vital and defining characteristic of giftedness (Albert & Runco 1986; Renzulli 1986; Runco 1993).

However, there is little agreement on what the term 'creativity' means. It is variously used to refer to *people* (who are said to *be* creative), products, and thinking processes (Cropley 1997; Ebert 1994).

Creative *individuals* are said by Guilford and Torrance to have four abilities (Wallace 1986b):

- *fluency*, which enables them to generate many ideas;
- *flexibility*, which allows them to change thought patterns;
- *originality*, which is the ability to produce an unexpected idea;
- *elaboration*, which is the ability to extend ideas, perceive detail and assess consequences.

These factors may not be entirely separate however: flexibility (the production of *alternative* ideas) and originality (the production of *unique* ideas) must, by definition, be closely related to the ability to produce *many* ideas (Borland 1986). In turn, this fluency is closely related to general ability (Borland 1986), suggesting perhaps a close link between creativity and intelligence, a theme to which I return shortly.

Creative *products* are of two types (Boden 1990, in Gallagher & Gallagher 1994), both of which require novelty. The first type is a product (such as an idea) that is novel to the person thinking it. The second type is socially acclaimed for being original and unique: no one else has ever produced it before. Products are judged socially to be creative when they are novel or original, but they must also be timely (i.e. relevant) and valuable (or effective) (Cropley 1997; Sternberg & Lubart 1991). However, the social judgment of the worth of a product may not accurately reflect the creativity of the thought processes involved in its discovery or invention, and may simply reflect the product's timeliness. Therefore Cropley (1997) and Runco (1997) reject evaluating creativity by its product, yielding the paradox that creativity implies producing something new and yet creativity cannot be judged with reference to that product.

Creative *processing* is said to involve a series of phases (Cropley 1997; Wallace 1986b):

- *intention*, during which the problem is identified and there is an urge to solve it;
- *preparation*, in which knowledge is accumulated and the problem is viewed in every conceivable way;
- *incubation*, when the problem is mulled over;
- *illumination*, when a solution is arrived at;
- *verification*, when the individual evaluates the new idea;
- *communication*, when the idea is made available to others;
- *validation*, when the idea is judged by its audience.

Cropley (1997) contends that different thinking skills, motivations and personality characteristics may be necessary at each of these phases, a proposal which he says could account for the conflicting research findings about the skills that are necessary for creativity.

According to some writers, it is the ability to think creatively that distinguishes giftedness from precociousness, or conservers of knowledge from producers of knowledge (Khatena 1992; Renzulli 1986). In one sense this is true, in as much as creative thinking is not reflected in IQ scores because IQ tests measure mainly only convergent thinking and conventional knowledge. This, however, does not mean that creativity is necessarily different from intelligence, as intelligence involves more than the attributes measured by IQ tests. Perhaps the omission from IQ tests of divergent thinking has contributed to an artificial schism between intelligence and creativity (Carr & Borkowski 1987), which sees the two skills as separate—not necessarily because they are, but because we have separate tests for each skill.

This leads us to Ebert's (1994) notion of creativity, which sees creativity as an inherent aspect of all thinking. The view from Ebert and the global ability camp is that scores on intelligence and creativity tests correlate highly with each other (Khatena 1992) and so are both tapping a general thinking ability. Ebert conceptualises creativity as thinking *processes*, whose *product* is novel or inventive for the person producing it. Ebert contends that *all* thinking is creative: if you have never had a particular thought before, then thinking it for the first time is creative—for you.

Thus, unlike Sternberg and Renzulli, Ebert does not differentiate between intelligence and creativity. He believes that creativity *is* intelligence—that creativity is involved in any thinking, as problem solving involves applying one's own unique experiences to the task at hand for the first time. This position is supported by research into metamemory (e.g. Carr & Borkowski 1987).

This yields a definition of personal creativity, which differentiates creativity from the social acclaim that is given to creative products (Runco 1997). However, this is not a perfect resolution—if a child knows nothing, then any new thought is creative, but it is difficult to accept that ignorance is a valid source of creativity (Cropley 1997; Runco 1997)!

In the early childhood years, notions that equate creativity with giftedness face the difficulty that very young children do not yet have an extensive enough knowledge base to manipulate ideas and facts creatively—certainly not in the 'social acclaim' sense (Sternberg & Lubart 1991, 1992). It is also apparent that creativity is not simply a function of individuals' abilities but requires a conducive environment (Cropley 1997). Children who are in an environment that discourages experimentation might fail to display creativity and so, by the creative definition, would not be identified as gifted.

DEFINITION 6: THE AFTER-THE-FACT DEFINITIONS

Another class is the after-the-fact definitions (Stankowski 1978, in Davis & Rimm 1998), which define giftedness as:

- a mature power rather than a developing ability (Morelock 1996); or
- eminent adult performances; or

- excellent (in contrast with eminent) performances (Feldman 1991, in Morelock 1996).

The main issue arising from the after-the-fact definitions is that they do not define young children as gifted: children are seen only to have the *potential* for giftedness. Yet adult giftedness clearly has its roots in early childhood (Tannenbaum 1983). The after-the-fact definitions also exclude gifted underachievers (Gallagher 1997).

As these definitions do nothing to identify in advance potentially talented children who could need special educational provisions, they are not useful in educational terms. More than this, they can be positively harmful, according to Gagné (1995): he asserts that a focus on eminent achievements creates an inflated view of giftedness, blinding teachers to the less eminent—but nevertheless gifted—children who are right in front of them and in need of special provisions.

At a wider level, the after-the-fact definitions have done a disservice, in my view, to the literature about gifted people. It is difficult to read a textbook on giftedness without coming across a study of Nobel Prize winners or eminent performers in particular fields. These studies typically make claims about how the subjects became eminent. Such retrospective analysis is fraught with error, which is best illustrated with an example about drug users. When illicit drug users are asked about their pattern of use, those on 'hard' drugs report having used marijuana first; this gave early researchers evidence that marijuana use led to hard drug use. But these users also drank coffee, and drinking coffee obviously does not lead to use of heroin. Thus, the only sensible direction for research is to ask marijuana users whether they 'graduate' to heroin. (Apparently, most do not.)

So it is with these ubiquitous studies of eminent people. Such studies have led to claims, for instance, that eminent adults were usually raised in families with at least one strong parent who was tough and not necessarily nurturing, had strong religious values and was a high achiever (Mares 1991; Walberg et al. 1981). However, this is the same as the marijuana and heroin error: there might have been any number of children raised in such families who did not turn out to be eminent, in which case these aspects of the environment would be irrelevant (Freeman 1993). The only way that we can make firm conclusions is to follow a group of gifted children through their childhoods and attempt to explain which differences in their backgrounds contribute to some becoming eminent and others not. This sort of study is not practicable, but the fact that it has not occurred means that our claims about necessary environments—or any other retrospectively gained conclusions about eminence itself—must be read with extreme caution.

Finally, after-the-fact conceptions of giftedness confuse the *expression* of a particular talent with the social judgment of its worth. Social acclaim can reflect the timeliness or usefulness of a product (e.g. the invention of penicillin), rather than how difficult it was to discover. Also, studies (e.g. Walberg et al. 1981) that rely on length of biographical records as an indication of eminence do not even reflect the degree of social acclaim but merely the availability of biographical data.

DEFINITION 7: GIFTEDNESS VERSUS TALENT

Some writers (e.g. Tannenbaum 1983) use the terms 'gifted' and 'talented' interchangeably. Others have defined the two terms separately, in a range of ways:

- Talent is seen to reflect a remarkable ability which, however, falls short of the superlative level characterised by true giftedness (Braggett 1998a; Morelock 1996).
- There is a hierarchical categorisation, with 'talent' referring to specialised aptitudes that are assumed to be unrelated—and inferior—to general intelligence and giftedness (Morelock 1996; Richert 1997).
- Recently, the term 'talented' has been used to replace the term 'gifted', which has become offensive as it implies 'getting something for nothing', having to put in little effort to achieve, and seeing oneself as better than other people (Colangelo & Davis 1997; Feldhusen 1996). It is a label that is applied to people, not skills, and it implies a hierarchy of talents, with academic talent being more important than other forms.

Gagné (1991, 1995) argues that if the two terms 'gifted' and 'talented' are used synonymously, then there is no need for both. Feldhusen's (1996) solution is to dispense with the term 'gifted'; while Gagné argues for the retention of both terms but for differentiating them by defining 'giftedness' as innate capacities and 'talent' as developed abilities or performances. His model goes further to describe the factors that contribute to the translation of gifted potential into talented performances (chapter 3).

Gagné's model is supported by arguments that we should move away from attempting to identify gifted *individuals* towards identifying and promoting gifted *behaviours* (Jackson & Butterfield 1986; Renzulli 1986). A second body of support comes from those who believe that the performances which are judged to be talented or of use to a culture will differ, depending on the culture's needs at the time. Thus, our definition of giftedness must reflect cultural diversity.

DEFINITION 8: OTHER CULTURAL VIEWS

Although the notion of giftedness and its basic elements are universal, the way in which talent is manifested will vary with a child's cultural and historical context (Passow & Frasier 1996). For instance, Bevan-Brown (1996) reports that traditional New Zealand Māori peoples value a broad range of qualities in the spiritual, affective, aesthetic, intuitive, creative, leadership and cultural domains in addition to Western culture's intellectual emphasis. The Māori emphasis is holistic and group-oriented. It is expected that individuals who excel in any domain will use their special abilities in the interests of others.

Similarly, Harslett (1996: 100) reports that traditional Australian Aboriginal peoples value talents in areas such as 'healing, lore, story telling, religion, music, crafts, hunting and tracking'. Individuals who are talented in these domains are expected to be humble and, although recognised for their talent, are not accorded higher status because of it (Harslett 1996).

It can be seen from these descriptions that Western culture's understanding of giftedness is increasingly approaching the multi-dimensional understanding of giftedness held by other cultures. Any definition needs to be liberal enough to recognise those talents that the child's particular culture considers valuable (Gibson 1998; Harslett 1996).

CLARIFYING THE TERMINOLOGY

As we can see from the discussion above, there is a startling array of definitions of what otherwise might have seemed a commonsense concept. This diversity of definitions arises from differences in the ideology and assumptions of their proponents (Coleman, et al. 1997). For this reason—and because giftedness is a dynamic concept which reflects changes in societies' needs and priorities—some discrepancy is inevitable. Diversity of opinion is also valuable, as it expands our scope of inquiry (Ambrose 1998). Indeed, according to Borland (1990: 166) 'giftedness *should* be defined differently in different settings, but in the manner that is logical and consistent with the realities that obtain in each of those settings'.

It is not possible to establish empirically whether certain definitions are the 'whole truth': definitions cannot be testable as valid or invalid, but can only be more or less useful educationally (Gallagher 1996;

Nevo 1994; Sternberg & Davidson 1986). Nevertheless, some working definition is necessary to enable the theories arising from it to be tested (Gagné 1997). Therefore, drawing on the conceptions summarised here, I propose the following definition:

> Gifted young children are those who have the capacity to learn at a pace and level of complexity that is significantly advanced of their age peers in any domain or domains that are valued in and promoted by their sociocultural group.

Some gifted children will be recognisable by their talented behaviours. Others will be hidden, and may not display their talents in everyday situations. Therefore, part two of my definition for children is:

> Talented behaviours are performances that are quantitatively or qualitatively exceptional compared with age mates.

Talent will be promoted by an optimal environment acting on the child's intellectual capacity. (I describe this process of translating gifts into talents in more detail in chapter 3.)

I put forward this dual definition in recognition that any definition must reflect diversity in children's development, differences in their personality, cultural diversity, underachievement among gifted children, and the changes in the expression and impact of giftedness throughout children's lives (Harrison 1995).

CONCLUSION

Definitions of giftedness will determine how we go about recognising advanced development in young children. Since it is clear that there is little agreement about a definition, we need to keep an open mind about which attributes characterise advanced development and how best to foster it. This is the subject of the next chapter.

SUGGESTED FURTHER READING

For detailed reading about the various conceptions of giftedness, I suggest Sternberg, R.J. and Davidson, J.E. (eds) 1986 *Conceptions of giftedness* Cambridge University Press, Cambridge, UK.

For a more recent and less technical overview of gifted education, my recommendation is Colangelo, N. and Davis, G.A. 1997 *Handbook of gifted education* 2nd edn, Allyn & Bacon, Boston, MA.

For a summary and overview of the various conceptions of giftedness, I recommend chapter 1 in Montgomery, D. 1996 *Educating the able* Cassell, London.

If you would like to refresh your understanding of how the brain functions,

I found Clark's description both useful and fascinating: Clark, B. 1997 *Growing up gifted* 5th edn, Merrill, Upper Saddle River, NJ.

DISCUSSION QUESTIONS

1. What is your opinion of the single and multiple definitions of intelligence? How would your understanding of these definitions affect your care or teaching of young gifted children?

2. What are your thoughts on the debate about whether giftedness is a quantitative or qualitative difference in intellectual and/or emotional capacities?

3. What are your thoughts about Gagné's contention that after-the-fact definitions blind adults to all but the very rare child prodigy and lead to an underidentification and underservicing of young gifted children?

4. How do you view the similarities and differences between high intellectual ability and creativity?

5. Focusing on the early childhood years, what would be your definition of giftedness and talent? In what ways does your definition reflect your own cultural heritage and present context?

that this 'sense of self' creates the motivation to learn and to achieve. In other words, Renzulli's aspects of motivation and creativity are regarded by Feldhusen and Hoover to be a *result* of a facilitating environment and adequate sense of self. They contend that, although motivation and creativity are worthwhile educational goals, these do not cause giftedness or talent, and therefore should not define it.

Renzulli's model does not identify underachieving gifted children (Gagné 1991), and so advocates services only for those children who are already succeeding academically (Gross 1993a). By way of a partial defence, Renzulli (1986) accepts that young children might not necessarily show all three characteristics of high ability, creativity and task commitment, but that they will still be defined as gifted if they are seen to be capable of later developing this cluster of traits. However, this leaves two problems. First, assessing this potential in young children would be difficult. Second, if their environment offers insufficient challenge, children often become unmotivated (Gross 1993a)—that is, they do not demonstrate task commitment.

Another issue relates to the debate about creativity (summarised in chapter 2). On the one hand, if creativity is distinct from above-average intelligence, then Renzulli's definition actually requires a child to be capable twice over (Gross 1993a; Jarrell & Borland 1990). On the other hand, if creativity is a characteristic of any thinking (Ebert 1994), the creativity criterion is superfluous.

Either way, it is clear that individuals need a good deal of information or knowledge about a field before they can begin to combine ideas in a new way—that is, before they can manipulate ideas creatively (Cropley 1997; Sternberg & Lubart 1991, 1992). This makes it difficult for young children to be regarded as creative, even though they might have this talent later in life.

These criticisms come about because Renzulli's model characterises talent as an internal trait of the individual. In contrast, another renowned authority on giftedness, Abraham Tannenbaum (1983, 1997), believes that talented performances or productivity will result from *both* internal and external influences on the child.

MODEL 2: TANNENBAUM'S PSYCHOSOCIAL MODEL

Tannenbaum has proposed five factors that must coincide optimally for an individual's gifted potential to be expressed in the form of achievements—that is, talents. These influences are: (a) general ability; (b) special aptitudes; (c) non-intellective factors; (d) environmental supports; and (e) chance. In his most recent model, Tannenbaum (1997) divides each of these factors into static and dynamic dimensions. The static dimension, as its title implies, refers to those forces that are fixed—always present in the individual's life; the dynamic factors refer to situations which can change.

Figure 3.2 Tannenbaum's psychosocial model

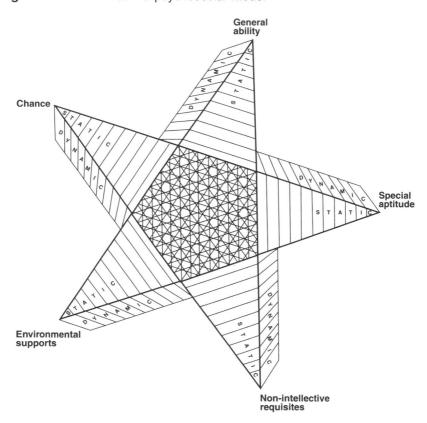

Source: Tannenbaum (1997: 31). Copyright © 1997 by Allyn & Bacon. Reprinted by permission.

General ability: static dimension. This refers to the power of one's neurological computer (the brain), whose biological structure and functioning is set down genetically (Plomin 1997) and environmentally (Clark 1997).

General ability: dynamic dimension. This dimension refers not to *what* the individual is able to do but to *how well* she or he is able to do it. Tannenbaum (1997) reports substantial research which concludes that gifted children possess distinctive styles of learning. (This research is summarised in chapter 4.)

Special abilities: static dimension. Many individuals will have particular talents that are more fully developed than their other skills. Expression of these special talents requires (a) above-average general ability, and (b) conducive influences, as detailed in the remainder of Tannenbaum's model.

Special abilities: dynamic dimension. This dimension refers to how the individual processes information in the domain in which she or he has a special aptitude. From Tannenbaum's (1997) description, this dimension appears to align with creativity in the individual's domain of special talent.

Non-intellective factors: static dimension. Obviously, the gifted child's personality traits may be both a result and a cause of giftedness, not least because they will have an impact on how the child copes with IQ testing and so will actually be part of what is being measured during a test. Three aspects of personality are highlighted by Tannenbaum (1997): internal versus external control; independence versus dependence; and present versus future orientation. Other writers also include motivation, self-esteem, flexibility and adjustment.

Non-intellective factors: dynamic dimension. The above personality factors are likely to change, depending on the situation. A child might have high self-esteem when it comes to academic tasks but be less confident at sport or socially, for instance.

The environment: static dimension. Children's family, school and social environments will all influence how their giftedness matures. A key influence is social class and the learning opportunities it affords (Tannenbaum 1997).

The environment: dynamic dimension. This dimension refers to how parents and teachers pass on their educational values to children: through their interactions with children; through encouragement of language and general learning; and by modelling an achievement orientation.

Chance factors: static dimension. These are random or accidental life circumstances which change the course of a person's history and over which there may be little control. This is the first type of chance factor which Austin (1978, in Tannenbaum 1997) described as the good or bad luck that strikes a person who happens to be in the right (or wrong) place at the time.

Chance factors: dynamic dimension. This refers to Austin's three other levels of luck (1978, in Tannenbaum 1997), all of which are influenced by individual action. At the first of these levels, a person increases the chance of good luck by being constantly on the move and on the lookout for positive circumstances. At the next level, the individual is uniquely equipped to realise the significance of a serendipitous event: as Louis Pasteur said, 'Chance favours the prepared mind' (Tannenbaum 1997: 39). (Cropley (1997) attributes this quote to Einstein.) Last, the talented individual persists with tinkering with ideas in what might be seen to be an eccentric obsession, until something finally falls into place.

Tannenbaum (1986, 1997) makes three points about the relative importance of each factor in his model:

1. each factor is necessary but on its own is insufficient for the realisation of gifted potential;
2. no combination of four factors can compensate for a serious deficiency in the fifth (Tannenbaum 1997: 30);
3. the relative importance of each of the five factors will differ across different talent domains.

MODEL 3: STERNBERG AND LUBART'S CREATIVITY MODEL

Whereas Tannenbaum focuses on resources that enable giftedness to be realised, Sternberg and Lubart (1991) focus on the resources to enable creativity. Nevertheless, their lists of facilitating factors are roughly compatible. Sternberg and Lubart's list comprises: intelligence; knowledge; intellectual style; personality; motivation; and a conducive environment. (Many of their ideas are included in the proposed model later in this chapter and so are not detailed here.)

Sternberg and Lubart (1991) add to Tannenbaum's discussion of these facilitating factors by noting that, in order to actualise potential, individuals need optimal levels of these resources. The term *optimal* implies that one can have too much of a good thing: for instance, although group acceptance is usually considered necessary for optimal personal growth, feeling out of step with others or with the current state of knowledge are necessary catalysts to the gifted person's search for a creative solution (Sternberg & Lubart 1991). A second example is supplied by Amabile (1990) and others (Kohn 1996; Ryan & Deci 1996) who state that external or extrinsic rewards can override and diminish intrinsic rewards, thus stifling creativity (although this view is by no means unanimous—see, e.g., Cameron & Pierce 1994, 1996; Eisenberger & Armeli 1997).

MODEL 4: DEVELOPMENTAL MODEL

The developmental model states that giftedness is not a personal characteristic that is fixed for life but, rather, a dynamic quality that is influenced over time (Braggett 1997). Horowitz (1987) poses a model which describes that children possess certain physical, intellectual and emotional characteristics that make them either invulnerable (resilient) or vulnerable to the quality of the stimulation which is provided by their familial, social, cultural and institutional environments. When these environments facilitate optimal development, both resilient and vulnerable children will prosper; when these environments are not conducive to optimal development, the resilient child will still prosper while the vulnerable child will not reach his or her potential.

Gifted children move through the same developmental stages as other children, but at a faster rate, to more advanced levels of mastery and to a greater depth of understanding (Feldman & Benjamin 1986; Stanley 1976). This higher level of achievement is facilitated by environmental conditions. Horowitz (1987: 167) states that: 'According to this model, there is no one set of conditions that accounts for all instances of giftedness.' This means that the environmental features that facilitate optimal development in one domain might not be the ones that promote optimal development in other domains (Horowitz 1987). For instance, Horowitz cites the parent who promotes early language development but does not equally foster spatial skills, or the child with musical talents who is never given a violin.

Similarly, the environmental features that are needed at one age might not be the ones that are required at another age. Development is dynamic, which is to say that individuals' needs change during childhood; in order to remain facilitating, the environment needs to alter in response to children's changing needs (Horowitz 1987). This accounts for the child whose early promise is not realised (which Horowitz puts down to the environment becoming less optimal over time), and the 'late bloomer' (resulting from an improved match between the environment's quality and the child's needs and abilities). Nevertheless, early identification of giftedness is crucial in planning for an optimally facilitating environment (Horowitz 1987).

This focus on the dynamics of development is what distinguishes the developmental model from the high-IQ and other static models (Braggett 1997; Feldman & Benjamin 1986). Rather than identifying gifted children and then offering these few youngsters a modified curriculum, the developmental model emphasises the power of the environment to develop giftedness (Braggett 1997). Under this model, the teacher's role is to provide a challenging and multi-dimensional curriculum to all children in order to allow those children to shine who have not already identified themselves as gifted through their advanced skills (Braggett 1997).

MODEL 5: GAGNÉ'S DIFFERENTIATED MODEL OF GIFTEDNESS AND TALENT

Gagné (1995) defines *giftedness* as untrained and spontaneous natural abilities (aptitudes) that exceed the norm. He defines *talent* as superior mastery of systematically developed abilities or knowledge. That is, giftedness refers to the individual's developmental potential, and talent refers to its expression. Where there is talent, there is necessarily a natural aptitude; but an aptitude can be hidden and not necessarily demonstrated in the form of a talent (Gagné 1991)—as is the case with gifted underachievers or children who have not been exposed to a domain in which they might otherwise have shown some talent.

Gagné's model has some notable features. First, as figure 3.3 shows, Gagné contends that various personal and environmental forces affect the translation of gifted potential into talented performances. He calls these forces catalysts, which enable or block the expression of the individual's natural aptitudes (Gagné 1991). In contrast with Renzulli's model, motivation here is a central catalyst of *talent*, not giftedness (Gagné 1991). Motivation determines whether the gift is expressed, but does not define gifted potential itself. The second feature worth emphasising is that Gagné divides both gifts and talents into various domains, reflecting the more recent multi-dimensional understandings of intelligence. Gagné's domains roughly align with Gardner's (1983) multiple 'intelligences' (adding further support to my contention in chapter 2 that these are content areas rather than 'intelligences').

A PROPOSED MODEL

In an attempt to marry the realisation of giftedness models with the information processing models described in chapter 2, I have proposed a model (see figure 3.4) which blends all of these (Porter 1997c). This is not an attempt to expound a new theory, but is a 'knitted' model (Kalmar & Sternberg 1981, in Sternberg & Lubart 1991) which draws together many of the theories discussed so far in this text. Its fundamen-

Figure 3.3 Gagné's differentiated model of giftedness and talent

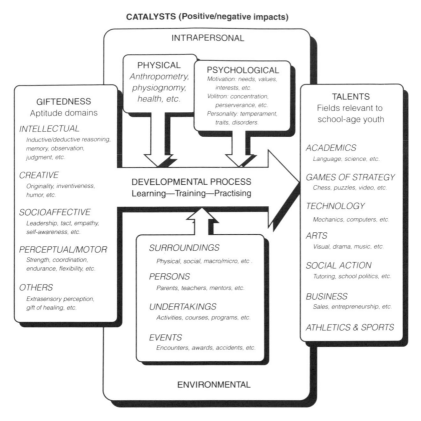

Source: F. Gagné, personal communication.

tal premise is that talented performances (which are evaluated and defined socially) arise from a rare and complex convergence of many factors (Haensly & Reynolds 1989; Sternberg & Lubart 1991; Tannenbaum 1997). Which combination of factors is regarded as optimal may alter throughout a child's life, in line with changes in the child's development (Horowitz 1992).

The proposed model aims to clarify the difference between gifts and talents and, in so doing, to include underachieving children within the definition of giftedness (but not talent). It is an attempt to describe the influences on performances, regardless of a child's developmental potential. It can equally well apply to children with intellectual disabilities as to advanced learners. This obviates the need to generate a separate model for giftedness and so allows us, when relevant, to transfer into the gifted field knowledge that is well recognised in other disciplines and fields of special education.

Figure 3.4 A proposed model for the realisation of gifted potential

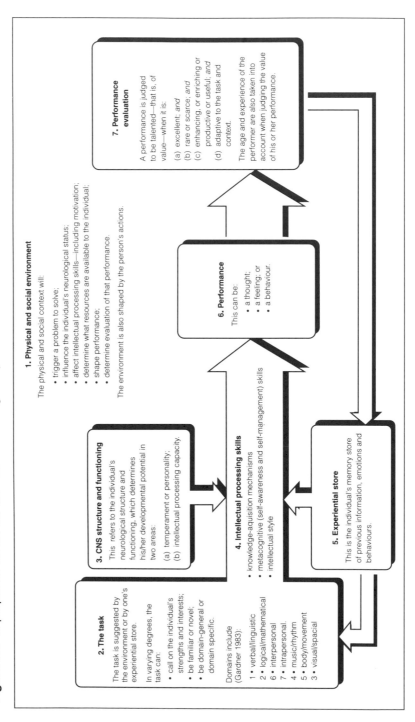

1. Physical and social environment

The physical and social context will:

- trigger a problem to solve;
- influence the individual's neurological status;
- affect intellectual processing skills—including motivation;
- determine what resources are available to the individual;
- shape performance;
- determine evaluation of that performance.

The environment is also shaped by the person's actions.

7. Performance evaluation

A performance is judged to be talented—that is, of value—when it is:

(a) excellent; *and*
(b) rare or scarce; *and*
(c) enhancing, or enriching or productive or useful; *and*
(d) adaptive to the task and context.

The age and experience of the performer are also taken into account when judging the value of his or her performance.

3. CNS structure and functioning

This refers to the individual's neurological structure and functioning, which determines his/her developmental potential in two areas:

(a) temperament or personality;
(b) intellectual processing capacity.

6. Performance

This can be:

- a thought;
- a feeling; or
- a behaviour.

4. Intellectual processing skills

- knowledge-acquisition mechanisms
- metacognitive (self-awareness and self-management) skills
- intellectual style

2. The task

The task is suggested by the environment or by one's experiential store.

In varying degrees, the task can:

- call on the individual's strengths and interests;
- be familiar or novel;
- be domain-general or domain specific.

Domains include (Gardner 1983):

1 • verbal/linguistic
2 • logical/mathematical
6 • interpersonal
7 • intrapersonal.
4 • music/rhythm
5 • body/movement
3 • visual/spacial

5. Experiential store

This is the individual's memory store of previous information, emotions and behaviours.

Source: Porter (1997c: 39, adapted from Gagné 1995).

Overview of the proposed model

When individuals are faced with a problem, the information processing skills they use to solve a problem draw on their neurological structure and functioning plus their knowledge base—that is, memory of previous experience. The environment affects all stages of task completion (as will be seen shortly). Together, all these factors affect performance.

These influences are identical across the full range of developmental potential, from intellectual disability to giftedness. However, gifted individuals have some distinct neurological and intellectual processing characteristics which improve their task performance.

Component 1: environment

The physical and social context determines what catalysts and resources are made available to support individuals' use of their personal skills, both short-term and ultimately. The environment influences all other components—by stimulating a problem to solve, by shaping individuals' neurological functioning through diet and early stimulation (Clark 1997; Freeman 1993); by affecting motivation (e.g. when a messy office makes working there less appealing); by affecting information processing skills (e.g. thinking is easier at home than in an exam room); by shaping performance (a cold room will affect a singer's voice production); finally, the social and cultural environment affects society's evaluation of the value or quality of a performance (Sternberg & Lubart 1992). As well, individuals' actions will shape their environment (Shore & Dover 1987).

The following environmental aspects can promote or obstruct the actualisation of one's developmental potential:

- the individual's physical health or constitution (Gagné 1991; Horowitz 1987; Sternberg & Lubart 1991);
- familial factors, such as family values, history, members' personalities and socioeconomic status (Albert & Runco 1986; Tannenbaum 1997);
- emotional nurturance received by the individual;
- educational opportunities that foster or stifle the development of skills and knowledge (Sternberg & Lubart 1991);
- peer relationships (Tannenbaum 1997);
- chance life events that (a) give the individual contact with a field in which she or he has particular skills (Walters & Gardner 1986) or (b) present obstacles to the actualisation of potential (Tannenbaum 1983, 1997);
- culture, including the individual's place and time in history

(Csikszentmihályi & Robinson 1986; Feldhusen 1986; Gruber 1986; Haensly, Reynolds & Nash 1986; Sternberg 1986a, 1997).

All children need similar physical, emotional and social resources in order to reach their developmental potential. However, it could be that gifted learners face different challenges whose existence implies the need for varied supports. This component of my model accepts the developmental premise that optimal environmental conditions will vary across different domains and ages (Horowitz 1987).

Component 2: the task

Tasks can be triggered by the environment or by one's experiential store—say, when new information challenges old ideas. Tasks are problems to be solved.

Task demands will vary: depending on whether the task is familiar or novel to the individual (Sternberg 1997); according to the domain or field to which it belongs; and depending on whether it requires that the individual apply his or her information processing skills and style with relatively equal efficiency across many domains (Sternberg et al. 1996) or in a more focused, specialised and domain-specific area—as with child prodigies (Feldman 1993).

There are probably many ways of classifying these domains but, notwithstanding my criticisms in chapter 2 of the confusion surrounding Gardner's (1983) domains, the lack of independent evidence for them (Matthews 1988) and the fact that others have suggested alternative content areas (e.g. those in Guilford's structure-of-intellect model), I consider Gardner's list to have at least face validity, and so I adopt them in this component of my model.

Component 3: central nervous system

An individual's neurological structure and functioning are set down genetically, but are also influenced by external factors such as trauma and prenatal insults (e.g. alcohol abuse leading to fetal alcohol syndrome) and stimulation during infancy (Clark 1997). As a result of these genetic and environmental conditions, there will be a ceiling on the individual's potential functioning.

Direct tests of neurological functioning that can distinguish gifted from average learners are in their infancy only. However, some studies have found, for instance, that some individuals who are later identified as being gifted have enhanced right-brain functioning and superior coordination and allocation of cortical resources within and between the cerebral hemispheres (Haensly & Reynolds 1989; O'Boyle, Benbow &

Alexander 1995, in Morelock 1996). Other studies show that choice response time differentiates between gifted and average learners (Grinder 1985).

Another line of research is followed by Eysenck (1986), who (as I report in chapter 2) has found differences between gifted and average learners in neurological error rate and resulting speed of their intellectual processing. While these and other data are still accumulating about differences in the nervous systems of gifted and average learners, this component of my model merely acknowledges that all people use their nervous system to think.

Component 4: information processing skills

Thinking (information processing) is not a passive process (Runco 1993): individuals actively select which aspects of a task to attend to and store, and what information from previous experience to retrieve from memory to apply to the task being undertaken. Individuals achieve this using three processes:

1. knowledge acquisition processes, which are used to learn how to solve problems (Sternberg & Lubart 1991). These are our thinking 'tools' (Tannenbaum 1991);
2. metacognitive skills, for thinking about one's learning. These comprise two components: (a) self-awareness of our own cognitive strategies, style and resources and of the compatibility between these and the task, and (b) self-management skills for controlling—that is, monitoring, coordinating, regulating and evaluating—our learning and performance (Cheng 1993; Hannah & Shore 1995; Shore & Dover 1987);
3. intellectual style, which is the proficiency with which we use thinking and metacognitive skills. Advanced learners tend to be highly motivated to understand, able to persevere, willing to take intellectual risks, and so on (see chapter 4). Nevertheless, as with environmental influences, in order to actualise potential individuals will need *optimal* levels of these elements of style (Katz 1995; Sternberg & Lubart 1991). For instance, while perseverance is usually a useful quality, it is inefficient to persevere past the point where a solution is possible.

Component 5: experiential (memory) store

As suggested by Ebert's (1994) cognitive spiral model, any new experience changes individuals' knowledge store or memory. Each experience is stored in memory and is used as data for the next experience. In this way, experiences (thoughts, feelings and behaviours) can simultaneously be *consequences* of previous experiences and *causes* of future performances; they energise individuals to exercise their intellectual processing abilities (Chan 1996). Naturally, individuals' memory store will expand as they get older.

Information

In order to produce an excellent performance, individuals need high-quality and extensive (both in terms of quantity and variety) knowledge in the field (Haensly & Reynolds 1989; Rabinowitz & Glaser 1985). However, while knowledge is necessary, it is not sufficient for competent performance (Rabinowitz & Glaser 1985). Sometimes, for instance, novices can be more creative than experts, because experts can be too constrained by the conventions of their field and may be less willing to take risks (Haensly & Reynolds 1989; Sternberg & Lubart 1991); on the other hand, novices often do not have enough knowledge to define worthwhile problems to solve, while experts clearly know where the issues lie in their field (Rabinowitz & Glaser 1985).

Remembered emotions

A crucial cluster of emotional factors are those which relate to self-esteem. Many authors (e.g. Chan 1996; Feldhusen 1986; Mulcahy et al. 1991; Tannenbaum 1983) have addressed gifted children's self-efficacy, self-confidence, self-concept or self-esteem but use these terms interchangeably when, although related, they do refer to different constructs. (Chapter 7 defines these terms and describes how to promote a healthy self-esteem in gifted children in order to facilitate the expression of their talents.)

Unlike Tannenbaum's star, the model in figure 3.4 has emotions not as a separate aspect of but instead as a part of memory. This is because I do not believe that it is possible to separate the intellectual (cognitive) processes from the emotions, as they cause each other. (For instance, I can tell whether my racing heart and perspiring palms are due to stress or to being in love by assessing my present context: that is, my emotions lead to thought. In reverse, thinking about a sad event can cause me to feel unhappy.)

Placing emotions within the memory store component has the disadvantage of appearing to 'bury' the emotions, making them seem less important. This is not my intention—indeed, I devote much of this text to addressing the emotional needs of gifted children. The point here is that, conceptually, emotions and thoughts cannot be separated.

Behaviours

Individuals develop a behavioural repertoire as a result of their previous performances and their assessment of the effects of these actions. When faced with a new task, individuals draw on their memory of previous actions to assess their behavioural options.

Feedback

The model in figure 3.4 illustrates that there is a feedback loop at work here also. When a task triggers an old memory, it might provoke a new problem to solve.

Component 6: performance

A performance can be a thought, feeling or behaviour. Using information processing skills, individuals will evaluate their own performance using standards that they have learned from the social environment and which are stored in their memory. This assessment, in turn, will expand their experiential store for future reference.

Component 7: social evaluation of a performance

Usually, outward behaviours are the only demonstrable signs of talent, and are thus the only aspect that is judged by the outside world. Their performance is the most common method observers use to infer that individuals are gifted. However, previous influences—the environment, motivation levels, experiential memory and even an overexcited CNS—can cause some gifted people to underachieve. Therefore, society might not recognise their giftedness.

In a synthesis of Tannenbaum's (1983), Renzulli's (1986) and Sternberg and Zhang's (1995) criteria for defining the value of a performance, my model contends that performances are judged to be talented when they are:

- *excellent* (Sternberg & Zhang 1995)—that is, of high quality according to the standards of expert judges (Sternberg & Lubart 1991); *or*
- *rare* (Sternberg & Zhang 1995) or *scarce* (Tannenbaum 1983). However, scarcity is not enough. Tannenbaum (1983) states that anomalous feats such as those recorded in the *Guinness Book of Records*, although rare, are not necessarily valuable and so should not be included in a definition of giftedness unless they also satisfy the remaining two criteria;
- *of value*—that is, are enhancing, enriching (Tannenbaum 1983), useful (Ebert 1994) or productive (Sternberg & Zhang 1995). The

product makes life easier, safer, healthier, more intelligible (Tannenbaum 1983) or more enjoyable; *and*

- adapted or *appropriate to the context* (culture, time and place), to the task or to the needs of the individual: the product will meet specified requirements and fit with the 'spirit' of the times (Feldhusen 1986; Gruber 1986; Haensly & Reynolds 1989; Sternberg & Lubart 1991; Tannenbaum 1983). This does not necessarily imply that the product must be novel, original or inventive (as if it is too avant-garde it will not be judged to be appropriate to the time and place), but neither does it have to adapt completely to the context: instead it can shape the environment to be open to the product (Shore & Dover 1987; Sternberg & Lubart 1991).

Ausubel (1978, in Haensly & Reynolds 1989) also states that judgments of talent have to be tempered by awareness of the individual's age and experience.

CONCLUSION

Early intervention can do much to set in place the conditions which foster young gifted children's optimal adjustment and development (Mares 1991). To that end, the next chapters examine how to recognise advanced development in young children in order that curricula can take account of and extend their prior learning.

SUGGESTED FURTHER READING

For more detail about most of the models presented in this chapter, my recommendation is Colangelo, N. and Davis, G.A. 1997 *Handbook of gifted education* 2nd edn, Allyn & Bacon, Boston, MA. You will need to go to the first edition of this text for a description of Gagné's model, as it is not included in the second edition.

DISCUSSION QUESTIONS

1. Which of the models introduced here most closely matches your understanding of how gifted potential is translated into talented performances?

2. Which aspects of the models appear most—or least—important to you? Why?

3. How could you improve on the models?

4. How does your understanding of the factors necessary for the realisation of gifted potential affect how you would care for and educate young children with advanced development?

4

RECOGNISING ADVANCED DEVELOPMENT IN YOUNG CHILDREN

The gifts of nature are infinite in their variety, and mind differs from mind almost as much as body from body.

Quintilian (in Laycock 1979: 59)

KEY POINTS

- It is important to remember that gifted children are not all alike and so, while descriptions of the signs of advanced development can assist with identification of young gifted children, such lists should be read with caution.
- Gifted children, by definition, display advanced cognitive (thinking) skills which are shown in how they acquire, recall and use their knowledge; they can also display certain characteristic intellectual styles.
- Gifted children's knowledge acquisition is hastened by their advanced speech and language skills and early mobility.
- Gifted children's social skills tend to be advanced compared with age peers, although they can resort to solitary play when age mates cannot play at their own sophisticated levels.
- Emotionally, young gifted children can sometimes appear to be immature, a fact that can disguise their giftedness.

INTRODUCTION

In this chapter I list a range of characteristics that children with advanced development might display during their early childhood years. Such lists are a mixed blessing, however. They can sensitise adults to the possibility of advanced development, but at the same time they can give a false impression that all gifted children are the same (Harrison 1995; Roedell et al. 1980). This is patently as untrue for gifted children as it is for any group of children, as the *gifted* label spans a broad range of ability from mild to exceptional giftedness, and because advancement can occur in a range of domains of human endeavour (Kitano 1985). Even two children with similar IQs (for want of a better measure) will differ in their stronger and weaker skill domains; in how evenly their talents are spread across domains; and in the extent to which their environment adequately meets their needs—with resulting implications for their emotional and social behaviours.

COMMON SIGNS OF ADVANCED DEVELOPMENT IN YOUNG CHILDREN

What we know about the characteristics of gifted children could be inaccurate, owing to three sources of bias in studies. The first source is the strong representation of middle-class children in many studies, such as Terman's longitudinal work (Hastorf 1997; Roedell et al. 1980).

A second source of bias arises from studies relying on teacher nominations of gifted children. This tends to lead to inclusion of only those children who are academically well adjusted while under-representing children who are experiencing school-based difficulties (Gross 1993a; Roedell et al. 1980).

The third form of bias is introduced by anecdotal evidence from clinical practitioners who, by definition, see children who are having difficulties. The result can be that practitioners gain a false impression about the prevalence of adjustment problems in gifted children.

COGNITIVE (THINKING) SKILLS

The defining characteristic of giftedness is advanced thinking and language skills (Davis & Rimm 1998). Advanced cognitive skills can be evident from as early as one year (Damiani 1997); by preschool age, gifted children show cognitive advances in a wide range of domains (Morelock & Morrison 1996). This is evidenced in their earlier progression through developmental milestones.

Knowledge base

Intellectually gifted children have wider and deeper knowledge than average learners (Kitano 1985), despite the two having experienced similar learning opportunities. This is usually thought to be an advantage, but it can propel gifted children into examining abstract issues before they have the emotional maturity to cope (Roeper 1977). Nevertheless, the fact of their more extensive knowledge raises the question of how it is acquired (Jackson & Butterfield 1986).

Knowledge acquisition skills

One likely answer to the question of how gifted children acquire more knowledge is that they are faster (more efficient) at storing information in their memory (Borkowski & Peck 1986; Haensly & Reynolds 1989; Perleth et al. 1993; Rabinowitz & Glaser 1985). This allows them to master a new skill with unusual speed (Moltzen 1996a).

Knowledge acquisition is an active process and, according to Ebert (1994), a creative one for the individual concerned. It involves perceiving that there is a problem, generating a range of potential solutions on the basis of past experiences, and selecting a course of action. The problem-solving skills of gifted individuals are often creative, allowing them to see the issue from a range of perspectives, sometimes yielding an original insight (Shore & Kanevsky 1993).

This facility with knowledge acquisition shows up even in very young babies, who can be keen observers of their environment. Even as babies they play an active role in eliciting stimulation from their physical and social environment (Damiani 1997; Morelock & Morrison 1996). Their insistent demands for 'input' can give the impression that parents are pushing children, but instead the reverse is true: most parents are following their children's interests and demand for increased stimulation (Damiani 1997).

Knowledge acquisition is helped when children are mobile early (as is common for many gifted children) and use language early. As they progress past the toddler years, many—but not all—begin to read, write or use numbers in advanced ways, which again helps them to acquire knowledge that is ordinarily considered to be advanced for their years (Baska 1989; Davis & Rimm 1998; Jackson 1992; Moltzen 1996a).

Not only might they be reading early, but young gifted children can have advanced preferences for books and films (Mares 1991), although their emotional sensitivity causes some to avoid the older themes in books or videos intended for older children. When their interests are advanced, this will give them access to still further information.

Knowledge retention (memory)

Not only are gifted children more efficient at storing information in memory—they are also more efficient at retrieving it. They characteristically have quick and accurate recall, allowing them to show competence in a skill they were taught some time ago. The result is that they have deeper knowledge than other children of the same age, even to the point of being able to teach other children.

Memory can be distinguished by three features: first is the *amount* of stored knowledge; second is how is it *organised*; and third is how *accessible* the information is (Rabinowitz & Glaser 1985). To explain these aspects it might help to think of memory as being like an office filing cabinet. In terms of the quantity of information that is stored, the number of documents in a filing cabinet grows with time; likewise, in memory, the amount that a child knows grows with age. In terms of organisation, if you toss documents into a filing cabinet until they fill the drawer, you are going to have difficulty locating the document you want when you need it. If, instead, you put each document in a hanging file devoted to that topic, then retrieving it again is simply a matter of locating the topic and finding the document that relates to it. So it is with memory. When we rehearse information or elaborate on it, we are ensuring that we 'park' that memory near other related information, which makes it easier to locate when we need to retrieve it later.

The third feature of memory is accessibility. Here, the analogy of dropping a stone into a pond might be useful. When a stone is thrown with force into the water, it disturbs or sends out ripples to nearby parts of the pond, in ever-widening circles. When the stone lands gently in the water, the ripples are smaller and they spread less far. In the same way, one memory can trigger or activate another, related concept. A person with a superior memory will have strong links between concepts and will activate a large number of related ideas (the 'ripples' will go out strongly from the original idea to a wide range of related memories). If, however, the associative links in memory are weak, then the activation (ripples) does not spread far enough or with enough strength to call up related ideas. In short, related memories are not activated automatically. The individual might be able to retrieve them, but only with effort. This ability of advanced learners to access a wide range of relevant information easily and quickly permits complex problem solving (Rabinowitz & Glaser 1985).

In summary, as individuals become more competent in a given domain, their *knowledge* of that domain grows, they *organise* their knowledge in memory in more sophisticated ways, and much of it can be accessed *automatically* (Perleth et al. 1993; Rabinowitz & Glaser 1985; Shore & Kanevsky 1993). This leaves processing capacity available for carrying out higher-order tasks, such as comprehending the meaning of a passage in a book rather than simply deciphering the words (Jackson & Butterfield 1986).

These findings lead to another question, namely: 'What mechanisms permit the faster memory storage and retrieval of gifted children?' As I indicate in chapter 2, the answer to this could be that their brain cells transmit information with few errors, and their high level of brain cell activity when at rest permits quick firing when a problem is to be solved (Eysenck 1986; Jausovec 1997). On the other hand, this enhanced brain efficiency could be a result, not the cause, of long practice and training (Perleth et al. 1993; Winner 1996).

Knowledge application

Having acquired broader and deeper knowledge than is usual for their age, gifted young children can often apply it to abstract or complex concepts, such as death or time, much earlier than their age mates. However, they cannot necessarily cope emotionally with the degree of information which they crave intellectually.

Summary: knowledge

So far, I have explained that gifted children are able to acquire, retain and use their knowledge more effectively than is usual at their age. The particular skills that enable them to do so include their advanced metacognitive abilities and their distinctive learning styles.

Metacognitive abilities

Metacognition refers to our awareness of our thinking processes and of what we know. We can monitor our own thinking at the same time as thinking. Metacognitive knowledge comprises knowledge about our abilities, how to use learning strategies, and when and why to use them. Metacognitive control comprises the planning, monitoring and evaluation that we use to regulate our thinking (Schraw & Graham 1997).

Gifted children's advanced language abilities and advanced understanding of cause-and-effect relationships allow them to display a high level of planning and to use metacognitive skills earlier than average learners (Borkowski & Peck 1986; Davis & Rimm 1998; Moss 1990, 1992). This contributes to their increasingly sophisticated performances throughout childhood (Moss 1990, 1992). Below is a box of some metacognitive skills that have been said to characterise gifted learners, although the evidence for all these features is as yet by no means substantial (Perleth et al. 1993).

METACOGNITIVE SKILLS OF GIFTED CHILDREN

The following metacognitive abilities have been identified as being advanced in gifted young children:

- the ability to focus their skills;
- the ability to select information that will help define the problem, to locate strategies for solving it, and to determine criteria by which to evaluate performance;
- use of meta-learning skills—that is, the ability to sense task demands accurately and quickly (sensing the 'ground rules' which determine what kind of solution is acceptable);
- the ability to set priorities and to allocate resources to addressing the most relevant features of a task;
- planning the approach to a problem;
- use of metamemory to scan for relevant information and possible solutions;
- selective encoding of information, which is the ability to notice information that could be relevant to solving the present problem. (It could be this skill that leads to apparently divergent thinking);
- a positive learning set—that is, a sensitivity to similarities between present and past tasks and a willingness to apply knowledge and strategies from previous experience. (This aligns with Sternberg's selective comparison; it enables children to generalise learning and transfer knowledge and strategies across domains);
- synthesis of information. (This aligns with Sternberg's selective combination of seemingly isolated ideas, which he regards as a component of insight and, in turn, creativity);
- elaboration of ideas—that is, the ability to embellish ideas;
- evaluation or monitoring of ideas and strategies to determine whether the product or thought is viable.

Sources: Borkowski & Peck (1986); Cheng (1993); Ebert (1994); Shore & Dover (1987); Haensly & Reynolds (1989); Moss (1990, 1992); Runco (1993); Sternberg (1986a); Sternberg & Lubart (1991); Tannenbaum (1983, 1997).

Self-awareness

Self-awareness involves knowledge of our strengths (Hannah & Shore 1995) and the ability to redefine tasks so that they employ our stronger skills (Shore & Dover 1987). In some studies, gifted children demonstrate more knowledge about how their mind works (Borkowski & Peck 1986; Carr et al. 1995; Schwanenflugel, Stevens & Carr 1997). This knowledge is crucial for selecting suitable problem-solving strategies (Borkowski & Peck 1986) and contributes to divergent or flexible thinking (Carr & Borkowski 1987).

Although many gifted children use imaginative strategies for accomplishing tasks, others may not be more capable than average learners of generating problem-solving strategies but appear to be able to use strategies more readily once they have been taught them (Borkowski & Peck 1986; Jackson & Butterfield 1986; Risemberg & Zimmerman 1992).

Self-management

Gifted children have a tendency to be more reflective and less impulsive in their thinking (Clark 1997). As a result of managing their own problem solving, they are more methodical in their approach. Kanevsky (1992) found that, when compared with older children of the same mental age or with same-aged average learners, gifted youngsters could better remember rules and apply former learning to a new task, which allowed them to learn from their errors and so improve their performance. These differences occurred only when the gifted children were interested in the task. Fatigue also set in more noticeably in the young, high-ability children, owing to the fact that they had invested so much energy in the task initially.

Their ability to generalise strategies from one task to another suggests that advanced learners can scan their memory efficiently (Borkowski & Peck 1986; Carr et al. 1995; Risemberg & Zimmerman 1992). This function is called metamemory, and is important for retrieving information and for being flexible in one's approach to difficult tasks (Carr & Borkowski 1987). Indeed, metamemory may be a better predictor of success than IQ (Carr & Borkowski 1987).

Metamemory can be demonstrated by an example. If I asked you to name the capital of Peru, you would *immediately* know that:

- you had never learned it;
- you had learned it but forgotten it;
- you would recognise it when I told you; or
- you could actually recall that Lima is the capital of Peru.

You might also be able to say where or how you learned this fact or why you could recall it. You can scan and assess your memory instantly and (usually) accurately. (Interestingly, this is partly why 5-year-olds so often say they know something that they clearly don't: they are beginning to be aware of their memory store but are not yet accurate in their assessment, and so claim to know more than they do.)

Gifted children's enhanced self-management means that their problem solving is more successful, as they can monitor the effects of their actions and adjust their actions as necessary (Shore & Dover 1987).

Learning style

Not only are gifted children able to learn more, but *how* they learn is typically different from less advanced children (Sternberg & Grigorenko 1993). The most useful learning style will depend on the task at hand (Grigorenko & Sternberg 1997; Martinsen 1997): there will be occasions when being reflective will be useful and other occasions when being quick and impulsive will be more productive (Martinsen 1997). Flexibility of style, then, is important to ultimate success (Shore & Dover 1987).

Motivation

When presented with a challenging and exciting environment, young gifted children are intensely curious: they seek to know and understand from an early age (Baska 1989; Greder 1986, cited by Ebert 1994; Perleth et al. 1993). They have a strong desire to master new skills, which may be due to their neurological need for heightened stimulation (Morelock & Morrison 1996). Given sufficient challenge, gifted children are willing to invest energy in and give attention to tasks in order to develop competence (Csikszentmihályi 1991; Renzulli 1986; Runco 1993; Sternberg & Lubart 1991; Vallerand et al. 1994).

Children will be motivated to attempt a task when they believe (from previous experience) that they will be able to cope with it and when the task matches their skills and interests. This can mean that they are not motivated to invest energy in tasks that are not intellectually demanding (Vallerand et al. 1994)—such as rote-learning tasks involving a high level of repetition. They might also not wish to invest energy in tasks where they do not expect to be successful (Chan 1996; Vallerand et al. 1994). That is, motivation has an 'expectancy component' (Chan 1996).

Motivation is thus thought by some to be both a characteristic of giftedness and necessary to spur the development of talent (Landau et al. 1996). Gifted children's intrinsic motivation is more powerful than extrinsic rewards (Amabile 1990; Clark 1997; Csikszentmihályi 1991; Sternberg & Lubart 1991, 1992) and will affect their effort, energy and persistence. As they grow older, gifted children strive to apply their skills meaningfully and to use their resources well (Gruber 1986; Sternberg & Lubart 1991). Their focus on a goal is especially apparent in areas of challenge or within their particular area of talent. This determined focus can be interpreted as either stubbornness or persistence, depending on how it is perceived by an observer (Kitano 1990a).

Attention skills

The picture of gifted children's attention skills is mixed, partly because of a confusion between various forms of attention. These forms have been described by Zentall (1989).

The first type of attention is maintaining a level of *arousal* in order to attend. On this dimension, gifted children are often described as being more alert than less advanced children (Morelock & Morrison 1996; Tannenbaum 1992), which is sometimes said to be associated with a poor sleeping pattern, although there is little evidence of this (Freeman 1983, 1991; Moltzen 1996a; Perleth et al. 1993).

The second type of attention is *coming to attention* to focus on an activity. From a few months of age, gifted children show a preference for novel stimuli and a tendency to habituate (i.e. lose attention) to stimuli that are repeated (Lewis & Louis 1991; Perleth et al. 1993; Slater 1995; Tannenbaum 1992). In short, gifted children's focus on an activity will depend on how intellectually stimulating it is.

The third type of attention is *maintaining attention over time*—that is, concentration span. Young gifted children may show intense absorption (a long concentration span) when engaged in a topic of interest; when an activity is not challenging, they may 'flit' from activity to activity without really becoming absorbed.

The fourth type of attention is *selective attention*. This involves scanning a range of stimuli to see which aspects of each are the most important and which can be ignored. This involves metacognitive skill at which gifted children commonly excel (as I have already reported). It is a crucial skill for beginning school, as children need to be able to listen to the next instruction while completing an earlier task, which involves alternating their attention selectively between what they are doing and the instruction they are receiving.

Locus of control

An important belief that children learn through experience is whether they themselves can control outcomes (this is termed having an *internal* locus of control) or whether luck, fate or other people control what happens to them (having an *external* locus of control).

There is some evidence that gifted children develop an internal locus of control earlier than less advanced children (Brody & Benbow 1986; Clark 1997; McClelland et al. 1991), especially when they are achieving near to their potential (Kammer 1986; Knight 1995; McClelland et al. 1991). It is thought that their strong belief in personal control underpins gifted children's enhanced self-management, and motivates them to use their problem-solving strategies effectively (Chan 1996).

There is a mixed picture of gifted children's locus of control with respect to accepting responsibility for their successes and failures, perhaps partly due to cultural differences (Perleth et al. 1993). One thread of evidence states that gifted children may be more willing to accept responsibility for their successes than their failures (McClelland et al. 1991). Bogie and Buckhalt (1987) found the reverse—that gifted children thought they were successful because the task was easy, and were discouraged by failure, although they still persisted at a difficult task. Chan (1996) found that, because gifted children regard themselves as competent, they do not blame failures on their own lack of ability but instead attribute them to their own inadequate efforts. This could account for their perfectionism: they might accept *too much* responsibility for their failures and so become disappointed in themselves.

When children believe that they are responsible for the outcomes of their actions (i.e. when they have an internal locus of control), they (Knight 1995):

- are more likely to learn from their mistakes;
- have more incentive to invest effort in a task and strive for success;
- have more effective communication skills and better interpersonal relationships;
- have superior concentration skills;
- are more persistent;
- are more reflective learners.

Independence

Gifted children's drive for independence can be paradoxical in early childhood. Many children prefer to work independently (Baska 1989; Clark 1997)—perhaps because of the discrepancies between their skill levels and those of their age mates. Others seek a lot of stimulation and, as infants, might have learned to rely on adults to supply this; they continue to do so even after they are capable of generating input themselves. Still others might fiercely insist on doing things (e.g. getting dressed) for themselves but, once they have mastered the task intellectually and it holds no further interest for them, might then might refuse to do it at all. They can be impatient with repetition of activities that they already understand (Clark 1997; Kitano 1990a).

ASPECTS OF INTELLECTUAL STYLE

The following lists the characteristic learning style of gifted children. (Those words referring to *how* they approach learning are in italics):

- *openness* to new experiences;
- *willingness* to take risks;
- discretion, *judgment*, self-censorship or taste in selecting a problem to which to devote one's efforts;
- *perceptiveness* or sensitivity to a problem (being more likely to recognise that a problem exists);
- *perseverance* in the face of obstacles;
- *speed* of information processing;
- *automatic* nature of problem solving;
- *adapting* speed to the task demands (i.e. being willing to *reflect* before acting in order to maintain *accuracy*);
- *efficiency* of processing;
- the ability to *immerse* oneself in a field to yield a superior breadth and depth of understanding and knowledge;
- *acuity* of perceptions;
- *initiative* and *imagination*;
- *tolerance* of ambiguity;
- use of *intuition* (i.e. allowing some of one's thinking to occur at a preconscious level);
- *fluency*, which reflects an ability to employ a range of ideas;
- *flexibility*, which alludes both to the quality of ideas brought to bear on the problem and to skill at adapting one's style to the task demands and goals;
- being *non-conforming* and rejecting limits;
- being willing to grow (i.e. not to stop at the first success but to enlarge on it);
- ability to be *independent*.

Sources: Amabile (1990); Anderson (1992); Borkowski & Peck (1986); Cheng (1993); Delisle (1992); Ebert (1994); Gagné (1991, 1995); Gallagher & Gallagher (1994); Haensly & Reynolds (1989); Haensly et al. (1986); Jackson & Butterfield (1986); Lovecky (1994); Morelock (1996); Piirto (1999); Rabinowitz & Glaser (1985); Runco (1993); Shore & Dover (1987); Sternberg (1988); Sternberg & Lubart (1991, 1992); Tannenbaum (1991, 1997); Tardif & Sternberg (1988).

SPEECH AND LANGUAGE SKILLS

Many studies report that gifted children speak much earlier than is typical, resulting in a wider and more complex vocabulary and sentence structure from an early age (Lewis & Louis 1991; Moltzen 1996a; Perleth et al. 1993).

Even more important than speech is the child's precocious comprehension of language. From an early age, receptive language ability is a robust indicator of intellectual ability (Freeman 1993; Guilford et al. 1981; Moltzen 1996a; Perleth et al. 1993; Robinson 1993; Smutny et al. 1989). Although it is not clear why intellectual ability and language skills are closely related, Davis and Rimm (1998) suggest that advanced language skills come about because of the children's advanced cognitive skills (i.e. abstract thinking ability).

Gifted children's advanced language skills allow them to communicate what they want from an earlier age; they understand adult explanations, which helps them to plan for events (Bromfield 1994). Their logical thinking can lead to constant questions to which they demand detailed, in-depth answers (Davis & Rimm 1998), while their constant talk can lead either to indulgence or to being ignored (Bromfield 1994).

Verbally gifted young children can comprehend adult conversations earlier than usual, with a resulting increase in the amount of information that is available to them but also an early interest in 'adult business'. Their advanced conversation can make them interesting companions but there is a risk that parents will confide too much in them, resulting in the children's becoming worried about adult issues or withdrawing from peers (Bromfield 1994). Another facet of this phenomenon is when their advanced language, being such an obvious sign of intellectual giftedness, tricks adults into expecting too much of them in other spheres.

In addition to their wide vocabulary, advanced verbal reasoning skills, accurate grammar and early comprehension, some specific signs of young gifted children's advanced language skills include their ability to:

- use metaphors and analogies;
- make up songs or stories spontaneously;
- modify their language for less mature children;
- use language for a real exchange of ideas and information at a young age;
- carry out instructions to do several things in succession.

Another demonstration of gifted children's advanced cognitive and language abilities is their early appreciation of humour. This comes about because their cognitive and language skills allow them to know what is typical and so they see exceptions—incongruities—as funny (Davis & Rimm 1998). For instance:

> When watching a cricket match on TV, a 5-year-old enjoyed the duck which walked across the screen when a batsman was out without scoring—that is, was out for 'a duck'. A few weeks later at the beginning of a match, a utility van with the sponsor's advertisement appeared across the bottom of the screen and she announced with amusement, 'He's out for a truck!'

Early talkers are not necessarily early readers (Perleth et al. 1993; Robinson 1993), although exceptionally early readers often are highly gifted (Gross 1993a). Early reading depends on motivation, socio-economic class and level of adult instruction: early readers do not 'teach themselves' (Perleth et al. 1993).

MOTOR ABILITIES

As with all other areas of development, children with advanced learning capabilities often acquire motor skills early, particularly skills that require cognitive control such as balance; less so, skills that rely on strength or endurance (Robinson 1993; Roedell et al. 1980). Young gifted children can learn new physical movements with ease (Moltzen 1996a) and can locate themselves in the environment. Their superior coordination, environmental perception and advanced planning skills contribute to a lowered rate of childhood accidents. These skills can also lead to early awareness of left and right.

However, gifted children's fine motor skills (eye–hand coordination) might not proceed earlier than the norm (Tannenbaum 1983), and their slower development of these skills can stand in the way of their other accomplishments (Davis & Rimm 1998). Nevertheless, interested children can be skilful in putting together new or difficult puzzles, taking apart and reassembling objects with unusual skill, or making interesting shapes or patterns with objects.

Their high physical energy levels and lack of attention to routine tasks is sometimes misinterpreted as attention-deficit hyperactivity disorder (Baska 1989; Baum, Olenchak & Owen 1998). (This issue is examined in chapter 12.)

Some gifted children have been reported to be more sensitive to physical sensations, such as temperature and pain, although evidence for this is anecdotal only.

SOCIAL SKILLS

Young children whose development is only mildly advanced appear to have few social disadvantages and some social advantages; it is not certain that the same can be said for children who are extremely gifted (Morelock & Morrison 1996). As a result of the discrepancy in interests and abilities, highly gifted children can experience social difficulties from early childhood onwards (Gross 1993a).

Empathy

Many gifted children are less egocentric (Shore & Kanevsky 1993) and more sensitive to the needs or feelings of other people than their age mates, as the following example illustrates.

> A child was told that her friend, Anna, could not come to her upcoming third birthday party because Anna's grandmother had died and she was going interstate for the funeral. Much later in the day, the almost-three-year-old was eating a sandwich with quiet tears rolling down her face. Her mother asked her what was the matter, thinking that she was disappointed that her friend could not come to her party. The reply was, 'I'm sad for Anna. She didn't get to say good-bye to her Nana before she died' and burst into piteous crying which lasted many minutes.

Gifted children are also more likely to be able to identify another person's internal (emotional) state and deduce that to be the cause of the other's behaviour (LeVine & Tucker 1986).

Play

Young gifted children often learn to play games with rules earlier than other children (Mares 1991), and incorporate academic and literacy activities spontaneously into their play (Kitano 1985). They have advanced play interests and behaviours (Robinson 1993), and so may attempt to structure the play of a group of age mates in too complex a way (Webb 1993). When less able children lose interest and wander off (Morelock & Morrison 1996), gifted children sometimes interpret this apparent lack of interest as a rejection of them, rather than attributing it to the fact that the other children cannot yet play at more sophisticated levels.

Friendships

Because of their ability to empathise with others and the scarcity of intellectual peers, young gifted children will often form strong attachments two friends (Baska 1989). Whereas young children usually regard s the children with whom they play the most, gifted children)e able to develop true reciprocal friendships far earlier.

This pattern is apparent, however, only when gifted children can find true (intellectual) peers. To do this, many seek out older children and adults for companionship, or seek to be alone more often than other children (Clark 1997; Davis & Rimm 1998; Lewis & Louis 1991). In order to meet their need for company, many have an imaginary playmate (Davis & Rimm 1998), although this is common also with imaginative children who are not gifted.

Although often sought out by other children (Clark 1997), gifted children might set too high standards of others, both as a reflection of the perfectionist standards which they apply to themselves and because of their advanced moral reasoning ability (Clark 1997; Gross 1993a).

Gifted children's social difficulties usually diminish when they find a true peer group (Morelock & Morrison 1996). Caregivers and teachers cannot expect them to display appropriate peer skills when they lack peers, and so it is often inappropriate to wait for gifted children to be 'ready' socially before moving them up to the next group in the centre or on to school. If moving up is impossible, it may be necessary to help gifted children find common ground with their age mates: developing relationships with others cannot be left to chance. (I discuss social needs in greater depth in chapter 9.)

Leadership

Young gifted children often show early leadership abilities (Clark 1997), such as being willing to accept responsibility, enjoying being part of a group, having respect for peers, use of clear communication, adaptability, flexibility, preference for directing rather than following activities, and self-confidence around others (Moltzen 1996a). They are often looked to by other children for their ideas and decisions. Their verbal and reasoning skills allow them to handle conflict non-aggressively by suggesting a number of solutions to social dilemmas (Morelock & Morrison 1996). They have the verbal abilities to influence other children's behaviour, although they might also use their skills manipulatively (Davis & Rimm 1998).

Moral judgment

Being less egocentric (Shore & Kanevsky 1993) and more empathic than is usual at their age, gifted children typically have an advanced sense of justice (Baska 1989; Clark 1997; Davis & Rimm 1998; LeVine

& Tucker 1986). This is expressed in their ability to make complex moral judgments earlier than their age mates (Gross 1993a), although they are not necessarily any better able to enact moral decisions in real life (Freeman 1993; Moltzen 1996a; Robinson 1993).

This advanced value system can present some problems for gifted children. First, it can intensify their feelings of being different (Gross 1993a). When other children do something which is developmentally normal but which they know to be 'wrong', gifted children can be offended and confused.

Second, their moral values can drive their personal interests, leading at times to a disdain for popular activities (e.g. sport) which have no 'meaning'.

Third, boys' altruism and compassion may be in conflict with the stereotypes of boys as 'tough guys' and so can lead to peer rejection or cause them to behave in ways that contradict their values, just so that they can fit in (Lovecky 1994b).

Fourth, gifted children's interest in social issues, especially those involving a violation of justice sometimes exceeds their emotional maturity and ability to cope, and can clash with their need to maintain their own growth (Baska 1989).

Finally, their sense of morality and intolerance of hypocrisy can mean that they are reluctant to tell those 'white' (social) lies that often oil the wheels of social interactions; their brutal honesty sometimes disturbs other people (Gross 1993a).

EMOTIONAL CHARACTERISTICS

As I mention in chapter 2, the Columbus Group of researchers use children's emotional characteristics as one of the defining criteria of giftedness. (Whether gifted children are actually more vulnerable to emotional difficulties than others is the subject of the debate in chapter 6.) Although the evidence about any unique emotional make-up is lacking, it would appear that their intellectual skills allow gifted children to be more perceptive than their age mates, which can result in displays of some atypical emotional behaviours.

Thus, it is important to be aware of the emotional traits that have been linked to giftedness, as some can impede accurate identification (Kitano 1990a). These traits often have the appearance of social or emotional immaturity, and can be misinterpreted as evidence that children are *not* gifted.

Emotionality

Gifted children are often described as being more emotionally sensitive, intense and responsive than average learners (Clark 1997; Miller et al. 1994; Morelock 1996; Piechowski 1997; Silverman 1993a). Some writers believe that the brain structure that permits advanced learning also leads to greater emotionality. Others put gifted children's emotional vulnerability down to their dissonant development (i.e. uneven development in their various developmental domains). These domains comprise cognitive or thinking skills; speech and language (understanding); gross motor (physical) skills; fine motor abilities; and social-emotional skills. Yet a third group believes that gifted children's emotional adjustment difficulties are due to being 'out of sync' with the rest of the world—a world which can be indifferent at best and hostile at worse to their needs.

Early development of fears

One result of their advanced cognitive and social awareness is that gifted children sometimes develop fears earlier than other children (Derevensky & Coleman 1989; LeVine & Tucker 1986; Robinson 1993), when they might be too young emotionally to cope with their precocious imagination (Chamrad & Robinson 1986). Another consequence of cognitive and social advances is that gifted children lose their innocence and their belief in magical thinking earlier (Roeper 1977).

Self-esteem

In gifted children, self-concept develops early (Delisle 1992), which, in turn, hastens their recognition that they are different from other children (Clark 1997; Harrison 1995). This awareness can lead them to assume that there is something 'wrong' with them.

On the whole, gifted children tend to be confident about the domain in which they are talented, but lack confidence in their physical or social skills (Chan 1988; Davis & Rimm 1998; Delisle 1992; Sekowski 1995; Tannenbaum 1997; van Boxtel & Mönks 1992) (see chapter 7).

Perfectionism

Despite a paucity of evidence for this (Stedtnitz 1995), and the methodological flaws in the few available studies (e.g. Orange's 1997 study of self-selected participants), gifted children are often described as setting high standards for their own performance and as demanding of themselves far more than do their parents or teachers (Clark 1997). This trait is commonly called perfectionism. However, it is important to distinguish between the various forms that this drive can take: as Hess (1994: 28) states, 'Not all perfectionists are created equal'.

The first form of perfectionism is a healthy drive, in which individuals take pleasure from making a real effort and achieving high-quality outcomes. The second type is a destructive form, in which individuals strive compulsively to achieve unrealistically high standards and are seldom satisfied, no matter how well they do. Their feelings of worth are linked to being successful (Hess 1994; Parker & Adkins 1995; Parker & Mills 1996). According to Roedell (1984, in Prichard 1985: 11):

> Setting high standards is not in itself a bad thing. However, perfectionism coupled with a punishing attitude towards one's own efforts can cripple the imagination, kill the spirit, and so handicap performance that an individual may never fulfil the promise of early talent.

Recent research (Parker & Adkins 1995; Parker 1996) describes gifted children's perfectionism in terms of striving for the excellence of which they are clearly capable, rather than the dysfunctional sense of never being happy with any of their achievements. But although this form of perfectionism is useful for children in that it helps them to achieve and may not be a problem for the children themselves, it might be misunderstood and poorly tolerated by other people (Silverman 1994a; Taylor 1996).

A third type of perfectionism is organisational. Individuals who seek to take charge of their lives (as is common with high achievers) have some protection against becoming depressed as depression is, in part, a reaction to feeling out of control (Lynd-Stevenson & Herne, in press).

The children perhaps most prone to perfectionism are those: with a wide spread of abilities (Kitano 1990a); who believe that giftedness means that they should be able to learn everything effortlessly (Mendaglio 1994); or who have perfectionist parents, whose caustic reaction to their own mistakes teaches their children how to respond to failure. Alternatively, they may fear failure partly because they have little experience of it (Hess 1994).

As a result of perfectionist tendencies, gifted children sometimes avoid taking intellectual risks (Kitano 1985; Webb 1993), and concentrate on their area of special talent, with the result that the gap between their upper and lower skills widens and they progressively lose confidence in their weaker areas. They might put off starting something in case they are not able to do it perfectly. They sometimes become workaholics, as their achievements are the only measure of their self-worth (Hess 1994). The route to helping children to harness the benefits of perfectionism while overcoming these negative effects is not to encourage them to lower their standards, however, but to boost their self-confidence so they will be willing to work towards their ideals (Silverman 1989b, 1994a).

Oversensitivity

Having high standards for themselves and being perceptive to others can make gifted children oversensitive, especially to criticism (Mendaglio 1994, 1995b). It is possible that while they are more perceptive to other people's signals, their limited life experience causes them to misinterpret these messages (Freeman 1983; Mendaglio 1994).

Frustration

While extremely gifted preschoolers tend to be precocious across all developmental domains, those with mildly advanced intellectual development achieve only slightly better than average in gross and fine motor skills (Tannenbaum 1992). The result is dissonant development between the various developmental domains, which can lead to frustration. They might be able to conceptualise what they want to do, but fail to make allowance for their child-level skills (Freeman 1983; Webb 1993), such as their lack of manual dexterity (Chamrad & Robinson 1986; Kitano 1986; Roedell et al. 1980; Whitmore 1980). The resulting outbursts of frustration can be intense, and are often misinterpreted as immaturity.

Maturity

On the one hand, gifted children often accept responsibilities that are usually given only to older children; on the other, they can have emotional or behavioural outbursts that seem very immature (Robinson 1993).

Behavioural non-conformity

Because of their independence, gifted children tend to resist external attempts to control their behaviour (Delisle 1992; Kitano 1990a) (an issue that I discuss again in chapter 11). Although their intellectual risk-taking is often reflected in advanced learning, it can result in breaking 'rules' in unusual and unanticipated ways and so can appear to be 'mischief-making' (Mares 1991). At the same time as not necessarily conforming to expectations themselves, young gifted children often want others to conform to rules (Kitano 1985).

Summary: emotional sensitivities

Davis and Rimm (1998) list some positive characteristics of giftedness with corresponding negative traits, most of which are social or emotional. To inject some personal philosophy here, my belief is that any trait can have either positive or negative effects in a person's life, depending on how it is disciplined. For instance, a normally positive trait of conscientiousness can, when ill-disciplined, result in stress from trying to do too much too well; in contrast, those of you who are or have been students will know the benefit of stubbornly refusing to 'let them get you down' when you hit those low patches in a course of study and want to quit. Stubbornness, when well-disciplined, can have its benefits.

Thus, it is not the characteristic or trait itself which is positive or negative, but how it is used. This is reflected in table 4.1, which details some emotional characteristics of gifted children extrapolated from lists by Davis and Rimm (1998), Moltzen (1996a), and Schetky (1981).

EXCEPTIONALLY GIFTED CHILDREN

Gross (1993b, 1993c) contends that not only must early childhood professionals be able to detect the signs of giftedness—they must also be able to recognise its differing levels. As Tolan (1998: 165) points out: 'Within the gifted range . . . there is a far larger span of cognitive difference than there is between normal and gifted.'

This is not to support a common myth, however, that the difference between an exceptionally gifted child (with an IQ of around 190) and a moderately gifted child (with an IQ of 130) is the same as the difference between a moderately gifted child and one with disabilities (an IQ of 70) (Lovecky 1994a; Webb et al. 1991). The reason that this rather attractive notion is not true is that the IQ scale has unequal intervals between its numbers (Sapon-Shevin 1994). Instead of each number being evenly spaced—as is the case, for instance, when measuring temperature in degrees—an IQ scale is more like the street numbers on letter-boxes, whose distance apart will depend on the size of each block of land.

It is likely, instead, that exceptionally gifted children display similar characteristics to children with lesser degrees of giftedness, although the characteristics occur earlier and sometimes more intensely (Lovecky 1994a). This means that exceptionally gifted children will have some unique needs and manifestations compared with other gifted children.

Exceptional giftedness occurs at the rate of around one in a million (Gross 1993a, 1993c). This fact makes such children difficult to identify,

Table 4.1 Positive and dysfunctional expressions of some common emotional characteristics of gifted children

Trait	Positive expression	Dysfunctional expression
Sensitivity	Perceptiveness Imagination	Overreaction to criticism or mistakes Early appearance of fears
Perfectionism	Striving for excellence High achievement Self-esteem from success	Procrastination Frustration Disappointment, whatever the standard of one's work High expectations of self High expectations of others
High task commitment	Exuberance Enthusiasm Curiosity Persistence	Boredom with repetitive tasks Underachievement with routine activities Overactivity Insatiability Fatigue
Independent thinking	Creativity Motivation	Behavioural non-cooperation Social isolation Lack of interest in details Stubbornness
Internal self-control	Learns from mistakes	May blame self for mistakes Self-deprecation
Social perceptiveness	Sense of humour Insight Leadership	Manipulation of others Alienation/isolation

Sense of justice and
    idealism
	Empathy
	Interest in social issues
		Disappointment/outrage that
		    other children do not
		    abide by rules
		Stress from helplessness to
		    effect social change
		Cynicism about authority

as caregivers and teachers will have little experience with them. Their scarcity and their extremely advanced play and leisure interests also mean that the social isolation of exceptionally gifted children is more pronounced than for children with lesser degrees of giftedness (Gross 1993a, 1993c; Gross & Start 1990).

Also, exceptionally gifted children often make the simple complex (Lovecky 1994a). If you ask them how many legs a bird has, they may think of exceptions and not come up with the simple answer of 'two'. Lovecky reports that this characteristic can be coupled with the need for extreme precision in order for the world to make sense, and so can result in extensive arguments or debates with others.

A reverse characteristic is that exceptionally gifted children make the complex simple (Lovecky 1994a). Once they have learned a concept, there is no need for further practice. But the material is mastered as a whole, which makes it difficult for these children to explain its parts, and explains the problem exceptionally gifted children have with peer tutoring. The same phenomenon is found with reading: once the children no longer need to sound out words, it is frustrating and difficult for them to be required to do so (Gross 1993a).

As with other gifted children, those with exceptional ability learn skills such as talking, walking and reading early, but advance through the developmental stages of each skill so quickly that some stages are virtually imperceptible. For instance, the participants in Gross's study went from walking with assistance to walking alone in one month instead of the usual three-and-a-half (Gross 1993a; Gross & Start 1990).

Early reading reliably differentiates between mild and high degrees of giftedness, with many exceptionally gifted children being keen readers by their third birthday and continuing throughout childhood to regard reading as their favourite form of recreation (Gross 1993a, 1993c; Gross & Start 1990). However, in order to fit in socially, these children may spontaneously stop reading when they begin school, having observed that other school entrants cannot read (Gross 1993a). Thus, many exceptionally gifted readers are not detected by their teachers, although their classmates often noticed their exceptional skills (Gross & Start 1990).

PRODIGIES

Child prodigies demonstrate adult-level performances in demanding areas at an extremely early age (Feldman 1993). Their skills are usually in specific domains such as chess and music, probably because these do not require much prior learning (Montgomery 1996). Not only do prodigies learn skills *earlier* (i.e. more quickly) but they achieve a *higher level* of performance than others, even those with the best training and most extensive practice. In contrast with savants, whose general abilities are usually below average, prodigies are usually very able intellectually, although not exceptionally so; however, like exceptionally gifted children, prodigies have a fierce determination to develop their talents (Feldman 1993).

Tannenbaum (1992) argues that prodigies appear not to be a product of genetics (their parents and siblings are seldom prodigies), but neither are they a product of their environment, as these very young children have not been alive long enough to benefit from even the most enriched environment. On the other hand, they do require environmental exposure in their area of special ability: in order to play the violin like a virtuoso, they need to have been introduced to the instrument (Tannenbaum 1992).

There appears to be higher than usual hostility to the special needs of prodigies within the education system, resulting in many parents choosing home schooling (Feldman 1993). At the same time there is a fascination with prodigies which, in my view, unintentionally ill-serves other gifted children. The frequent mention of prodigies in the media and literature (vastly out of proportion to the prevalence of prodigious children) can create an inflated view of giftedness and so blind educators to the more common forms that giftedness can take.

SUMMARY OF COMMON INDICATORS OF ADVANCED DEVELOPMENT IN YOUNG CHILDREN

Cognitive (thinking) skills

- Early achievement of developmental milestones
- Quick learning
- Keen observation of the environment
- Active in eliciting stimulation from the environment
- Reading, writing or using numbers in advanced ways
- Advanced preferences for books and films, unless too sensitive to older themes
- Quick and accurate recall
- Recall of skills and information introduced some time ago
- Deeper knowledge than other children
- Ability to teach other children
- Understanding of abstract concepts (e.g. death or time)
- Imaginative, creative
- Advanced sense of humour.

Learning style

- Motivated, curious, in search of understandings
- Intense focus on an area of interest, as long as there is sufficient challenge
- Wide-ranging interests

- Alert
- Responsive to novel stimuli
- Longer than usual concentration span on challenging topics of interest (but may 'flit' from one activity to another if activities are not challenging enough)
- Early use of metacognitive skills to manage own thinking processes
- Clear understanding of cause-and-effect
- Good planning skills
- Internal locus of control
- Reduced impulsivity
- Independent work at challenging, non-routine tasks
- Logical thinking.

Speech and language skills

- Early comprehension
- Advanced speech, in terms of vocabulary, grammar and clear articulation
- Use of metaphors and analogies
- Ability to make up songs or stories spontaneously
- Ability to modify language for less mature children
- Use of language for a real exchange of ideas and information at an early age
- Ability to carry out instructions to do several things in succession.

Motor abilities

- Early motor development, particularly in skills that are under cognitive control
- Ability to locate themselves within the environment
- Early awareness of left and right
- Fine motor skills may lag behind other developmental domains
- Ability to put together new or difficult puzzles
- Ability to take apart and reassemble objects with unusual skill
- Ability to make interesting shapes or patterns with objects
- High levels of physical energy.

Social skills

- Less egocentric
- Highly developed empathy for others
- Advanced play interests
- Early ability to play games with rules
- Early ability to form close friendships
- Seeking out older children or adults for companionship
- Withdrawal to solitary play if intellectual peers are not available
- Often sought out by other children
- Leadership skills
- Early development of moral reasoning and judgment
- Early interest in social issues involving injustices.

Emotional and behavioural characteristics

- Emotionally sensitive, intense and responsive
- Early development of fears
- Early development of self-concept and awareness of being different
- Self-confidence in strong domains
- Perfectionism, in the sense of having high standards
- Oversensitivity to criticism
- Frustration, which can lead to emotional or behavioural outbursts
- Acceptance of responsibility usually given only to older children
- Non-conformity.

Sources: Baska (1989); Borkowski & Peck (1986); Chamrad & Robinson (1986); Chan (1996); Clark (1997); Damiani (1997); Davis & Rimm (1998); Delisle (1992); Gross (1993a); Haensly & Reynolds (1989); Jackson (1992); Jackson & Butterfield (1986); Kanevsky (1992); Kitano (1985, 1990a); Klein (1992); Knight (1995); Lewis & Louis (1991); McClelland et al. (1991); Mares (1991); Meador (1996); Mendaglio (1994); Miller et al. (1994); Moltzen (1996a); Morelock & Morrison (1996); Moss (1990, 1992); Parker & Adkins (1995); Parker & Mills (1996); Perleth et al. (1993); Rabinowitz & Glaser (1985); Renzulli (1986); Roedell et al. (1980); Silverman (1993a); Smutny et al. (1989); Sternberg & Lubart (1991, 1992); Tannenbaum (1983, 1992, 1997); Whitmore (1980); Winner (1996).

SUMMARY

Based on detailed observations, Eyre (1997: 32) classifies gifted children into four patterns of behaviour:

- the verbal, knowing, independent child;
- the curious, moving and doing, explorer child;
- the quiet, focused, unexpectedly humorous child;
- the socially interactive, engaging, 'on stage' child.

While these patterns may fit many children, however, it is also important to be aware that some children might not conform to any of these descriptions. Stereotypes about gifted children can blind parents and teachers to children who do not fit their preconceived image. Thus, it is well to be aware that not all gifted children:

- are highly capable in all areas of development (Silverman 1989);
- are high achievers;
- have superior language abilities;
- prefer to learn independently;
- are early readers;
- are highly motivated.

Few fit the stereotype of the genius, 'little professor' or nerd; none can split the atom or invent a cure for cancer. They look like other children and may not come forward to demonstrate their skills. They might not complain when they have insufficient challenge (Eyre 1997); they might not even create disruptions when bored. But if not challenged, their skill development may decline.

CONCLUSION

There are no unique combinations of skills found in gifted children that are not found in average learners: it is a matter of the degree of advancement (by age) of children's skills, and the combination of skills that the children display (Gallagher & Gallagher 1994). This quantitative view suggests that gifted children are similar to older children of the same mental age.

The qualitative approach, in contrast, suggests that gifted children's intellectual processes might not be displayed by older children of the same mental age. An example is Gross's (1993a) tale of a 22-month-old who, when asked, was able to tell his mother that they had been walking for $26\frac{1}{2}$ minutes. Even a child twice this age (as his mental age was assessed to be) would not be able to perform such accurate time-keeping.

Looking ahead . . .

As children move through the primary (elementary) and high school years, their social and emotional characteristics and needs will alter. The expression at later ages of many of the characteristics listed here can depend on how well the children's educational and social contexts meet their needs.

SUGGESTED FURTHER READING

For more detail on exceptionally gifted children, I recommend Gross, M.U.M. 1993 *Exceptionally gifted children* Routledge, London.

DISCUSSION QUESTIONS

1. What accounts for the common myth that many parents of young gifted children push their children to excel? Does something in the children's make-up or an aspect of the parent–child relationship give rise to this myth?

2. Do you see a conflict between gifted young children's thirst for knowledge and their need for independence?

3. What is the significance of young gifted children's earlier use of metacognitive skills? What does this imply for educational practice?

4. Which characteristics of their learning style do you judge to be most fundamental for gifted young children?

5. What does the information about locus of control imply for educational practice?

5

ASSESSING DEVELOPMENTAL ADVANCES IN YOUNG CHILDREN

The most important prerequisite of [identification systems] is that they should fit neatly with the existing structures and systems so that the identification of ability and talent can be an integral part of the [centre's] activities . . . It is only in [centres] where the identification is embedded in [centre]-based systems that it has significant impact on . . . practice. Otherwise, the link between identification and provision is tenuous: although certain pupils may have been identified, this process has not led to a change in classroom provision for these children.

Eyre (1997: 11)

KEY POINTS

- Accurate measurement of the extent of children's developmental advances is particularly difficult during the early childhood years owing to the inadequacies of our measures.
- Assessment involves gathering educationally relevant information from a variety of sources, only one of which is formal tests.
- Parents and caregiver-teachers can be accurate in their identification of children's developmental advances, particularly when they have a checklist to guide their observations and they are attuned to non-traditional manifestations of high ability.
- Despite the many limitations of IQ tests and their frequent misuse for purposes for which they were not designed, they can assess the extent of children's cognitive advances, but will be less useful at assessing other developmental domains and the skills of children from educationally disadvantaged backgrounds.

INTRODUCTION

The assessment of children with a view to determining whether their development is advanced rests on three assumptions: first, that all children have a right to an education that meets their needs; second, that gifted children are likely to have some particular needs that are not automatically met by a regular program; third, that the earlier we can identify that particular children have special needs, the sooner we can meet these needs through curricular modifications (Feiring et al. 1997).

This last point deserves some expansion. The early years are crucial in establishing children's interest in learning. If children's time is being wasted in an unchallenging program, they are at risk of developing learning, emotional, behavioural and social difficulties (Whitmore 1980). The opposite pattern can be conformity to low expectations (Shaklee 1992). Both can result in underachievement and lowered self-satisfaction.

SOME KEY TERMS

Educational *assessment* is a systematic process of gathering information which is relevant to making educational decisions regarding goals, curricula content and strategies, classification and placement (Assouline 1997; McLoughlin & Lewis 1994; Taylor 1997). It involves gathering information from a range of sources (Wright & Borland 1993).

Testing, in contrast, elicits children's responses on a series of questions posed under structured conditions (McLoughlin & Lewis 1994). A test is a tool—but only one of many—which is used to arrive at a complete assessment. Increasingly, testing is seen to have a relatively minor role in assessment, with the growing emphasis on curriculum-based measures such as portfolios.

The widespread dissatisfaction with formal tests arises from the fact that by their nature they tend to measure rote learning and recall, rather than higher mental functions such as analysis and evaluation of information. This can become a curriculum issue when it causes teachers to focus on teaching only those things which can be easily tested rather than teaching more complex abilities (Taylor 1997). The move away from formal testing also reflects the trend towards a more dynamic, holistic, multi-dimensional and continuous assessment that focuses on processes rather than products (Taylor 1997).

Evaluation is a related term, which refers to establishing the effectiveness of a program—as distinct from focusing on the progress of particular children (Cook et al. 1996). *Formative evaluations* involve collecting information as the program is continuing, in order to evaluate its effectiveness and to plan program modifications, while *summative evaluations* occur at the end of a program, to assess its effects (Cook et al. 1996).

TYPES OF ASSESSMENT ERROR

There is necessarily a debate about how to be *as accurate as possible* in the assessment of young children's development. (We will never be 100% accurate with testing, as no human endeavour is perfect.) The dilemma is, given the limitations of testing, how to combine objectivity with flexibility (Rimm 1984). Given that error is inevitable, we must choose the type of error we are prepared to tolerate.

The menu comprises two types of errors. The first is false positives, in which children will be identified as having particular needs which they in fact do not. This is termed *inefficient* identification. The second type of error is false negatives. This type is regarded as *ineffective* identification (Tannenbaum 1986), because it involves failing to detect children's special needs.

When identifying gifted children, false negatives are the more likely and the more serious error (Robinson & Chamrad 1986). The reason that false negatives are a real risk is that it is relatively easy to depress children's attainment by a suboptimal environment or inadequate assessment techniques, but rarely can children demonstrate more skill on a test than they are capable of achieving (examiner bias notwithstanding) (Robinson & Chamrad 1986; Smutny et al. 1997). The effect of false negatives is to deny some gifted children access to special educational provisions from which they would benefit. This can have obvious personal costs for individuals, and denies society the expression of those individuals' talented achievements if as a result of not having their needs met they later underachieve.

Although false positives sound a better option, they are inefficient (Tannenbaum 1986) and so do have costs—mainly in economic terms of providing special programs for individuals who might equally profit from a regular program.

All assessment techniques, therefore, will represent a trade-off between effectiveness (lack of false negatives) and efficiency (avoidance of false positives) (Tannenbaum 1986).

PLANNING ASSESSMENT

When planning assessment procedures, there are three questions to ask (Miller 1978, in McCormick & Schiefelbusch 1984): why assess, what will we assess, and how?

Why are we assessing the child?

With respect to children who are suspected of having advanced development, assessment can serve many purposes (Taylor 1997).

Screening. Initial screening aims to identify children who might need additional evaluation, and will occur before a child is referred for more specific testing. Screening measures will be broader and more naturalistic than the detailed and individualised assessments that are used for the remaining purposes.

Assessment of current skills. Determining gifted children's current performance level and corresponding educational needs is a fundamental goal. It will involve assessment of their strengths and relatively weak skill areas, as a guide to both their educational and social-emotional needs.

Curriculum planning. Another fundamental goal of assessment is to guide decisions about what and how to teach, based on a detailed understanding of children's level of functioning and the processes they use to deal with content.

Classification. This is a common reason for the assessment of children who are suspected of being gifted. It is a controversial function of assessment although, by definition, giftedness is a comparative label and so issues of classification are inevitable. This notion of inevitability implies that classification is necessarily negative, yet it can perform a social justice function: it can highlight the plight of certain sectors of the community who are known to be educationally disadvantaged compared with the dominant sector; it can target individual children for special educational provisions; and it can direct educational funds to the most needy children. Nevertheless, it is a process that is fraught with errors and misuses (which I examine later in this chapter).

Decisions about program placement. Placement decisions might involve planning early entry to school for young gifted children. If the child's program will be the same regardless of the assessment results, there is little point in assessing for this purpose. When the purpose of testing a child is to choose an appropriate educational placement, the test needs to tap the skills which are promoted in the programs being considered (Smutny et al. 1989). If you wanted to know whether a young child needed an enriching musical experience, for instance, you would not use an IQ test to find this out; but if you needed to know about the child's academic development prior to modifying an academic program, an IQ test would be appropriate.

When making decisions about program placement, the timing of the assessment is important. For instance, if the results will inform a decision about early entry to school, parents will need enough time to consider their schooling options before the child is due to start, and so the assessment needs to be done well in advance. On the other hand, if the assessment is to serve a dual purpose of informing the child's new teachers about his or her present skills, the assessment needs to occur as close as possible to the intended school starting date. These two needs have to be weighed up in a decision about when to carry out an assessment.

What are we going to assess?

The answer to this question will be guided by your earlier informal observations of a child's development. When you are assessing for suspected giftedness, the assessment method/s will need to be able to identify what skills the child possesses and whether these are significantly advanced for age.

How are we going to assess?

How to assess will depend on the answers provided to the first two questions. The chosen assessment method will need to be capable of generating a picture of a child's particular strengths and relatively weak skill domains, in order to design a suitable program. To achieve this, assessment should be an ongoing process rather than a one-off event (Fatouros 1986).

When assessing children whom we suspect of having significantly advanced development, the range of tools to use includes checklists, which outline some of the signs of advanced development. These are *criterion-referenced measures*: that is, they indicate whether the child does or does not display certain behaviours that fulfil our criteria for defining gifted attainment. Criterion-referenced measures tell you what a child is achieving, although not how well that achievement compares with other children's of the same age.

Because the notion of giftedness is linked with the notion of exceeding the norm, there are times when educators need to compare a child to the norm (or average) for his or her age. This is done using a *norm-referenced test*, typically a developmental or 'intelligence' test. Usually only a psychologist can administer these tests, and so they constitute the final stage of the assessment procedure.

PRINCIPLES OF ASSESSMENT

Seven principles should guide assessment for gifted children: advocacy, defensibility, equity, pluralism, comprehensiveness, pragmatism (Davis & Rimm 1998; Richert 1987), and programming relevance (Bergan & Feld 1993).

Advocacy. Assessment should uphold the interests of all children. Methods should be selected on the basis of whether they meet children's needs, rather than being administratively convenient.

Defensibility. Assessment methods should be based on the best available research and knowledge. This guideline is the basis for an accusation which is often levelled at standardised (normed) tests in particular—namely, that they are being used to assess abilities they were not designed to measure (Richert 1987). Another criticism is that various assessment procedures are being used at inappropriate stages of the identification process (Richert 1987)—for instance when screening measures are used to diagnose, when they are not powerful enough to achieve this.

Equity. Assessment methods should not disadvantage any groups within the community. (I shall discuss this issue in more detail later in this chapter.)

Pluralism. The broadest definition of giftedness should be adopted. Although recent research supports a pluralistic view of gifts and talents, there continues to be too much credence given to the single IQ score (Jenkins-Friedman 1982; Kitano 1990a). The result is that identification procedures commonly oversimplify the complexity of giftedness (Richert 1987).

Comprehensiveness. A related point is that as many gifted children should be identified as possible. False negatives need to be minimised.

Pragmatism. Assessment methods should be efficient in terms of the financial and personnel resources that they require. There is no point in relying on tests which can be administered only by psychologists, for instance, if there are too few of them to perform the assessments. Such scarce resources can be saved by identifying children by means other than standardised tests and reserving these tests for the minority of children whose skill levels are difficult to assess in more naturalistic ways (Gallagher & Gallagher 1994).

Programming relevance (utility). Assessment methods need to be able to do more than diagnose (i.e. identify who is gifted). They must also be able to identify children's strengths and needs, to help plan learning opportunities and to inform educational decisions (Bergan & Feld 1993; Rimm 1984; Treffinger & Renzulli 1986).

DIFFICULTY OF IDENTIFYING GIFTED YOUNG CHILDREN

Many parents and professionals are unwilling to label children—and young children in particular—as gifted. Even when they *are* willing to identify giftedness in very young children, accurate assessment remains a difficult task. Some young children are never identified as being gifted, for the following reasons.

- Young gifted children vary considerably in their outward behaviour, some of which can be interpreted negatively rather than being seen as part and parcel of being gifted (Kitano 1982, 1990a).
- Children can be gifted in a range of domains, and our ability to identify giftedness is likely to be better in some areas than in others (Robinson 1987). For instance a verbally talented child can be more obvious than a child with advanced mathematics or creative abilities.
- The detailed knowledge of child development which is the hallmark of early childhood care and education can unwittingly set a ceiling on our expectations of children, with the result that we do not offer sufficient challenge either to keep gifted children stimulated or to provide the opportunity for them to demonstrate their advanced skills (Shaklee 1992).
- Some young gifted children are aggressive or withdrawn because their social-emotional development does not match their advanced cognitive skills or because they are bored with the regular program.
- Some have not yet had experiences in the domain in which they might later develop special talents (Fatouros 1986).
- Some young children's advanced skills are hidden by their as yet immature social or emotional behaviours (Kitano 1990a) or their inability to direct their own learning: they might not concentrate for long enough to display their talents, for example (White 1985).
- The behaviour of young children often changes markedly in various environments, giving observers in different settings an inconsistent view of their skills (Fatouros 1986).
- Although it is crucial that teachers and caregivers be aware that talent can occur in any domain, there is a risk of overdifferentiation: that is, adults may not expect children who are talented in one domain (such as verbal skills) to be talented in another domain

(e.g. the arts) as well, and so might fail to identify a child's multiple talents (Guskin et al. 1988).

The variation in the outward behaviours of young gifted children makes it difficult to discriminate giftedness from other conditions. Parents and professionals can be forgiven for not thinking that giftedness could explain a child's stubborn refusal to dress her- or himself, lack of cooperation with adult instructions, apparent inability to play with children of his or her own age, and sometimes half-hearted attempts at activities. If anything, adults are likely to think that the child has some developmental delays!

The US literature (e.g. Burns et al. 1990; Sandel et al 1993; Tannenbaum 1983) often talks of beginning assessment with a broad-based screen of all children for the purpose of placing preschool-aged children in gifted programs. However, broad-based screening is not the practice in Australia, and there are few preschool gifted programs, making broad-based screening unnecessary. Nevertheless, it is important to identify early any children who would benefit from modifications to the regular early childhood curriculum. We thus need to rely in the first instance on parental reports and later on caregiver and teacher observations. This is entirely appropriate, as to do the reverse—that is, test children and then seek parents' and teachers' input only for those children who pass the screening test at a specified level—is to pay mere lip-service to the notion of using multiple assessment criteria. When done in that order, the achievement test is the pre-eminent measure and the use of other sources of information simply cosmetic (Jenkins-Friedman 1982).

PARENTAL REPORTS

Parents have detailed knowledge of their child's milestones, motivation and personalities, allowing them to be skilled reporters of their child's abilities (Feldhusen & Baska 1989; Louis & Lewis 1992; Robinson 1987; Roedell et al. 1980; Silverman et al. 1986). Indeed, in two studies (Ciha 1974; Jacobs 1971), parents correctly judged their child's giftedness 76% of the time, compared with 22% and 4.3% for early childhood teachers' ratings in the respective studies. These findings are similar to those of Louis and Lewis (1992) who found that 61% of parents correctly identified their preschoolers' advanced development, with the remaining 39% correct in that the children were advanced but not to the extent of being gifted.

Ciha and colleagues' study (1974) reported a much higher rate of parents' overestimation, perhaps because the questionnaire to which parents were responding comprised irrelevant indicators and because of the inadequate IQ measures to which parental reports were being compared. When parents were given a more accurate checklist of indicators, over 90% correctly identified their child's giftedness when the cut-off score was an IQ of 120 and 66.6% when the cutoff score was an IQ of 132 (Silverman et al. 1986). (A surprising finding of this study was that 100% of the children who were nominated by their parents but who were not identified as gifted on the IQ test had histories of recurrent ear infections. The researchers concluded that these children could be considered gifted-learning disabled as indicated by their sequential learning difficulties and the marked disparities between their strengths and weaknesses. If so, then the parents' nominations could be regarded as 100% accurate!)

Despite the accuracy of parents' reports of their child's developmental milestones, parents' impressions are often dismissed as biased (Robinson 1996). Some people think either that parents typically exaggerate their child's accomplishments or that they are pushy and might exploit their child (Delisle 1992; Harrison 1995). Contrary to these popular myths, parents do not tend to think that their child is gifted (Davis & Rimm 1998). It is more usual for them to underestimate their children's abilities than to overestimate them (Chitwood 1986), especially when the parents are well-educated (Roedell et al. 1980).

Underestimation can come about: when parents do not have another young child with whom to compare their own child's skills; when they do not notice their child's developmental advances; when their child's advanced skills follow less well-defined developmental sequences (e.g. spatial abilities) (Robinson 1993); or when, although they notice their child's advancement, they do not realise its extent. Other parents have an inflated view of giftedness based on an image of the child prodigy; while acknowledging that their child is 'bright', they do not realise that she or he might indeed be gifted (Mares & Byles 1994). Thus, even though parents can often judge the *direction* of their child's atypical development, they do not necessarily have the skills to judge the *extent* of any advances (Smutny et al. 1997).

More than this, some parents do not *want* their child to be gifted. Some mistakenly think that gifted children are not well-adjusted, and thus deny the talent that is right in front of their eyes (Davis & Rimm 1998; Mares & Byles 1994). Parents also worry about the effects of the 'gifted' label on the identified child and on his or her siblings (Colangelo & Brower 1987). Finally, some parents, and some members of particular minority cultures, can be reluctant to single their child out from the group by applying the gifted label (Feldhusen & Baska 1989).

For these and other reasons, many parents are reluctant to raise the issue of their child's precocity, and many teachers will not raise it with them. The result is an underidentification of giftedness, especially during the preschool years (Chamrad & Robinson 1986; Mares & Byles 1994).

This can be overcome when early childhood professionals seek parents' information about their child's milestones, needs and interests. This can be done at enrolment simply by asking parents questions about their child. A second possibility is to provide parents with a checklist of gifted behaviours (Roedell et al. 1980). Both approaches supply information which the centre does not have about a child, while your early childhood knowledge and gifted training can allow you to interpret whether or not the behaviours reported by the parents represent developmental advances. In this way, parent nomination is strengthened by collaboration with early childhood staff.

TEACHER OBSERVATIONS

Teacher nomination is the most widely used means of identifying gifted children (McBride 1992). However, early studies indicated that teachers were unable generally to identify gifted children, especially with children from minority cultural groups (Hadaway & Marek-Schroer 1992). In an early meta-analysis of studies about the accuracy of teacher identification of gifted children, Gear (1976) reports accuracy rates of between 4.4% and 48%, while Jacobs (1971) found that teachers' ability to identify gifted children was lowest during the early childhood years, when their accurate identification was just below 10%.

Some of the reasons for this low accuracy rate are the following.

- Caregivers and teachers who have not been actively involved in gifted education might have inflated views about how exceptional a child has to be in order to qualify as being gifted (McBride 1992).
- Inexperienced teachers of gifted children tend not to have positive views of giftedness (Cramond & Martin 1987) and, according to McBride (1992: 20), showed 'at best, indifference to the idea [of identification] and, at worst, outright antagonism and rejection'.
- Inexperienced teachers of gifted children can be particularly unwilling to label children at such an early age (McBride 1992).
- In McBride's study (1992), inexperienced teachers reported 'not knowing what they were doing' with respect to gifted education, and preferred to leave identification of gifted children to psychologists and special educators (who, however, are often not accessible enough).
- Teachers tend to stereotype giftedness, focusing only on intellectual or academic giftedness (Hany 1993).

- Teachers tend to underidentify slow-to-warm-up gifted children who hang back and only gradually become involved in activities and to disregard creative, non-conforming children, while overestimating the intelligence of children who plunge into activities readily and are cooperative and conforming to adult expectations (Jacobs 1971; Roedell et al. 1980; Westby 1997).
- Early childhood teachers might be better at identifying moderately gifted than highly-gifted children (Roedell et al. 1980), possibly because of how rarely they come across highly gifted children.
- When teacher nomination leads to referral to a segregated gifted program, teachers tend to 'play safe' and avoid disappointing children and their parents by nominating only those children who are certain to be admitted (Hunsaker 1994).
- Research into the accuracy of parent and teacher nominations typically compares their nominations to an IQ score, and assumes that the IQ score is the better and more accurate measure (Renzulli & Reis 1986; Tannenbaum 1983). Sometimes, though, the parents or teachers are correct and the IQ score is in error.

Recently, however, the early studies have come under criticism (see, for instance, Gagné 1994). It has been found that teachers' accurate identification can double without raising the rate of false positives when:

- they are trained to recognise advanced development (Gear 1978; Roedell et al. 1980), including atypical manifestations of giftedness in a range of domains, with children from minority cultures, and for those whose giftedness is not evident in their behaviour (Richert 1987; Yarborough & Johnson 1983);
- they can refer to a list of the signs of advanced development (Borland 1978);
- the children are given sufficiently challenging activities so that their talents can show up; and
- teachers have time to observe these talents (Denton & Postlethwaite 1984).

These findings hold for children from minority cultural groups (Hunsaker et al. 1997), for those who are underachieving at school (Borland 1978) and for creative abilities (Schleblanova 1996).

It is also important to remember that accurate assessment is not the responsibility of the caregiver or teacher in isolation. Identification should be a collaborative endeavour between professionals and parents: a teacher's job is simply to know which questions to ask parents about their child's development (McBride 1992).

Structured observation

Many young children virtually identify themselves through their advanced performances (Braggett 1997; Casey & Quisenberry 1976). Structured observation can enhance the picture of skills of this group of children and it can help to identify those children whose abilities are more mixed—those who, perhaps, have advanced knowledge but are unable to demonstrate it because of how they approach tasks.

Observation involves describing in specific terms what a child does, either in spontaneous situations or in activities which you have contrived in order to observe specific skill domains. When observing, it is important to avoid diagnosing or inferring reasons for the behaviour. (For instance, an observation is that Michael hit Sam following a dispute over a toy in the sandpit; an inference or diagnosis is that 'Michael was aggressive towards Sam', or even 'Michael is an aggressive child'.) As well as focusing on individual children, you can observe the educational program in order to assess its appeal and effectiveness, in general, for particular children, or for fostering particular behaviours such as co-operative play (Taylor 1997).

The research (reported in chapter 4) about gifted children's more efficient and effective use of metacognitive skills suggests that these could be useful identifiers of advanced development (Horowitz 1992). Therefore, you could instigate and observe activities that require the children to use and report on their metacognitive processes (see, for instance, Lowrie 1998).

Checklists

One estimate has 250 million normed tests being administered in US schools every year (Caplan & Caplan 1983, in Sisk 1998). The use of standardised tests is not so entrenched in the Australasian and British school systems, and this cultural difference has two implications. First, the American debate about testing in schools mainly questions its prevalence and pre-eminence as a tool for assessment (see, for instance, Haladyna et al. 1998). When standardised testing is targeted at referred children and used to supplement other sources of information—as is more often the case outside the USA—much of the controversy abates.

Second, it means that, in Australasia at least, parent and teacher referrals are the first method of identification of young gifted children. However, as already discussed, unguided nominations are likely to underidentify many children, particularly children from disadvantaged backgrounds. This means that the onus is on early childhood caregivers and teachers to be particularly attuned to the signs of advanced development, especially in children from non-typical families, so that these children can receive the assessment and subsequent educational provisions that they require. As Tannenbaum (1983: 360) observes: 'The use of nomination to help locate the gifted should not be an exercise of solving riddles without clues.' For this reason, checklists can be a useful way to sensitise parents, caregivers and teachers to typical gifted or talented behaviours.

A number of these checklists are reproduced in Appendix I. All appear to be straightforward, but they have a number of flaws. At the theoretical level, most have not established their reliability or validity (Hadaway & Marek-Schroer 1992) but rely instead on commonsense descriptors of giftedness. (An exception to this criticism is the list proposed by Silverman et al. (1986), which has since been slightly expanded and updated (Silverman & Maxwell 1996). This is reproduced in Appendix I.)

At the practical level and in terms of using checklists as identification tools, the first issue is that it is difficult to know how *much* of each characteristic a child has to display to qualify as being gifted. The items in a checklist indicate the *types* of advances gifted children can display, but not the *degree*. It can be difficult for parents to assess what 'learning *quickly*' means, or what 'most of the time' or 'often' means (Roedell et al. 1980).

Second, checklists do not indicate how *many* of these characteristics children have to demonstrate in order for the judgment to be made that their development is advanced. Some checklists are so broad that almost anyone could appear to be gifted, while other lists are so restrictive that no child would meet all or most criteria (Hadaway & Marek-Schroer 1992).

Third, checklists can incorrectly imply that all gifted children are the same, when they can display any combination of the attributes described in the lists.

Fourth, checklists rely on children's performances to identify giftedness, when we know that many gifted children underachieve and so would not be identified by observation of their behaviour. Children with behavioural difficulties are also unlikely to be identified by using a checklist (Roedell et al. 1980), particularly one leaving out the emotional or behavioural signs.

For these reasons, ultimate confirmation of advanced development will still have to rely on a normed test, in which a child's abilities are compared to the typical skills of children of that age. Unfortunate as it may be, the very notion of *giftedness* implies a comparison to what is average. A checklist does not refer to average development and so can only signal the need for further testing to compare a child to the norm (the average) for his or her age. Such a test is called a *standardised, normed* or *norm-referenced* test.

PORTFOLIOS

Recent enthusiasm in the US literature for portfolios is a response to this system's extremely high reliance on standardised testing and the resulting counter-trend to more naturalistic and ongoing assessment. Few countries share the US's reliance on testing (Walker & Barlow 1994), particularly in the early childhood years (Barbour 1992), so portfolio assessment is an answer to a problem that is by no means universal. Nevertheless, the literature on portfolio assessment can remind us not to assess only what children have been 'taught' (Bergan & Feld 1993) but to document children's growth in skills in real-life activities (Kingore 1995; Seely 1996; Shaklee & Viechnicki 1995).

Portfolios are not merely a collection of children's products but are a systematic compilation of their progress in all developmental domains, particularly in complex mental skills (Hadaway & Marek-Schroer 1992; Johnsen et al. 1993; Paulson et al. 1991; Seely 1996; Shaklee & Viechnicki 1995; Taylor 1997; Wright & Borland 1993). They are a structured file, documenting children's efforts and progress (Kingore 1995). As such, portfolios can offer evidence of advanced development— especially in non-traditional domains (Coleman 1994; Wright & Borland 1993). As an ongoing assessment technique, they can also help teachers to develop and enrich the curriculum through reflecting on its impact on the children (Seely 1996).

Depending on the target audience—usually the child's parents and next teachers—a portfolio could include (Wright & Borland 1993):

- observational notes about children's language and behaviour which might signal their interests and thinking;
- typical examples or photographs of their work;
- notable examples of their work which might indicate their ability, potential or progress, particularly in their use of learning strategies— that is, metacognitive skills (White 1985);
- child-selected examples—preferably of pieces of work that are special to the children (rather than examples of their 'best' work). Included in these examples will be the children's reflections on the work, which they can dictate for you to write out;
- notable moment records, which can be small file cards on which you record illuminating occurrences that help to round out the picture of the child's skills;

- let-me-tell-you-about-my-child cards, which are the parents' contributions to the portfolio. Given that children can behave differently at home from in the early childhood setting, these cards add significantly to information about the child, involve parents in the early childhood program and can help them focus on positive aspects of their child;
- finally, an exit summary report written by the caregiver or teacher on the basis of the contents of the portfolio.

While it is argued that portfolios can be useful in the early years, it is a leap of faith to assume that they can be useful in diagnosing giftedness. The products in individual children's collections must still be evaluated, which involves making sense of the information that has been gathered (Seely 1996).

For evaluation to be meaningful, you will need to be aware of the normal developmental stages so that you can recognise any departure from the norms. In order to identify advanced development (or giftedness), your attention could focus on four categories: exceptional knowledge acquisition, comprehension and application abilities, generation skills, and motivation (Coleman 1994; Shaklee & Viechnicki 1995).

- Exceptional *knowledge acquisition* abilities comprise quick and easy learning, exceptional memory for and retention of knowledge, and advanced understanding.
- Exceptional *use, comprehension* and *application* of knowledge comprise advanced use of symbol systems (language or numbers) and advanced reasoning abilities.
- Exceptional *generation* of knowledge involves creative, atypical thinking, self-expression, a keen sense of humour and curiosity.
- Exceptional *motivation to pursue knowledge* involves perfectionism (in a striving-for-excellence sense—see chapter 4), initiative, reflective style, long attention span on challenging tasks, leadership skills and intensity.

Despite such categorical systems to aid in the evaluation of portfolios, the reliability of evaluations is still questionable, and may be vulnerable to the teacher's cultural and class biases. For this reason, it is possible that culturally diverse children may be *less* rather than *more* likely to be identified through portfolios.

Of the few studies of the reliability of portfolio assessments, Johnsen and colleagues (1993) found little correlation between portfolio scores and the children's IQs, although portfolio scores predicted relatively well who would be placed in a gifted program. These researchers offered no data on whether the children were successful in the program, however.

Therefore, it is too early to say whether portfolios are reliable enough to be used when making important decisions for a child (Herman & Winters 1994)—such as about early entry to school. Thus, for such purposes, portfolio evaluation will still need to be supplemented by standardised ability measures (Hadaway & Marek-Schroer 1992; Wright & Borland 1993).

NORMED TESTS

The major purpose of norm-referenced tests is to give information about how a child compares with other children of the same age. You might need this type of comparative information about a child whose development appears to be advanced when:

- you would like a formal assessment to investigate your hunch that a child might be gifted (Braggett 1998a);
- you believe a child to be gifted but need to determine its degree in order to plan for meeting the child's needs (Braggett 1998a);
- you suspect a developmental reason for a child's behavioural or other difficulties;
- a child's development seems uneven, either in any one skill domain or across domains. This pattern can cause you to be unclear about what type of program would best suit the child's needs.

A norm-referenced test can determine (within the test's limitations) whether children's skills are significantly ahead of the norm (the average) for their age. The conservative tradition defines as gifted any children who are learning around one-third faster than usual—or, put another way, those whose abilities fall in the top 3%–5% of their age group.

INTELLIGENCE TESTING

Although it is accepted that IQ tests are inadequate as the sole or even pre-eminent measure by which to assess advanced development in all domains (Yarborough & Johnson 1983)—and that this is especially so in the preschool years (Barbour 1992; Robinson 1993)—young children are increasingly being referred for standardised assessment for suspected giftedness. The goal of IQ testing these children is to identify those who may require special educational provisions. Another, non-educational but equally valid, purpose is to help parents understand their child's dissonant development and any accompanying emotional or social difficulties.

In Australasia, most young children are referred for formal testing for giftedness only after parents or early childhood caregivers or teachers have observed the child's skills and formed an opinion that these appear to be advanced. In other words, formal testing is usually the third phase of assessment for giftedness, following parental or professional nominations and completion of formal checklists.

When identifying academic giftedness, the most common normed test is the 'intelligence test'. Its results are reported as an 'intelligence quotient', thus yielding the abbreviated name of 'IQ test'. (Owing to the controversies surrounding the term 'intelligence' as operationalised by these tests, I have chosen to refer to them from now on by their abbreviated title of IQ tests.) The average (or *mean*) intelligence is 100 IQ points. Traditionally, intellectual giftedness has been defined as any score that is two standard deviations or more above the mean, which translates to an IQ of above 130 on the Wechsler tests and above 132 on the Stanford-Binet. However, Gagné (1998) argues that this system does not translate well to other types of tests or forms of giftedness other than the academic, and so proposes a categorisation based on percentile ranks. (See Appendix II for an explanation of this statistic.)

In recognition that there is little difference in achievement between the top 5% of children and the 5% who fall just below them on IQ measures (Reis & Renzulli 1982), Gagné (1998) proposes a 'metric' classification system in which the top 10% are regarded as being mildly gifted, while the top 10% of that group are classified as moderately gifted, and the top 10% of them as highly gifted, and so on. Gagné's full categorisation is given in table 5.1. (The traditional classification is given in Appendix II.)

Table 5.1 A proposed categorisation of the levels of giftedness

Level	Percentage	Proportion of population	IQ score	Standard deviation equivalent
Mildly	10	1:10	120+	+ 1.3
Moderately	1	1:100	135+	+ 2.3
Highly	0.1	1:1000	145+	+ 3.0
Exceptionally	0.01	1:10 000	155+	+ 3.7
Extremely	0.001	1:100 000	165+	+ 4.3

Source: Adapted from Gagné (1998: 90).

Debates about the use of tests

Since their inception almost 100 years ago, IQ tests have been surrounded by controversy, much of it well-deserved. The advantages and disadvantages of these tests are summarised in table 5.2. In examining the issues, I follow the path suggested by Robinson and Robinson (1992), who ask the following questions:

- Are IQ tests dependable—that is, reliable?
- Are their findings meaningful—that is, valid?
- Do they reveal anything that is not already known about a child's abilities?
- How well do the tests describe a child's current developmental level?
- Can they predict children's future functioning?
- Are there groups of gifted children we are failing to identify by relying on IQ tests? (Gallagher & Gallagher 1994).

Table 5.2 Advantages and disadvantages of IQ tests

Advantages	Disadvantages
IQ test scores predict academic performance	IQ tests do not sample non-academic skills
IQ tests can identify gifted underachievers and those with learning disabilities	IQ tests underidentify creativity
IQ tests can serve a social justice role of highlighting the educational disadvantage of particular minority *groups*	IQ tests underidentify gifted *individuals* from minority cultures
IQ tests provide a profile of children's developmental strengths and needs	IQ tests can be poor guides for educational planning because their items are not necessarily functional
Observation of how children approach items during the test supplements the diagnostic information provided by the results; children with low confidence or motivation can thus be identified	IQ tests will disadvantage children who are not confident at taking tests and for whom too much might be read into the results on the basis of observations during a single assessment session
IQ tests avoid the biases inherent in purely subjective assessments	IQ tests introduce their own errors
The IQ test is a quick, relatively inexpensive way to sample reliably a broad range of academic skills	IQ tests inadequately sample evaluation and divergent thinking skills and the multi-dimensional nature of intelligence (while the tests are reliable, they are not necessarily valid)
IQ tests are more reliable and valid than any alternatives yet designed	IQ tests are acknowledged to be reliable, but are valid only with respect to intellectual giftedness
IQs allow comparison between children, thus allowing educational programs to target the most needy	IQ scores imply that one's ability is innate, stable and fixed, which can become a self-fulfilling prophecy

Reliability

Reliability relates to the stability of test results over time. There are two lines of evidence on this issue. First, as long as children's environments are stable (so that their natural rate of learning is not altered), IQ scores will be similar from one testing to the next. The actual score will change by perhaps five to nine points over one to six years (Cahan & Gejman

1993; Spangler & Sabatino 1995) but, overall, children's rankings within a group will alter very little (Tannenbaum 1992). Second, children who are identified as being gifted in the early childhood years are highly likely to maintain their advanced skills, at least into the early primary (elementary) years (Cahan & Gejman 1993; Spangler & Sabatino 1995).

Tests produce less reliable results with young children than they do for their older counterparts, however. The very rigour that makes these tests reliable also makes them inflexible and unresponsive to the requirements of young children, who can find the testing process demanding. Their test-taking behaviours (attention to instructions, concentration span and so on) can impair their test performance, although fewer gifted than average learners are untestable at young ages (Morelock & Morrison 1996). These and other contaminants of the testing situation can lead to unreliable measurement, especially with very young children. These cautions aside, many writers contend that the tests are still the most accurate method of assessing children's intellectual development (Assouline 1997; Kaufman & Harrison 1986; Stanley 1976; Tannenbaum 1983).

Validity

The issue of validity—whether IQ tests measure anything meaningful—is the crux of the debate about these tests. There is a danger that precision of scores (reliability) will be confused with validity (Sternberg 1982). This tension between reliability and validity is exemplified by Pruzek (in Jenkins-Friedman 1982: 26):

> It is better to provide imprecise answers to the right questions, than precise answers to the wrong ones.

In other words, critics claim that, although IQ tests are reliable, they do not necessarily measure anything worthwhile. They sample a narrow range of intellectual abilities in a single domain, as chosen to represent mainstream society's definition of giftedness (Davis & Rimm 1998; Grinder 1985; Matthews 1980; Sternberg 1982; Sternberg et al. 1996), making them valid 'for some of the people some of the time' (Sternberg 1982: 157). This leads to the claim that culture-fair tests cannot exist because culture influences all learning opportunities and, in turn, test performance (Masten 1985).

As well as sampling a narrow range of content, IQ tests are accused of tapping a narrow range of processing skills (Sternberg 1986b). They do not ask children to apply, extend, analyse, synthesise or evaluate information in creative ways but simply to generate superficially correct responses on cue (Davis & Rimm 1998; Sternberg 1986b; Sternberg et al. 1996; Wiggins 1993, in Assouline 1997). Advocates for testing agree with this assertion but claim that these higher-order skills are less amenable to reliable measurement (Gallagher & Gallagher 1994; Robinson & Chamrad 1986). Also, although higher-order skills are essential for creativity and are clearly part of intelligent behaviour, they are not highly valued in the school system and so do not predict academic success. This observation causes Sternberg (1986b) to criticise schools for rewarding lower-order skills, which might ultimately be detrimental to society, in that it deprives us of original thinkers.

Do tests reveal any new information?

The first significant benefit of IQ tests is their ability to identify children's strengths, thus shifting the focus from a deficit orientation (Vialle & Konza 1997). This can be particularly important when children have been referred for behavioural, emotional or educational difficulties—that is, when some explanation other than giftedness has so far dominated the understanding of their behaviour. Underachievers and gifted children with learning disabilities can be identified as well (Kaufman & Harrison 1986; Pyryt 1996).

A second, related benefit is that children's test-taking behaviour and scores can alert the examiner to the potential for certain emotional difficulties. For example, children (either with gifts or disabilities) who have an uneven profile of abilities can have low self-esteem because they expect themselves to do equally well in all skill areas, and are disappointed in themselves when they cannot.

Third, normed tests allow us to identify an individual whose development is significantly advanced of the normal pace and who therefore might benefit from an enriched program. In contrast, a checklist or other criterion-referenced measure will document what a child is achieving but will not indicate the extent of the advancement, and therefore might fail to recognise children who need a modified program.

Fourth, normed tests also rank children by severity of need. These results are used by agencies to allocate support services to those children who demonstrate the most need. Whether or not this is ideal, it is reality. It protects taxpayers from funding unnecessary services, and ensures in a crude way some justice in the allocation of tax-funded services. If the child is eligible for services, the normed test is of direct benefit to the child and family. If because of the results a needy child remains a low priority for services, society needs to examine its fund allocation. The fault does not lie with the test.

Finally, IQ tests have served the social justice function of making educators aware of the relative educational disadvantage of many minority groups (Pyryt 1996).

Do IQ tests accurately describe children's skills?

The question to be answered about IQ tests is not whether they are perfect—as they clearly are not—but whether they describe children's abilities better than alternative measures (Robinson & Chamrad 1986). The response to this is a qualified 'yes': they do give a fair indication of an individual's expected success on academic tasks, as Gardner (1983: 3) concedes:

> The importance attached to the [IQ score] is not entirely inappropriate: after all, the score on an intelligence test does predict one's ability to handle school subjects, [al]though it foretells little of success in later life.

However, tests are more likely to underestimate than overestimate children's abilities (Smutny et al. 1989), both because factors unrelated to ability can lower children's test scores, and because of the tests' low ceilings (see Burns et al. 1990; Davis & Rimm 1998; Kaufman 1992).

Despite these limitations, Kaufman and Harrison (1986) contend that until something better can be devised, the IQ test is still the most technically sound measure of academic ability and should not be replaced by a less sound instrument because of an aversion to the misuses of IQ tests.

Future predictions

Much of the discussion about the merits of IQ testing examines whether the tests predict excellent performances later in life. However, it has always been a vain hope that IQ tests could predict later achievement, given the many emotional and external factors that contribute to the actualisation of an individual's potential (see Gagné 1995; Sternberg & Lubart 1991; Tannenbaum 1997). Indeed, as might be expected, children's voluntary leisure activities are a better predictor than an IQ test of later achievement in a particular area (Freeman 1998a).

It is widely accepted that IQs obtained in the preschool years are less robust predictors of future performance than scores obtained later (Robinson & Chamrad 1986). This is mainly because at younger ages the items in the tests bear little resemblance to problem-solving tasks in later life, and so young children's scores are less likely to tally with their adult performances (Gallagher & Moss 1963). Nevertheless, if children score in the extremely high or low ranges, it is likely that their score will remain within that realm throughout life (Sattler 1988). Also, after the age of 5 years, the tests improve in their predictive power—except for children who become sensitive to the testing situation as they get older and offer only responses of which they are certain (Silverman

1991). In these cases, an earlier assessment might be more accurate than a later one. A final caution: correlations between scores in early life and functioning in later life are based on *groups*, not individuals (Worthen & Spandel 1991). Therefore, important decisions should never rest on a single assessment and early tests will need to be repeated at significant decision-making times throughout a child's life.

Are we failing to identify some children?

Most children have advances in many skill domains, and so will be relatively easily identified by tests (Robinson & Robinson 1992) but those who have advanced skills in just one domain may not be recognised if there is continued reliance on IQ tests alone. It is also likely that if we continue to rely solely on IQ tests for identification of gifted children, we will continue to underidentify minority cultural group members, rural children, children with disabilities, and children who live in poverty (Borland 1996b; Braggett 1998a; Davis & Rimm 1998; Gallagher & Gallagher 1994; Maker 1996; McKenzie 1986; Richert 1987, 1997; Scott et al. 1996; Sternberg 1982; Tannenbaum 1983). These children might be burdened by their family situation such that they cannot focus on their own learning, they might lack sufficient stimulation at home, or they might have gifts or talents in domains which are not well-recognised by the dominant sector of society (Richert 1987).

The underidentification of disadvantaged gifted children brings accusations of test bias arising from inappropriate test content, language bias and norming bias (Masten 1985). The first is an issue of validity, with which we have already dealt. In terms of language bias, children from minority cultures often perform less well on ability tests that are designed for the dominant culture. This is likely to be a result of their lack of facility in the spoken or written language of the mainstream culture and will in turn affect both their real-life performances and their test-taking abilities (Brooks 1998; Frasier 1997; Henriques 1997; Robisheaux & Banbury 1994; Tyler-Wood & Carri 1993).

As to norming bias, most modern and reputable tests are normed on a sample that matches the racial and socioeconomic make-up of the country in which the test is developed—usually the USA—and so norming bias is a less serious issue, as long as the test is used in its country of origin. Nevertheless, some writers (e.g. Pendarvis & Howley 1996) argue for using local norms so that disadvantaged children are compared with people who are similar to themselves, although this approach could compromise the reliability of the instrument and result in the overemphasis of cultural or economic differences (Bailey & Harbin 1980; Passow & Frasier 1996).

An alternative view is that differential results by children who are experiencing educational disadvantages are not due to flaws in the tests or in testing but to the fact that society—not the tests—disadvantages minorities (Borland 1986; Richert 1987; Pyryt 1996; Tannenbaum 1983; Taylor 1997). The tests accurately reflect the fact that these children *are* less likely to excel at school and beyond (Pyryt 1996), but this is a social flaw, not a fault of the tests.

Finally, it must be said that using test results to plan educational programs for children is a vast improvement on using subjective impressions of the children's learning abilities and general demeanour, which simply perpetuates the inequalities that children bring to school (Rist 1970). The 'old boy' network has served disadvantaged children even less well than standardised testing presently does (Worthen & Spandel 1991). Bias would not be eliminated by abolishing testing and would still leave us with many decisions to make, with less defensible bases on which to make them (Pendarvis & Howley 1996; Worthen & Spandel 1991). Thus, we need to:

- increase teachers' awareness of atypical manifestations of giftedness, in a range of domains, and in children from diverse backgrounds (Bailey & Harbin 1980; Pendarvis & Howley 1996);
- improve tests by ensuring that their content reflects the everyday meanings and events to which children are exposed (Scott et al. 1996) rather than relying on dominant language experiences (Tyler-Wood & Carri 1993);
- use information from multiple sources and about a range of adaptive skills that are valued by non-majority cultural groups (Bevan-Brown 1996; Maker 1996; Passow & Frasier 1996; Plucker et al. 1996; McKenzie 1986; Renzulli & Reis 1997; Scott et al. 1996; Tannenbaum 1983).

Our best assessment instrument is human (Borland & Wright 1994): tests do not allow us to see everything and so we must supplement their objectivity with sensitivity for atypical manifestations of giftedness (Passow & Frasier 1996; Smutny et al. 1989).

Choice of test

There is a range of assessment tools available in the early childhood age range. In most common use for testing 3 to 6-year-olds in Australia are the Wechsler Preschool and Primary Scale of Intelligence—Revised Edition (WPPSI-R) and the Stanford-Binet (Fourth Edition). In less common use (in Australia, although not necessarily elsewhere) are tests such as the Kaufman Assessment Battery for Children (K-ABC) and the

McCarthy Scales of Children's Abilities (Perleth et al. 1993). Only rarely would a child be referred for formal testing before the age of 2 years, in which event the Bayley Mental Scales of Infant Development or the Griffiths Mental Development Scales might prove useful.

In order to select an appropriate assessment instrument, testers must know when testing would be appropriate, how to select an appropriate test for the given purpose, how to interpret the findings accurately, and how to communicate those findings appropriately to both lay and professional readers of the assessment report (Hansen & Linden 1990). A normed test for assessing advanced development can be selected on the criteria of whether the test:

- measures skills that are relevant either to an intended gifted program or in the child's life (Feldhusen & Baska 1989; Hansen & Linden 1990)—that is, whether the information gained will be educationally useful (Fallen & Umansky 1985). This is the utility criterion, which says that testing must aim to improve services for children (National Association for the Education of Young Children 1988);
- is valid and reliable—that is, technically sound in its construction (Hooper & Edmondson 1998; NAEYC 1988). This criterion acknowledges that the younger the child, the more difficult it can be to obtain reliable and valid results on a standardised test (NAEYC 1988);
- samples a wide range of behaviours in a range of settings, gathering information from sources other than standardised measures to supplement test scores (Hansen & Linden 1990), especially when placement decisions rest on the findings (NAEYC 1988);
- has few limitations, particularly with respect to the purpose to which the test is being put (Hansen & Linden 1990);
- is culturally fair, which is to say that assessment must not underestimate the skills of children from any given culture (Hooper & Edmondson 1998);
- has a design and format that is suitable for the age of the children being tested (Fallen & Umansky 1985);
- can be administered by personnel who are skilled at and familiar with assessing young children (NAEYC 1988);
- can be interpreted accurately by available personnel (Hansen & Linden 1990);
- can avoid the negative effects on children (Hansen & Linden 1990) that arise through misuse of the findings or from labelling children;
- is used only for the purpose for which it was designed;
- is efficient in terms of administration time and cost and does not

unduly burden the child with prolonged assessments (Fallen & Umansky 1985).

A PROPOSED ASSESSMENT MODEL

Figure 5.1 illustrates a proposed series of steps for assessing young children's abilities and needs. It could be called an 'identification by provision' approach: by providing an enriched curriculum, the caregiver or teacher gives children the opportunity to display their talents (Braggett 1997; Passow & Frasier 1996; Wallace 1986a; Zorman 1997). The model thus begins not with the child but with the program. The program is not altered in response to the identification of giftedness; rather, the identification of giftedness occurs when teachers and caregivers recognise the advanced way in which a child is responding to the curriculum.

A basic requirement of the model (figure 5.1) is collaboration (at phase II) between parents and caregivers or teachers in order to identify which children need special provisions or more in-depth assessment. This phase will be informed by formal checklists or ongoing measures such as observations and portfolios.

Those children whose developmental status is still a puzzle—plus those who, for eligibility or placement reasons, need a standardised assessment—will be referred (usually to a child psychologist) for normed testing. Children whose developmental status is unclear might be those with dissonant development across domains; children with disordered development (e.g. gifted children who also have a specific disability); and children whose approach to tasks limits their performance (Braggett 1997).

The proposed model refers for standardised assessment only those children whose developmental status is uncertain. This avoids tying up scarce resources (e.g. psychologists' time) in the quest to avoid false positives, while still aiming to minimise false negatives by giving credence to parents' and teachers'/caregivers' everyday knowledge of children (Gibson 1997).

The main benefit of such a model is that it avoids neglecting talented children who do not identify themselves by high scores on IQ tests (Davis & Rimm 1998). This will particularly benefit children from educationally disadvantaging backgrounds and those with both gifts and learning disabilities (Passow & Frasier 1996). In this model, interpretation of scores from standardised tests is tempered with more authentic assessment information from parents and teachers and, if the two are at odds, more data will be gathered. The IQ score will not be trusted over

Figure 5.1 A proposed model for the identification of advanced development in young children

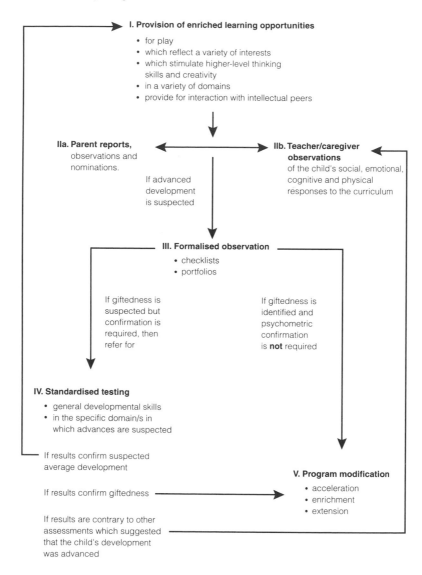

the other measures (Borland 1986): tests are more likely to underestimate than overestimate children's abilities (Gibson 1997) and children's talents may emerge later in their development (Eyre 1997). IQ scores will thus be used to verify that a child is gifted, but scores alone should never be used to define a child as 'not gifted' (Borland 1986; Mares 1991; Rimm 1984; Yarborough & Johnson 1983).

This approach will ensure that the focus is on *assessment*, not on *testing* (Hebert 1992). In accordance with Eyre's advice (1997), the model also ensures that assessment information can be used directly within the curriculum, as most of the assessment is carried out by the people who are responsible for programming. Eyre (1997) reports that once teachers are aware of children's high abilities, they tend to provide more educational challenge and, as a result of observing children's responses to these challenges, become more adept at identifying high abilities in future.

CONCLUSION

It is an overstatement to say that IQ tests measure 'intelligence' (Borland 1986). Nevertheless, when information is required about a child's academic functioning, these tests can be a useful tool.

Having said this, there is virtually unanimous agreement that the IQ test should not be the only assessment measure (Kaufman & Harrison 1986; Robinson & Chamrad 1986). There is a limit to what an examiner can find out about a child in a 90-minute session, even when looking not only at the scores the child ultimately achieves but also at how the child goes about the test tasks.

Rowe (1990) suggests that many professionals rely on testing as a drunk relies on a lamp-post: more for support than illumination. Gardner (1983: 16) echoes this implied caution and offers the following conclusion on the merits of intelligence testing:

> Most scholars within psychology, and nearly all scholars outside the field, are now convinced that the enthusiasm over intelligence tests has been excessive, and that there are numerous limitations in the instruments themselves and in the uses to which they can (and should) be put.

Shaklee's (1992) advice is to use a single evaluation strategy— namely, *knowing the child well*. This will be achieved by collecting information from a range of sources and interpreting that information on the basis of sound knowledge about child development.

Looking ahead . . .

Some gifted children are particularly creative, which is unlikely to be identified by an IQ test (Davis & Rimm 1998). In the early childhood years creativity is difficult to measure; at later ages it might be possible to recognise it with a test of creativity, although there are serious questions about these tests' reliability and validity (Tannenbaum 1983).

Any IQ test that is administered in the preschool years will need to be repeated at later ages. This is because development is dynamic, and so the child's strengths and needs might change with maturation. You would not prescribe glasses for a child on the basis of an old vision test; similarly, you should not design an educational program on the basis of a dated intellectual assessment (Gallagher & Moss 1963).

Peer nominations are often recommended for identifying older gifted children who demonstrate leadership skills (Richert 1987). Self-nominations are also valuable. These can be used only to a limited extent in the early childhood years; both can usefully supplement information from other sources by the late primary (elementary) school years onwards.

SUGGESTED FURTHER READING

Almost any text on assessment would give additional background about the issues covered in this chapter, although few specifically concentrate on assessment of giftedness. My suggestion is Taylor, R.L. 1997 *Assessment of exceptional students: educational and psychological procedures* 4th edn, Allyn & Bacon, Boston.

If you would like a detailed treatment of intelligence testing, the text on which psychologists often rely is Sattler, J.M. 1992 *Assessment of children* revised 3rd edn, Jerome M. Sattler Publishing, San Diego, CA.

DISCUSSION QUESTIONS

1. In your experience, what is the most common reason for assessing young gifted children's suspected giftedness? Is this reason valid?

2. In your experience, what are the most common assessment methods used? Are there viable alternatives that would expand your knowledge of children's skills?

3. How would you suggest overcoming the difficulties of identifying gifted young children?

4. How could portfolios be used in your present setting to expand awareness of young children's skills?

5. Referring to the characteristics of giftedness described in chapter 4, how could you improve on your effectiveness and efficiency of identification of giftedness in young children?

6. What are your impressions of the proposed model for assessing giftedness? Is it practicable? Can you see any constraints on its implementation?

6

EMOTIONAL ADJUSTMENT OF GIFTED CHILDREN

[For gifted children], nearly everything matters, and it matters that it matters.

Kline and Meckstroth (1985: 25)

KEY POINTS

- The literature on gifted children's social and emotional adjustment focuses mainly on their friendships, popularity with peers and self-esteem.
- Gifted children tend to be at least as well adjusted emotionally as average learners, although there are contradictory findings on the issue.
- Those who believe that gifted children do have additional emotional difficulties cite as reasons gifted children's neurological sensitivity, the lack of a true peer group, or the mismatch between their needs and the regular environment.

INTRODUCTION

It is assumed that to be well-adjusted, individuals need to have a healthy self-esteem, to feel satisfied with their relationships, and to have some control over what happens to them (Porter 1996). Since Terman's finding that gifted individuals were well-adjusted (Terman et al. 1947) was compared with Hollingworth's conclusion that gifted children are vulnerable emotionally and socially, there has been an ongoing debate about their emotional status (Grossberg & Cornell 1988). Naturally, gifted children can experience the same traumatic life events—such as their parents' divorce or deaths in their family—that all children experience (Grossberg & Cornell 1988). But the issue here is whether they have additional problems as a direct result of being gifted.

DEBATES ABOUT GIFTED CHILDREN'S EMOTIONAL ADJUSTMENT

There are three claims made about whether gifted children have unique emotional characteristics which in turn make them vulnerable to emotional difficulties. The first is that the qualitative differences between gifted and average learners are largely emotional and contribute to gifted individuals' heightened social-emotional vulnerability; the second claim accepts the emotional differences between gifted and average learners but contends that the difference advantages gifted individuals; a third view is that there is no qualitative difference at an emotional level.

To test these claims it will be useful to introduce two terms: endogenous and exogenous factors. *Endogenous* factors are characteristics of an individual that affect his or her functioning, while *exogenous* factors are external events that influence a person's adjustment (Webb 1993).

Qualitative differences leading to emotional vulnerability

The first view is exemplified by the Columbus Group, which believes that gifted individuals' highly attuned nervous system (their brain) contributes both to advanced learning and to an increase in their emotional sensitivity, intensity and responsiveness (Geake 1997; Lovecky 1992; Miller et al. 1994; Morelock 1996; Piechowski 1997). This endogenous explanation holds that gifted young people's potential for intrapersonal and interpersonal conflict arises from many factors, which include their: divergent thinking ability, insightfulness, need to understand, excitability, sensitivity, perceptiveness, need for logical precision, non-conformity, and need for self-determination (Lovecky 1993; Silverman 1993a).

Geake (1997) gives a biological explanation for the link between giftedness and emotional intensity. He describes that gifted individuals have more efficient links between the limbic system—which is the seat of emotions in the brain—and the pre-frontal lobes, which are responsible for the executive functions or metacognitive abilities that oversee our learning. Therefore, when a child demonstrates a special ability to learn, which involves superior use of metacognitive skills, it is likely that the child also has more ready access to his or her emotional store (Geake 1997).

A variant on this qualitative hypothesis is that as IQ rises the uniqueness of gifted individuals becomes more pronounced (Davis & Rimm 1998; Delisle 1992; Gross 1997; Harrison 1995; Kline & Meckstroth 1985; Kline & Short 1991; Tannenbaum 1992; van Boxtel & Mönks 1992; Whitmore 1980). This is the curvilinear model of social-emotional adjustment (Grossberg & Cornell 1988; Oram et al. 1995). This model hypothesises that from the average to some point in the highly gifted range children's emotional adjustment will increase, but that adjustment will decline with growing ability beyond the highly gifted range (see figure 6.1).

Figure 6.1 Hypothesised curvilinear relationship between IQ and emotional adjustment

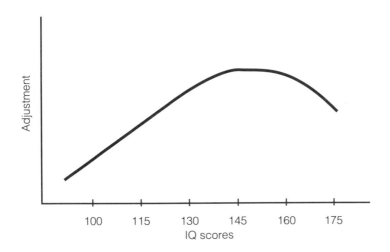

However, even if gifted individuals are shown to be more emotion-ally vulnerable than the norm, another, exogenous explanation is equally plausible. This holds that gifted individuals are at risk of social and emotional difficulties not because their nervous system is created qual-itatively differently, but because their atypical needs are met either with negative reactions or indifference (Freeman 1997; Webb 1993). As a result, gifted children are forced to adapt to society, instead of the reverse (Taylor 1996). Their giftedness makes it difficult for them to fit into the usual social and educational structures that suit their averagely develop-ing peers (Culross 1995; Grossberg & Cornell 1988; Kline & Meckstroth 1985; Taylor 1996; Whitmore 1980). According to this exogenous explanation, if services were to supply what gifted children needed intellectually and socially, the children would be better adjusted emotionally. The source, then, of their emotional difficulties is seen to be the mismatch between their environment and their special needs, not the neurological and psychological make-up of the children as such (Webb 1993).

Qualitative differences leading to improved adjustment

The second view is that gifted children's social-emotional development actually proceeds *better* than that of average learners (Clark 1997; Grossberg & Cornell 1988; Janos & Robinson 1985; Kunkel et al. 1995; Moon et al. 1997; Nail & Evans 1997; Olszewski-Kubilius et al. 1988; Parker 1996).

The findings of better social-emotional adjustment have both an exogenous and an endogenous explanation. The exogenous one is that in many studies (e.g. Terman's) the children came from homes with high socioeconomic status and strong backing for achievement. The children's family and school environments provided the necessary support both for the development of their talents and for their emotional adjustment (Stedtnitz 1995). The second, endogenous, explanation is that most gifted children can use their sophisticated cognitive skills in order to solve any problems they face and so can make satisfactory adjustments to being gifted (Freeman 1997; Webb 1993; Whitmore 1980). Gifted children's internal locus of control and high levels of organisational perfectionism would also protect them from emotional difficulties such as depression, since depression arises from feeling helpless (Lynd-Stevenson & Hearne, in press). Clark (1997: 145) summarises this argument when she says that 'the very ability that creates the problem can supply the solution'.

No differences

The final position states that there is *no* qualitative difference between gifted and average learners emotionally. Hence, there is no increase in emotional adjustment problems in gifted children (Feldhusen & Nimlos-Hippen 1992; Freeman 1991; Gallucci 1988; Grossberg & Cornell 1988; Lehman & Erdwins 1981; Robinson & Noble 1991; Rost & Czeschlik 1994). Some writers (e.g. Lehman & Erdwins 1981) qualify this by noting that, when compared with older children of the same mental age, gifted children's adjustment is similar; when compared with same-aged children their adjustment is better, particularly in the social skills domain.

Other authors (e.g. Manaster & Powell 1988) argue that, while overall adjustment is similar, gifted children face *different* issues from average learners. These writers contend that gifted children's atypical development has three effects:

- developmentally, they are out of stage, which is to say their cognitive development proceeds ahead of others, resulting in talents that differ from the average;
- socially, they are out of phase, which means that these advanced abilities make it less likely that they will have interests in common with age mates;
- psychologically, they are 'out of sync'—some gifted young people feel different and, as a consequence, believe that they *cannot* fit in with others.

It is possible that, while developmental dissonance and social asynchrony are inevitable for gifted children, feelings of being emotionally or psychologically 'out of sync' could arise from how the children interpret their circumstances and so could be changed with a change in their thinking.

THE EVIDENCE ABOUT GIFTED CHILDREN'S EMOTIONAL ADJUSTMENT

The first thing that needs to be said is that there is little research evidence to support the 'current wisdom' that gifted individuals are more emotionally vulnerable than the rest of the population (Gallagher 1990, in Lewis et al. 1992; Gust 1997). Gust contends that most of the debate is based on folklore or professional anecdotes. The latter can be good places to start, but continued reference to them as if they reflect common experience is a mistake that contributes to parents' reluctance to identify their children as gifted and to ongoing misconceptions and misunderstandings of gifted children's characteristics and needs (Gust 1997).

The debate often refers to Dabrowski's theory about gifted individuals' 'overexcitabilities' and their drive towards a 'deeply meaningful life' (Piechowski 1997: 372). The latter is more a personal philosophy of life than a testable theory, and space precludes addressing it; instead, I examine the evidence for these 'overexcitabilities'. In order to do so, it is important to realise that the term 'overexcitability'—which, to many, would have negative connotations of neurosis—is in fact taken by Dabrowski and his adherents to mean an abundance of psychic energy which provides 'positive potential for further growth' (Tucker & Hafenstein 1997).

One source of evidence about these excitabilities comes from Lewis and colleagues (1992), who found that gifted children did characterise themselves as being more intense on many of Dabrowski's five dimensions (intellectual, emotional, imagination, psychomotor and sensual). They confirm Dabrowski's definition that these traits provide positive potential for growth in that the children reported that these intensities had actually enriched their lives.

Kitano (1990b) found no relationship between scores on IQ and creativity tests and Dabrowski's 'overexcitabilities' for preschool children, although she did find that as the children's IQ scores rose, their parents increasingly reported them to be intense intellectually. Like Lewis and colleagues, Kitano observed that this 'intensity' does not signify emotional difficulties. However, it could be hypothesised that thwarting an intense need could bring about a stronger than usual reaction (Freeman 1983), in which case it is not the intensity as such but inappropriate responses from others that can create difficulties for gifted children.

Ackerman (1997) found evidence of psychomotor, intellectual and emotional excitabilities (in that order) in gifted adolescents. She hypothesised that motor intensity supplies the necessary energy to achieve, particularly for the 12 to 14-year-age group that she studied. On the other hand, one-third of the 'non-gifted' children resembled the gifted children in their pattern of excitabilities, while a quarter of the gifted students matched the 'non-gifted' ones. Ackerman took this to mean that these children had been mislabelled: some were identified to be gifted when they really weren't, while others' giftedness had not been recognised. However, it could equally mean that the 'excitable' emotional profile is neither unique nor essential to giftedness.

A further source of evidence comes from a study by LeVine and Tucker (1986). These researchers found that gifted 6 to 8-year-olds showed greater awareness of others' feelings, had more sophisticated moral reasoning and a more internal locus of control than average learners. However, the children's interpersonal *perceptiveness* could be regarded as a cognitive skill, rather than a sign of emotional *sensitivity*. On the other hand, when combined with limited life experience, precocious perceptiveness can cause children to misinterpret events and this, in turn, can lead to emotional difficulties (Freeman 1983).

Finally, Tucker and Hafenstein (1997) asked teachers to nominate a child (aged 4–6 years) who fitted the description of each of Dabrowski's five types of overexcitability. The researchers gathered assessment data about each child, questionnaires from parents, interviews of teachers and observations of the children in class. They concluded that the nominated children exhibited characteristics of intellectual, imaginational and emotional overexcitability—which is not to be wondered at, given that this pattern was what led their teachers to nominate them for the study.

Unfortunately, these results tell us nothing about whether gifted children in general possess overexcitable characteristics.

EXPLANATIONS FOR CONFLICTING FINDINGS

Despite the paucity of evidential support, the clinical literature describes some emotional risk factors for gifted children (Lewis et al. 1992). The two views can perhaps be reconciled by considering the country of origin of the studies: attitudes to giftedness, the resulting educational provisions, and thus the children's own responses to being gifted are likely to vary between cultures (Webb 1993). Against this background, the following additional factors may give rise to the disparate conclusions.

Group versus individual perspective

While it may be true that some *individuals* experience emotional issues about being gifted, it may be equally true that, on the whole, gifted children *as a group* are well-adjusted (Gallagher 1997; Schauer 1976).

Dissonance versus asynchrony

While many advocates of Dabrowski's theory would accept that gifted children are not 'out of sync' with their age mates in terms of their emotional wellbeing, nevertheless these children have above-average intellectual skills alongside average emotional development, resulting in internal dissonance (Shore & Delcourt 1996). This could be countered by observing that, if it were such a problem to the children themselves, then it would show up in their reduced emotional adjustment, and this does not seem to be the case.

Bias in subject selection

Another explanation lies in how the research into emotional sensitivities has been conducted and how subjects are selected for studies on the issue of emotionality. For instance, Dabrowski based his theory on clinical and biographical studies of patients and eminent intellectuals and artists (Ackerman 1997)—that is, those who stood out for their performances. However, they might also have been easily identifiable because of their pattern of emotionality, in which case the finding that they were more emotional would not be surprising.

Similarly, clinical studies—such as Lovecky's (1992)—which focus on gifted individuals who have been referred to counselling services for emotional difficulties are naturally going to find a higher rate of emotional problems (Gagné 1997; Webb 1993). The reverse is also true:

children who are well-adjusted are less likely to be recognised as being gifted (Freeman 1991, 1997).

Another form of bias comes about because children in gifted programs are most often studied because they are easy to locate. However, there is a bias in who is admitted to such programs, which favours academically well-adjusted children from well-educated families with a high standard of living (Webb 1993). This makes it difficult to tease out which factors are due to giftedness and which to socioeconomic status (Robinson & Noble 1991).

Finally, children who are achieving academically so highly that they are identified as gifted are likely also to be functioning well in other areas of life; those whose giftedness has not come to the fore may be experiencing some social or emotional difficulties (Webb 1993).

Age of children

With research on children, age may have a bearing on the findings. There appears to be a downturn in young people's confidence during the middle high school years, which improves thereafter (although not necessarily reverting to former high levels) (Klein & Zehms 1996; Kline & Short 1991; Kunkel et al. 1995; van Boxtel & Mönks 1992). Therefore, when middle high school students are studied, problems become apparent; while older and younger subjects do not evidence as many difficulties.

Placement of children

The preponderance of studies of children attending gifted programs could result in sampling children whose educational and social needs are being more adequately met than in regular programs, or who were already displaying good adjustment which resulted in their selection for the gifted program. Either of these explanations could account for the research findings that these children show more favourable adjustment compared with the broader population of gifted children.

On the other hand, children in gifted programs appear to experience lowered academic self-concepts as a result of having more able classmates with whom to compare themselves (Craven & Marsh 1997; Gross 1997; Wright & Leroux 1997). Nevertheless, the academic self-concept of children in gifted programs is still above average (Gross 1997, 1998) and so does not represent maladjustment.

Levels of ability

There is some tentative evidence that gifted children's social and emotional difficulties grow with their intellectual ability (Brounstein et al.

1991; Gross 1993c). However, a study by Oram and colleagues (1995) did not support this curvilinear model. Perhaps this was because their study sampled few individuals in the highly gifted range; nevertheless, their caution is valid—namely, that teachers and parents cannot equate gifted children's adjustment with their level of giftedness but must look to other social, familial and personal explanations for adjustment problems.

Types of ability

Children with high verbal abilities may be at greater risk of adjustment difficulties than children with talents in other domains (Ablard 1997; Brody & Benbow 1986; Dauber & Benbow 1990; Swiatek 1995). This is probably because verbal abilities are more obvious in social situations than, say, mathematical skills, making the verbally gifted child more likely to stand out.

IQ tests measure *both* intelligence and emotional qualities

Another perspective is offered by Tannenbaum (1983), who mounts the argument that 'non-intellective' or personal qualities contribute during testing to the resulting IQ score that is used to denote children's level of intellectual functioning. Therefore, an IQ score is *both* a measure of children's level of intellectual functioning *and* their emotional status; thus, it should not be surprising that high IQs correspond to emotional status.

A similar conclusion is reached by Freeman (1983, 1991) by a slightly different route. She found that parents' and teachers' stereotypes of gifted children as social misfits caused adults to identify as gifted those children who were experiencing social-emotional difficulties—and to fail to recognise as gifted those children who were well-adjusted socially and emotionally. This creates a pool of gifted children who are not necessarily typical of all gifted children and who thus bias our studies (Freeman 1983, 1991, 1993).

Exogenous factors

Schauer (1976) reports that, while gifted children are more independent and less conforming in their behaviour, they seem to be well-adjusted. Perhaps well-adjusted individuals are more likely to grow up in an environment that accepts their independence and does not demand that they conform; children who are less well-adjusted might be reared in a setting that is critical of their emotional characteristics.

Other predisposing problems

It could be that, just like anyone else, when gifted individuals experience adjustment difficulties, these are a result of conditions other than their giftedness. Schauer (1976), for instance, reports that the majority of gifted individuals who were showing signs of poor adjustment in fact had undetected learning difficulties.

IMPLICATIONS OF THE DEBATE

Although written with the intention of supporting parents in their quest to find appropriate provisions for their exceptionally gifted children, claims (e.g. by Webb et al. 1991: 31) that gifted children are 'fundamentally' different from others are not warranted by the evidence. Rather than helping, such claims could depower parents and professionals, who could doubt their ability to handle an unusual child. Instead, it seems plain to me that most of what we know about meeting the needs of all children will apply equally well to gifted youngsters (Shore & Delcourt 1996). With this as my basis, the recommendations in the next chapters draw on practices from both gifted and general education.

CONCLUSION

The notion of the 'mad genius' still permeates lay understandings of giftedness, despite evidence that ongoing mental illness and gifted productivity are incompatible (Yewchuk 1995a, 1995b). One analysis concluded that around 10% of highly gifted people have psychiatric disturbances for at least some of their lives (Simonton 1984, in Yewchuk 1995b). Even this figure might be an overestimation, as reviews of biographies of famous achievers are contaminated with the superstitions and limited medical knowledge of the times (Yewchuk 1995b).

The first thing to be said, then, is that the incidence of emotional disturbance in gifted individuals is probably the same as for the rest of the population. Given that 9%–10% of all children experience some emotional difficulties (Gallucci 1988), and that some of these children will be gifted, we know that *some* gifted children are at risk of emotional difficulties and are therefore worthy of special attention (Konza 1997).

The second conclusion is that, probably predominantly for exogenous reasons, the rate of social-emotional problems *might* indeed be higher for gifted children than in the general population (Silverman poses a figure of 20%) and, if so, then a particular focus on gifted children's emotional needs is warranted.

The third conclusion is that, even if this estimate proves to be in error and gifted children indeed have a similar *rate* of emotional adjustment difficulties to others, the issues which they confront are *different* from the issues for their peers (Manaster & Powell 1983). Thus, we need to be aware of their special challenges and ensure that they adjust with the minimum of distress.

Looking ahead . . .

The debate presented here tells us that the social and emotional adjustment of young children will depend largely on the extent to which their environments are responsive to their changing needs throughout childhood. Any negative emotional reactions are likely to reflect these external factors rather than any personality characteristics that are peculiar to gifted children.

DISCUSSION QUESTIONS

1. What is your conclusion about the social and emotional adjustment of young gifted children? Does being gifted pose extra difficulties for them?

2. Do you think your conclusion would differ if you were considering older children or adults? In what way does age affect children's adjustment?

3. Is any increased vulnerability due to internal (endogenous) features of the gifted child or a result of external factors?

4. What do your conclusions imply for educational practice?

GIFTED YOUNG CHILDREN'S SELF-ESTEEM

Self-esteem is not a trivial pursuit that can be built by pepping children up with empty praise, extra pats, and cheers of support. Such efforts are temporary at best, and deceptive at worst. Our children need coaches, not cheerleaders.

Curry and Johnson (1990: 153)

KEY POINTS

- Self-esteem is both an effect of former learning and a cause of our approach to the tasks that we attempt in future.
- Self-esteem is a comparison between our concept of ourselves and the standards which we uphold for ourselves; these separately encompass our social, emotional, academic, family and physical capabilities.
- Gifted children generally have positive global and academic self-concepts but they may feel less positively about themselves in other realms, such as the social domain.
- Self-esteem can be promoted by expanding children's self-concept and helping them to adopt realistic ideals for themselves. A third and fundamental route to a healthy self-esteem is promoting children's competence at worthwhile activities.

INTRODUCTION

There are two ways of looking at self-esteem. Some writers see it as a filter through which we evaluate our achievements and assess our coping skills. In this way, it determines how we approach future tasks. A second way of looking at self-esteem is that it is a *result* of achieving at relevant and worthwhile activities.

My conception is that it is both. We develop a healthy self-esteem from knowing that we have formed successful and accepting relationships and that we are learning. This sets up an *expectation* about our future learning. In this way, self-esteem is both an *effect* of past learnings and a *cause* of future learning (Chapman et al. 1990).

This means that enhancing self-esteem is desirable both in itself and because it contributes to other favourable outcomes such as improved academic achievement (Craven & Marsh 1997). It also means that children's self-esteem will not be improved by making them feel better about their achievements: it will be necessary to ensure that those achievements are worthwhile. Success—at something meaningful— breeds confidence.

WHAT IS SELF-ESTEEM?

Individuals' self-esteem is largely set in place in the very early years of life. Children learn about themselves from their parents' reactions to them. By a process called 'reflective appraisal', children interpret these judgments and build this feedback into a picture of the type of people they are. As time goes on, their earlier experiences act as a filter which distorts the information that they receive from other people (Adler et al. 1995).

In their first two years or so, when young children are learning to trust their caregivers, their self-esteem relies almost entirely on whether they feel loved and *accepted*. After that age, their self-esteem begins to be fed by how much *control* they can exercise over their lives. They use adults' reactions to their attempts at independence to feel pleased—that is, *morally virtuous*—or guilty about their efforts, and they begin to define themselves as *competent* or as failures (Curry & Johnson 1990).

So self-esteem is learned. Adults' reactions to children tell them about the type of people they are and also the type of people we want them to be. Children then judge how much they measure up to this ideal. That is, self-esteem has three parts (Burns 1982; Pope et al. 1988): the self-concept, the ideal self, and self-esteem itself.

The self-concept

This is our picture or description of ourselves. (This aspect is also termed self-perception.) Children's self-concept becomes more comprehensive as they get older, mainly owing to their accumulated self-knowledge, a process that can be expected to begin earlier for gifted children because of their earlier self-awareness (Hoge & McSheffrey 1991; Sekowski 1995; van Boxtel & Mönks 1992). Young children's self-concept describes how they look, what they wear, their state of health, and their possessions; as they get older, they begin to describe themselves in terms of their relationships, abilities and talents at sport and academic work, temperament, religious ideas, and ability to manage their lives (Burns 1982). Their ancestors, family and cultural membership will also be part of children's self-concept.

These characteristics together make up the global self-concept. Global self-concept is an amalgam of five relatively distinct facets: social, emotional, academic, family, and physical (Hoge & McSheffrey 1991; Pope et al. 1988; van Boxtel & Mönks 1992). Each of these aspects is further divided into subfacets, which are lower in the hierarchy and become less stable over time and more situation-specific (van Boxtel & Mönks 1992). I would equate these to 'self-confidence', which is very skill- and situation-specific.

The ideal self

This is our beliefs about how we 'should' be. This set of beliefs comes about from actual or implied critical judgments by significant people in our lives or by a process called social comparison, in which we compare ourselves to other people and evaluate ourselves accordingly (Adler et al. 1995). It is clearly important to choose realistic models with whom to compare ourselves, lest we generate an unduly lax or harsh set of ideals. These ideals can be explicit, such as wanting only distinctions in one's study, or implicit, with standards that the individual hardly knows she or he is imposing and which therefore can be more difficult to identify and challenge (Pope et al. 1988).

Self-esteem

Not all of the characteristics that we possess are equally important to us. Feedback from others allows us to rank our characteristics according to how important or valued they are to other people; we then usually internalise those value systems. Self-esteem thus reflects how much we *value* our characteristics: it is a judgment about whether our abilities and qualities meet or fall short of the standards that we believe are ideal. (For example, I will not feel badly about my lack of swimming prowess if I come from a family that does not value swimming; if, however, I come from a family of Olympic swimmers, then being able to swim would be central to my self-esteem.)

Our self-esteem—the comparison of our performance with our

ideals—has both an intellectual and an emotional component (Pope et al. 1988). That is to say, how we *think* about our achievements affects how we *feel* about them. If our thinking highlights our deficiencies and ignores our achievements, our emotional reactions to these supposed deficiencies are likely to be unrealistic or extreme.

Summary: the nature of self-esteem

It is clear that self-esteem is multi-dimensional. The self-concept contains many descriptors of ourselves, while the ideal self ranks these traits according to how highly we value each one. Our self-esteem is a measure of the extent to which our self-concept and ideal self overlap (see figure 7.1).

Figure 7.1 Diagram of self-esteem as the congruence between the self-concept and ideal self

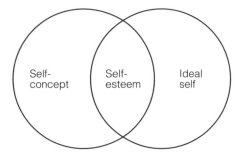

An unhealthy or low self-esteem can come about in either of two ways. First, our beliefs about the type of person we are (i.e. our self-concept) might not be accurate because we do not notice enough of our positive attributes. Second, our expectations of ourselves (our ideals) could be too high, and as a result we believe that we have few of the characteristics we 'should' have.

CHARACTERISTICS OF INDIVIDUALS WITH A HEALTHY SELF-ESTEEM

A healthy self-esteem is one that 'realistically encompasses shortcomings but is not harshly critical of them' (Pope et al. 1988: 2). People with healthy self-esteem have more accurate perceptions of their positive qualities and more realistic expectations of themselves; there is thus a high degree of overlap between how they think they are and how they want to be. (The self-concept and ideal self will never overlap entirely, of course; otherwise individuals would have no ambitions or goals for which to strive.) The following list describes these and other characteristics of individuals who have a healthy self-esteem (Adler et al. 1995; Clark 1997; Curry & Johnson 1990). They:

- lead others spontaneously;
- make transitions easily;
- approach new and challenging tasks with confidence;
- set goals independently;
- have a strong internal locus of control;
- assert their own point of view when opposed;
- trust their own ideas;
- initiate activities confidently;
- cope with criticism and teasing;
- tolerate frustration caused by mistakes;
- describe themselves positively;
- make friends easily;
- accept the opinions of other people;
- cooperate and follow rules, remaining largely in control of their own behaviour;
- show pride in their work and accomplishments;
- make good eye contact (although this can vary across cultures).

Signs of low self-esteem

Young children who have low self-esteem can display a wide range of less adaptive behaviours, such as being reliant on the approval of others. This can show in constant requests for declarations of love, or when children are constantly helpful in the belief that they have to 'earn' adult approval rather than deserving it just for being themselves. They might overreact when they fail or are gently chastised, cannot report any positive characteristics of themselves, or constantly say negative things about themselves and their abilities, such as 'I'm hopeless', or 'I can't'.

Their pessimism can mean that they are not able to have any fun, are withdrawn, and are not able to enter a group without being either too self-conscious ('shy') or too boisterous. Finding and keeping friends can be a problem, and negotiating conflict can be difficult because they do not have enough confidence to stick up for themselves. They are easily bullied or led. At later ages they might develop and maintain relationships with other children who are also experiencing difficulties, almost as if they think that they are not capable or worthy of better relationships.

When young children expect too much of themselves, they are often hard on other people as well. They might tell tales on their friends because they cannot break rules themselves and believe that no one else should. Potential friends can be put off by their competitiveness, and peer rejection then feeds their low self-esteem.

Children with low self-esteem might rely so much on adults that they cannot separate from their parents at an appropriate age, and so do not develop independent play and self-care skills at the usual age. (Alternatively, this can result from a mismatch between the child's needs and the environment in which he or she is being left, rather than being due to the child's low self-esteem.)

Finally, some individuals are motivated not so much by the desire to succeed as by the desire to avoid failure (Davis & Rimm 1998). This will yield one of two patterns of behaviour: underachievement as a result of not seriously challenging their skills; or compulsive high achievement, in which their self-esteem is tied so closely to success that they cannot bear to fail (Davis & Rimm 1998). Thus, young children with low self-esteem might:

- avoid trying something new, refuse to take risks or be adventurous;
- give up easily;
- play the same game over and over because they are afraid of failing at something else;
- refuse to work without instructions in case they make a mistake;
- get frustrated with their mistakes;
- lack initiative;
- be uncertain about making decisions.

EFFECTS OF LOW SELF-ESTEEM

In truth, we do not really *know* what effects low self-esteem has. There are problems with defining self-esteem and difficulties with conducting research into such a pervasive but ill-defined concept (Craven & Marsh 1997). All we can say is that we assume that the behaviours that we associate with low self-esteem can have an effect on individuals' success because their self-doubts detract from their ability to perform. In terms of social adjustment, children with low self-esteem can be rejected by other people partly because they do not have the emotional resources to be supportive to others.

Keeping in mind the lack of evidence on the issue, the following statement by Clark (1997: 159) is nevertheless instructive:

Low self-esteem results in higher levels of anxiety, more frequent psychosomatic symptoms, less effectiveness, and more destructive behavior. Children with low self-esteem find it hard to believe that any personal action can have favourable outcomes. Instead, they believe themselves powerless and unworthy of love or attention.

SELF-ESTEEM OF GIFTED CHILDREN

Most of the information that we have about gifted children's self-esteem comes from school-aged children and adolescents. These findings are summarised here, but we have to be cautious when applying them to young gifted children. One thing we do know, however, is that the quality of children's relationship with their parents is fundamental to their self-esteem, from the early childhood years (Windecker-Nelson et al. 1997) right through adolescence (Walker & Greene 1986).

Gifted children of all social classes, ethnicity and gender tend to have high global and academic self-esteems (Ablard 1997; Brounstein et al. 1991; Chan 1988; Chapman & McAlpine 1988; Hoge & Renzulli 1993; Karnes & Wherry 1981; Pyryt & Mendaglio 1994; Robinson & Noble 1991; Tidwell 1980; Van Tassel-Baska et al. 1994; Wright & Leroux 1997). That is, in terms of figure 7.1, most gifted children's global and academic self-concepts are congruent with their ideal self (Jenkins-Friedman & Murphy 1988). They set realistic expectations for themselves, are willing to risk failure, and can notice their achievements.

As well, gifted children usually feel most positively about their area of talent (Chapman & McAlpine 1988; Davis & Rimm 1998; Hoge & Renzulli 1993; Sekowski 1995; van Boxtel & Mönks 1992). However, as many as 20% seriously underestimate their abilities (Phillips 1984, 1987) while, for many (but not all), high academic self-concepts are offset by their lower opinion of their other abilities—such as physical skills and social relationships (Ablard 1997; Brounstein et al. 1991; Kelly & Colangelo 1984; Tannenbaum 1997). This can cause gifted individuals to focus on developing their intellectual skills, with the results that their interests become more narrow and other people's perceptions of them become negative (Sekowski 1995).

Performance and self-esteem

Having high potential is not enough to bolster children's self-esteem: they must be performing well too (Delisle 1992; van Boxtel & Mönks 1992; Vespi & Yewchuk 1992). This means that underachieving gifted children generally have lower self-esteem than high achievers, which can be both a result and a cause of their underachievement. As Delisle

(1992: 117) states: 'A child who learns to see himself or herself in terms of failure eventually begins to place self-imposed limits on what is possible.'

Developmental differences

Age might play a part in gifted young people's emotional adjustment although findings about this are not uniform (Hoge & Renzulli 1993). It appears that a need for social conformity temporarily lowers mid-adolescents' self-esteem (Kunkel et al. 1995; van Boxtel & Mönks 1992), while younger and older children and adolescents are less subjected to peer pressure and so experience a higher social self-esteem (Klein & Zehms 1996; Kline & Short 1991).

Placement

Some studies (e.g. Feldhusen et al. 1990; Kolloff & Moore 1989; Maddux et al. 1982) report neutral effects on gifted children's self-esteem from their involvement in gifted programs, while others demonstrate that the children's self-esteem is improved. A closer look reveals that children's social and physical self-appraisals are enhanced—probably as a result of making friends with children who have similar interests to themselves—while their academic self-esteem may be lowered (Chan 1988; Craven & Marsh 1997; Gross 1997; Olszewski et al. 1987). Importantly, Chan (1988) and Carter (1986) found that there was no decrease in the self-esteem of students who were not selected into the gifted program.

At first, the finding of neutral effects with respect to academic self-esteem seemed surprising since the children were thought to be receiving an academic program which better reflected their needs. However, it is now realised that children who are placed in gifted programs have more capable youngsters with whom to compare themselves (Chan 1988; Jenkins-Friedman & Murphy 1988). Increased expectations arising from being identified as gifted and the children's change in ranking within the more able group can result in a lowered—although perhaps more realistic—picture of their own academic skills (Coleman & Fults 1982; Craven & Marsh 1997; Hoge & Renzulli 1993; Marsh & Craven 1998; Marsh et al. 1995; Schneider et al. 1989; Wright & Leroux 1997). Craven and Marsh term this 'the big-fish-little-pond effect'.

It is also apparent that, in terms of their academic self-esteem, children who are interested in *doing* their best appear to fare better in gifted programs than children who are interested in *being* the best (Craven & Marsh 1997; Gross 1997).

Gender differences

There are no consistent differences between the self-esteem of gifted girls and boys that are not apparent in average girls and boys (Czeschlik & Rost 1994; Hoge & Renzulli 1993; Tong & Yewchuk 1996). Boys may have higher physical self-esteem than girls, while younger girls might have higher academic self-esteem than younger boys (Chan 1988; Feldhusen & Nimlos-Hippen 1992; Lea-Wood & Clunies-Ross 1995). However, because they may be concerned about the social stigma attached to being gifted and female, girls' academic self-esteem lowers as they get older, while boys appear to adjust increasingly to their abilities and their academic self-esteem improves (Kline & Short 1990). The result is that the self-esteem of the two genders balances out—both in terms of their overall or global self-esteem and throughout childhood.

Although being successful is probably more acceptable for boys, many gifted girls are likely to have strong role models in their talented mothers and so do not regard themselves as misfits (Howard-Hamilton & Franks 1995). Girls are also likely to achieve through conformity, but might be disadvantaged later in life by being trained to be conventional (Loeb & Jay 1987; Kline & Short 1991).

METHODS TO ENHANCE SELF-ESTEEM

Lilian Katz (1995: 34) has this to say about enhancing children's self-esteem:

> Self-esteem is most likely to be fostered when children are esteemed. Esteem is conveyed to them when significant adults and peers treat them respectfully, consult their views and preferences (even if they do not accede to them), and provide opportunities for real decisions and choices about events and things that matter to them.

Early childhood is an ideal time to inoculate gifted children against developing feelings of low self-worth. This can be done by teaching young children how to think of themselves in constructive terms and how to set realistic standards for themselves, and by ensuring that they can be successful at worthwhile tasks.

Promote a constructive self-concept

Some children's perception (or view) of themselves is dysfunctional and unduly negative. These youngsters are probably the ones to whom we are referring when we talk about children with low self-esteem.

Accept yourself

Children will watch how you react to your own successes and mistakes. If you accept yourself—even your own imperfections—children will learn from you how to be gentle with their own failures. If you acknowledge your successes, they will learn that it is okay to notice their own. So, instead of only ever saying negative things about yourself, try saying some positive things, such as: 'I'm really good at . . .'. The children will copy your positive attitude to self.

Accept children

Their behaviour. When a child has made a mistake, you can accept the person without having to accept the behaviour (Rodd 1996).

Their feelings. It is crucial that you accept children's feelings, even when they are different from yours. Fields and Boesser (1998) make the point that some adults believe that 'little people have little feelings', which is clearly not so. Children's feelings are as meaningful to them as ours are to us, and it is important that you accept what they are feeling even if you do not understand why they feel that way.

Their backgrounds. Another part of accepting children is accepting their cultural backgrounds. You will need to do more than give children information about the exotic customs and dress of other cultures: you should demonstrate acceptance of children's diverse backgrounds in your day-to-day interactions with all the children. By accepting diversity of all kinds, you make it possible for the children to accept other differences, such as varying rates of development among them.

Talk to children respectfully

To let children know that you value and respect them, you will need to talk to them courteously, regardless of their age or ability levels. It is also important to talk to children about things that interest them and to gain information that you do not already have, rather than just giving instructions or asking instructional questions such as 'What colour is that?'.

Listen

When children are disappointed in their performance, it is tempting to try to reassure them. However, this can be an inadvertent message to 'Get over it'. Reflective listening can show them that you understand and that you know they can cope with feeling disappointed. You might say something like 'I can see that you're disappointed in your model', perhaps followed by a question, such as 'Do you want to do anything to improve it, or leave it as it is?'.

PERMISSION TO BE YOURSELF: FIVE FREEDOMS

The freedom to see and hear what is here
Instead of what should be, was, or will be.
The freedom to say what one feels and thinks
Instead of what one should.
The freedom to feel what one feels
Instead of what one ought.
The freedom to ask for what one wants
Instead of always waiting for permission.
The freedom to take risks on one's own behalf
Instead of choosing only to be 'secure' and not rocking the boat.

Virginia Satir (1976), reprinted with permission of Celestial Arts

Foster belonging

Because children need to feel connected to others, your relationship with the children in your care is important to their self-esteem. Your relationship needs to involve the five As—acceptance, attention, appreciation, affirmation, and affection (Albert 1989, in Rodd 1996).

Children also need to feel connected to each other. Their friendships matter as much to them as adult friendships matter to us. Friendships not only meet their social needs but feed their self-esteem and protect them from stress. Thus, it is important that a child finds at least one true peer with whom to relate. Age groupings in early childhood centres can work against this, as finding an intellectual peer for a gifted child often means finding an older child. (I discuss how to overcome this obstacle in chapter 9, which looks at children's social needs.)

Encourage autonomy (independence)

All individuals need to feel that they have some degree of control over their lives (Rodd 1996). Sometimes our good intentions to help children makes us do things for them which they could do for themselves (Brown 1986). Children need opportunities to exercise choices, initiative and autonomy. Therefore, it is important to provide some structure for children, while also giving them some freedom to make choices within the framework (Hay 1993).

There are three levels of choices that we can offer children (Porter 1997a, 1999). When the activity has to be done—such as washing hands before a snack—then we cannot give a choice of *whether* to do it, but we can give options about *how* (using the hand-dryer or paper towels, going with a friend etc.). If there is no choice about how, then we can give a choice about *how to feel* about it. For instance: 'It is time to wash your hands. You can get upset about that, or you can get on with it happily. It's up to you.'

Give specific feedback

Especially when children are becoming discouraged about their performance, it will be necessary for you to acknowledge and support their efforts. Jones and Jones (1995) report that teacher feedback is often too vague and does not specify success or failure accurately. They advise that adults need instead to give feedback which specifies exactly what the child has achieved. Children might also need help to notice positive feedback and not to take negative feedback too much to heart.

Not only does feedback need to be specific—it also needs to be *authentic* (Curry & Johnson 1990). This injunction raises the issue of praise, whose authenticity is sometimes questioned.

Give acknowledgment

Underlying praise is an attempt to manipulate children into repeating a behaviour of which we approve, as if they would not otherwise choose to behave considerately (Porter 1997a, 1999). It is difficult to deliver praise fairly, because we cannot really judge how much praise a child deserves. The result is that children can learn to resent praise or can become competitive with each other so that they receive more praise than others (Hitz & Driscoll 1988; Porter 1997a, 1999). At the same time, outside rewards such as evaluative praise—in contrast with informative feedback—can detract from children's own natural motivation (Kohn 1996; Ryan & Deci 1996) and can promote unrealistic standards for their behaviour. (For a contrary opinion, see Cameron & Pierce 1994, 1996; Eisenberger & Armeli 1997.) These and other potential disadvantages of praise are summarised in the box on p. 130.

On the basis of these disadvantages, I contend that it is less risky to avoid praise and instead to show children how to acknowledge their own successes (Porter 1997a, 1999). Acknowledgment is different from praise in the following ways:

1. Acknowledgment teaches children to *evaluate their own efforts*. ('What do you think of *that*?' . . . 'Was that fun?' . . . 'Are you pleased with yourself?' . . . 'You seem pleased that you did that so well'.) In contrast, praise approves of work that meets *adult* standards.

SUMMARY OF DISADVANTAGES OF PRAISE

Effects on the child's self-esteem

- Praise and other rewards imply that the adult knows everything in all domains and so has a right and is able to judge whether someone else's achievements are adequate.
- Children will not feel accepted when they know that they are being judged.
- Rewarded children might expect themselves to 'be good' all the time, which lowers their self-esteem when this is impossible.
- Praise teaches children that other people's opinions of them are more important than their own. This can stifle self-reliance.

Interference with learning

- Praised children may engage in 'adult-watching' to assess which behaviours the adults will approve. This distracts them from their own developmental tasks.
- Praise causes children to focus on external rather intrinsic rewards; it inhibits self-motivation.
- Praise can interrupt children's concentration.
- Praised children may strive to please and fear making mistakes, and so may avoid being creative and adventurous.

Provoking misbehaviour

- Discouragement from being unable to meet unrealistic expectations may cause some children to behave disruptively.
- Praise does not teach children to monitor their own successes, and so does not give them the skills to regulate their inappropriate actions.

Ineffectiveness of praise

- Praise can be automatic for the adult and thus delivered in a meaningless way.
- Adults and their praise will lose credibility if children's evaluation of their work does not match that of adults.

Praise can be unfair

- Adults need a high level of technical expertise to use praise well.
- While some children can 'pull' praise from adults, other children cannot, and receive less praise than they deserve.
- Praise encourages competition between children.
- Their experience that praise is unfair causes children to reject the adults who administer it.
- Many children come to resent being manipulated by praise.

Source: Adapted from Porter (1996).

2. Unlike praise, acknowledgment *does not judge* children or their work, although we still might choose to tell them what we think or feel about the work. (For example, 'I like the colours you used' replaces the praising statement that a painting is 'beautiful'.)
3. Acknowledgment focuses on the *process* rather than the outcome. You can comment on children's effort, rather than on the end product. ('Looks like you're having fun over there', or 'I can see you're enjoying drawing', or 'I'm impressed at how long you have been working on that'.)
4. Acknowledgment is a *private* event, which does not show children up in public or compare them with each other. Unlike praise, it does not try to manipulate other children into copying a child who has been praised. Acknowledgment simply describes—in private—the behaviour that you appreciated. ('Thanks for being quiet while I found a book to read', or 'I appreciate that you tidied up the home corner'.)

Self-esteem is literally a *self*-evaluation. By acknowledging rather than praising children, you will be helping them to evaluate their own achievements and will be adding to their self-concept without feeding their ideal self. In this way, there is more chance that their self-concept and ideal self will match more closely, with the outcome that their self-esteem will be safeguarded.

Instigate activities to help children notice their qualities

It is important for children to have a realistic picture of themselves. Partly because of their age but sometimes also because of a pessimistic outlook, many young children see themselves in black-and-white terms: either they are completely hopeless, or totally wonderful. These children need help to appreciate their qualities in a more balanced way.

If children are perfectionists or are not noticing their own qualities sufficiently, you can help them to make a list of things they can do. You can begin with a heading, 'Jake can . . . ', and then make a list of all his thinking, physical, social, play, self-care, speech and caring-for-others skills. Some of the items on the list could be: 'Jake can run, listen, answer the telephone, help set the table, wash his own hands, feed the cat, smile, make friends, be happy, pick up toys, feel angry', and probably a hundred other, very specific skills.

List *anything* that he has ever done: a single instance is enough to tell you that he can do it, even if he does not do it all the time. And do not qualify these statements with 'sometimes' or 'when he tries', or with descriptions of how well he does the activity. But if the child insists that you write down that, for example, he can run fast, then you make that two items ('Jake can run', and 'Jake can run fast'). Remember also that the skills you list must be appropriate for the child's age (e.g. he can feed a pet, but he cannot be responsible for its total care; he can give his mother a hug when she's upset, but he cannot be responsible for looking after her).

Other activities include the 'All about me' books, in which children draw themselves and write down their favourite things. These activities are intended to expand children's self-concept—that is, to broaden their description of themselves. But such activities will not improve their self-esteem if they do not value the characteristics on their list. Katz (1995) advises focusing on enduring skills and traits, such as being able to try when a task gets difficult or being a considerate friend, rather than such skills as being able to ride a bike, which virtually every child can do. Similarly, if you acknowledge a child's inherited characteristics, his self-esteem will not improve because he had no control over those characteristics and cannot take the credit for them. Instead, you will need to acknowledge *effort* rather than cleverness, *personality* rather than appearance, learning *style* rather than outcome (Katz 1995).

Promote realistic ideals

Individuals' self-esteem is likely to be high when their ideals are realistic. After you have made children more aware of their positive qualities (i.e. helped to expand their self-concept), you can help them to set realistic expectations of themselves.

Self-expectations

Self-esteem is the measure of how well we achieve the standards that we expect of ourselves. Part of having realistic ideals is having a valid reference group (Adler et al. 1995). If we compare ourselves to people who are very different from us, we will be setting unrealistically deflated or inflated standards for ourselves.

Expectations from others

Gifted children in one study (Ford 1989) complained that their parents expected them to do their best all the time, and that parents highlighted deficiencies in their performance rather than what was good about them. These children felt obliged to make their teachers look good by achieving well, and were annoyed at the expectation that they be perfect. They also felt annoyed at receiving so much 'constructive feedback' while their less able classmates received extensive praise for lesser achievements.

It is thus important for adults to convey realistic expectations of gifted children. However, individuals will perform down to low expectations, and so you must communicate your faith in every child's ability to be successful (Jones & Jones 1995). We need to teach gifted children that they can 'dare to dream' (Jenkins-Friedman & Murphy 1988)—to have lofty ideals for which to strive—as long as these are their own dreams and not someone else's.

Accept mistakes

It is important to teach children from an early age that no one has to get things right every time and that not all mistakes have to be corrected. Balson (1992) notes that most of us focus on children's mistakes in the erroneous belief that this is how to help them to learn. This focusing on children's deficiencies and not noticing their strengths discourages effort and contributes to continued failure. Mistakes indicate a lack of skill, and skill is acquired only through practice, but a discouraged child refuses to practise and so does not learn. Therefore, you should not require children to fix every mistake. Most mistakes do not really matter, and most children realise that making mistakes is a part of learning, in the same way that falling over was a part of learning how to walk.

When a child has not been as successful as you would have expected, it is still important to comment on what that child *did* achieve. (Instead of asking Jake what went wrong when he wrote his name backwards, you can congratulate him for beginning to understand how to write his own name.) It is helpful to teach ourselves and others to live by the rules:

- Strive for excellence, not perfection.
- Have the courage to be imperfect.
- On worthwhile tasks, strive to *do* your best, but not to *be* the best.

As well as accepting natural mistakes, you can actively teach children how to make deliberate mistakes by doing something together and failing at it badly, as long as no one gets hurt. You might try to lose at a game. It will also help when you make light of your own mistakes so that children learn that errors are okay—and can even be funny.

Teach children to cope with negative feedback

At some time everyone will fail at something or will be snubbed or rejected by other people. It is important that children notice this sort of negative feedback about themselves, especially when it is valid. But it is also important that they do not let a single failure define them as failures as people, or take other people's opinions of them more seriously than they take their own (Katz 1995). Your first response when children are disappointed in themselves, should be to listen and accept what they feel. They will think that you do not understand them if you insist on reassuring them that things are not so bad or if you tell them to cheer up.

On the other hand, if children are reacting to an invalid criticism or are expecting unrealistically high performances of themselves, you might gently ask them whether they are being realistic, without giving advice or telling them off for feeling that way. (You could, for example, say gently, 'You seem disappointed that you can't do that well. But do you think you're as good at it as a 4-year-old? Isn't that all you can expect when you are four?') Another possibility is to explain that they cannot do something because they have not been taught it yet. Or you could agree with a child's judgment that she or he is not especially good at that particular activity but then point out that, with practice, she or he will still be able to improve.

Promote competence

Children's academic self-esteem is largely a function of how successful they are in school, regardless of all other variables, such as home background (Chapman et al. 1990). Once established, academic self-esteem will be both a result of earlier achievement levels and a cause of future achievement.

If children lack confidence because they are being unsuccessful in important ways, you do not want to boost their self-esteem artificially but instead build their skills (Curry & Johnson 1990). Their low self-esteem is both valid and functional, because it might motivate them to achieve.

Remember that you cannot fool children by making the task too easy. Achievement of a trivial task will not make any difference to children's self-esteem (Bandura 1986). It might actually do harm by teaching them *helplessness*: that no matter what they do, they will always get it right because the task has been made so easy; instead, they need tasks that increase their perception of their personal skill (Seligman 1975). Children will feel best about themselves and their abilities when they are meeting meaningful challenges and putting in some real effort (Katz 1995). This makes developmentally appropriate programming an important part of promoting children's healthy self-esteem (see chapter 10). Hay (1993: 16):

> Self-perception and motivation are improved when [children] work on tasks that have personal meaning, purpose and choice, in a learning environment that is orientated [sic] towards higher level thinking, problem solving and decision making.

To encourage them to achieve to their maximum, you will need to teach children how to apply themselves, to work independently at times, to explore and solve problems, and to enjoy learning and achieving (Curry & Johnson 1990; Knight 1995; Yong 1994). At the same time, you should ensure that the children have a sufficient history of success, so that they are willing to attempt a task that carries a risk of failure (Whitmore 1980).

Establish priorities

If children are rightly dissatisfied with their present skills, help them to decide which skills they would like to learn. With your help, they can then set priorities for themselves and plan each step. Self-esteem will be most directly enhanced if children are able to achieve in skills that are useful and of interest to themselves.

Record improvement

Recording children's progress is a valuable technique for allowing them to appreciate change that otherwise might be too small to notice or which they might ignore because they feel discouraged. Dieters know this strategy well. However, it is not wise to reward improvements, as outside reinforcers can reduce children's natural motivation to learn (Amabile 1990; Csikszentmihályi 1991; Kohn 1996; Ryan & Deci 1996; Sternberg & Lubart 1992) (see chapter 11). You can use a star chart or some similar method simply as visible *evidence* of the child's progress—as long as the stars are not seen to be external rewards either in themselves or to be traded in for a special privilege (Porter 1997a, 1999).

Place realistic limits on children's behaviour

Children will feel proud of themselves when they know that they can control themselves (Pope et al. 1988). When they can behave within fair limits, they will be well-accepted by other people; when they can manage their own emotions, they will feel safer.

This does not mean imposing controls on children. The type of discipline that you use will need to appeal to children's pride, competence and concern for others (Clarke-Stewart & Friedman 1987, in Curry & Johnson 1990)—that is, it should foster considerate rather than compliant behaviour. (In chapter 11 I discuss the issue of behaviour management in more detail.)

CONCLUSION

Children's self-esteem is both a result of former learning and a cause of their future approaches to social and academic challenges. We need to help children to acknowledge their achievements so that they will be willing to apply themselves in future. Also, we have to help them to be successful at worthwhile tasks, and not placate them with platitudes to help them feel better about unsatisfactory performances (Seligman 1995). Remember that individuals' self-esteem will fluctuate from time to time and across different areas of their skills. An occasional low period is no cause for alarm.

Looking ahead . . .

In the long term we need to teach children to draw a distinction between those standards which they *want* for themselves and those which have been imposed on them. Imposed standards usually contain compelling words such as *should*. Most of us learn these imperatives from our parents and other people who are important to us. They reflect standards that worked *for them, at that time*. They might never have been relevant for anyone else.

SUGGESTED FURTHER READING

For a detailed look at self-esteem, I recommend Curry, N.E. and Johnson, C.N. 1990 *Beyond self-esteem: developing a genuine sense of human value* National Association for the Education of Young Children, Washington, DC.

You might also like to refer to Porter, L. 1999 *Young children's behaviour: practical approaches for caregivers and teachers* MacLennan & Petty, Sydney.

A lay title, which discusses perfectionism and its relationship to self-esteem for gifted children and other individuals, is Adderholdt-Elliot, M. 1992 *Perfectionism: what's bad about being too good* Hawker Brownlow Education, Melbourne.

Discussion questions

1. In your view, what causes children to develop low self-esteem?

2. Using as your clues the four distinctions between praise and acknowledgment listed in this chapter, convert the following praising statements into acknowledgment:
   - You're a good helper.
   - That's terrific!
   - Good boy for putting the toys away!

3. What activities do you find useful for expanding young children's self-concepts?

4. In which skill domains do you think most children value high achievement? Which contribute most to their self-esteem?

5. How can you help children to cope with setbacks and negative feedback from others?

8

PROMOTING RESILIENCE IN GIFTED YOUNG CHILDREN

We want more for our children than healthy bodies. We want our children to have lives filled with friendship and love and high deeds. We want them to be eager to learn and be willing to confront challenges . . . We want them to grow up with confidence in the future, a love of adventure, a sense of justice, and courage enough to act on that sense of justice. We want them to be resilient in the face of the setbacks and failures that growing up always brings.

Seligman (1995: 6)

KEY POINTS

- Gifted children may be more vulnerable to stress reactions because their environments might not meet their atypical needs.
- Their increased awareness of wider issues can lead to early exposure to stress but, in the longer term, they are likely to be able to resolve their worries because of their sophisticated problem-solving abilities.
- They can be protected from stress by their personal temperament and skills, and by supportive relationships within and outside of their family.
- Children can be resilient when they have a healthy self-esteem and can use some specific strategies for coping with stress.

INTRODUCTION

Reviewing in chapter 6 the evidence about gifted children's vulnerability to emotional difficulties, I draw the conclusion that it is unlikely that any higher incidence of difficulties would be due to being gifted as such;

more probably it would be due to other people's reactions to the atypical characteristics and needs of gifted children. At the same time, gifted children can suffer the negative life events and accompanying stress that any other children can experience.

My assumption is that there may be little we can do to change the personality or neurological make-up of gifted children; thus, even if endogenous factors are in future shown to play a large part in gifted children's sensitivities, it is the external events on which we can have more influence and which therefore deserve our attention.

One of these external factors is the dual message our society gives them. Corrigan (1994) argues that we set gifted children up when we demand that they contribute in meaningful ways to society because of their talents yet at the same time belittle those talents and leave the children without social supports. Not only is this exploitation but it will lead to stress and a decision to withdraw from demands.

DEFINITIONS

The stress literature is replete with definitions of terms that have both lay and particular meanings and which, therefore, call for some clarification.

Stressors

Stressors are specific external or internal demands that we believe tax or exceed our ability to cope (Compas 1987). They are an everyday part of childhood experience and reflect children's need to cope with the demands of reality and with differences between adult and child perceptions (Dickey & Henderson 1989).

Most events that are considered to be stressors are negative changes in children's lives, which are largely beyond their control (Slee 1991). These can be everyday hassles or traumatic life events (Luthar & Zigler 1991). As to the latter, traumatic life events will have different effects depending on when they occur in a child's life, how recently they occurred, whether they are one-off events or chronic life conditions such as poverty, and whether they are internal to the child (e.g. an illness) or arise from external sources such as parental separation or inadequate educational provisions (Goodman et al. 1993; Honig 1986a; Slee 1991, 1993; Rutter 1985).

The stress reaction

The stress reaction is a *physical* response in the body involving four stages: an adrenalin-based alarm reaction; cognitive appraisal of the situation; search for a coping strategy; and implementation of a selected strategy (Honig 1986a). When individuals are stressed, they can experience social or emotional difficulties both at the time and in later life (Slee 1993), probably because of what the events teach them about who is in control of what happens to them (Rutter 1985). In turn, adjustment difficulties can themselves create stress (Luthar & Zigler 1991).

Selye and other writers have believed that we need a certain amount of stress to function optimally. In figure 8.1 it can be seen that an individual operating on the left-hand side of the peak would feel challenged, stimulated and excited. To have insufficient of these feelings is indeed stressful, particularly for gifted individuals. However, Beck (1976) believes that this side of the graph equates with feeling aroused and should not be termed 'stress' at all: stress arises only when demands exceed our capacity to cope. This will result in a reduction in our performance ability.

Figure 8.1 Performance at various levels of stress

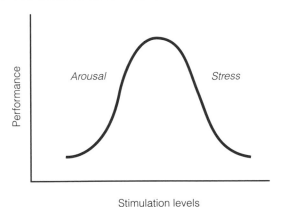

Stimulation levels

Anxiety and worry

In contrast to stress, *anxiety* has emotional, behavioural, physical and cognitive components. Stress is a reaction to events that have actually occurred, whereas anxiety is a response to anticipated events—events that might not even happen at all (Silverman et al. 1995).

Worry is the cognitive component of anxiety. Worry can be adaptive: by anticipating events, children can rehearse an adaptive response; but if the worry is not resolved and the danger is being rehearsed without a solution ever being found, then worry is maladaptive (Silverman et al. 1995).

Coping

Coping is the process of changing our thinking or behaviour to manage stressors—that is, to minimise our distress and maximise our performance (Compas 1987). This occurs in a number of stages, as we first appraise the stressor and our own resources for coping with it and then take action (Ryan 1989).

The coping strategy that we use can try to change our circumstances (that is, the strategy is *problem-focused*); it can be directed at our own emotional reactions (that is, *emotion-focused*); or it can comprise changing our behaviour to *adjust* better to circumstances that we cannot change (Compas 1987; Sowa & May 1997). Emotion-focused coping includes methods such as accepting, tolerating, avoiding, distracting, reframing, and relaxation, as well as emotionally distancing ourselves from a bad situation that we cannot change (Rutter 1985).

Individuals' methods of coping might vary with time and context, depending on the nature of the stressor (Compas 1987). Children will use different strategies at different stages of development and in different phases of problem solving—before, during and after the event (Ryan 1989). Children use problem-focused strategies most when they perceive that they have some control over a situation, whereas they will use emotion-focused strategies or behavioural adjustment to deal with issues that they cannot change (Spirito et al. 1991). The most effective coping style is likely to be one that is flexible and adaptive to circumstances (Compas 1987) and which balances the need to fit into the environment with the need to be true to oneself (Sowa & May 1997).

Resilience

Another concept that we need to define in order to discuss stress in children is the notion of *resilience*. Even with the most high-risk children, fewer than half who experience multiple stressors go on to experience adult adjustment problems (Rutter 1985; Zimmerman & Arunkumar 1994). The fact that so many people cope with adverse circumstances is often attributed to their 'resilience'. Resilience refers to the ability to avoid maladaptive responses to risk or adversity even when one feels distressed or upset (Zimmerman & Arunkumar 1994). It is the ability to bounce back from adverse experiences (Bland et al. 1994).

Children become resilient as a result of both their temperament and their experience with surmounting obstacles (Rutter 1990; Zimmerman & Arunkumar 1994). Resilience does not come about by avoiding stressors, but by encountering them *at a time* and in a way that enhances children's self-confidence through their experience of mastery and taking

141

of appropriate responsibility (Rutter 1985). In short, successful coping can strengthen the individual.

Although resilience seems to be a positive attribute, apparent resilience might in fact be masking distress, or children can appear to be resilient in one domain—say, by maintaining a good school record—but be experiencing difficulties in other areas, such as at home (Luthar & Zigler 1991; Zimmerman & Arunkumar 1994).

Stress and gifted children

As with the study of self-esteem, most studies of stress in gifted children focus on adolescents, so we have to be cautious about applying these results to the early childhood years.

Research has suggested that gifted young children would be less stress-prone than average learners (Scholwinski & Reynolds 1985), despite potentially being under more pressure to succeed. As well, it is generally thought that preschool children have lower stress levels than older children, perhaps because the child-centred preschool environment more closely meets their needs than is the case for children at school (Slee, pers. comm.).

However, the early childhood setting might not be meeting *gifted* children's social and academic needs as well as it meets those of other children. And although very young children are normally protected from stress because they do not understand the meaning of stressful events, intellectually gifted children, in contrast, might be aware of stressors from an earlier age while still being too young to cope emotionally (Sowa et al. 1994). It is only as they get older that their advanced cognitive abilities will help them to resolve normal concerns more quickly, resulting in their eventual superior adjustment (Sowa et al. 1994).

Ability levels and stress

It is clear that more sensitive children need to cope with a greater number of situations than less sensitive children. They will have to cope with both internal and external stressors (Compas 1987).

Although high IQ helps children to cope with stress (Slee 1993), it is possible that exceptionally gifted children do experience more stress than mildly gifted children (Miller et al. 1994). Another possibility is that highly gifted children tend to internalise their stress rather than engaging in acting-out behaviours, and so mask their difficulties (Luthar & Zigler 1991).

Gender differences

Girls rate stressful events as more upsetting than boys, while boys report more such events occurring in their lives (Slee 1991, 1993) and may be more vulnerable to such stressors as separation from caregivers (Zimmerman & Arunkumar 1994); however, findings on boys' vulnerability to stress are mixed (Goodman et al. 1993).

Boys who are under stress tend to have more learning and internalising problems than girls under stress, although boys might still maintain their academic competence (Goodman et al. 1993). This is contrary to expectations that boys would 'act out' when under stress and suggests that it is important for teachers to be sensitive to girls' and boys' internal difficulties, not just to disruptive behaviour.

In terms of coping, one study found that boys were more likely to blame others for problems they were having with friends and siblings, while girls were more likely to use problem-solving strategies (Spirito et al. 1991). Boys may use more physical activity to help them cope than girls do, while girls use more social support and emotional behaviours (Ryan 1989). On the other hand, helplessness has been observed to occur more often in girls, probably as a result of socialisation practices (Compas 1987). Helplessness can put girls more at risk of underachievement (see chapter 12).

SOURCES OF STRESS FOR GIFTED YOUNG CHILDREN

The particular sources of stress that can affect young gifted children include uncertain expectations of them, and their early interest in social issues.

High expectations

Adults' expectations of gifted children can become inflated when they use children's achievement levels to guide what they expect of the children (Freeman 1995b). Uneven development can result in over-generalised high expectations—on the part of either adults or gifted children themselves (Kline & Meckstroth 1985). The stress of living up to high expectations can lead children to stretch to cope at an advanced level; then, when the stress gets too much, they behave even more immaturely than their years.

Stress can differ depending on the child's context—that is, depending on the demands. This, in part, accounts for changes in children's behaviour across settings (Robinson & Robinson 1992).

Young children are particularly vulnerable to everyday stressors such as tiredness or feeling overstimulated, and so young gifted children are more likely than older gifted children to get emotionally out of control. The result can look like a behavioural difficulty, when instead it is a young child's normal reaction to everyday stressors combined with the added stress of being gifted.

Low expectations of gifted children

Knowledge of normal developmental milestones or a fear of pushing children can set a ceiling on adults' expectations of them, resulting in adults not providing suitably challenging activities in the belief that, because of their age, the children are 'not ready' for more advanced experiences (Harrison 1995). Not only can adults' expectations be too low, but peers (particularly during the school years) can actively discourage high achievement. Trying to appear non-gifted or having insufficient challenge can induce stress.

Involvement in adult issues

Because verbally gifted children understand adult issues and conversations, they sometimes involve themselves in adult business (Delisle 1992). They might argue with adults about their instructions, and might even think that adults have no 'right' to tell them what to do. This gives children too much power, and can result in stress levels that are revealed in inappropriate behaviour. (Ways of overcoming these sorts of difficulties are discussed in chapter 11.)

Gifted children often worry about the big social issues as well (Galbraith 1985). They feel responsible for fixing the environment, for poverty and wars but have no power to do anything about these problems, and so they can become stressed, lose confidence in themselves, or become depressed about their helplessness (Galbraith 1985).

PROTECTIVE FACTORS

Three factors have been linked to children's resilience to stress: the disposition and skills of children; the family supports available to them; and the availability of a supportive and nurturing relationship outside of home (Compas 1987; Garmezy 1985, in Luthar & Zigler 1991; Rutter 1985; Zimmerman & Arunkumar 1994).

Children's disposition and personal skills

Children's coping styles are affected by their temperament, self-perceptions, whether they have an internal or external locus of control, how able they are to deal with change, and the quality of their problem-solving skills (Compas 1987; Rutter 1985).

However, we need to beware of notions that focus on individuals' personal coping skills, as these can lead to a value judgment that children are somehow deficient if they are not coping with stressors (Zimmerman & Arunkumar 1994). It will be more humane to look at the settings that provoke stress reactions and that fail to help children compensate for or protect themselves against risk than to focus on increasing individuals' possibly already satisfactory coping skills (Zimmerman & Arunkumar 1994).

Hardiness. Hardiness is the cognitive (thinking) component of resilience. Hardy individuals (Bland et al. 1994):

- have a strong commitment to self;
- are willing to take action to deal with problems;
- have a positive attitude towards their environment;
- are optimistic;
- hold a strong sense of purpose;
- have a strong internal locus of control (Hébert 1996) or self-efficacy;
- appraise challenges realistically.

Cognitive appraisal. Because of their advanced cognitive development, gifted children can use cognitive appraisal earlier than average learners as a way of coping with stressors (Bland et al. 1994).

Locus of control. Highly achieving gifted children are more likely to have an internal locus of control than are underachieving gifted or average learners (Knight 1995). Having an internal locus of control involves believing that one's own actions affect outcomes; this is often called having a sense of self-efficacy (Bandura 1986). People are said to have an external locus of control, or to display 'learned helplessness' (Seligman 1975), when they believe that events outside of their control are responsible for what happens to them.

Helpless children display ineffective coping in terms of reduced levels of effort, high discouragement, and deteriorated performance (Compas 1987). They either make no attributions regarding the cause of their failures, or blame aspects of themselves such as their own lack of ability. Mastery-oriented children, in contrast, attribute their failures to aspects of the task or changeable factors such as effort. This avoids discouragement and directs their energies towards finding a solution (Compas 1987). Nevertheless, a helpless cognitive set is not fixed, and can change with circumstances (Rutter 1985).

Family environment

Aspects of a supportive family environment include parental warmth, cohesiveness, order, organisation, and supervision. Gifted children flourish best in family environments in which achievement is fostered although not in a competitive sense (Cornell & Grossberg 1987).

I have already mentioned the dangers of focusing solely on individuals' coping skills because it blames them for not coping. The second reason is that internal explanations ignore children's social context. If children are showing persistent signs of distress, it might not be due to their temperament but to the persistence of relationship disturbances or outside stressors such as poverty (Rutter 1985).

A supportive relationship

Gifted children in particular can benefit from supportive relationships with at least one individual within or outside the family, who provides nurturing and a positive role model at an optimal developmental stage or during trauma. Social contacts are not enough to protect children against stress: it is the quality and range of those relationships—how satisfying they are—that counts.

METHODS TO PROMOTE RESILIENCE

The factors that promote resilience also promote the realisation of giftedness (Bland et al. 1994). The above section on protective factors gives rise to some recommendations for ways of helping stressed children. Given the importance of children's self-esteem to their coping capacity, the measures for promoting a healthy self-esteem (in chapter 7) will help them to cope with stress. In addition, the following suggestions target stress in particular.

Structure a cooperative setting

Adults can choose to take part in activities and to associate with people who bolster their self-esteem, but children are at the mercy of the contexts in which we place them (Katz 1995). This means that children rely on us to create an accepting environment in which they can feel emotionally safe and confident about their ability to meet the demands being placed on them.

Children need a psychologically safe environment (Jenkins-Friedman & Murphy 1988) which supports experimentation, so that their mistakes are taken to be part of the learning experience rather than a measure of their worth as people. Cooperative activities in early childhood centres and at home can ameliorate stress by reducing competition between children and, in turn, help gifted children's overall adjustment.

Promote children's autonomy

In chapter 7 I detail the types of choice we can give young children. Here it is worth noting that allowing children to contribute to decision making about issues that affect them will both enhance their self-esteem and raise their confidence in their coping skills.

Identify early

Caregivers and teachers need to be able to identify early those children in particular who are exposed to multiple stressors. You can do this by watching out for the signs of low self-esteem which can indicate that children are internalising their stress. External signs include behavioural difficulties, underachievement, a lack of age-appropriate independence, withdrawal, and impulsive behaviour.

Be emotionally available

Children need to feel connected to the adults who work with them. Emotionally meaningful relationships between adults and children are important protective factors for children of all ages. Relating to children at an emotional level protects them from developing stress reactions and fosters their healthy self-esteem.

Be sensitive to children's stress

Furman (1995) observes that teachers should not avoid managing stressful situations because the challenges that they provoke offer useful learning experiences; also, the successful management of stressors can remove impediments to children's participation and learning. Adults need to be sensitive to what a stressor *means* for individual children (Honig 1986a) and to help children to deal with the realities that impinge on them from the outside world, so that they learn to manage their feelings about stressful events (Furman 1995).

Restrict children's responsibilities

To minimise children's concerns about adult issues, it is sometimes helpful to discuss with them only those issues about which they *can* do something. When we tell young children something, they are likely to judge that (a) we want them to do something about it; (b) it is their fault; or (c) it is important, when it may actually be quite trivial. Given gifted children's tendency to take on early responsibilities it is wise to censor discussions with them, using their emotional response as a guide to how much information they can cope with.

It can be useful to explain that adults are taking care of adult business, and that it is children's job to be children and to grow up at their own speed. They will be adults for a lot longer than they will be children and so they will have plenty of time to act to set the world to rights later. It is not their turn yet to be older. At the same time, gifted children can be encouraged to do age-appropriate things (e.g. write a letter to a politician) to allow them to feel satisfied that they have done what they can in the meantime.

Attribution training

An attribution is an explanation of the cause of an event (Pope et al. 1988). To promote resilience, it is important to teach children to see themselves and interpret their actions accurately so that they can accept responsibility for what they do (Seligman 1995). In this way, they learn that they have control over their own lives.

When children are unsuccessful, they need to define the event as *temporary* rather than permanent, *specific* to the event rather than a sign of a general or all-pervasive failing on their part, and they need to take personal responsibility without taking blame. That is, they need to explain the event in terms of their *behaviour*, not personality (Seligman 1995).

When you hear children blame their personality for failings (such as when they say 'I'm hopeless at this') and when they assume that the problem is permanent ('I'll *never* be able to do it'), you can gently correct their statements (with something like, 'You're right. It hasn't worked out, has it? What could you do to make it better?'). Children must learn about the link between their own actions and the outcome. You do not have to confront them with failure, but to deny it is not helpful either.

Provide intellectual peers

Children will choose friends who are at their developmental level. Therefore, you will need to do what you can to provide older playmates for a young gifted child. If this is not possible, then it can help to put parents in touch with the local Gifted and Talented Children's Association, which might run sessions where young gifted children can meet. Without social support, gifted children are at risk emotionally and academically.

Provide mentors

Introduction to a well-adjusted and happy adult whose 'brain also learns quickly' (just like theirs) can give stressed children hope that they too will overcome the obstacles they now face. Although this approach is most commonly recommended for gifted adolescents (see, e.g., Freeman 1998b), early childhood professionals can do much to support young gifted children, especially those who are living in stressed families (Weinreb 1997). In these circumstances, it is tempting to feel powerless to help because it is difficult to change children's stressful home circumstances. However, we can strengthen children by believing in them, providing warmth, and offering 'incidental' (but deliberate) comments which guide them in how to cope. As Weinreb (1997: 16) states: 'Resilient children are children who have hope and a positive outlook that they can deal with problems.' We can give them this hope.

Encourage special interests

At later ages, extracurricular activities can be useful to promote resilience in young people. Recreational activities provide a refuge from the pressures of daily life and of being gifted, engage children in a social group, and offer a source of self-esteem (Hébert 1996; Swiatek 1995). At earlier ages you can encourage young children's special interests either in the centre (Weinreb 1997) or by mentioning to parents special outside activities in which their child might participate—as long as these activities reduce the demands the children are facing rather than adding to them.

Teach coping skills

It does not so much matter *how* children cope but *that* they take action about a stressful event (Rutter 1985). Doing so teaches them that they are in command of their lives. Nevertheless, rather than teaching children some specific coping strategies, it will be more useful if you can identify what skills they are already using successfully and help them to improve on these (Ryan 1989).

Teach self-control

When children can control their own behaviour and can trust that they will be protected from the behavioural excesses of other children, they will be less vulnerable to stress. Therefore, behaviour management makes life more predictable and manageable for young children. However, the methods used must be congruent with the aims of the overall program rather than encouraging intellectual risk-taking at the same time as insisting on behavioural conformity (McCaslin & Good 1992). (I discuss behaviour management in chapter 11.)

Introduce fun

Fun is the intangible joy that we experience when our learning and emotional needs are met (Glasser 1986) and is thus a natural byproduct of the other measures for meeting children's needs. Nevertheless, adults can ensure that they are playful in their interactions with young children in order to balance out the many demands children can experience.

Provide counselling support

I regard most early childhood staff's 'counselling' as incidental comments aimed at boosting children's faith that they can surmount obstacles. These comments can occur during play, or be suggested by children's books that discuss coping strategies or provoke discussions about stressful events. Referral to a child psychologist or similar professional might be necessary on rare occasions.

CONCLUSION

Children's ability to adjust to stressful events is more related to their self-esteem and self-efficacy than to their cognitive problem-solving skills. This is particularly relevant to preschool children, who might lack a comprehensive range of cognitive strategies (Rutter 1985). It also highlights the importance of the recommendations in chapter 7 about enhancing children's self-esteem.

In addition to those suggestions it will be important to identify individual children who are at risk of stress reactions. This will include gifted children, both as a result of their negotiating a world which makes few allowances for their needs and because, like all other children, gifted children can experience everyday problems and traumatic life events. Their responses to these stressors might be atypical because of their earlier self-awareness, and so they might be more vulnerable to experiencing stress reactions. On the other hand, their precocious cognitive skills can help them to resolve their worries at an earlier age than averagely achieving children.

Looking ahead . . .

As children grow older there are changes in the types of situations that they find stressful. Older children's stress relates mainly to their relationships (Slee 1993), personal adequacy, and the future (Rutter 1985).

Competition at school can be particularly stressful for all children (Humphrey & Humphrey 1985). In one study, gifted children stated that competition at school was no fun for anyone: 'For those who had little hope of winning or for those who had little chance of losing, contests were boring at best' (Ford 1989: 132). The gifted children said that competition tended to scapegoat them and promoted cheating and jealousy between classmates. However, they found competition between equally matched participants exciting and challenging. In a similar vein, Cropper (1998) reports that competition may actually lower the achievement of children who consistently win. These findings have implications for how schools present cooperative and competitive activities in their curricula.

SUGGESTED FURTHER READING

A lay discussion of resilience is provided by Seligman, M.E.P. 1995 *The optimistic child* Random House, Sydney.

DISCUSSION QUESTIONS

1. What signs would you associate with stress in children?

2. What could make gifted young children more prone to stress reactions?

3. How do you conceive of resilience, and how could you promote it in an early childhood setting?

9

MEETING GIFTED YOUNG CHILDREN'S SOCIAL NEEDS

My life is spent in a perpetual alternation between two rhythms, the rhythm of attracting people for fear I may be lonely and the rhythm of getting rid of them because I know that I am bored.

Joad (1948, in Gross 1993a: 233)

KEY POINTS

- Although well-adjusted in other respects, the area that presents most concern for gifted children is their social relationships with their age mates.
- Gifted children's social problems can be most acute during the early childhood years because older playmates are not accessible to them.
- We can identify socially at-risk children by observing whether they appear to have friends, can play at appropriately sophisticated levels given their age or have particular skill deficits, or by administering a sociometric measure.
- Adults can promote gifted young children's social skills and satisfaction by providing them with intellectual peers for some of the time.
- Additional measures include ensuring that the environment is caring and that there is respect for differences between children; instituting cooperative games to involve isolated children; teaching children how to enter a group; and coaching social skills.

INTRODUCTION

Gifted children may view their talents positively but simultaneously believe that other people do not (Colangelo 1997; Coleman & Cross 1988;

152

Cross et al. 1991, 1992; Kerr et al. 1988; Swiatek 1995; Tidwell 1980; van Boxtel & Mönks 1992). Even very young gifted children are sensitive to the perceptions of others (Swiatek 1995), and learn early that they are different from other people (Clark 1997; Harrison 1995).

Children report that the presence of other children is the most important factor to them in their early childhood setting—more important than toys, activities and staff (Langsted 1994, in Pugh & Selleck 1996). This finding verifies that friendships are important to young children, and that making friends is the most important developmental task of early childhood (Cooper & McEvoy 1996).

Children choose friends whose skills are at the same level as their own and who share their interests (Clark 1997; Oden 1960, cited in Delisle 1992). So, although gifted children are often sought out by their age mates because of their social skilfulness (Clark 1997), many gifted young children prefer to play with older children or adults. They may feel less comfortable and be less skilful at interacting with their age mates (Silverman 1997).

ELEMENTS OF FRIENDSHIPS

Friendship is a voluntary, ongoing bond between individuals who have a mutual preference for each other and who share emotional warmth. In relating to peers, three issues are involved: inclusion/exclusion, control, and affection (Schutz 1958, in Webb et al. 1991). The most basic of these for children is whether they are included in the group. This sense of belonging can be threatened for gifted children who are already aware that they are different.

At the next level, the group establishes who is a leader and who is a follower. This jostling for position in a hierarchy occupies a good deal of time when a group is newly formed, but then the group changes its focus once the hierarchy has been established. Gifted children, on the one hand, often have the developmental maturity to act as leaders; on the other, they may not have the emotional maturity to handle that role with grace, or their leadership might not be accepted by others in the group.

At the third level, the issue arises about whether the individuals in the group feel any lasting affection for each other. As Webb et al. (1991: 146) observe: 'Typically you feel affection only for those whom you can count on, and whose behaviour is predictable.' As I discuss later in this chapter, gifted children might find other young children's less mature behaviour confusing and even upsetting, making it more difficult for them to establish affectionate ties in a group of age mates.

BENEFITS OF FRIENDSHIPS

Friendships serve many important functions. Developmental benefits of friendships are that they help children to develop social skills; teach self-control; give children experience at problem solving; provide practice at using language; and allow them to exchange skills and information which they do not readily learn from the adults in their lives (Asher & Parker 1989; Asher & Renshaw 1981; Hartup 1979; Johnson & Johnson 1991; Kohler & Strain 1993; Perry & Bussey 1984; Rubin 1980). These cognitive and social benefits in turn enhance other skill domains (Swetnam et al. 1983).

On an emotional dimension, friendships supply reassurance, promote a healthy self-esteem, enhance confidence in stressful situations, avoid loneliness, provide fun, and foster individual happiness. Friends also offer practical and emotional support through information, advice and counsel. Intimacy is necessary to sustain one's drive to excel and contributes significantly to individuals' perception of satisfaction with their lives (Gross 1996).

EFFECTS OF ISOLATION

Low peer acceptance may have more damaging consequences than low academic achievement (Frosh 1983). Children who are isolated miss out on the important benefits that friendships offer, and are lonelier and less satisfied with the relationships they do have. Isolated children will have fewer supports for coping with the daily stresses of life, and less confidence in and experience at eliciting support from others. These effects can carry over into adult life (Asher & Parker 1989).

SOCIAL ADJUSTMENT OF GIFTED CHILDREN

Most of what we know about gifted children's social skills and peer relationships is based on studies of upper primary (elementary) school children (Austin & Draper 1981). Nevertheless, the metacognitive skills of self-management, planning, monitoring and evaluating that enhance gifted children's cognitive performance are the same skills that also enhance their social problem-solving abilities (Freeman 1995b; Jones & Day 1996; Moss 1992). This being so, it can be expected that gifted youngsters are more socially adept at earlier ages than average learners, although their advanced social knowledge is not necessarily reflected in more advanced social behaviour (Austin & Draper 1981).

Despite their intellectual advantages, it is possible that gifted children are emotionally vulnerable, because they need to adjust socially to being different (Whitmore 1980) even when their difference is a source of pride and so feeds their self-esteem (Freeman 1993, 1997). Some gifted children feel conflict between their need to achieve and their need for intimacy, since remarkable achievements can lead to peer disapproval or even complete ostracism, especially beyond the early childhood years (Gross 1996).

Gross (1996) contends that, at a younger age than normal, gifted children move from measuring themselves against their own standards to comparing themselves to others. Gifted children thus develop their self-concept and feel peer pressure earlier than usual.

Most gifted children are socially accepted by their peers: they are less disliked and are identified as being less aggressive than others (Austin & Draper 1981; Cohen et al. 1994). Their popularity, of course, does not necessarily mean that the gifted children themselves are satisfied with the intimacy of their relationships. Even though they can relate well to their age mates, they tend to form best friendships with other gifted children (Cohen et al. 1994). Also, they might be popular because they have prestigious skills or are useful academically (Austin & Draper 1981).

Ability differences

The majority of moderately gifted children have positive peer relationships even when they lack intellectual peers (Janos & Robinson 1985). When comparing moderately and extremely gifted children, Janos et al. (1985) found that children of both ability levels said that they preferred to play with other children to playing with adults or playing alone. Very few reported that it was hard for them to make friends, and all thought of themselves as being 'about as friendly or friendlier' than other children.

The picture is not so uniformly positive for highly gifted children (Brody & Benbow 1986; Silverman 1997). Compared with the more moderately gifted, extremely gifted children report that it is harder for them to make friends, an observation that is verified by their parents (Brody & Benbow 1986; Dauber & Benbow 1990; Janos et al. 1985). Therefore, it does appear that a significant minority of highly gifted children—perhaps 20%–25% (which is twice as many as average or moderately gifted children)—experience social difficulties (Janos & Robinson 1985; Janos et al. 1985). Possible causes include adults' emphasis on intellectual pursuits to the detriment of social experiences, or the children's own perceptions of their differences from their age peers (Janos et al. 1985). The problem might be inherent not in the psychology of highly gifted children but in the mismatch between their needs and their social environment.

The other side of the coin is that this still leaves the vast majority of highly gifted children experiencing satisfactory social relationships (Janos et al. 1985).

Talent profile

The social experiences of gifted children can depend on the skill domain or domains in which they are advanced. For instance, verbally gifted children may be less socially accepted than mathematically gifted children, perhaps because extreme verbal talent is more obvious in more social situations (Ablard 1996; Brody & Benbow 1986; Dauber & Benbow 1990; Swiatek 1995, 1998). A second issue is that when children's developmental level varies across skill domains it is likely that they will require different peers for different pursuits (Webb et al. 1991).

Age differences

There appear to be two periods of development that are particularly challenging socially for gifted young people: the early childhood years, and adolescence. However, these two critical times occur for slightly different reasons. In the early childhood years, gifted young children are isolated because they do not have access to older children who would be their intellectual equals. Adolescents, on the other hand, are more likely to have access to older intellectual peers but could experience more pressure to fit in with their age mates, with the result that they must choose between hiding their talents or facing isolation.

Gender differences

Gifted girls report receiving fewer social supports from their classmates and friends than gifted boys (Van Tassel-Baska et al. 1994). Girls appear to feel more keenly than boys the conflict between displaying their talents and winning social approval. The risk is that gifted girls will underachieve to gain social status and conform to peer group expectations (Luftig & Nichols 1991).

Wolfle (1991) contends that teachers often emphasise boys' achievement at the expense of their socialisation. She says that the best way to assist gifted boys is to help them to increase their social supports. This might involve improving their social skills or simply providing them with some true peers.

SOCIAL ISSUES FACING GIFTED YOUNG CHILDREN

Hollingworth (in Whitmore 1980) reported that friendship problems are most acute in early childhood, because same-aged peers do not share gifted children's interests and level of organisational and conceptual play, but older children regard them as infants and so do not want to play with them. Also, older children are either in another group in a child care centre, or are already at school when the young gifted child begins preschool.

Especially in the later preschool years, young gifted children's play can become solitary because they lack a true, matched-ability peer group. The upshot can be that they become increasingly aware of the differences between themselves and other children.

Loneliness

Solitude can be a choice—a way of coping with stress (Readdick 1993); whereas loneliness results from being rejected by one's peers (Bullock 1993). Gifted young girls are less likely than other girls to play with dolls and instead favour games involving structure and logic, which makes their play styles incompatible with those of their age mates (Gross 1996). Also, gifted children tend to show less interest in competitive games (Janos & Robinson 1985), perhaps because they feel empathy for the loser. This can make it hard for them to find friends, and so they spend a good deal of time alone. As Webb et al. (1991: 21) report, 'solitude, [al]though necessary, can become a prison instead of a retreat'.

Alternatively, gifted young children's play becomes a compromise between their own interests and the need to maintain relationships (Gross 1996: 116):

> Thus, even play, which for the average child is one of the most important aids to socialisation, serves to underscore the differences between the gifted child and his age-mates, rather than acting as a link between them.

Lost friends

When gifted children's older playmates move up to the next group in the child care centre or go to school, they have to make new friends. At the end of the next term the same thing happens again, which can be discouraging. (This effect is more pronounced when schools have intakes at the beginning of each school term, and less pronounced in states or districts where children enter school only at the start of each school year.) Meanwhile, as gifted children themselves near the age to move on there are fewer and fewer older children available to provide the stimulation they need, and so their last terms in preschool can be a particularly lonely time.

High demands of others

Because gifted children can have the verbal abilities to direct play and because their play ideas are sophisticated, they might manipulate or intimidate other children into playing games their way (Clark 1997; Hay 1993). Their high expectations of others might deter their companions, which can have two effects: the first is that the gifted children might feel still more isolated and lonely; the second is that they might stop showing how bright they are so that other people will like them (Delisle 1992). If they stop trying to achieve, they might lose some of their skills and not achieve to their potential.

Misunderstandings of other children

The reverse can also occur. Gifted children can be intimidated when other children do not abide by the same social rules as themselves. They can mistakenly assume that another child's aggression, lack of empathy, or lack of planning are a deliberate attempt to hurt them (instead of the normal developmental ignorance that it is), and so they are more deeply hurt than usual. For example, the gifted child who plans ahead and can consider other people would not start down a slide until the previous child was safely off the equipment; a child with normal development might forget to plan this far ahead, go down while another child was still on the slide and kick him in the back. The gifted child who is injured will not understand that it was accidental because he or she thinks first and simply does not have accidents like that.

Need to learn tact

It is often said that gifted children need to be tactful about displaying their abilities in front of others. However, Swiatek (1998) reports that many young gifted people—especially girls and the exceptionally gifted— are often *too* reticent about showing their true abilities. Other researchers conclude that this is due to their awareness of the social stigma that is attached to being gifted (Cross et al. 1991, 1992), although it is equally possible that the children are merely being tactful with peers, since they are happy for peers to know that they are interested in learning but are careful not to parade their academic accomplishments (Cross et al. 1991).

Either way, in order to maintain their achievement levels, these children need support to recognise their talents. When they understand their own abilities, they will also understand that other children are different from them, without regarding this as a deficit. Instead of thinking that other children are being 'deliberately stupid' (Delisle 1992), they will be more likely to accept individual differences.

Leadership

Gifted young children's early sensitivity to the needs of others and mature moral reasoning skills enable them to lead their peers (Clark 1997; Hensel 1990, 1991; Rothman 1992). Their leadership skills are enhanced by an early development of verbal skills, which allow them to convey their ideas to their playmates; a precocious imagination, which allows them to envision possibilities; problem-solving skills; and organisation abilities (Hensel 1990, 1991). These same traits can conversely be enhanced by being placed in leadership roles (Rothman 1992).

These advanced social and intellectual skills might mean that other people are willing to confer leadership status on gifted individuals, whether or not they seek it. Leadership occurs when others voluntarily follow (Smith 1995). However, Ford (1989) found that some school-aged gifted children resented always being expected to take leadership roles in the class. And, unlike their older counterparts, young gifted children might not have the emotional resources to handle social dilemmas; so adopting leadership roles might place them under stress.

Nevertheless, leadership skills can be taught (Hensel 1990), by: teaching children to understand others' perspectives; modelling caring behaviours; practising making decisions and coping with their consequences; allowing children to talk about their feelings and ideas; and offering opportunities for them to work or play collaboratively (Hensel 1990).

Effects of identification of giftedness

Some writers report that gifted children find it difficult to live up to the gifted label once they have been so identified. However, it is not clear whether it is the label which they find difficult to bear, or whether it is the circumstances that caused parents to request an assessment (e.g. the observation that their child was bored, was not fitting in socially, or had perfectionist tendencies).

Buescher (1985) says that, while giftedness can give young people status, it can also create a barrier between them and their age mates. (I return to this issue in chapter 13.)

Family conflict

Intellectual discrepancies between siblings can lead to exaggerated competitiveness and jealousy between them (Chamrad & Robinson 1986; Freeman 1995b). This can be exacerbated by parents' uncertainty about how to respond to each child and to the relationship difficulties between them.

Exceptionally gifted children

If gifted young children are at risk socially because of a lack of intellectual peers, then young exceptionally gifted children are more so. They have fewer intellectual peers and are less mobile than older children and adults, and so cannot easily locate the few in their vicinity. Rural children with exceptional advances are penalised still further. Nevertheless, their social isolation does not represent an emotional disturbance or lack of social skill, as their difficulties disappear when true peers can be located (Gross 1992, 1993c).

SOCIAL SKILL AND SOCIAL COMPETENCE

Kerr and Nelson (1998) define social *skills* as specific social behaviours, whereas social *competence* refers to the ability to use those skills in the right time and place. To relate cooperatively and competently together, children need to be able to:

- communicate their feelings;
- give information;
- ask for information or help;
- manage their own feelings;
- negotiate differences in opinion with their friends;
- deal with conflict constructively;
- achieve what they want without hurting anyone else;
- respond to provocation, such as teasing or bullying;
- evoke favourable responses from other people;
- deal with people in authority.

In short, children need the skills for dealing with the impact of the world on themselves and for influencing that world. They will use these skills when establishing, maintaining and elaborating friendships.

The skills comprising social competence change as children get older (Asher & Renshaw 1981). Preschool-aged children need the specific social skills to establish and maintain contact, the language and communication skills for accurate exchange of information (past the age of $2^1/_2$), and the motor skills to engage in the favourite activities of the peer group (Finch & Hops 1983). Ability to share feelings will be paramount at later ages.

IDENTIFYING SOCIALLY AT-RISK CHILDREN

You might be concerned about children's social skills for a number of reasons:

- They have very few friends.
- They spend very little time playing with other children.
- Their type of play is inappropriate for their age.
- They appear to be unhappy with their friendships or say that they feel lonely.
- You notice that they have particular difficulties with certain types of social dilemmas.
- You are aware of the subskills that make children socially competent and see particular children displaying less successful interaction patterns.
- You have administered sociometric measures which have highlighted that certain children are neglected or rejected by most others in the group.

None of these measures is perfect. First, the number of friends can be misleading. Most people of all ages have just one or two friends (Porteous 1979), and the number of children's friendships is less important than their quality. Children might have few friends but appreciate and enjoy the ones that they have (Webb et al. 1991).

Second, children might spend little time playing with others, but when they do, they play entirely appropriately. In contrast, socially engaged children might be aggressive (Perry & Bussey 1984). The important measure is *how*—not *how much*—children play socially.

As long as children can enter a group when they want to, there is unlikely to be a social problem (Frosh 1983). These points are confirmed by Perry and Bussey (1984: 305), who note:

> If children are wasting their time while alone—if they are unoccupied or are doing something that is better done in a group—then high rates of solitary play may be detrimental for the children's development. But if children are spending their time alone wisely, then solitary play may be beneficial.

Finally, sociometric measures—which ask children to report on who are their friends—are not entirely practicable in early childhood settings, despite being the most common measure for school-aged children (Hops & Lewin 1984).

Therefore, in the early childhood setting, direct observation will be the best measure of children's social skills. Direct observation lets you appreciate the conditions that gave rise to a child's social behaviour and so allows you to change features of the environment that could avoid a recurrence. On the other hand, a judgment about whether behaviour is appropriate to the context is subjective, and can lend bias to observations.

METHODS TO PROMOTE SOCIAL INCLUSION

It may be more viable, relevant and benign to change the environment that gives rise to social problems than it is to attempt to change individual children—such as through social skills training. Perhaps children already have the necessary social skills but do not feel safe to experiment socially, or feel different from the other children and so do not use skills of which they are capable.

Locate intellectual peers for children

The single most important intervention for promoting gifted children's social satisfaction is to find them some intellectual peers with whom they could play at least occasionally (Galbraith 1985; Gross 1996; Janos & Robinson 1985). Without this, they are at risk of not understanding their own abilities, concealing their true potential, and blaming themselves for not fitting in with their age mates (Gross 1996).

Coleman (1995) believes that being with intellectual peers changes gifted children's sense of who they are; what they can achieve; their ability to make contact with strangers; whether they are accepted by people whose opinions they value; whether they are free to express themselves; and their ability to find others who are excited about the same things. The children no longer feel that they are in a minority of one (Coleman 1995). At later ages their academic self-esteem may decline somewhat, through comparing themselves with more able peers, but their social self-esteem will improve as a result of having more successful relationships with the other children (Gross 1997).

Cohen et al. (1994) agree that gifted youngsters need to relate to their intellectual peers but say that negative outcomes are related to a lack of relationships with age mates. Therefore, a blend of relationships is necessary: when gifted children find acceptance within an intellectual peer group, their social confidence grows and they find themselves better able to relate to other children as well (Silverman 1997).

Cooperative learning

Cooperative learning involves highly structured group activities in which the children rely on each other to achieve a common goal and common reward (Robinson 1990). Within the school sector, there is an active debate about using cooperative learning with gifted children, mainly centred on the fact that it usually involves mixed-ability groupings (Johnson et al. 1990; Slavin 1987b; Snowden 1995), although it does not necessarily have to (Fiedler et al. 1993; Joyce 1991). Advocates of cooperative learning (e.g. Slavin 1991) claim that gifted children can gain socially and learn more in a mixed-ability group by leading or teaching the less able children; its critics (e.g. Colangelo & Davis 1997; Feldhusen 1998; Robinson 1990, 1997) say that this 'Robin Hood' method (Montgomery 1996) of robbing time from the able so that they can help the less able amounts to exploitation of gifted children, restricts their access to more advanced learning, and can frustrate them if their group mates do not understand or are less motivated than them (Matthews 1992).

The conclusion of this debate is that the effects of cooperative learning will vary according to the children's ages and ability levels, and the type of activity being undertaken (Li & Adamson 1992). Thus, Rogers and Span (1993) advise that structured cooperative activities should be restricted to the social sphere. In early childhood, this implies the use of cooperative games.

Cooperative games aim to involve isolated children and to pair up those who do not ordinarily play with each other. In this way, they expand the pool of each child's potential friends; help children to form a cohesive group; teach cooperation skills, turn-taking and sharing; decrease aggressiveness; and provide a non-threatening context for modelling and rehearsing social skills (Bay-Hinitz et al. 1994; Hill & Reed 1989; Orlick 1982; Sapon-Shevin 1986; Swetnam et al. 1983). They can produce the social benefits of structured cooperative learning activities without, however, incurring any of their disadvantages.

Like cooperative learning exercises, cooperative games require co-ordinated effort by all members of the group for all participants to achieve success. However, participation is voluntary and the children's only reward is the fun of taking part. Examples include non-elimination musical chairs, which involves removing a chair—not a player—whenever the music stops, so that all the children end up having to fit on the one remaining chair; or the frozen-bean bag game, in which children walk with small bean bags on their heads, standing still if their bag falls off until a companion replaces the bean bag. (For further examples of cooperative games, see Porter 1999.)

Competitive games, in contrast, are games where there are winners and losers, and individuals aim to win and to see their opponents fail. They may involve taunting or teasing (e.g. 'King of the castle'), grabbing or snatching at scarce toys (e.g. musical chairs), monopolising or excluding other children (e.g. 'piggy-in-the-middle'), or games involving physical force (e.g. tag ball) (Orlick 1982; Sapon-Shevin 1986).

It can be difficult at first to engage children in cooperative games (Hill & Reed 1989). Some children prefer competitive games, and are reluctant at first to participate in cooperative activities or to touch other children if that is part of the game (Bay-Hinitz et al. 1994; Hill & Reed 1989). Nevertheless, children still benefit from even low participation rates (Bay-Hinitz et al. 1994), and can be encouraged to participate by gentle persuasion and by seeing that the other children are enjoying themselves (Hill & Reed 1989).

Another difficulty is that simply playing cooperative games will not ensure that the children generalise their enhanced social skills to other activities. You will need to supplement cooperative games with instruction that helps the children understand how to be cooperative in their natural play (Sapon-Shevin 1986).

Teach group entry skills

To enter a group, children first need to recognise when is a good time to ask to enter. Having chosen an appropriate time, socially capable children typically follow a series of steps: first, they approach some other children and quietly observe their game. Next, they wait for a natural break to occur and then they begin to do what the other children are doing. That is, they imitate the other children's play. (Adults do the same thing at parties: we shoulder up to a small group of people who look as if they might not reject our advances, wait quietly until there is a suitable break in the conversation, and then contribute something on the topic that the group is discussing.)

In contrast, when less competent children try to enter a group, they disrupt the group's play by calling attention to themselves, asking questions, criticising the way the other children are playing, or introducing new topics of conversation or new games. The group members will usually reject these disruptive attempts to join them, and so unsuccessful children learn yet again that other people do not like them.

If the others say that they can't join their play, competent children will have the confidence to try again; less adept children appear to need to save face but, in their attempt to do so, behave in ways that are more likely to lead to repeated rejection (Putallaz & Wasserman 1990).

Social skills coaching

Social skills are usually (not always) learned naturally. Natural cues will be enough for most young children to acquire and practise appropriate social skills. However, social skill deficits—and aggression in particular—are unlikely to disappear spontaneously (Schneider 1989). Individual children with these deficits can benefit from additional coaching; otherwise they will lack both the social skills to form relationships and the relationships in which to practise their social skills.

Training methods generally comprise: teaching children about social goals, such as having fun together (Mize 1995); giving them opportunities to practise new social skills; and supplying feedback (Ladd & Mize 1983; Mize 1995; Rose 1983). For instance, Mize used hand puppets, asking a pair of children for ideas of how to teach the puppets to have fun together. The children then acted out their ideas with the puppets, with other toys and then in their natural play. (For a fuller description of this program, see Mize 1995, or Porter 1999.)

We need to keep in mind that gifted children might not be displaying peer relationship skills simply because they lack real peers, rather than because they lack social skills. To repeat my earlier advice, in most cases it will be better to begin with changing the children's social environment than to target individual children for social skills training.

CONCLUSION

Moderately gifted children are often more popular than their age mates, as measured by the number of times that they are nominated on class sociometric measures (Roedell et al. 1980). However, the typical question on such measures is: 'With whom would you most like to work?' On such a question, most children would nominate a bright child, not because he or she is necessarily popular but because he or she is useful. This was verified by Ford's (1989) study, in which gifted children complained that their classmates used them for their abilities on special projects but did not remain friends with them afterwards.

It is clear that our satisfaction with our relationships depends not on how many relationships we have, but on how close we feel to our companions. Popularity is more superficial than friendship. Thus, adults need to help gifted children to distinguish between popularity and friendship so that they can be true to themselves rather than conform to their peers, sacrificing their personal goals in order to win popularity (Keirouz 1990).

Looking ahead . . .

Social challenges can become particularly apparent again during adolescence, when young people both separate from their family of origin and establish themselves personally, socially and occupationally with respect to others (Buescher 1985; Swiatek 1995). This integration into the adult world is complicated by gifted youths' anxieties about being different from other people (Buescher 1985; Whitmore 1980).

Many older gifted children report having been teased by their less able peers. Those who cope best, according to Galbraith (1985), are those children whose sense of self is intact and thus can withstand verbal jibes, who can express their feelings and communicate these to others, and who can search out people with whom they can communicate honestly.

Ring and Shaughnessy (1993) report that when gifted children learn to use their gifts positively, their peers view them positively, but when gifted children are ashamed of their abilities or behave differently from their peers, their peers start to look down on them. (These writers report this as if it were a positive finding, yet having to fit in with the peer group in order to be accepted is the very thing which gifted children report as a problem.)

In an effort to reduce their uncertainty, gifted adolescents might make hasty decisions about relationships and careers. They might be less willing to take social risks because of being more able to recognise possible repercussions, and may become 'control freaks' in order to stay in charge of as many aspects of their lives as possible (Buescher 1985). These responses imply the need for ongoing social guidance throughout childhood.

SUGGESTED FURTHER READING

For more detail on social skills programs and cooperative games for young children, you could refer to Porter, L. 1999 *Young children's behaviour: practical approaches for caregivers and teachers* MacLennan & Petty, Sydney.

For a more technical overview of social skills training, see Porter, L. 1996 *Student behaviour: theory and practice for teachers* Allen & Unwin, Sydney.

For suggestions for cooperative games, you could consult Hill, S. 1992 *Games that work: cooperative games and activities for the primary school classroom* Eleanor Curtin, Armadale.

DISCUSSION QUESTIONS

1. How can early childhood teachers or caregivers assist in the social development of young gifted children?

2. Do talented performances make children less socially accepted? If so, how would you respond to the gifted children themselves and to their age mates?

3. Which is more important, social acceptance or individual achievement? Are the two necessarily incompatible?

4. What distinguishes popularity from friendship? Is popularity important?

5. How do notions of inclusion of children from other cultures and with disabilities help with the social inclusion of children with gifts or talents?

10

MEETING GIFTED YOUNG CHILDREN'S LEARNING NEEDS

It remains a source of astonishment . . . that the same sane and caring adults who would not dream of forcing a child [who was] growing at a faster rate than average into shoes too small for her feet will nonetheless insist on forcing a child whose mental growth is faster than average into a learning programme too small for her mind and imagination.

Cathcart (1996: 124)

KEY POINTS

- Gifted young children need their curriculum to be guided by the same philosophy as any early childhood curricula. Much of what is offered all children will be suitable for gifted children as well.
- However, some adjustments to a regular program will be needed in order to cater for gifted young children's precocity, complexity and intensity.
- Curriculum planning will need to promote a two-way exchange between teachers and parents so that teachers can learn from parents about their child's interests, needs and abilities and can inform parents about the aims of the curriculum.

INTRODUCTION

The basic premise of this chapter is that giftedness *can* develop in an optimal environment: 'The quality and character of . . . curriculum are vital ingredients to the eventual realization of a child's capacity'

(Van Tassel-Baska 1997: 126). Teachers' responsibility is not to impart information to children, but instead to provide a curriculum that facilitates their acquisition of knowledge and problem-solving skills (Barclay & Benelli 1994; Shaklee 1998). By enriching the general curriculum, all children will have the opportunity to develop talents according to their potential.

AIMS OF AN EARLY CHILDHOOD CURRICULUM

Early childhood programs aim to (Kilmer & McFarland 1988, in Wolfle 1990; Wright & Coulianos 1991):

- develop children's curiosity about the world and enthusiasm for learning;
- impart basic learning skills to children and conceptual knowledge of the world around them;
- facilitate the development of higher-order thinking and problem-solving skills;
- give children the opportunities to be expressive and creative in many domains;
- encourage children's growth in all developmental domains;
- help children to establish satisfying and successful social relationships;
- develop in each child a healthy self-esteem.

With these goals in mind, I have deliberately placed this chapter on curriculum after the chapters dealing with emotional and social needs because children will not learn unless their emotional needs are met first (Jones & Jones 1995). The goals of enhancing children's self-esteem, teaching them resilience, and fostering their friendships are both ends in themselves and ways to advance their learning. (I do not repeat the guidelines for promoting children's emotional and social adjustment here, but refer you to chapters 7–9 for the suggestions they contain.)

EDUCATIONAL CHALLENGES FOR GIFTED YOUNG CHILDREN

Gifted children's advanced intellectual skills, plus their social and emotional needs, create some special challenges for curriculum planning. On the one hand, these young children need the intellectual stimulation that is typically given to older children; on the other, their physical size and emotional immaturity might mean that some activities for older children are not suitable for them. Thus, the curriculum that is planned for them cannot simply be an adapted early school program: it must take account of their atypical interests and constellation of abilities (Parke & Ness 1988; Wolfle 1990).

Reliance on adults

Gifted young children crave high levels of stimulation. The further advanced their development, the less likely they are to receive this stimulation from peers (Harrison 1995) and the more likely they are to learn to rely on adults to teach them directly. At home, this can be demanding but manageable; in a centre, it has to be balanced with the needs of the other children. And in both settings it needs to be balanced with children's natural requirements for self-directed exploration.

Threatened self-efficacy

Self-efficacy is individuals' judgment about their ability to organise and execute a chosen action (Bandura 1986) and, in this context, refers to children's awareness that they know how to learn. This awareness may be impaired in gifted children because their learning can be so swift that they do not recognise the strategies they are using (Delisle 1992). Thus, they will need help to notice their own achievements (see chapters 7 and 11) and to develop their thinking (metacognitive) skills (discussed later in this chapter).

Boredom

The quick information-processing capacity, high levels of energy, and curiosity of gifted children (Chamrad & Robinson 1986) can make it difficult to keep them stimulated. Boredom occurs when a task is too easy or too difficult. A teacher's knowledge of child development—which is valuable in all other circumstances—can be a handicap for gifted children if it sets a ceiling on expectations of them in the belief that, because of their age, they are not ready for more advanced experiences.

Perseverance

Because gifted young children are often able to complete age-level tasks quickly and because they are often interested in global issues rather than the fine detail (Roeper 1995a), they might not naturally learn how to persevere with more demanding tasks and see them through to completion (Chamrad & Robinson 1986; Mares 1997). Another pattern leading to low perseverance is when children doubt their abilities (Phillips 1984, 1987). To teach perseverance, it will be necessary to supply activities

...at are neither too easy nor too difficult so that the children can rise to an attainable challenge (Mares 1997).

Attention span

Their ability to solve problems quickly can mean that gifted young children appear to have a short attention span; in fact, they are refusing to repeat an activity which they were able to master the first time. Given that most gifted children concentrate well, if they are restless this may be a sign that they need more challenge. This, however, is not the same as needing harder or even more work, just more *appropriate* work. They are likely to resist if we insist that they do more than anyone else (Braggett 1994).

CURRICULUM

The curriculum comprises a selection of knowledge and skills that a culture regards as worthwhile for its members to acquire (Montgomery 1996). It is 'all of the interactions, experiences and routines that are part of each child's day' (Department of Education and Children's Services 1996: 16). Taking each of these aspects in turn, interactions are 'all of the interpersonal communications that promote learning, caring relationships and positive self-esteem' (DECS 1996: 16); experiences are the result of planned or spontaneous opportunities to consolidate and extend learning; while routines are 'the regular activities associated with the comfort, health and well-being of the children' (DECS 1996: 17).

While all children should be provided with challenging, novel and stimulating activities, it is also important that we accept where the children are now, not just to have an eye on where we want them to be (Stonehouse 1988). It is important not to rush children to learn the next developmental skill as if their present developmental state is deficient in some way, but instead to give them time to consolidate what they already know.

PRINCIPLES OF CURRICULUM PLANNING

The stages of curriculum planning are identical for all children, whatever their ability levels. Curricula will be developed:

- in light of guidelines and policy directions provided by education and other authorities;
- drawing on teachers' training and experience;

- on the basis of assessment of each child's interests, experience a
  abilities in a range of domains (Krechevsky et al. 1995); how ea
  child learns; and with whom each child plays (Theilheimer 199
  and
- taking into account resources and constraints.

However, while planning processes are the same for all children, the
actual *content* of the program will reflect the children's differing ability
levels.

CURRICULUM DIFFERENTIATION

Curriculum differentiation refers to the provision of different learning
activities for same-aged children who have different learning needs and
preferences (Kulik & Kulik 1997). When planning to differentiate the
curriculum, it is necessary to consider what we want to cover for the
more able children that is not already provided for everyone (Eyre 1997).
However, any curricular differences need to be justifiable educationally,
rather than being something faddish that titillates rather than educates
(Callahan 1996). In other words, entertainment is fine but it should not
be mistaken for academic rigour (Sawyer 1988).

In chapter 4, I reported on gifted children's precocious learning
abilities and style. A differentiated curriculum must take into account
these differences (gifted children's external asynchrony) as well as
their uneven developmental levels (internal dissonance) (Morelock &
Morrison 1996; Piirto 1999). It must allow for differences in both
the pace (quantity) and depth (quality) of children's learning (Piirto
1999).

Thus, when most writers discuss curriculum differentiation measures,
they describe three main modifications:

- acceleration of the *pace* of instruction;
- enrichment, which refers to the provision of *broader*, more varied
  educational experiences to reflect the needs and interests of atypical
  children (Braggett 1994; Braggett et al. 1997; Schiever & Maker
  1997; Van Tassel-Baska 1997);
- extension, which refers to a *deepening*, in contrast to a broadening,
  of the curriculum (Braggett 1994; Braggett et al. 1997).

These three approaches give rise to the general curriculum guidelines
that are listed in the box, opposite.

In a practical sense, however, there is uncertainty about what activities
constitute true enrichment, rather than merely 'busy work' (Townsend
1996). There is some confusion between enrichment measures that would

GENERAL CURRICULUM GUIDELINES

Given gifted learners' advanced thinking skills, the early childhood curriculum will need to offer open-ended activities which:

- encourage higher level thinking skills such as analysis, synthesis, evaluation and problem solving;
- allow the children to pursue their own interests to a depth that satisfies them;
- involve less repetition and a faster pace than usual for their age;
- promote intellectual risk-taking—that is, creativity—and divergent thinking;
- offer a high degree of complexity and variety in their content, process and product.

Holden (1996) suggests that these same guidelines can also apply to parents' choice of toys for their gifted young child.

benefit all children and those that are uniquely suited to gifted children (Shore & Delcourt 1996; Tomlinson 1996; Wallace 1986a). Some content will be aimed at cultivating the talents of all children and will enhance their confidence in themselves as learners; some will comprise broader and deeper learning experiences for those children whose performances demonstrate that they can engage in advanced levels of thinking; and some content will be designed for those children whose development is advanced in non-traditional domains (e.g. creativity), whose giftedness is manifested in non-typical ways, or who need additional stimulation for their advanced skills to emerge (Braggett 1992; Cooper 1990).

To help distinguish common from targeted curricular provisions, the remainder of this chapter adapts Tomlinson's (1996) format by first discussing aspects of the regular curricula that are common to all children and then suggesting modifications that will be necessary for gifted learners. (These measures are summarised in table 10.1.) Using the regular curriculum in this way as a basis for differentiation is crucial because, as Callahan (1996: 160) states: 'It is extremely difficult to build a strong differentiated curriculum on a weak basic curriculum.'

Curricular modifications fall into four categories: modification of the learning *environment*, curricular *content*, curricular *processes* (Harrison 1995; Montgomery 1996; Van Tassel-Baska 1997), and the *products*

173

Table 10.1 Common and differentiated features of curricula for young children

Environmental organisation	Content	Process	Product
Common elements			
• structured yet flexible organisation • supportive climate • encouragement of exploration • acceptance of mistakes • high but realistic expectations • high-quality teaching	• optimal opportunities for all • adherence to developmental theory and quality guidelines • domain-specific and interdisciplinary content • integrated curriculum • curriculum based on children's interests • experience in multiple domains	• children need to be active learners • opportunities for autonomous learning • adult involvement	• application of key knowledge and skills • a range of mediums • a range of domains
Differentiation methods			

• flexible time allotment
• supplementary resources
• increased flexibility
• systematic planning
• specialised teacher training
• ability grouping
• early entry to school
• grade skipping
	• tailored activities:
	  – simple vs complex
	  – concrete vs abstract
	  – small vs large steps
	  – factual vs conceptual
	  – uni- vs multi-dimensional
	  – structured vs open-ended
	  – breadth vs depth
	• tiered activities
	• curriculum compacting
	• telescoping
	• promoting children's interests
		• mediated learning
		• mediated sociodramatic play
		• metacognitive training
		• teach thinking skills
		• enhance motivation
			• tiered products
			• teach expressive skills

Source: Adapted from Tomlinson (1996).

through which children demonstrate their learning (although in the early childhood years, variety of products is routinely built into the curriculum for all children).

ENVIRONMENTAL ORGANISATION

The environment refers to the physical structure of a setting, its organisation, and its social climate.

Common environmental features

The learning environment needs to be responsive to the cognitive, emotional and social needs of the children (Clark 1997). As you do for any children, you will need to plan how the centre will be organised in order to facilitate the children's optimal growth. Aspects to consider include the type of outdoor and indoor spaces that are available, grouping practices, and time-tabling (Braggett 1997).

The learning environment needs to be structured and yet allow the children some freedom and choice (Berk 1997; Hay 1993; Whitmore 1980). This is nicely put by Smutny et al. (1997: 28):

> It's essential that structure be used not to define learning goals but, like a sturdy ladder, to provide the stability and direction the child needs to reach as high as possible.

That is, young children need a safe, well-organised but flexible learning environment, whose structure permits them to pursue their own interests and to integrate their learning (Clark 1997). They need consistent challenge (Freeman 1995a) to meet high but realistic expectations (Emerick 1992) and, when they expect more of themselves, these pressures need to be balanced by the provision of extra supports. The children must feel safe about making mistakes and using trial-and-error approaches for solving problems, as when teachers set great store by doing things right, the children are likely to underachieve (Eyre 1997; Harrison 1995; Harrison & Tegel 1999). Children need to accept that failure is a natural part of the learning process (Prichard 1985); if they aren't making mistakes, they are only practising.

High-quality teaching

Some writers contend that caregivers and teachers of gifted children require a number of special qualities, including the capacities to be: mature; self-confident; achievement-oriented; accepting, understanding and respectful of children; well-organised and yet flexible; imaginative and creative; spontaneous; enthusiastic; broadly cultured; and in possession of a sense of humour (Anderson 1985; Baldwin 1993; Feldhusen 1985, 1997; Wendel & Heiser 1989). Teachers are said to require a positive attitude to catering for children with diverse abilities—including those who are educationally disadvantaged—so that children feel safe about being different. They must *want* children to explore, defy boundaries and express opinions (Anderson 1985; Clark 1997; Wendel & Heiser 1989) and must be willing to question some basic assumptions about how to meet children's diverse needs (Cathcart 1996).

However, this list seems equally relevant for all teachers, regardless of the children's age or ability levels (Baldwin 1993; Sapon-Shevin 1987a): high-quality teaching is a necessity for all children.

Environmental differentiation methods

The above elements of the physical and social environment can be adapted to cater more effectively for children with advanced development.

Allotted time

At times, gifted children need an accelerated pace of curriculum delivery because they can learn more quickly than usual. At other times, they need prolonged periods in which to develop their play themes, generate ideas, and deal with content creatively and with appreciation of its subtleties and profundities (Harrison & Tegel 1999; Klein 1992; Tannenbaum 1983; Ward 1996). Therefore, either because of their need for an increased pace of learning, or because they need to become deeply absorbed in a single topic, the theme-a-week concept might be inappropriate for gifted children. Patton and Kokoski (1996) describe this as the 'less is more' rule, which is to say that we need to teach fewer concepts but in greater depth.

Supplementary resources

You will need to provide more than the usual resources and you will need to be prepared for these resources to be used in creative or unusual ways (Harrison & Tegel 1999). One resource is reference material and interest centres that allow the children to explore their interests in depth. Another is parents and other community members who have special expertise and interests: they can be invited into the centre to contribute to enriching activities. Other resources involve community walks and field trips which allow the children to experience concepts in the 'real world' (Braggett 1998a; Harrison & Tegel 1999; Willard-Holt 1994).

Increased flexibility

Individualisation of the curriculum necessitates greater flexibility in teachers' role, organisation of the setting and structure of the curriculum

(Wallace 1983). You will need to take advantage of spontaneous opportunities to extend children's learning, rather than adhering slavishly to planned activities (Eyre 1997).

Systematic planning

Modifications to curricula need a clear rationale and should be planned systematically so that changes satisfy gifted children's need to learn in greater depth and breadth, rather than merely offering them trivial additional exercises (Schiever & Maker 1997). As Eyre (1997: 41) concludes: 'Bolt-on, one-off extension ideas are of limited value and effectiveness.' Once modifications have been enacted, the curriculum needs to be monitored or evaluated as a way of building in accountability (Clark 1997; Wallace 1983) and to enable its continued refinement.

Teacher training

Curriculum differentiation measures are not employed widely in regular classes (Archambault et al. 1993; Westberg, Archambault & Brown 1993; Westberg et al. 1993). Many researchers conclude that this is due to teachers' inadequate training for meeting the needs of gifted children. Teachers of gifted children need to be knowledgeable about offering challenging curricula, and must understand the uneven developmental profiles of gifted children and their atypical emotional and social characteristics (Anderson 1985; Feldhusen 1985, 1997; Feldhusen & Hoover 1984; Fraser 1996; Renzulli 1973; Wendel & Heiser 1989). Most writers agree, therefore, that caregivers and teachers require some additional professional knowledge and skills, which can be acquired through specific training in gifted education (Christie 1995; Feldhusen 1985, 1997; Hansen & Feldhusen 1994; Moltzen 1998; Reis & Purcell 1993; Reis & Westberg 1994; Van Tassel-Baska 1995).

Ability grouping

Research tells us that placing gifted children together with other children of similar abilities and subsequently making instruction more complex improves the children's achievement, attitude to learning, social skills, and self-esteem (Allan 1991; Gamoran 1992; Hallinan 1990; Kolloff & Moore 1989; Kulik & Kulik 1982, 1992; Lando & Schneider 1997; Rogers & Span 1993; Shore & Delcourt 1996; Rist 1970; Slavin 1987a, 1990a; Van Tassel-Baska 1992). This is probably because the starting point for the task can be higher (Eyre 1997). At the same time, removal of gifted children from a group does not reduce the less able children's self-esteem (Carter 1986; Chan 1988) or achievements, as these children regard gifted children as dissimilar to themselves and so do not model themselves on them (Schunk 1987).

The concept of ability grouping is often mistaken for tracking or streaming, in which children of similar ability are grouped together for relatively long periods (Feldhusen & Moon 1992; Fiedler et al. 1993; Gamoran 1992); in contrast, ability groups have flexible memberships, depending on the activity. Tracking has been criticised on the grounds that it confers high status on the fast tracks and low status on those in the slower groups (Kulik & Kulik 1982). This, it is claimed, results in poorer instruction in the low tracks and, consequently, progressively increases the academic disparities and inequalities between the high and low groups, the latter of whom are often already disadvantaged in terms of their social background (Carey 1994; Gamoran 1992; Hallinan 1990; Rist 1970; Sapon-Shevin 1994; Slavin 1991). However, this criticism is less relevant to flexible ability groupings.

In early childhood, this debate is somewhat academic since ability grouping (particularly tracking) is seldom available in preschools and child-care centres (Hall 1993; Kitano 1982; Wolfle 1990) because of their size. This can be turned into an advantage in that heterogeneous grouping requires teachers to focus on enriching the curriculum for all children, so that they all have opportunities to demonstrate their strengths.

Meanwhile, in order to meet gifted children's social needs, some centres can offer multi-age grouping, in which children of a wide range of ages are educated and cared for together. This gives teachers the flexibility to create both homogeneous and heterogeneous groupings as required by the children and the activity (Lloyd 1997). Although multi-age grouping can be a challenging teaching arrangement (Mason & Burns 1996), and is not always possible because of the restricted age range in a centre, it has many advantages (Katz et al. 1990; Lloyd 1997; Milburn 1981; Pavan 1992; Porter 1999; Tanner & Decotis 1995), the main one of which is that it allows younger children to access older friends and so to find peers whose developmental level matches their own. Also, the presence of children of a wide range of ages can sensitise adults to each child's present developmental status and to meeting each child's individual needs (Bouchard 1991). The outcome can be that children feel less pressure to conform developmentally, which can be especially beneficial for children with learning difficulties or advances, uneven levels of development across domains, and those who are under-achieving (Bouchard 1991; Katz et al. 1990; Lloyd 1997).

Nevertheless, multi-age grouping alone has a neutral effect: simply placing children of different ages together will not be enough to ensure that they benefit from the experience (Mosteller et al. 1996; Veenman

1995, 1996). The benefits appear to come from the adults' philosophical commitment to meeting individual children's needs without regard to age norms (Lloyd 1997).

Thus, a multi-age class is not the same as a composite class, in which children of two year-levels are 'housed' in the one classroom but are taught separately (Lloyd 1997). In a true multi-age centre or classroom, the children are not seen to be members of a grade or year level, but instead are all taught similar content and processes. The children engage with this curriculum at their own level and progress at their own rate. The result is that they remain in the class for as long as it takes them to master the curriculum.

The conclusion from this debate is that gifted children benefit academically and socially from spending some time learning alongside other children of similar ability levels to themselves. However, it can be difficult to provide intellectually similar peers in early childhood centres, in which case it may be useful for parents to make contact with the local Gifted and Talented Children's Association to ensure that their child can receive this social contact outside of the centre.

Early entry to school

Just as children with intellectual disabilities might need to delay starting school, children with developmental advances often need to begin school early. This is one form of *acceleration*, which means increasing the pace at which the curriculum is presented in line with gifted children's natural rate of learning, so that the curriculum is better tailored to their developmental levels (Bailey 1997; Elkind 1988; Schiever & Maker 1997; Townsend 1996). The term appears to imply an attempt to speed up the children's development itself, however, and so should perhaps be replaced with the title of *developmentally appropriate placement* (Elkind 1988; Feldhusen 1989; Feldhusen et al. 1996; Rogers & Kimpston 1992; Southern et al. 1993).

Aims of acceleration

The intention of developmentally appropriate placement (or acceleration) is to enhance children's achievement by providing a closer match between their needs and abilities and the curriculum that is delivered to them (Benbow 1991). In so doing, its aims are:

- to avoid boredom, along with any resultant behavioural difficulties (Holden 1996; Rogers & Kimpston 1992);
- to promote the children's development of good study skills such as

higher-order thinking skills and motivation (Benbow 1991; Braggett et al. 1997);

- to allow gifted children to mix socially more successfully, by placing them with children who differ from them in age but who share similar interests. Early entry to school can prevent later acceleration with its resulting dislocation from the peer group (Rogers & Kimpston 1992);
- to capitalise early on young children's interests and abilities (Rogers & Kimpston 1992).

Effects of acceleration

Research consistently reports that acceleration meets all of these academic, social and emotional aims. One study found that, compared with their classmates, early entrants' relative academic standing increased as they progressed through school (Proctor et al. 1986). Accelerants mostly adjust well socially and emotionally (sometimes after some initial minor difficulties), and they report preferring to be with the older children who are their intellectual peers.

Most studies have found that accelerants display equivalent adjustment compared with equally gifted children who have not been accelerated (Sayler & Brookshire 1993; Swiatek & Benbow 1991), and thus no benefit seems to have accrued. However, children who elect to be accelerated might have experienced harm had they *not* been allowed to accelerate: they might have become bored and unmotivated, with a consequent decrease in achievement (Heinbokel 1997; Montgomery 1996; Swiatek & Benbow 1991).

Finally, it appears that the resulting early exit from school is not a problem for accelerants, who continue to do well into university and beyond (Swiatek & Benbow 1991).

On the other hand, a few authors (e.g. Freeman 1991) have found some harmful academic, social and emotional side-effects of acceleration. With respect to early school entry, one specific finding was that 20% of early entrants performed poorly in school as assessed by teacher ratings (McCluskey et al. 1996), although this might not have been caused by their early entrance—they might still have performed poorly even if they had started school on time. It is also unclear whether subsequent difficulties are due to acceleration as such, to negative attitudes by teachers which result in accelerated children receiving little support in their new placements (Heinbokel 1997), or to the fact that acceleration is used so rarely that an accelerated child feels abnormal (Southern et al. 1993).

Despite evidence of the mainly positive effects, many parents are reluctant for their child to begin school early because they believe that its structure is incompatible with young children's social and emotional needs (Kitano 1982). They do not want their child to be one of those who experiences difficulties arising from acceleration (Bailey 1997). They may seek to hold a child back because of his or her apparent social or emotional immaturity. But, rather than signalling that the child is not ready for school, this behaviour can be a result of being in a socially and educationally inappropriate setting and can improve once the child is more appropriately placed (Braggett 1992).

This discussion gives rise to some recommendations for how best to assess which children are most likely to profit from early entry to school.

Guidelines for early entry to school

Children and their anticipated school have to be carefully screened before early entry is contemplated. The following are important considerations.

- The school has to be willing to accept the child early (Braggett 1993; Mares & Byles 1994).
- The classroom that the child is entering needs to be flexibly structured and the receiving teacher must be sympathetic to the idea of early entry (Braggett 1992).
- The school must be willing to fill any gaps in a child's skills that have resulted from entering school early (Bailey 1997; Heinbokel 1997).
- The child will need sufficient fine motor skills for academic activities such as handwriting (Braggett 1992; Mares & Byles 1994; Robinson & Robinson 1992).
- Reading readiness is a crucial factor (Braggett 1992).
- The child must be interested in starting school early, although adults must be careful not to give him or her the impression that it will solve all difficulties (Bailey 1997).
- The child will need to be comfortable about mixing with older children and being one of the youngest in the class, if not the school (Braggett 1992).
- The parents' wishes and support are crucial (Braggett 1993; Mares & Byles 1994; Robinson 1990b) as their comfort with acceleration will affect how well their child copes (Braggett 1992; Robinson 1990b).

To follow are some less important issues to consider: these should not rule out early entry to school if all of the above factors indicate its potential value to the child, but they can help smooth the transition to the next placement.

- The children need to be socially and emotionally mature enough to cope with school. Having said this, there is clearly a wide range in school entrants' social and emotional maturity (Braggett 1992) and younger children tend to 'grow into' the social-emotional levels of those around them (Vialle 1998). Lack of maturity may thus not be an impediment to early entry.

- It helps if children are not small for their age so that they can participate in the other children's physical games and sports and do not look physically out of place among older classmates. This is desirable but not crucial (Rimm & Lovance 1992b).

- The children will also need the physical stamina to cope with a longer day (Schiever & Maker 1997). On the other hand, if they become tired, they could attend schools for four days a week: their absence on the fifth day would seldom excite attention.

- It can help if the children have attended an early childhood centre for at least six months prior to school entry so that they have learned to separate from their parents, to delay gratification, to cope with conflict with other children using negotiation rather than aggression, and to concentrate (Mares & Byles 1994).

Nevertheless, the uneven development of gifted children means that few will be equally mature in all these domains. Therefore, consultation between early childhood staff, parents and the selected school will be necessary to decide what is best for each individual child (Morelock & Morrison 1996). The decision to enrol a child at school early should be treated as a trial, and its effects monitored closely (Braggett 1992).

Limitations of acceleration

Some gifted educationists contend that acceleration will not be a complete solution to children's needs: offering gifted learners the same curriculum sooner reflects a quantitative approach, they say, and does not take account of the children's qualitatively different learning abilities (Mares & Byles 1994; Schiever & Maker 1997). This view holds that, on its own, acceleration is not likely to be sufficient to meet gifted children's needs unless they are offered an enriched curriculum as well (Feldhusen et al. 1996). Others (e.g. Pendarvis & Howley 1996) do not agree, and so place greater faith in the efficacy of acceleration.

Grade-skipping

A second key method of acceleration involves allowing gifted school-aged children to skip a grade, or to go up to a higher grade for certain subjects (which is termed 'partial acceleration' or 'subject acceleration').

This can be organisationally attractive since it seems to avoid the need to provide special curricula for accelerated children (Bailey 1993; Eales & de Paoli 1991; Willard-Holt 1994): the children do all the adjusting to their new placement. However, the school will still need to adapt its curricula to meet the children's needs, regardless of their class placement (Heinbokel 1997; Shore & Delcourt 1996).

CURRICULAR CONTENT

As already mentioned, it is not required that the whole curriculum should be differentiated for gifted children. Some experiences are equally valuable for all children; others will be suitable for a group of bright students; while still others will be unique to a particular child (Braggett et al. 1997; Shore & Delcourt 1996).

Common elements

The following guidelines for curricular content are applicable to all children.

Optimal opportunities for all

All children should be provided with opportunities that allow them to attain optimal levels of learning.

Adherence to developmental theory and quality guidelines

The curriculum must cater for all of the intellectual, social, emotional, physical, intuitive and creative needs of children (Clark 1997) in a way that is not only developmentally appropriate but also 'humanly, culturally and individually appropriate' (Stonehouse 1994a: 76).

Domain-specific and interdisciplinary content

As well as teaching knowledge that is specific to particular fields, the curriculum needs to be interdisciplinary (Jacobs & Borland 1986; Nidiffer & Moon 1994). As its title implies, this means that topics are examined from a range of perspectives—through different lenses, as it were (Jacobs & Borland 1986). The most suitable topics for examination from a range of perspectives are ones that are conceptual in nature, of interest to the children, and sufficiently broad to lend themselves to study from many perspectives while not being so broad that they are limitless (Jacobs & Borland 1986).

An integrated curriculum

An integrated curriculum is first one where traditional content areas are incorporated naturally into all activities (Barbour 1992; Nidiffer & Moon 1994). Second, it is one where the whole child is the focus—that is, the curriculum is sensitive to children's intellectual, physical, emotional and social needs, rather than their intellectual skills alone (Barbour 1992; Holden 1996; Van Tassel-Baska 1995). Third, integration implies an integration of the children's worlds—home, the school or preschool, culture and community (Holden 1996). Finally, integration implies that processes such as solitary exploration are integrated with social activities (Diezmann & Watters 1997).

Curriculum based on children's interests

Curricular content should be drawn from the children's interests and educational needs, rather than a predetermined sequence of instruction. Teachers need to guide children to identify their areas of interest and help them to learn the strategies and thinking skills that are necessary for addressing the issues and problems in their chosen area.

Experience in multiple domains

Gardner's (1983) multiple intelligence theory (which, as described in chapter 2, refers to multiple content areas) is a useful guide for checking that the curriculum covers all developmental domains. Other guides are provided by local authorities. For instance, in South Australia the Department of Education and Children's Services (1996) issued a curriculum framework entitled the *Foundation Areas of Learning,* which outlines nine fundamental areas of learning: self-concept, communication, creativity, critical thinking, cultural understanding, environmental understanding, health and physical development, social development, and technology. Like Gardner's multiple intelligence theory, such guidelines direct teachers to consider the multiple ways in which children can be challenged.

Content differentiation methods

Some curricular content will need to be modified so that it is responsive to children's disparate developmental levels.

Tailored activities

The following features of activities can be varied in line with the ability levels of the children and the complexity of the learning task (Tomlinson 1996).

Simple versus complex tasks. When children are dealing with content or processes that they are only just ready to learn, they will need the content to be simple; when the children are working comfortably within their developmental level, they will be more motivated by tasks that are complex.

Concrete versus abstract examples. At entry level, children will need concrete learning experiences; if children are advanced in the task at hand, they will be more able to apply their more sophisticated knowledge to abstract problems.

Small steps versus larger leaps. When a task is intellectually demanding, children will need it to be broken into smaller steps; when children already possess the requisite subskills, they can take larger leaps in their learning.

Knowledge acquisition versus concept mastery. Gifted learners will often have more prior knowledge than their age mates. Therefore, they will need less repetition, revision and consolidation time than less able children (Braggett 1998a; Kanevsky 1994; Plucker & McIntire 1996). Thus, there can be less need to teach them isolated facts, leaving time for them to focus on broader concepts.

> A 4½-year-old came home and reported that she didn't think her preschool teachers' brains 'learned very quickly'. When asked why by a puzzled mother, the child reported that the teachers put the same activities out on Tuesday that they had put out on Monday and that they read a book today which they had read last week. The child's conclusion was, 'I don't think they remember that they have read it to us already'. The repetition, usually necessary for young children to learn, was a main contributor to this child's need to enter school early.

Unidimensional versus multifaceted. When children are novices within a field of interest, they might need to explore it along a single dimension; when they already grasp the basics, they can explore it in a more multidisciplinary manner, making more connections between ideas and examining issues from various perspectives.

Structured versus open-ended. When children are comfortable with an area, they can cope with open-ended activities; when they are not sure of their grounding in a domain, they are likely to prefer more structured activities, otherwise they may underperform in an attempt to stay safe (Burton-Szabo 1996; Eyre 1997; Stewart 1981). Very unstructured tasks, such as 'Go and find out all you can about . . .' activities, are not likely to appeal to many children, will underutilise their skills and could lead to discouragement or disruptions (Eyre 1997).

Breadth versus depth. All children will need to acquire a broad range of skills across domains; when they have attained these, they can be encouraged to achieve deeper understanding (Patton & Kokoski 1996; Van Tassel-Baska 1997).

Tiered activities

The provision of tiered activities takes two forms (Montgomery 1996):

- differentiation of *inputs*, whereby teachers provide different activities at different levels of difficulty but which share a common theme. The children could self-select which activities suit them or teachers could target certain children and support them to attempt the more demanding tasks;
- differentiation of *outcomes or responses*, whereby teachers set a common task which children enter at their own level and then respond to according to their level of sophistication. Both the product and learning processes will vary commensurate with the children's abilities (Hertzog 1998).

Offering tiered activities requires that teachers establish appropriate starting points for the children, based on their identification of the children's prior knowledge (Eyre 1997). This identification can be facilitated by brainstorming, concept mapping or observation of the children's achievement on open-ended tasks (Eyre 1997; Shore & Kanevsky 1993).

Curriculum compacting

Curriculum compacting simply means delivering curricular content at a faster pace to reflect gifted children's more efficient learning. It occurs in three phases: first, identifying the goals and outcomes of a given activity; second, determining who can already achieve those goals; third, providing these children with extension activities instead (Reis & Renzulli 1992; Willard-Holt 1994). These activities might comprise special projects on topics in which the children are passionately interested.

Curriculum compacting places extra demands on teacher time and skills (Schiever & Maker 1997) but is thought to be beneficial in some instances because it keeps children within their same-aged peer group (Braggett 1993), while still allowing them to progress through the curriculum at their own pace. Studies of this form of acceleration show that, rather than reducing children's understanding of the concepts covered, the increased speed of delivery does not detract from mastery; in some cases, it may even promote better understanding (Reis & Renzulli 1992; Reis et al. 1998; Townsend 1996). Curriculum compacting tends to work best in hierarchical subjects such as mathematics but, even in this domain, the findings of improved performances by gifted students are by no means resounding (Reis et al. 1998).

Telescoping

Telescoping is a related method of curriculum acceleration. It involves teaching the curriculum at a faster pace to the whole group, with the result that they all cover, say, three years' work in two, and graduate to the next educational setting at a younger age (Braggett 1992). This is unlikely to be used in early childhood settings, but can occur in the junior primary (elementary) years, say, by telescoping the first year of school into half a year for those children who enter school in the middle of the year.

Like other accelerative measures, telescoping hastens progress through school but does not alter the curriculum and so does not address gifted learners' need for an enriched curriculum as well as a faster pace of delivery (Braggett 1992).

Promoting children's interests

Gifted children often develop a series of passionate interests. These interests are significant because they help the children to resolve inner conflicts, and so it is important that adults help them to explore their topics rather than redirecting them to more traditional tasks (Cohen 1998). Focusing on these interests avoids their erosion and children's consequent underachievement (Whitmore, in Cohen 1998). It also avoids the deficit model of education, in which the focus is on what children *cannot* do (Cohen 1998).

While children's interests change over time, their underlying themes are remarkably similar throughout childhood (Cohen 1989, 1998). Cohen (1998) has identified six major themes:

- control—which refers to children's drive to be in control of themselves and their world, to master tasks, and to understand how things are organised;
- nature-nurture—where the children's interests centre on the natural world and on nurturing others or belonging;
- putting it all together—where the children are interested in the meaning, function and origins of things and in transforming objects;
- people and relationships—where they seek to understand other people and roles and to make friends;
- aesthetic-expressive—where they are interested and sensitive to beauty and the arts and express themselves artistically and emotionally;

- symbols and symbol systems—where the children are interested in learning words, numbers, grammatical symbols and body language.

Cohen (1989) reports that because gifted young children are aware of their environment earlier and attempt tasks earlier, they experience from a younger age the traps or dangers inherent in performing tasks for which they are cognitively ready but for which their bodies might be too immature. As a result, she says, their play tends to be centred on a control theme. This begins with a thirst for knowledge, which must be satisfied, as knowledge confers power. Next comes the need to 'put it all together' and to understand cause-and-effect. Alongside these themes might be the child's need to express ideas, perhaps aesthetically (e.g. through music) or symbolically.

Children's interests can be encouraged by helping them to gather resources, asking them questions, and extending an interest into a new area when the time is right (Cohen 1998). Having determined which theme or themes are driving a child, teachers can generate tasks in a range of curricular areas which address that theme and demonstrate the relationships between areas of content (Cohen 1998; Shaklee 1998). For instance, a child who seeks to control, master and understand could be helped to research an interest such as dinosaurs and then to explore this interest through science, maths, story-writing, art, and teaching the other children about dinosaurs.

TEACHING AND LEARNING PROCESSES

As with the other elements of the curriculum (environment and content), there are elements of teaching and learning processes that are common to all children.

Common principles

Early childhood curricula are guided by a range of principles that are equally relevant to all children.

Children need to be active in their learning

The program needs to give children freedom to manipulate and explore worthwhile interests extensively and in depth (Tannenbaum 1983). Therefore, the curriculum should encompass play as an outlet for expression and a vehicle for learning (Harrison & Tegel 1999; Parke & Ness 1988; Snowden 1995).

Children need opportunities for autonomous learning

Children should contribute to decisions about their curriculum so that they learn how to take responsibility for their own learning, are more motivated to take part in the activities that they selected for themselves, and can develop their initiative (Willard-Holt 1994). This can be done by brainstorming sessions in which the children volunteer information that they already know about a topic and, in doing so, signal what interests them (Patton & Kokoski 1996). (In the early childhood years, brainstorming might best be done in pairs or small groups of three to four children as younger children tend to forget their idea if they have to wait a long time while others present theirs; see Paulus & Paulus 1997.)

Adult involvement

The main strategy for teaching children is to interact with them. Although teachers usually prefer active to passive (supervisory) roles, they tend to spend most of their time offering guidance (including praise and directives) and the least time asking divergent questions and elaborating on children's play. This pattern is sensitive to caregiver or teacher training and to group size: the better trained the teacher and the smaller the group, the less directive adult–child interactions become (Kontos & Wilcox-Herzog 1997).

Many gifted children are left to their own devices because their teachers know that they are capable and well-behaved and they do not 'look stuck' and in need of help (Eyre 1997; Wolfle 1989). This is not unique to gifted children: although teachers spend the majority of their time interacting with children, research shows that nearly one-third of children receive no individual attention on a given day (Kontos & Wilson-Herzog 1997).

In light of this and given that the adult–child ratio prohibits a large *quantity* of interaction, teachers have to make a conscious effort to spend high-quality time with individual children. Teachers' involvement can be characterised on four dimensions: the *amount of time* spent interacting with individual children; the *role* adopted during those interactions (e.g. giving directions, being co-players, or monitoring the children); the *sensitivity*, warmth or responsiveness of interactions with the children; and the *intensity* of involvement with them (Kontos & Wilcox-Herzog 1997).

Process differentiation methods

Teaching methods will differ at different stages of children's development. This is illustrated in table 10.2 which adapts Belgrad's (1998) suggestions.

Table 10.2 Young children's modes of learning and corresponding modes of teaching

Developmental level	Modes of play or learning	Modes of teaching
0–18 months	Imitation	Direct instruction • showing • telling • describing
18–30 months	Exploration Discovery	Provision of a safe environment Questioning
30–48 months	Prediction testing (trial-and-error learning) Discovery	Mediation Explaining cause-and-effect
4+ years	Construction	Facilitation Opportunities for learning Mediation

Source: Adapted from Belgrad (1998).

Mediated learning

Mediated learning—as distinct from direct learning through the senses—occurs when adults interpret the environment for children, reflecting the children's interests, needs and capabilities to make the task demands compatible with these (Klein 1992). This takes considerable teacher skill: to set the stage, to recognise the children's responses, and to follow through with support in order to advance their thinking skills (Barclay & Benelli 1994).

In mediated learning, adults initially direct children's thinking processes towards a higher level than they can achieve alone, and then the children progressively acquire the ability to take over this executive control function themselves (Moss 1992). That is, children first experience problem solving as an interpersonal process—in a dyad with a parent or other adult—and then develop the ability to solve problems independently (Moss 1992). To achieve this transfer, children need opportunities to participate actively in the joint problem-solving process (Moss 1992; Wallace 1983).

Prior to school age, young children are dependent on adults to regulate (i.e. mediate) their approaches to tasks (Moss 1990). So, although early childhood curricula are based on children's exploration and discovery, teachers will need to guide children's learning. You should invite children's ideas and suggestions, provide cues, ask questions, identify problems, and offer and ask for feedback. This can be done through comments and open-ended questions (Wallace 1983). These will incorporate the following five key strategies (Klein 1992).

Focus. Teachers can select salient aspects of the activity and help children to focus on these through accentuation or exaggeration (Klein 1992; Moss 1992). (With young babies, a toy might be 'danced' to within easy reach; with older infants, teachers could point out important features: 'Hey, look at this! What do you think it's for?')

Meaning. Teachers can convey intellectual interest in and emotional excitement about an activity. Children will then internalise (learn) to find such activities interesting, and develop the commitment that is necessary for sustained effort and success.

Expansion. Teachers can expand children's cognitive awareness beyond their immediate activity by making spontaneous comparisons, pointing out strategies for memory storage and recall, and so on.

Feedback. Teachers can express excitement and satisfaction with children's achievements by, for example, making explicit, positive statements about their efforts (e.g. 'Look how well it's going!'). This teaches children how to monitor and judge outcomes for themselves and will enhance effort and reflection (Moss 1992).

Organisation. Teachers can help children to plan, regulate and monitor their activities by matching the task to their developmental levels and interests. This can be done in the infant years by working on tasks jointly until the youngsters gradually acquire the ability to use their organisation skills independently. Once children reach a developmental level of around 4 years (regardless of their actual age), they will begin to internalise directives in the form of self-talk, which is the beginning of metacognitive control (Moss 1992).

Eyre (1997) suggests instituting a 'teaching bubble' when using formal mediated learning, whereby you create a physical cue to signal to the other children that the group cannot be interrupted, in which case they must ask another adult when they need help. Reduced interruptions enables participating children to maintain their attention.

Mediated sociodramatic play

Young children do not play or work: they simply *do* (Hein 1973, in Snowden 1995). Their play experiences teach them knowledge and learning processes that they could not readily acquire through outside instruction. However, teachers will need to set the stage so that high-quality play—and hence high-quality learning—can occur (Ward 1996).

When children are engaged is sociodramatic play, the temptation is either to interrupt their play to make it more 'educational' or to leave them to their own devices for fear of stifling or disrupting their ideas (Ward 1996). In most instances, it is important to allow the children to direct their own play and remain involved until they have resolved its issues (Harrison & Tegel 1999). However, at other times, teachers will need to help children to enrich their play (Harrison & Tegel 1999). Ward suggests the following strategies.

- Teachers can play in parallel with children who, through observing what they are doing, begin to copy their play. This adds to or extends children's own play ideas.
- At the invitation of the children, teachers can become a co-player, joining in their existing play and responding to their comments or actions, thus complementing and extending their ideas.
- At the next more intrusive level, teachers might take more control of the direction of the play, either by making suggestions from the side or by participating actively.
- Teachers can initiate play for children who appear not to be able to engage in advanced play without adult prompts. Then teachers can ease out of the play as soon as the children assume control of its direction themselves (Ward 1996).

At all of these levels teachers can pose questions, make suggestions, and add to the children's processing and cooperative skills through careful observation of their play and assessment of the type of guidance they need. By providing help in the children's zone of proximal development (i.e. at the level just beyond what they can achieve independently), teachers can promote further learning in all developmental domains.

Metacognitive training

The main task of the early childhood years is the acquisition of metacognitive thinking—that is, control of one's learning. Their superior use of metacognitive skills distinguishes gifted from average learners (Horowitz 1992; Schwanenflugel et al. 1997). Therefore, a major focus with intellectually gifted youngsters will be on promoting metacognitive skills, which comprise planning, monitoring and evaluation of their approach to tasks (Berk 1997; Freeman 1995; Schraw & Graham 1997). Teaching these skills is achieved through synchronous, contingent and reciprocal interactions between adults and children. This means responding to children's cues, engaging them in a two-way exchange of ideas and information, and responding contingently rather than randomly to their actions.

Teach thinking skills

The first level of thinking skills comprises domain-general skills such as comprehension, summarising, identifying main ideas, and asking questions. Gifted children need knowledge before they can manipulate it and, thus, it is important to foster these basic skills (Bailey & Leonard 1977; Sawyer 1988). In addition, gifted children's ability to deal with abstract and complex material earlier and gain knowledge in greater depth and breadth than is usual for their age (Morelock & Morrison 1996) means that they will also benefit from early training to think at higher levels (Pohl 1997). They will need to learn to:

- apply knowledge;
- understand and analyse ideas;
- synthesise information by solving problems and creating, inventing and constructing original products;
- evaluate outcomes (Braggett 1998a; Wallace 1986a).

Critical thinking entails evaluating one's thinking 'to make it more precise, accurate and relevant, consistent and fair' (Paul 1990, in Montgomery 1996: 91). As well as promoting critical thinking skills, teachers will need to foster the enabling attitudes of curiosity, persistence, tolerance of ambiguity, and confidence (especially about taking intellectual risks).

Enhance motivation

Just as it is a mistake to view intelligence as a trait of the individual, so too is it a mistake to view motivation as an inherent part of children's personality. Motivation refers to children's willingness to invest time, effort and skills in tasks that we define as educationally significant (Ben Ari & Rich 1992). If some children are choosing to invest their energies elsewhere, this will have at least as much to do with the way educational activities are structured as it has to do with the children's personality (Ben Ari & Rich 1992).

If children do not understand the concept or value the task, they come to believe that learning is meaningless and full of unpredictable traps (Katz 1988). They learn by rote instead of understanding the principles; despite gifted children's phenomenal memory, this will not work in the long run as their skills, interest in learning and confidence in their abilities will deteriorate.

In order to be motivated, all children need to feel responsible for their own learning, to believe that what they are achieving is worthwhile and exciting, to experience success and to receive authentic feedback about their efforts (Jones & Jones 1995). Gifted children's non-conformity and intellectual drives may accentuate these needs. In addition, they will need extra supports for the intellectual risks they are capable of taking earlier than usual.

One key way to stimulate motivation in children is to explain the rationale for a task. This takes seriously their (often unspoken) queries about a task's benefits and teaches them to be aware of their own learning. (For instance, I once explained to a group of school entrants that the reasons they were making a flower with shredded crepe paper were that it gave them practice at using their hands when they were drawing and cutting the flower outline and shredding the paper; it gave them practice at planning how to make something; it taught them to notice whether their plan was working; and it was pretty. They enthusiastically set about the task which had previously been puzzling them.)

THE MARRIAGE OF CONTENT AND PROCESS

Although process is regarded conceptually as being different from content, in practice we cannot and must not attempt to teach children how to learn without teaching some content that is worth learning. In a critique of 'enrichment' activities, Sawyer (1988: 8) asserts that 'problem solving is in fact meaningless if in fact there is no problem to begin with'.

To ensure that problem solving and other thinking skills are applied to worthwhile content—and that the content can be examined at various levels of sophistication—teachers could create a grid comprising content domains (be they Gardner's or some list of their own) on one axis, and a range of processing skills on the other axis (be they Bloom's or a similar list), and then plan their curriculum to include elements from all cells in the grid (see table 10.3). This can seem cumbersome at first but, once familiar with planning content to be covered at a range of depths, the method soon becomes more automatic (Eyre 1997).

The aim of such an approach is not to fragment children's learning, to make planning and education more complex than it already is, or to suggest teaching separately to each cell in the grid. A *blend* of these skills is the goal, not their fragmentation so that, overall, the curriculum will give children multiple chances of understanding and retaining what is taught (Smerechansky-Metzger 1995).

PRODUCT

Common to all children is their need to demonstrate the knowledge and learning skills that they have acquired. It is important that they can

Table 10.3 Sample form for planning curricula to include a range of processes applied to many content domains

Process skills	Domains							
	Linguistic	Logical-mathematical	Musical	Spatial	Kinaesthetic	Interpersonal	Intrapersonal
Knowledge								
Comprehension								
Application								
Analysis								
Synthesis								
Evaluation								

negotiate in which mediums and domains they will express their learning. Early childhood centres routinely offer this opportunity and so enlargement here is unnecessary.

Product differentiation

Gifted children will also need some form of differentiation to take their product beyond the level normally achievable by other children and, thus, to make it more satisfying for them.

Tiered products

Some children will be interested in and capable of producing mature expressions of their learning; others will be at the typical early stages of drawing and other handicraft work. Advanced production will require supplementary resources (discussed earlier).

Teach expressive skills

In the early childhood years, children's reading and writing skills will limit their ability to record and express what they have learned. In the linguistic domain, therefore, it may be necessary to allow individual children to dictate stories to an adult scribe, or to use keyboards if they are able to write but are held back from handwriting by their less developed fine-motor skills. If they are ready to learn to read and write and are desperate to do so, it could be necessary to teach them these skills so that their lack does not block their achievement. In other domains, children may seek to express their learning through musical expression and dance or drama and so these will be necessary components of the program.

USE OF COMPUTERS

Computers offer a suitable medium for adapting the content, process, product and learning environment (Berger & McIntire 1998).

Content. Computers give children access to databases to support their research (Knight et al. 1997; Spicker & Southern 1998). They provide access to a wider variety of information and more abstract and complex information (Berger & McIntire 1998).

Process. Computers provoke children to construct and organise their knowledge, and teach them to adapt to emergent technologies. Also, children and teachers can learn together, rather than the teacher being the expert (Berger & McIntire 1998).

Product. Computers can help young children to produce written material when their fine motor skills would otherwise preclude handwriting.

Learning environment. Computers allow isolated gifted children to form electronic links with other children who share their interests. Computers facilitate collaborative work as well as independent study (Berger & McIntire 1998).

EXCEPTIONALLY GIFTED CHILDREN

Whereas older children reject as playmates children who are in lower grades at school, they will play with those same children when they are in the same class as them (Gross 1993b). This verifies the findings (reported in chapter 7) that acceleration will not harm young, exceptionally gifted children's social wellbeing.

Their degree of advancement makes even radical acceleration or enrichment alone inadequate for exceptionally gifted children (Gross 1992, 1993a, 1993b, 1993c). They will need both of these measures, plus opportunities to work alongside similarly gifted children and to meet with mentors in their field of interest (Gross 1993a, 1993c).

A problem that exceptionally gifted young children face is a lack of resources at their developmental level in early childhood venues. This can be overcome by borrowing advanced books and other resources from the local library or special education resource centre. The main challenge is maintaining these children's motivation to excel (Gross 1993a: 21): 'Underachievement may be imposed on the exceptionally gifted child through the constraints of an inappropriate and undemanding educational program.'

PARENT COLLABORATION

Parents are an integral part of their children's learning environment (Hanninen 1998). Therefore, rather than regarding them in a similar way to one's in-laws (i.e. potential hindrances who, however, 'come with the territory' [Riggs 1998]), teachers will need to respect and respond to parents' assessment of their children's interests and abilities (Knopper 1998), and welcome their contributions to their children's education. Parents' knowledge can inform curriculum planning and delivery, and will promote children's participation: children are more likely to participate in activities that their parents support (Holden 1996).

While most parents are confident that they can meet the needs of typical children, those whose children are gifted might want or need suggestions about how to support their young children's learning and emotional adjustment. Traditional ways of explaining the educational program and involving parents include individual meetings, interactive newsletters, display boards, posters describing the activities in each activity centre and how they contribute to children's learning, portfolios of children's work, and photos of children's products (especially of sand sculptures or block constructions for which there is otherwise nothing to show at the end of the day). Other suggestions for providing support and information to parents are given in chapter 13.

CONCLUSION

Parke and Ness (1988: 197) conclude:

> Much of curricular decision-making and planning comes down to a question of balance. The curriculum must be balanced to respond to the unique learning needs of the gifted and their unusual make-up.

This quote implies that no single approach will suit every child: it is important to be flexible about meeting individual children's needs and to be aware that their abilities and needs are likely to differ across the various developmental domains (Holden 1996). On the other hand, sometimes the various differentiation methods appear to be more different than they are: acceleration is said to focus on the quantity of children's learning; enrichment and extension on the quality. Yet, by moving gifted children more quickly through content (acceleration), they will necessarily be exposed to more varied educational experiences (enrichment); allowing children to study more broadly and deeply will inevitably expose them earlier to new knowledge, demanding its synthesis and evaluation (Southern et al. 1993).

In striving to provide a high-quality education that is responsive to children's needs, teachers should be aware of the constraints under which they are functioning. The first of these is that, although the small size of early childhood centres is the best setting for young children, it has the side-effect of isolating children from their intellectual peers and teachers from colleagues. The former can lead to social difficulties for the children (Whitmore 1980); the latter results in a lack of cross-fertilisation of ideas for teachers (Harrison 1995).

Yet, on the positive side, early childhood professionals are inherently child-focused, have a flexible enough structure to allow them to cope with the demands of a mixed-ability group, and are aware of the imperative to focus on children's social, emotional and physical needs as well as their intellectual skills. Just as primary (elementary) teachers are more flexible in their programming than secondary teachers (Kerry & Kerry 1997), so too I believe that early childhood professionals are advantaged over school personnel, as their natural philosophy is integrated and interdisciplinary. Meeting the needs of gifted children is thus a much more natural step in early childhood settings than it can be further up the education system.

Looking ahead . . . The transition to school, and beyond

In the disability field, it is common practice to integrate gradually children from a special facility into regular school, sometimes on a part-time basis for one or two terms. My practical observations have been that this can lead to a prolonged period in which the child feels out of place in both settings and is regarded by peers (and teachers) as not truly part of either group. For this reason, when early entry to school is being contemplated for gifted children, it is necessary to plan the transition to school carefully. It is best if this planning includes some school visits before the child begins full-time, but I suggest that these visits do not span more than a few weeks, if for no other reason than that, once gifted children get a taste of school, preschool can become comparatively unattractive and it will be difficult to motivate them to continue to attend.

When gifted children are in school they may still experience a mismatch between their needs and the curriculum. Their atypical needs will necessitate ongoing curriculum differentiation throughout school: early entry to school or grade-skipping (acceleration) alone will not be enough to sustain them, especially those who are exceptionally gifted.

Another problem that can surface during the school years is under-achievement. This and other issues are discussed in chapter 12.

SUGGESTED FURTHER READING

The following text describes the curriculum planning process for young children, although it makes no reference to gifted children: Arthur, L., Beecher, B., Dockett, S., Farmer, S. and Death, E. 1996 *Programming and planning in early childhood settings* 2nd edn, Harcourt Brace, Sydney.

The following texts contain extensive advice on curriculum modifications for young gifted children: Harrison, C. 1995 *Giftedness in early childhood* KU Children's Services, Sydney; Morelock, M.J. and Morrison, K. 1996 *Gifted children have talents too: multidimensional programmes for the gifted in early childhood* Hawker Brownlow Education, Melbourne; Smutny, J.F., Walker, S.Y. and Meckstroth, E.A. 1997 *Teaching young gifted children in the regular classroom: identifying, nurturing, and challenging ages 4–9* Free Spirit Publishing, Minneapolis, MN.

For a list of resources for science, maths and technology extension programs in early childhood settings, see Patton, M.M. and Kokoski, T.M. 1996 'How good is your early childhood science, mathematics, and technology program?: Strategies for extending your curriculum' *Young Children* vol. 51, no. 5, pp. 38–44.

For suggested activities during the first year of school for gifted children who have been admitted early, you might like to refer to Mares, L. and Byles, J. 1994 *One step ahead: early admission of, and school provisions for, gifted infants* Hawker Brownlow Education, Melbourne.

For curricular suggestions for school-aged gifted children, which will have to be adapted for early childhood settings, you might like to consult: Bailey, S., Knight, B.A. and Riley, D. 1995 *Developing children's talents: guidelines for schools* Hawker Brownlow Education, Melbourne; Braggett, E., Day, A. and Minchin, M. 1997 *Differentiated programs for primary schools* Hawker Brownlow, Melbourne; Clark, B. 1997 *Growing up gifted* 5th edn, Merrill, Upper Saddle River, NJ; Eyre, D. 1997 *Able children in ordinary schools* David Fulton, London; Piirto, J. 1998 *Talented children and adults: their development and education* 2nd edn; Merrill, New York; Pohl, M. 1997 *Teaching thinking skills in the primary years: a whole school approach* Hawker Brownlow Education, Melbourne; Van Tassel-Baska, J. 1994 *Comprehensive curriculum for gifted learners* 2nd edn, Allyn & Bacon, Boston, MA.

For an overview of the curriculum planning process, you might refer to Braggett, E.J. 1994 *Developing programs for gifted students: a total-school approach* Hawker Brownlow Education, Melbourne.

DISCUSSION QUESTIONS

1. How could you adapt your present curriculum to take account of gifted children's needs?

2. What are your views about acceleration/appropriate developmental placement? Can you suggest any reasons why research about its effectiveness is so positive and yet many practitioners are hesitant to allow young children to enter school early?

3. On what domains or content areas do you focus when you program for young children? How could you extend or enrich that curriculum for gifted children?

4. Think about how you encourage children's cognitive and metacognitive skills. In what additional ways could you advance children's awareness and regulation of their own thinking?

5. Do you experience any impediments to best educational practice for gifted young children? If so, what are these?

11

TEACHING GIFTED CHILDREN CONSIDERATE BEHAVIOUR

Passive children are more likely to decline in intellectual status as they grow older, while more active, curious ones are more likely to show a rise [. . .] Yet the passive, conforming child is valued in many families and schools, and is likely to be rated a much easier child to rear.

Robinson and Robinson (1992: 163)

KEY POINTS

- Behaviour management involves mainly the prevention of disruptions by ensuring that children's social, emotional and learning needs are largely met. (These issues are detailed in chapters 7–9.)
- Young gifted children do not have *more* behavioural difficulties than others, but they do present with *different* behavioural issues.
- A range of theories of behaviour management guide practice in early childhood. The choice of a theory can be made on the grounds of eclecticism, the goals of each theory, ethical considerations, or the special needs of gifted children.
- These criteria give rise to some recommendations for teaching children how to manage their feelings so that they can behave considerately.

INTRODUCTION

Behaviour management is not an interruption to normal duties: it is 'the professional responsibility to socialise young children and help them learn to become responsible, competent fully functioning members of their culture and society according to their developmental capability'

(Rodd 1996: 6). This definition implies that behaviour management is based on protective, nurturing, encouraging and educational relationships between adults and children (Rodd 1996).

RATIONALE FOR A FOCUS ON BEHAVIOUR MANAGEMENT

There are many reasons why I focus in this text on behaviour management with gifted children.

1. If we want children to experiment intellectually, we must also be ready for them to experiment behaviourally—even though this sometimes results in mistakes.
2. Gifted young children's dissonant development, in which their emotional development has not caught up with their intellectual precocity, can sometimes lead to emotional outbursts which look immature—compared both with their age and their ability levels. This behaviour is sometimes misinterpreted as a sign that the children are not gifted, and can provoke inappropriate responses from adults.
3. Parents may be inexperienced during their children's early childhood years, and may respond with uncertainty to gifted children's atypical behavioural patterns. Your advice to them at this early stage in their relationship with their child can be particularly valuable.
4. The call for moral education for all children—and sometimes for gifted children in particular—requires that we teach children *how* to think in moral terms (but not necessarily *what* to think). Teaching children right from wrong is inextricably linked to how we discipline their behaviour.

TYPES OF DISRUPTIVE BEHAVIOUR

Behaviours to which adults will need to respond include:

- a normal behaviour which occurs excessively (i.e. that occurs too often or beyond the age at which a child could be expected to have learned more appropriate behaviour) (Herbert 1987);
- a constellation of normal behaviours which by themselves would not make management difficult but in combination present some management problems (Herbert 1987);
- an appropriate behaviour that is mistimed (e.g. dancing and walking around are appropriate acts, but not during a group storytime).

These 'primary' behaviours (Rogers 1991) might affect the child by making other children avoid him or her; they might harm another child or adult; or they might interfere with both the child and others having their needs met (Gordon 1991). In any case, adults will need to take some action, as someone is being harmed.

Very young children behave inappropriately on occasion mainly because they lack more mature skills. Either they do not have the more appropriate behaviour in their repertoire yet, or they know the skill but cannot use it because of temporarily being overwhelmed emotionally (Porter 1997a, 1999). This is normal. However, the adults' response can then provoke some 'secondary' behavioural difficulties, such as resistance, rebellion, aggression directed at the adult, verbal abuse, defensiveness, and refusals to cooperate (Gordon 1991; Rogers 1991), which can be more disruptive than the original behaviour. It is thus crucial that the methods we use to respond to an initial disruptive behaviour do not provoke these secondary reactions.

BEHAVIOURAL DIFFICULTIES OF GIFTED CHILDREN

Many researchers (e.g. Clark 1997; Cornell et al. 1994; Gallucci 1988) report a low incidence of behavioural problems among gifted students. Delisle et al. (1987: 38, in Clark 1997: 491) report:

> Gifted students generally do not develop behavior problems when they are: (a) placed with a teacher who enjoys teaching gifted children and learning with them; (b) afforded frequent opportunities to learn with intellectual peers; (c) actively engaged in learning that is appropriately complex, challenging and meaningful; and (d) provided guidance in how to understand and cope with their giftedness in society.

Because they are able to anticipate outcomes at young ages, gifted children tend to be more careful and less impulsive than other children (Roeper 1995b). Nevertheless, some do evidence behavioural difficulties:

- as a way of coping with boredom (Freeman 1995a; Plucker & McIntire 1996);
- to prove to peers that they are not so smart after all (Clark 1997);
- because of their heightened activity levels (Whitmore 1980);
- as part of an underachievement syndrome (Clark 1997; Delisle 1992; Freeman 1995a);
- as a reaction to their heightened sensitivities and other stresses of adjusting to being different (Whitmore 1980);
- when their emotional development has not caught up with their intellectual precocity.

The resulting outward behaviour in these cases can be emotional outbursts which look immature, compared both with the children's age and their ability levels. As well as these outbursts, other emotional and behavioural issues were identified by Damiani (1997), who found that of the 32 parents of gifted young children who participated in the study, 38% reported sufficient behavioural difficulties at home to warrant their seeking professional advice. The behaviours of concern comprised being unable to be distracted from something that was forbidden, arguing at length over parents' directives, being bossy, and becoming frustrated with other children.

Nevertheless, these difficulties arise mainly from the children's attempts to think independently, rather than being motivated by their desire to be deliberately disruptive (Silverman 1997). The behaviours are not outright challenges to parental authority, unless parents interpret them as such. Even so, when parents do feel that their authority is challenged, they are more likely to become coercive in their behaviour management (Whitmore 1980). They might chastise gifted children for feeling passionately (when this is often part and parcel of being gifted) or might perceive that the children's non-conformity is a threat to them (Clark 1997). Alternatively, inappropriately lax discipline can come about when parents and teachers:

- have too much reverence for gifted children's advanced skills (Freeman 1995a) and so fail to offer appropriate behavioural guidelines;
- believe that gifted children are so exceptional that they do not have to abide by normal social rules (Prichard 1985);
- are confused by the children's dissonant skills and so do not know what to expect of the children, or of themselves (Freeman 1995a). As Silverman (1997: 391) states: 'When a child talks and reasons like a much older person, it is easy to forget what is age appropriate';
- accord higher status to a gifted child, compared with siblings and, sometimes, compared with the parents themselves (Keirouz 1990);
- allow children who are perceptive or gifted verbally to use these skills to manipulate and manage their parents and siblings;
- when parents become their children's peers as a result of being their main play partner and their medium for interpreting the world (Roeper 1995b).

When there are insufficient guidelines for children's behaviour, parents' reduced authority and gifted children's increased power can put too much pressure on children, leave them feeling unprotected (Kitano 1986); it can also create resentment in the other siblings who sometimes feel as if they have three parents (Chamrad et al. 1995; Hackney 1981) and put pressure on the parents' marriage, particularly when the spouses disagree about their roles with respect to the children (Keirouz 1990).

This tension between too little and too much discipline can be resolved by referring back to theories of behaviour management. The next section describes these and then offers some suggestions for choosing between them.

THEORIES OF BEHAVIOUR MANAGEMENT

Four theories of behaviour management are in common use in early childhood centres. These are: applied behaviour analysis, cognitive-behaviourism, neo-Adlerian theory, and the democratic theories. I believe the main difference between the theories to be the amount of power they give to the adults versus the amount of autonomy that they give to children. With this distinction in mind, I have arranged the theories along a continuum, shown in figure 11.1 (Porter 1996). On the left are the authoritarian theories in which the adult has control over children, of which applied behaviour analysis is probably the most common. At the other end of the continuum is the permissive or laissez-faire approach which grants children a free rein, with very few adult-imposed restrictions. No professionals endorse this approach. The middle ground is occupied by the authoritative theories—humanism and choice theory—which promote children's self-control. These are also referred to as the democratic theories, although adults and children do not share power equally: adults still act as leaders and, when necessary, make executive decisions on the children's behalf.

Figure 11.1 The theories of behaviour management

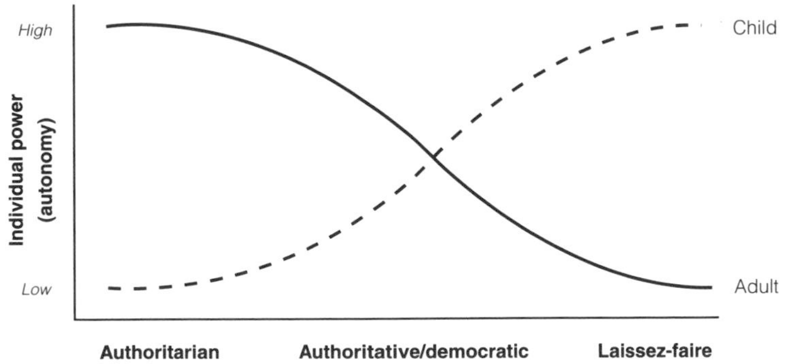

Theories	Applied behaviour analysis	Cognitive behaviourism Neo-Adlerian	Humanism Choice theory	
	Authoritarian	Authoritative/democratic		Laissez-faire

Source: Adapted from Porter (1996: 11).

Applied behaviour analysis

Applied behaviour analysis (ABA) is the new term for behaviour modification. According to this theory, individuals acquire new behaviours through imitation and through a process called shaping, in which a complex skill is learned by mastering a series of small steps that together make up the total task. Once children have learned a behaviour, they will repeat it if it works or if, in the language of ABA, it is 'reinforced' (i.e. it earns them something they value). This consequence makes it likely that they will repeat the behaviour.

Therefore, if you want a child to stop engaging in a particular behaviour, you have to prevent it from working—from receiving a positive response. To do this, you increase the rewards you give to an alternative, more desirable behaviour so that (comparatively) the behaviour that you are targeting no longer works for the child. The kinds of rewards from which you could choose include: social reinforcers such as praise, hugs or a smile; the opportunity to do a favourite activity; a sticker or some other tangible reward which the child values for itself; and food rewards (although these are not recommended; see Birch et al. 1995).

If rewarding an alternative behaviour does not increase the rate of a desirable behaviour, then under ABA the adult can punish the undesirable behaviour. Strictly speaking, the term *punishment* means to reduce the rate of a behaviour, and so anything which achieves a reduction in the behaviour is a punishment. There are two types of punishment: taking away something that the child wants, or administering something the child does not like.

Taking away something that the child likes includes withdrawing privileges and time out—probably the most widely used punishment. Time out is based on the assumption that something in the environment is maintaining (reinforcing) the child's undesirable behaviour and so, if you remove the child from that environment and place him or her where she or he cannot receive any reinforcement, the behaviour will stop.

The second class of punishment—delivering something aversive or unpleasant—includes verbal aversives such as reprimands and physical aversives such as smacking. (Experts agree that physical aversives should never be used. Besides being ineffective in controlling behaviour, they prompt anger and resistance in children and can spiral into serious abuse.)

So far, I have introduced two central themes of applied behaviour analysis: first, that rewards will increase the rate of children's desirable behaviours; second, that punishment will reduce the rate of children's undesirable behaviours. The third key principle is that, when using ABA, it is absolutely crucial that you observe and record the circumstances that precede the behaviour (its antecedents) and what happens after the behaviour (the consequences). This allows you to choose an appropriate reward or punishment. Careful recording of the behaviour rate before and during the selected intervention also allows you to evaluate whether the behaviour management program is working, and to change it immediately if it is not. Systematic observation guards against frustration, which can cause you to feel mistakenly that the child's behaviour is not improving; and will ensure that unwanted side-effects of punishment are detected early, so that the program can be changed if these occur.

Cognitive-behaviourism

A recent variation of ABA is cognitive-behaviourism, which I have placed between the authoritarian and authoritative positions on figure 11.1 because the adult remains partly in control of the child but at the same time involves the child somewhat in managing his own behaviour.

Cognitive-behaviourists believe that individuals' behavioural choices are affected by the consequences of behaviour, but also by their planning skills, emotional state, developmental stage and the environment (Kendall 1991). When a child's behaviour appears to be inappropriate, cognitive-behaviourism attempts to identify and remediate deficiencies in any of these elements, looking for possible causes of the behaviour both within the child and within the environment.

This theory focuses on how children feel about a task by:

- improving their *self-esteem*, mainly through praise;
- ensuring that they believe their actions can make a difference to the outcome, which is termed having an *internal locus of control*;
- teaching them to believe in their ability to organise and execute a chosen behaviour, or *self-efficacy*;
- teaching them to apply to a new activity knowledge that they have gained from a related activity, which is termed a *learning set*;
- improving *motivation* by ensuring that what they are being asked to do is relevant for them and therefore has intrinsic or built-in natural rewards for them.

Cognitive training involves teaching children to manage how they learn and behave. The first aspect of self-management is teaching children to notice or *monitor* their own behaviour. They can monitor themselves formally (e.g. with a chart) or by being given informal cues (e.g. 'What are you doing? Is it a good idea?').

Next, cognitive-behaviourism aims to teach children how to give themselves helpful *instructions* about their approach to tasks or their behaviour, rather than talking to themselves in ways that make success less likely. (For instance, instead of saying, 'This is too hard. I can't do it', the child might say, 'This is tricky, but I can do it if I think about it'—or a simplified version of this for very young children.)

Then, children are taught to *evaluate* whether their behaviour has met an agreed standard. When it has, the adult delivers a reward, then the adult and child together administer a reinforcer, and finally the child reinforces herself or himself independently (although this last stage may be too ambitious for preschool-aged children).

These general approaches can be used to teach children specific behaviours—such as how to adhere to routines, follow instructions and manage frustration. The methods focus on the children's thinking and planning processes and on teaching children that they can regulate their own behaviour. Children can also be taught specific learning strategies, such as how to solve problems.

Neo-Adlerian theory

Another theory that falls between the authoritarian and authoritative positions (see figure 11.1) is neo-Adlerian theory, which is thus called because it represents modern writers' refinements of Alfred Adler's writings early in this century. This theory was originally popularised in the USA by Don Dinkmeyer and his colleagues (Dinkmeyer et al. 1980; Dinkmeyer & McKay 1989), and subsequently in Australia by Maurice Balson (1992, 1994) for school-aged children and Jeannette Harrison (1996) in the early childhood age group.

Neo-Adlerian theory has two distinct parts. Its preventive aspect focuses on creating warm relationships with children, listening to them, fostering cooperation and reducing competition between children, and encouraging rather than praising them. Of this list, most features have been borrowed from the democratic theories to be discussed below, although the use of encouragement instead of praise is a unique contribution of this theory. (The distinctions between praise and encouragement are given in chapter 7, although I use the term *acknowledgment*.) Encouragement aims to overcome the disadvantages of praise which arise when children resist being manipulated into repeating behaviour of which the adult approves or when, conversely, they become compliant and submissive.

In contrast to its preventive component, the neo-Adlerian approach to intervention with disruptive behaviour is largely under adult control. That is, the adult diagnoses children's motivation for their behaviour and subsequently chooses an intervention. Neo-Adlerians believe that all children are striving to belong and that when they cannot do so through prosocial behaviours they resort to antisocial behaviour by seeking attention, power, or revenge or by withdrawing from adult demands. Adults can diagnose which of these goals is motivating the child by noting their own feelings about the child's behaviour, how they normally discipline the child, and how the child responds to that discipline. Table 11.1 summarises these clues.

Table 11.1 Neo-Adlerian clues to the goals of inappropriate behaviour

If the adult feels	If the adult responds by	If the child's response to correction is	Then the child's goal is
Annoyed	reminding, coaxing	stopping but then repeating the behaviour	Attention
Angry	fighting or giving in	confronting or ignoring authority	Power
Hurt	wanting to retaliate or get even	becoming devious, violent or hostile	Revenge
Despairing or hopeless	agreeing with the child that nothing can be done	refusing to participate or cooperate, being uninterested	Withdrawal

Source: Porter (1996: 101).

Having diagnosed which goal is motivating the child's antisocial behaviour, the adult can then plan an intervention, which will differ for the various goals. For instance, adults are advised to ignore attention-seeking behaviour, or apply logical consequences (defined below) when ignoring is not possible. At the same time, they are to give the child extra attention for appropriate behaviour.

Instead of punishment (as used by ABA) to curb undesirable behaviour, neo-Adlerian theory employs natural or logical consequences. Natural consequences are those which—as their title implies—occur naturally, without adult manipulation. Logical consequences are arranged by the adult but unlike punishment, which can be arbitrary, they are related to the act. For instance, a natural consequence for children who throw sand in the sandpit might be that they are asked to play somewhere else so that everyone can be safe; a logical consequence might be that they are banned from the sandpit for a specified period; a punishment might be sending them to time out to consider their actions.

The democratic theories: humanism and control (choice) theory

The democratic writers include humanists Carl Rogers, a leader particularly in humanistic counselling for 50 years until his recent death;

Thomas Gordon; Haim Ginott; Dan Gartrell, a writer in behaviour management in early childhood; and choice theory's author, Bill Glasser. (In all his writings Glasser has called his approach *control theory*, but he recently changed the title to *choice theory* in recognition of the fact that individuals' choices are central to how they behave.)

All these theories are categorised as democratic, although adherents do not believe that adults and children are the same. Children and adults have different roles and exercise different responsibilities, but they have equal rights to have their needs met. Under a democratic system, the adult facilitates children's learning by acting as a leader (or expert) rather than a boss, who has power over others (Glasser 1992; Gordon 1991).

The democrats believe that most of children's difficult behaviour can be avoided by creating a child-centred program that meets children's learning, social and emotional needs for self-esteem, autonomy, belonging and fun (Glasser 1986; Rogers & Freiberg 1994).

Before making a decision to intervene with a disruptive behaviour, Thomas Gordon reminds adults that we must understand children, so that we can accept most of their behaviour as being normal for their stage of development. If we accept little of what they do, our expectations are unrealistic. But when a behaviour interferes with someone's rights, then it is unacceptable, and it is crucial to everyone's happy adjustment that we intervene to change it.

The first step to doing so is to decide who the behaviour is inconveniencing. When the behaviour interferes with children's ability to function, then the adults *listen* to the children's words or behaviour for a clue about how to help them meet their own needs without hurting themselves or anyone else.

When a child's behaviour negatively affects other people, the adult must speak up, must state honestly and *assertively*—but not aggressively— what effect the behaviour is having.

A third communication skill—*collaborative problem solving*—is used when both the child and the adult are being affected by the child's behaviour (except if someone is in danger, in which case the adult takes charge unilaterally). Collaborative problem solving involves listening to the child's needs and being assertive about your own, following which you agree on a solution that satisfies you both. This process might result in a contract, or 'deal', with the child, but with the unique feature that the contract is reciprocal. A reciprocal contract specifies not only what standards the child must achieve, but also states how the adult will help the child to meet those expectations. The process might also result in the adult's adjusting his or her demands, instead of simply requiring the child to comply with what is being expected of him or her.

The democratic writers do not use praise, rewards, logical conse-

quences or punishments. However, if children break a reasonable agreement or cannot behave appropriately, then Glasser (1977) advises adults
to isolate children until the issue can be worked out. Unlike time out,
however, this 'time away' would be in pleasant surroundings where
children could occupy themselves enjoyably, but they would not return
to the group until they could find a way to behave considerately.

STRENGTHS AND WEAKNESSES OF THE THEORIES

The following is a summarised critique of the theories; see Porter (1996)
for a more detailed analysis.

Applied behaviour analysis

The great strength of ABA is its emphasis on unbiased observation of
the child's behaviour and careful monitoring of the success of a management program. But it requires detailed recording that is difficult to fit
in with one's other tasks.

Second, the approach works: it changes individuals' behaviours
(Alberto & Troutman 1999), although perhaps mainly in tightly con-
trolled conditions that cannot be duplicated in natural contexts.

This leads to my assessment of ABA's weaknesses. First, because ABA
is highly technical (more technical than this brief summary suggests), it
takes a great deal of skill and training to use effectively. Second and more
fundamental is the philosophical objection to ABA, which concludes that
its behavioural gains come at a high price to the individual child, to
onlookers, and to the adults who oversee a controlling regime. These
disadvantages of punishment are summarised in the box below.

SUMMARY OF THE DISADVANTAGES OF
PUNISHMENTS

Limited effectiveness

- Children must infringe someone's rights before action is taken.
- Children learn to behave well only to avoid punishment, rather
  than developing a 'conscience'.
- Adults must constantly be vigilant to detect misbehaviour;
  failure to identify the full circumstances leads to error in
  administering punishment.

- The effects of punishment are not permanent.
- Punishment may not replace an inappropriate behaviour with a more desirable one.
- Punishment works only for those who do not need it.

Effects on children

- Punishment can decrease children's ability levels (Webb et al. 1991).
- Punishment can produce negative emotional side-effects, including low self-esteem in children who receive repeated punishment.
- Punishment can teach children to copy controlling behaviour.
- Children may avoid punishing situations either by withdrawing or by being compliant.
- Punishment may provoke inappropriate behaviours, such as telling lies to get out of trouble. These in turn tend to attract more punishment.
- Punishment can intimidate onlooking children, even if they themselves are never punished.
- Punishment can cause onlookers to define a punished child as 'naughty'; as a result, they might exclude him or her from their friendship group.

Effects on adults and society

- Punishment can become addictive and can escalate into abuse.
- Punishment can teach children to ignore adults who threaten punishment but do not deliver it.
- Children may push adults who threaten punishment to see how far they will go, or to force them to back down from an empty threat.
- Children are likely to withdraw emotionally from their relationship with a punitive adult.
- Violence at home or school leads to a violent society.

Source: Adapted from Porter (1996).

Cognitive-behaviourism

The cognitivists (e.g. Rogers 1994; Wragg 1989) claim that ABA is inefficient because it does not harness the child's skills and motivation to change (Fontana 1985). Cognitive methods aim to teach children to manage themselves without adult supervision so that their behavioural improvements will be maintained across settings.

Another advantage is the efficiency and comprehensiveness of the cognitive approach. Children often present with a constellation of difficulties in three areas: underachievement, behavioural difficulties, and low self-esteem. By promoting self-discipline through self-monitoring, self-instruction and self-evaluation, caregivers and teachers can deal simultaneously with all three problems (Porter 1996); see figure 11.2.

Figure 11.2 Interrelatedness of achievement, behaviour and self-esteem

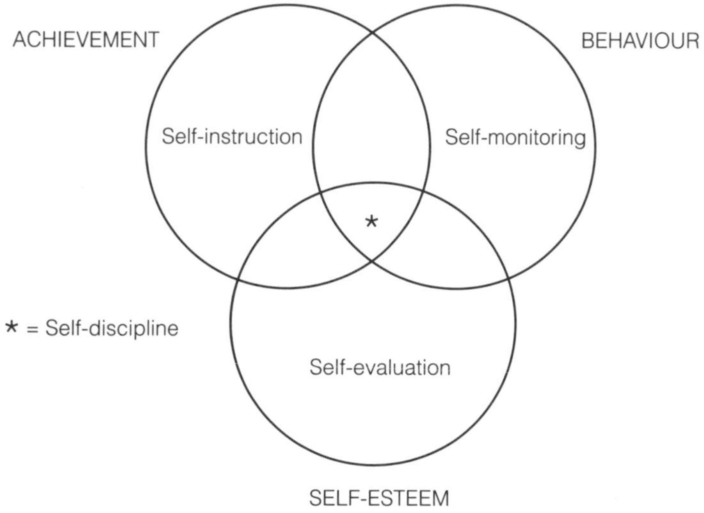

Source: Porter (1996: 187).

Although behaviourists accuse cognitive methods of being vague and imprecise (Benson & Presbury 1989; Lee 1993), cognitivists reply that this makes the methods adjustable to the circumstances and to individuals (Dobson & Pusch 1993; Dyck 1993).

Neo-Adlerian theory

The strengths of neo-Adlerian theory lie in its preventive aspects and its use of encouragement instead of praise (although I prefer the term 'acknowledgment'). Although by no means a unanimous viewpoint, many researchers conclude that informative feedback enhances children's self-esteem while evaluative feedback can lower it (Kohn 1996; Lepping et al. 1996; Ryan & Deci 1996).

However, I have two criticisms of this theory's interventions. First, they are based on illogical assumptions that a child's behaviour *makes* the adult feel a certain way and that how the adult feels is a reliable indicator of the child's motivation. It is obvious that adults can feel disturbed by a child's behaviour for reasons other than the actions themselves. For instance, the adult might be tired, or the particular behaviour might be the last of a series of disruptions, causing the adult to feel more irritated than if the behaviour were an isolated incident.

Second, because the neo-Adlerian interventions are adult-directed, they contradict the democratic flavour of the theory's preventive component. Children are likely to doubt that they are truly respected if, when they do not behave appropriately (as judged by the adult), the adult steps in and imposes control on them.

Humanism and choice theory

By meeting children's developmental and emotional needs, the democratic/authoritative approaches aim to prevent most instances of disruptive behaviour. The humanists argue that their theory's strength is that it does not provoke children to rebel against a denial of their autonomy. By refusing to punish or reward children, the humanists say that they safeguard the adult–child relationship, stimulate children's motivation to follow reasonable rules, and retain children's selfresponsibility. The rights of the child, victims of the behaviour, onlooking children, and adults are all protected by a response that does not blame or shame anyone (Ginott 1972).

The strengths of this theory are also its weaknesses. By rejecting all forms of punishment, the democrats have few interventions to use for disruptive behaviour. They do believe in natural consequences, but at very young ages, even these can be inappropriate. (Their theory does, however, provide a basis for many of the specific suggestions that are introduced in the final part of this chapter.)

CRITERIA FOR EVALUATING THE THEORIES

To guide your practice, you will need to evaluate these theories on some criteria. Your options include: blending attractive elements of each theory; choosing a theory whose goals match your own; examining the research evidence for the various approaches; judging them according to ethical guidelines; or—in the case of gifted education—taking into account the special needs of this population of children.

Eclecticism

When choosing a theory to guide your practice, it might be tempting to select elements of all the theories to arrive at an eclectic blend. To be eclectic means to select the best practices from various theories. This can occur in three ways (Young 1992). The highest form, *synthetic* eclecticism, is an attempt to synthesise or draw together compatible ideas, resulting in a more complex and comprehensive theory than any of the original theories alone. The second form, *technical* eclecticism, utilises one organising theory and borrows some approaches from other theories. The third form is *atheoretical* eclecticism, in which the practitioner lacks a theory base and so uses whatever methods 'seem a good idea at the time'.

The theories of discipline introduced in this chapter differ in their goals and in the resulting status of adults versus children, making many of their practices incompatible with one another. Like Corey (1996), I advocate a blend of only those theories that have compatible philosophies, because transplanting management strategies into a framework which differs in intent from their parent theory renders their effects uncertain.

Goals of the theories

Rather than being eclectic, you might choose a theory that shares your discipline goals. The various theories of behaviour management have different goals (as detailed in table 11.2).

1. To create order so that activities can flow smoothly. This is a managerial goal (Doyle 1986); the remaining four goals are educational.
2. To teach children *self-discipline*, so that with support they learn to take responsibility for their actions, and can be trusted to make wise decisions about their behaviour, whether they are being supervised or not (Glasser 1986; Rogers 1991).
3. To teach children to *express their feelings appropriately*, without getting themselves distressed and without upsetting the people around them (Gartrell 1994).
4. To teach children to *cooperate* with other people (Hill & Hill 1990; Johnson & Johnson 1991; Johnson et al. 1990).
5. To give children the *integrity* to make moral decisions and the *confidence* to enact them. These ethical choices will be based on an empathy for others and children's commitment to exercising their social responsibilities as well as their rights (Gartrell 1994; Ginott 1972; Glasser 1986, 1992; Gordon 1970, 1974, 1991; Greenberg

1992a, 1992b; Knight 1991; Porter 1996, 1997a, 1999; Rogers 1951, 1978; Rogers & Freiberg 1994). Although this is a long-term aim, it begins when adults teach the moral principles behind children's decisions, and encourage children to empathise with other people.

It can be seen from table 11.2 that the democratic theories have a more comprehensive range of goals than the authoritarian theories. This is clearly an advantage—discipline must do more than foster order alone, as order is necessary but not sufficient for learning to occur (Doyle 1986).

Table 11.2 Goals of each theory of discipline

Theory	Goal
Applied behaviour analysis	Compliance/order
Cognitive behaviourism	Compliance/order
	Self-discipline
	Cooperation
Neo-Adlerian theory	Self-discipline
	Cooperation
Humanism	Self-discipline
Control (choice) theory	Appropriate emotional expression
	Cooperation
	Integrity
	Order

Ethics

When assessing which theory is the best guide to behaviour management practices, in my view, the issue of justice or ethics is fundamental. This criterion requires that adults manage children's behaviours in ways that are just, rather than merely practical, expedient or convenient (Katz 1995). I believe that the democratic approach best satisfies these criteria.

Special challenges of gifted children

Authoritarian discipline can have many negative effects on all children, but is particularly risky for gifted children.

Self-esteem

Authoritarian discipline can threaten gifted children's self-esteem because their earlier development of self-concept means that some will be hypersensitive to cues of acceptance or rejection from others. Also, their tendency towards perfectionism implies that we should not be imposing unrealistically high standards on them, as can happen when we praise or punish. Children will have healthy self-esteem when they know that we accept them unconditionally, not just when they meet our standards for them. This is explained by Rimm (1997: 416) who says:

> The profuse praise [which gifted children] receive . . . may cause them to feel as if they are expected to accomplish the goals that are so admired or valued by others. They not only may feel pressure to achieve, but they also may acquire a dependence on attention and find it difficult to function without continuous praise and reinforcement.

Sense of justice

Gifted children's advanced moral development, with its standards of fairness and justice, will demand fair and ethical disciplinary practices (Delisle 1992).

High expectations

The stress that can result from having to live up to inflated expectations can lead to emotional outbursts. However, to expect stressed children whose behaviour is disruptive to 'grow up' would be insensitive to the pressures under which they are functioning. Instead, we have to help them to 'grow down' a little and become less attuned to adult issues and less concerned about meeting externally imposed standards. Only when freed from having too much responsibility will they be able to take on responsibility for their own behaviour.

Promotion of achievement

Children of all ability levels are more likely to think divergently and take academic risks if they are given sufficient structure balanced with some autonomy (Berk 1997; Windecker-Nelson et al. 1997). Recent research confirms earlier findings by Baumrind and colleagues (e.g. Baumrind 1967) that authoritative discipline produces children who are more self-controlled, self-confident, independent and socially competent, both in preschool and in later years (Berk 1997; Niebrzydowski 1997; Windecker-Nelson et al. 1997). The authoritative system of discipline produces demands that are fair and reasonable rather than arbitrary, making it more likely that children will accept and voluntarily observe the standards expected of them. In contrast, authoritarian discipline—which demands compliance—produces withdrawn, anxious, unhappy children who become hostile when frustrated and are unwilling to persist at tasks (Berk 1997). Robinson and Noble (1991: 59) offer this succinct conclusion:

> Parents with authoritarian (high control, high demands) patterns are likely to produce children with high achievement but also high degrees of conformity and lack of originality.

So, if we want children to experiment intellectually, then we must be ready for them to experiment behaviourally as well, even when this sometimes results in mistakes. If our response to those mistakes quashes their explorative spirit, it will repress their intellectual exploration as well. This may lower their achievement levels. As McCaslin and Good (1992: 13) state: 'We cannot expect that [children] will profit from the incongruous messages we send when we manage for obedience and teach for exploration and risk taking.' Also, gifted girls in particular are likely to be socialised into being compliant, which might result in their being under-ambitious as they conform to the dependent female role model (Kline & Short 1991). This fact makes discipline practices that promote compliance a double hazard for gifted girls.

Summary: the case for a democratic approach

It is my judgment that the special needs of gifted children and the requirements that disciplinary practices be educational, ethical and effective in managing behaviour all favour the authoritative or democratic approach to behaviour management.

PREVENTION OF DISRUPTIVE BEHAVIOUR

Whitmore (1980) contends that disruptive behaviour in gifted children stems from the conflict that is generated when their personal needs are not being met. Like the democratic theorists, most researchers believe that the majority of children's disruptive behaviour can be prevented by creating a child-centred program that meets children's academic needs as well as their emotional needs for self-esteem, belonging, autonomy and fun (Glasser 1986; Rogers & Freiberg 1994). (These preventive approaches are discussed in chapters 7–10.)

INTERVENTION: TEACHING CHILDREN TO BEHAVE CONSIDERATELY

The tension between the authoritarian and authoritative discipline styles can be resolved when adults aim to teach children to be considerate rather than forcing them to comply (Porter 1997, 1999). Considerate

Loan Receipt
Liverpool John Moores University
Learning and Information Services

Borrower ID: 21111090163114
Loan Date: 06/02/2009
Loan Time: 11:37 am

Beginning qualitative research :
111009601897
Due Date: 13/02/2009 23:59

Gifted young children :
111009837210
Due Date: 27/02/2009 23:59

Please keep your receipt
in case of dispute

behaviour will comprise four of the goals that were listed earlier—self-discipline, appropriate expression of emotions, cooperation with others, and integrity (Porter 1997, 1999).

Response to considerate behaviour

The democratic approach does not believe that children need rewards or manipulation to behave considerately. But, like adults, children need acknowledgment of their considerate behaviour (see chapter 7 for a description of the difference between praise and acknowledgment). Whereas praise judges the worth of a behaviour or piece of work, acknowledgment expresses appreciation of considerate behaviour, celebrates achievements and asks children's opinion of their own work so that they can develop their own standards for their behaviour and learn to appreciate their achievements. Acknowledgment is one of a range of natural positive consequences which also help children to consider the needs of other people.

Response to inconsiderate behaviour

Under the authoritarian discipline approach, the adult acts as the boss who has power over children and so imposes rules on them. In contrast, the democratic adult acts as an authoritative leader who guides children to behave considerately (Glasser 1992; Gordon 1991). Leaders do not take a child's disruptiveness personally or regard it as a threat to their own power. At the same time, they take responsibility for themselves and will speak up when their rights—or the rights of other children in their care—are being infringed.

A developmental view of behaviour

The democratic or authoritative adult realises that learning to behave considerately is a developmental task like any other, although it is far more complex than any other skill that children will learn. Just as children need to learn how to walk, so too do they need to learn how to be considerate. When a behaviour is disruptive, instead of viewing it as 'naughty' or 'misbehaviour' the democratic adult regards it as developmentally normal for children to lack maturity, and sets about teaching them the required skill. The democratic adult will also realise that children might have a particular skill and yet are temporarily unable to use it because they are overwhelmed by their feelings. This, too, is a normal developmental event.

This normalising attitude will allow you to give children an escape route (Baum 1986) when they have made a mistake. There is no need to blame or shame them (Ginott 1972): simply use the error as an occasion for guiding them about how to behave more considerately.

Changing the demands

Authoritative adults will listen to what disruptive behaviour is telling them about children's needs. They might be willing to change what they expect of the children, instead of forcing them to comply with unrealistic expectations. This is clearly beneficial to those children whose emotional sensitivity makes them vulnerable to stress.

Assertiveness

Authoritative adults are honest when children's behaviour is having a negative effect. They are not aggressive and do not blame children—neither do they force themselves to be patient with inconsiderate behaviour. To tolerate it would teach children that they can behave inconsiderately with impunity, and would allow the behaviour to continue to harm its victims. The adults assert their own needs and the needs of other children in their care.

Collaborative problem solving

Democratic adults offer children choices about their behaviour, and may negotiate—using a collaborative problem-solving approach—to find ways that they can meet their needs without violating the needs of other people. Gifted children's advanced intellectual skills would enable them to participate meaningfully in negotiations, even from a very young age.

Flexibility

Adults who believe in controlling children are inflexible about their discipline, so that they are not seen to have 'lost' a power battle with a child. Instead of changing a discipline approach that is not working, they attempt to apply it more rigidly or 'consistently'. Adults using an authoritative or democratic approach are concerned not with winning or losing but with meeting everyone's needs. Therefore, they are willing to change their minds about a directive—as long as doing so will not violate their own rights.

Teaching emotional self-control

At around the age of 2 years, children begin to display more mature social behaviour. But their behaviour fluctuates considerably

(Stonehouse 1988); hence the 'terrible twos' label. They can show very capable behaviour one minute and very disorganised behaviour the next. Temporary tiredness, illness, hunger or distress can overwhelm very young children, with the result that even when they know what to do they cannot do it. Their feelings get out of control and their behaviour becomes 'disorganised'. Although this stage begins at around 2, it can last for many years, especially when children are stressed by other factors in their lives, among which can be giftedness.

When children are feeling overwhelmed, the authoritarian approach is to punish them, which amounts to punishing them for *being* children. The democratic adult would not punish children for a natural childhood state but instead would help them to calm down—perhaps by giving them some time away (not time out) to regain control by themselves if they enjoy solitude, by cuddling them until they are calm again if they respond to adult comfort (Porter 1997a), or by showing them how to breathe deeply and relax before returning to a demanding situation (Porter 1997a, 1999; Whitmore 1980). These nurturing methods are not used in the authoritarian approach because they appear to give children attention for inappropriate behaviour; under the democratic approach, the aim is to teach children how to manage their feelings, so that they can return to considerate behaviour.

Once children are calm again, the adult could teach them the appropriate skill to use and explain how that skill will benefit them or other people. (Sometimes a later explanation is unnecessary: the children already had this information but were simply unable to act on it at the time.)

Natural consequences

Rather than administering a punishment, the authoritative adult might choose to employ a natural or logical consequence. Logical consequences fit less well than natural consequences within the democratic framework (Gordon 1991), although some authors (e.g. Balson 1992, 1994) continue to endorse them. However, not all natural consequences are necessarily superior. For instance, you would not make young children suffer the social rejection (a natural consequence) that was brought about by their aggressive behaviour; instead, you would make sure that they knew the necessary social skills and encourage them to use these appropriately.

Time away

Instead of incurring the disadvantages of time out, time away is a recognition that everyone needs solitude, and children's disruptive behaviour signals that this is one of those times. Therefore, when children are overwhelmed, you can invite them to go off by themselves to somewhere pleasant until they can cope again. This is not a punishment but simply accepts that they are not feeling sociable right now.

Reframing

Your response to children's behaviour will depend on what you think the behaviour *means*. If you think that they cannot help it, then you will not expect them to take charge of themselves; if you think that they are 'doing it deliberately', you are likely to get into power struggles with them. When a problem has become chronic, however—that is, when your solution is not working—this is a clue that your explanation of the behaviour is not helpful (Molnar & Lindquist 1989). To change the behaviour, you will need first to find a new way of looking at it. A new view of the problem is called a *reframe*.

Reframing is the process of producing a new description or understanding of the behaviour but one that is still plausible to those who are experiencing problems with it. The reframe must make sense to everyone involved with the behaviour and should help in designing an intervention. If it does not, then you need to find yet another way of explaining the behaviour. The new interpretations are usually positive, as if we are critical of others they are less likely to change. At the same time, the new view must not downplay the significance of a problem, because to call it something nice without suggesting how it could improve would only allow the disruptive behaviour to continue unabated, which is not fair to anyone.

The steps involved in reframing are (Molnar & Lindquist 1989):

1. You describe exactly what the child does, when, and in what circumstances. You also identify who else is involved.
2. Next, you describe how you usually respond to the behaviour and what effect that has. This effect will mainly be on the child's relationships with others.
3. Then you identify your present explanation for the child's behaviour, taking special note of any explanations which blame the behaviour on something that happened in the past or on the child's personality. Because these tend to blame someone for the problem, they will not help to solve the difficulty.
4. Create a range of positive alternative explanations for the behaviour. This is the reframing step.
5. Next, select a positive explanation that will seem plausible and honest to those involved with the problem—mainly yourself, colleagues, and the child's parents.
6. Finally, act in the new way suggested by the new explanation.

Doing something different

Unlike reframing, which is based on changing how you think about a problem, doing something different merely requires doing the opposite of your usual response to the problem (Amatea 1989), even though you might not understand in advance how that could help. There is an old saying that a chain is only as strong as its weakest link. We can break the chain of events surrounding disruptive behaviour, producing in its place a new interaction pattern. We can disrupt the old, dysfunctioning pattern by (Durrant 1995):

- changing the location of the behaviour;
- changing who is involved;
- changing the sequence of the steps involved;
- adding a new element;
- introducing random starting and stopping;
- increasing the frequency of the behaviour.

For example, if your earlier response has been to try to get children to stop behaving in a particular way, then doing something different could mean allowing them to continue with the behaviour (although you will impose certain constraints to limit its impact on everyone else). If in the past you have thought that they could not help themselves, then doing something different might mean telling them that you have faith that they can learn a new behaviour.

This suggestion to do something different is based on the advice: 'If something isn't working, don't do it again' but do something else instead (de Shazer & Molnar 1984; de Shazer et al. 1986). Or, put another way, 'Always change a losing game' (Fisch et al. 1982).

Having fun

When a child has been behaving disruptively for some time, usually the adults involved have become desperate and distressed. The problem seems serious and intense—and no one is having any fun. Normally successful solutions have not worked. Having some fun can be the key to unlocking the problem. If you cannot think of anything else to do, do something silly. When children throw a tantrum, dance the highland fling beside them or throw a tantrum yourself. It cannot do any harm, it will be fun, it could provide some relief from all this seriousness, and it just might work.

CONCLUSION

Gifted children's emotional vulnerabilities mean that our discipline methods must support rather than censure them, so that they learn to cope with the demands that giftedness can bring. Their advanced intellectual skills mean that they are particularly prone to reacting to unjust discipline approaches and to rebelling against authoritarian methods that rob them of their autonomy (Berk 1997; Niebrzydowski 1997). Also, gifted girls in particular are likely to be socialised into being compliant, which might result in their being underambitious as they comply with the dependent female role model (Kline & Short 1991). This fact makes discipline practices promoting compliance a double hazard for gifted girls.

These particular needs reinforce the argument that discipline of any children needs to promote their regulation of their own considerate behaviour, rather than requiring compliance with adult instructions. The specific skills used in authoritative approach are summarised in table 11.3.

Table 11.3 Summary of authoritarian versus authoritative discipline skills

Discipline style	Authoritarian/control	Democracy/guidance
Goals	Order Compliance	Considerateness • self-discipline • handling feelings • cooperation with others • integrity
Adult's status	Boss	Leader
Response to considerate behaviour	Praise Rewards	Acknowledgment Natural positive consequences
View of disruptive behaviour	Naughty Inappropriate	Developmental Natural
Response to inconsiderate behaviour	Intervention Change the child Aggression Patient Impose a solution Inflexible Punishment	Prevention Change the demands Assertiveness Honest Find a solution collaboratively Responsive to circumstances Teach mature skills Teach emotional self-control Natural consequences

Source: Porter (1999: 38).

The promotion of considerate behaviour ensures that society will be protected from the behavioural excesses of its members as, like everyone else, gifted children will be required to consider other people, to accept responsibility for themselves, and to satisfy their own needs without violating the needs of other people (Gordon 1991).

Looking ahead . . .

Behavioural disturbances at school age can take the form of clowning, withdrawal or conforming to low expectations (Clark 1997). The authoritarian approach of many schools, with its rewards for compliance and punishments for rule infractions, is at odds with the methods outlined here. This means that if you adopt the authoritative approach that I have described here, when children move into the new system they may have trouble adjusting. It might be necessary for you to explain the debates about discipline, to give the children continued confidence to assess their own achievements independently of external rewards and to have the courage to be imperfect so that, if they receive censure or punishment in an authoritarian classroom, they do not feel devastated.

SUGGESTED FURTHER READING

If you would like an expanded discussion of behaviour management with young children, my approach is detailed in Porter, L. 1999 *Young children's behaviour: practical approaches for caregivers and teachers* MacLennan & Petty, Sydney.

A more detailed look at the theories introduced here is included in Porter, L. 1996 *Student behaviour: theory and practice for teachers* Allen & Unwin, Sydney, and Charles, C.M. 1996 *Building classroom discipline: from models to practice* 5th edn, Longman, New York.

DISCUSSION QUESTIONS

1. What are or have been your goals for discipline? How do they equate with the goals (managerial and educational) described in this chapter?

2. In your view, which theory has the best potential for meeting your goals?

3. Which theory has goals that best match your educational goals for children?

4. Is it necessary to blend two or more theories to develop a comprehensive approach consistent with your own philosophy? If so, how could you account for any discrepancies in the philosophy and practices of the theories comprising your blend?

5. Think about a troublesome child behaviour that you have encountered. How did you explain it at the time you were dealing with it? Is there another possible explanation? In what ways would this new explanation change how you responded?

12

CHILDREN WHOSE
GIFTS ARE DISGUISED

The problems of identifying and nurturing talent potential are not resolved by formulating constructs of giftedness solely for minority and economically disadvantaged students that differ from those for the majority populations, or by watering down the criteria or standards for excellence . . . The challenge is one of creating paradigms that take culture and context into account in order to enhance the possibilities for identifying potential of many kinds in all populations.

Passow & Frasier (1996: 200)

KEY POINTS

- Gifted girls are prone to underachieving as a result of the contradiction that many of them perceive between being feminine and being gifted.
- Gifted boys may be under more pressure to use their talents, sometimes at the expense of meeting their needs for socialisation. Gifted boys will also experience dual exceptionalities more often than gifted girls; as disabling conditions combined with giftedness are often unrecognised, this places boys at greater risk of receiving inappropriate educational provisions.
- Gifted children who are experiencing educational disadvantages as a result of their backgrounds or disabilities may express their talents in ways that are not easily recognisable; teachers will need to be alert to non-traditional manifestations of giftedness if they are to provide for these children.

226

INTRODUCTION

Many gifted young children are easily recognisable by their extraordinary performances. Others are not so easy to recognise: they might not be willing to perform, or their environment might not be offering optimal conditions for learning. Children whose abilities are manifested in non-traditional or atypical patterns are at risk of being overlooked within the education system, with the result that their curriculum will not be responsive to their needs. Some of these atypical patterns combine giftedness with a disadvantaging condition—such as poverty, attention-deficit disorder, or physical disabilities—and have an early impact on young children's skill development. Other forms of 'disguised giftedness' are less obvious in the early childhood years. The difficulties that are associated with underachievement, learning disabilities, and the special challenges experienced by boys and girls separately, may not be manifested until the early to middle primary school years.

Whether they show up early or later, the seeds of later difficulties can be sown during the early childhood years. Later problems can be avoided when adults are aware of the early signs and enact appropriate preventive and interventive measures during early childhood.

GIFTED GIRLS

Although much of the research on gifted girls is dated and modern girls' experiences may differ from those of their predecessors (Callahan 1991; Davis & Rimm 1998; Kerr 1997), it is clear that gifted girls and boys face challenges that are specifically related to their gender. The pressure to fit in with their peers is the same, but they have different gender roles.

Despite the fact that giftedness is evident at an earlier age in girls than in boys and that gifted girls outperform gifted boys throughout primary school, gifted young women's aspirations and achievements decline when compared with males' (Butler-Por 1993; Freeman 1996, 1998a; Kerr 1985, 1996, 1997; Reis & Callahan 1989). Many mature women look back with regret on lives of unrealised potential (Holahan 1996; Reis 1987). Despite diminishing gender differences in abilities, and despite gifted girls having less sex-stereotyped interests than average girls, males still achieve to higher levels educationally and in their careers; this gender difference is most pronounced among the highly gifted (Callahan 1991; Lubinski et al. 1993; Randall 1997). Gifted girls are less willing than gifted boys to take intellectual risks, are more prone to perfectionism, and more often attribute their successes to outside forces such as luck or effort rather than to ability (Callahan et al. 1994; Jacobs & Weisz 1992; Kerr 1997; Lubinski et al. 1993; Randall 1997; Smutny 1998).

Gifted girls might do well in their school work as a result of being compliant and doing what is expected of them—that is, conforming to the female gender role—but these same behaviours can disadvantage them in adult life (Kerr 1985; Kline & Short 1991). Their low achievement in adulthood can be put down to five factors: (a) their reduced expectations that they can be successful; (b) their lowered perceptions of how important academic and career goals can be; (c) their concern about the social stigma and isolation that can be associated with being gifted and female; (d) their focus on outside reinforcement such as grades and teacher or parental approval, rather than motivation to achieve for their own fulfilment; and (e) the suppression of girls' giftedness in schools (Callahan et al. 1994; Davis & Rimm 1998; Fitzgerald & Keown 1996; Freeman 1996; Kerr 1997; Lea-Wood & Clunies-Ross 1995; Leroux 1988; Randall 1997; Smutny 1998). Although these factors are usually regarded as deficits, it is worth keeping in mind that girls tend to be less narrowly focused than boys in their abilities, interests and values, resulting perhaps in their lowered career aspirations but not necessarily diminishing their life satisfaction (Delisle 1998; Lubinski et al. 1993).

Nevertheless, Kerr (1985) believes that 'a culture of romance' encourages girls to value their relationships over the fulfilment of their personal dreams; in contrast, boys and men are able to have both. Women have been expected to experience satisfaction second-hand, by supporting their male partners' achievements (Davis & Rimm 1998). Reis (1987) relates this romance culture to girls' lack of planning for independence. She says that many gifted young women fail to plan to be self-sufficient because they believe that a man will come along and support them.

Kerr (1997) assumes that gifted girls are happiest when they challenge their intellectual potential and can attain their goals and dreams. In order to enhance awareness of their options, we need to help young girls challenge sex stereotypes and to counsel them so that they understand their own capabilities, interests and values (Kerr 1985, 1996, 1997; Kline & Short 1991). To help gifted girls reach their personal potential it is not enough to raise their aspirations: they need help to become deeply committed to their dreams (Kerr 1996; Kline & Short 1991).

This begins in early childhood, not least by questioning gender stereotypes on TV, in books, and with respect to toys; providing successful female role models; giving girls the confidence to persevere; accepting assertive behaviour from girls to the same extent as we do from boys;

and giving girls an equal share of teacher attention (Davis & Rimm 1998; Fitzgerald & Keown 1996; Freeman 1996; Kelly 1988; Kerr 1997; Reis & Callahan 1989; Smutny 1998). It involves admitting girls to school early and other accelerative measures; providing access to peer groups of other gifted girls; counselling them about their advanced abilities; and counselling parents in order that they allow their daughters' natural talents to flourish, regardless of whether these are in traditional female domains or not (Butler-Por 1993; Delisle 1998; Fitzgerald & Keown 1996; Freeman 1993, 1996; Jacobs & Weisz 1992; Kerr 1996, 1997; Lubinski et al. 1993; Smutny 1998) (see chapter 13).

GIFTED BOYS

While gifted girls can feel that it is not feminine to be talented, gifted boys who are emotionally sensitive can feel out of place among a 'macho' male culture (Lovecky 1994b). As reported in chapter 9, adults might encourage—even pressure—boys to pursue their talents independently, while neglecting their social skills, with the result that boys can become increasingly isolated and consequently lack social supports and friendships (Wolfle 1991).

Boys are more likely than girls to clown around in class—even when doing so attracts teacher sanctions (Luftig & Nichols 1991). This can help boys' popularity with peers, but can affect their achievement levels. Gifted boys' achievements may also be affected by the fact that boys in general are more prone than girls to learning and other disabilities (Moltzen 1996b). The lack of attention to gifted children with learning disabilities will thus disadvantage boys more often than girls. On the other hand, underachieving boys are more likely to be recognised than underachieving girls (McCall et al. 1992, in Freeman 1996).

GIFTED CHILDREN FROM MINORITY CULTURES

We must guard against the stereotype that children from minority groups suffer from deficient backgrounds that will disadvantage them educationally (Barclay & Benelli 1994; Frasier 1989; Sapon-Shevin 1994). This is the *individual* picture: difference does not mean deficiency.

On the other hand, *as a group*, children from minority cultures are educationally disadvantaged in being underidentified as gifted (Braggett 1998a; Butler-Por 1993; Davis & Rimm 1998; Frasier 1989, 1997; Gallagher & Gallagher 1994; Maker 1996; Renzulli 1973; Richert 1987, 1997; Scott et al. 1996; Tannenbaum 1983), which is clearly inequitable, given that giftedness is assumed to occur at equal rates in all cultures

(Borland & Wright 1994; Casey & Quisenberry 1976). Minority cultural membership will be an educational disadvantage when it is compounded by poverty, isolation, limited language exposure or reduced experiences (Frasier 1993).

The reduced recognition of gifted children from minority backgrounds comes about in part because, although all cultures accept that individuals possess advanced skills, the skills which are particularly valued differ across cultures and environments (Harslett 1996). Teachers in general are not attuned to non-traditional signs of giftedness (Frasier 1997).

Another reason for the underidentification of non-majority gifted children is that many teachers' stereotyped low expectations of culturally and linguistically different children can become a self-fulfilling prophecy (Brooks 1998; Butler-Por 1993; Frasier 1997; Gibson 1998; Rist 1970).

Also (as discussed in chapter 5), children from minority cultures often do perform less well on ability tests designed for the dominant culture. This is likely to be a result of their reduced facility in its spoken or written language (Brooks 1998; Frasier 1997; Henriques 1997; Renzulli 1973; Robisheaux & Banbury 1994; Tyler-Wood & Carri 1993).

CHILDREN IN POVERTY

Whereas children from minority cultures have a *different* range of learning experiences, children in poverty typically are exposed to a *restricted* range of learning experiences. These restricted opportunities for learning will often reduce their abilities compared with more advantaged children (Kitano & Perez 1998). It is thus more suitable to compare their development to other children with similarly disadvantaging backgrounds: a relative rather than an absolute measure of giftedness is necessary.

At the same time, just as we have to guard against stereotypes about children from other cultures, so too we need to be aware that knowledge of children's backgrounds can be a two-edged sword: it can help us to understand disadvantaged children's developmental patterns but it can also cause us to lower our expectations of them (Spicker et al. 1987). Contrary to urban myths, socioeconomic status has very little impact on *individual* children's academic achievement: parents' encouragement of learning, which is independent of family income, has most impact (Freeman 1993; White 1982). Also, even when individuals are disadvantaged by their family circumstances, many of these children are nevertheless resilient, especially when significant adults in their lives teach them the skills to be so (see chapter 8). These two facts together mean that educators do not need to feel helpless about assisting children who live in poverty.

RURAL CHILDREN

Gifted children who live in rural areas can be disadvantaged for a range of reasons, some of which relate to developing their talents in the first place and some to being recognised as having advanced development and subsequently receiving suitable educational provisions. These disadvantages include the following (Bailey et al. 1995; Knight et al. 1997; Lupowski 1984; Spicker & Southern 1998; Spicker et al. 1987).

- Living in areas with a sparse population gives rural children a restricted range of social contacts from whom to learn.
- Distance will preclude exposure to a breadth of experiences which can promote their development, although findings about IQ differences between rural and urban children are not uniform.
- There will be fewer opportunities for rural children to come together with their intellectual peers.
- There will be too few gifted children to justify the provision of a gifted program in a rural school and perhaps some resistance to innovation will make it difficult to initiate such programs.
- In rural areas, resources such as educational spending, libraries and school support personnel may be scant.
- There tends to be a more limited curriculum in rural than in metropolitan schools, and teaching staff tend not to be able to specialise in curricular areas or develop new curricula in line with latest practices.
- Teacher turnover in rural areas may be higher than in metropolitan schools.
- Giftedness might be discouraged in conservative communities, especially if it is seen to violate gender norms.
- Excelling at school might be discouraged if it will lead to leaving the area in order to receive a tertiary education.
- There is a high incidence of poverty in rural communities, and this will disadvantage rural children in the same way that it does urban children.

Nevertheless, rural students may have skills in non-traditional domains (e.g. spatial skills). They may be able to develop independent skills and learn at their own rate (Lupowski 1984), and may have dedicated parents on hand to assist them with their education (Bailey et al. 1995; Spicker & Southern 1998). Rural living can offer a range of hands-on experiences that are not as readily available in metropolitan areas, and can create the need for small groupings of able children, thus facilitating the development of a tailor-made program to suit their needs. Also, computers can link up rural children electronically with other gifted students even when they cannot physically meet, and can give them access to databases to support their research (Knight et al. 1997; Spicker & Southern 1998). Computers can also allow rural teachers to form relationships with distant colleagues, thus permitting an exchange of expertise to enrich their programs (Spicker et al. 1987).

In order to facilitate the development of skills by rural children, teachers will need to emphasise that the development of giftedness can preserve the best features of the local community (Spicker & Southern 1998). They will also need to ensure that rural students have access to computers and are computer-literate from a young age, to avoid exacerbating the differences between wealthy and poor children and between girls and boys in computer skills (Spicker & Southern 1998).

GIFTED UNDERACHIEVERS

Despite claims to the contrary, the school dropout rate for gifted children appears to be around the same as for average-ability students—namely, 17% (Irvine 1987). Nevertheless, given their abilities, gifted young people would be expected to achieve better than average at school, and so their equivalent dropout rate could be termed underachievement.

This would represent a loss to gifted young people themselves and to society, not least because of their forfeited contributions. For instance, a higher rate of delinquency can be associated with underachievement (Moltzen 1996b) or learning disabilities (Lajoie & Shore 1981). This is not to say that underachievement *causes* delinquency: both delinquency and underachievement themselves appear to have a prior cause—namely, nonconformity to social norms, or antisocial attitudes and values (McCord 1993; Tremblay et al. 1992). If gifted children's underachievement arises instead from inappropriate educational provisions (as opposed to antisocial nonconformity), any link between their underachievement and delinquent behaviour would appear less likely.

Manifestations of underachievement

Gifted underachievers represent a paradox. On the one hand, they display exceptional abilities in intellectual or memory skills and creativity, especially in non-traditional areas. On the other hand, they also display the following characteristics (Butler-Por 1993; Davis & Rimm 1998; Diaz 1998; Dowdall & Colangelo 1982; Fine & Pitts 1980;

Hishinuma 1996; Hishinuma & Tadaki 1996; Moltzen 1996b; Montgomery 1996; Whitmore 1980):

- avoid rote learning;
- are inconsistent in their application to tasks;
- have poor organisational or time management skills when uninterested in an activity;
- have an external locus of control;
- use avoidance behaviour, such as arguing that school is irrelevant or too boring to justify making an effort;
- produce better oral than written work;
- apply themselves to extracurricular activities but not to school work;
- demonstrate conceptual understanding but shun detailed work;
- experience social problems;
- suffer from low self-esteem.

The result can be performances that are adequate but nevertheless well below the children's potential. These behaviours occur without any identifiable disabling condition or family trauma (e.g. their parents' divorce), and can show up in the first years of school. Attention to the signs of underachievement in early childhood years is thus crucial (Karnes & Johnson 1991; Karnes et al. 1985; Wolfle 1990).

Identification of underachievement

Identification of underachievement is complicated by the fact that children's gifts can compensate for or mask an inconsistent approach to work, just as is the case when giftedness hides a learning disability (Hishinuma 1996). Indeed, these children's giftedness is often identified coincidentally; often they are originally referred for other difficulties (Hishinuma & Tadaki 1996).

Identification of these children involves detecting a discrepancy between their potential and their performance (Butler-Por 1993; Moltzen 1996b). This is not as easy as it sounds because (Butler-Por 1993; Dowdall & Colangelo 1982; Moltzen 1996b):

- it is not possible to measure potential;
- teachers will not be aware that children could achieve at higher levels if the curriculum offers few opportunities for them to do so;
- it is not certain if a discrepancy between potential and performance is significant or whether it is just due to testing error;
- children might appear to be underachieving when actually they have unrecognised learning difficulties.

Children's current performance and test scores both may be depressed by their chronic lack of engagement with school and so, where possible, present performance needs to be compared with earlier test results (Davis & Rimm 1998).

Causes of underachievement

Underachievement can have at least four causes (Baum et al. 1994, 1995; Butler-Por 1993; Diaz 1998). These include (in order of significance):

- emotional difficulties such as low self-esteem, family difficulties and perfectionism;
- an unstimulating curriculum, where success is possible without effort or perseverance, or where conformity is encouraged over creativity;
- undiagnosed learning disabilities, poor self-regulation strategies (to which highly-able children do not want to admit) or ineffective coping strategies, such as withdrawal and procrastination, which surface once school work finally becomes challenging (although these patterns have set in many years prior to this);
- social and behavioural factors, such as peer group pressure, lack of behavioural controls and social skills.

Rimm (1986) says that underachievement can be set in place in the preschool years, if a child's parents either underachieve or model that hard work is exhausting; when the child is overly dependent on parents or dominates them; or when the home is so disorganised that persistent effort is well-nigh impossible. However, underachievement is a school problem and teachers have little influence over children's home environments. Thus, interventions need to focus on the educational setting (Montgomery 1996).

Alternative views of underachievement

Delisle (1994b) says that the 'underachieving' label is unfortunate because it focuses the blame on 'troublesome' gifted children and burdens them with the sole responsibility of reversing their 'academic neglect'. It is hurtful and disrespectful, kicking children when they are down and already well aware that their performances are disappointing the important people in their lives. If the children themselves are not blamed, instead they are turned into helpless victims of an 'inadequate' home or curriculum; neither focus is helpful (Delisle 1994b).

Inappropriate learning environment

When applied to individuals, the label 'underachieving' distracts us from the need to correct an educational setting that may not be motivating children sufficiently (Delisle 1994a, 1994b; Moltzen 1996b; Seeley 1993). Many children are blamed for being lazy and not trying hard enough, or are diagnosed with emotional or behavioural problems when instead they are reacting to inappropriate educational provisions (Clark 1997; Hishinuma & Tadaki 1996; Moltzen 1996b; Rivera et al. 1995).

Non-producers

Underachievement is not the same as being non-productive (Freeman 1995a). Some children do not conform to expectations of scholastic achievement but instead channel their energies into extracurricular activities or their areas of special interest, where their productivity is excellent and personally rewarding (Richert 1990, in Piirto 1999; Whitmore 1986); others choose not to produce as a deliberate way of coping with pressures to excel (Corrigan 1994).

Underachievers are likely to be emotionally distressed individuals with low self-esteem, whereas non-producers are self-confident people who decide not to conform for reasons of their own but who can achieve at high levels when they are motivated. We should not blame children for being interested in unconventional areas of learning (Delisle 1994b).

The myth of realised potential

Few of us can be said to ever achieve to our full potential, even if that could be measured (Delisle 1994a)—we balance our academic striving with other demands and interests. If we do not reach the level of academic or career attainment that others believe we could or 'should' achieve, then perhaps we have sought and found our fulfilment else-where.

GIFTED CHILDREN WITH DISABILITIES

The possibility that gifted children could also have specific learning disabilities was first recognised in 1937 by Samuel Orton, who found that a group of dyslexic children spanned the full range of general intellectual abilities (Weill 1987). But it was not until 1963 that Kirk coined the term 'learning disabilities' to describe learning difficulties that have no apparent cause (Baum et al. 1991) and that are inconsistent with a child's other skills (Montgomery 1996).

It is thought that around 5%–10% of gifted children—that is, somewhere between 1 in 200 and 1 in 400 children—could also have a learning disability (Dix & Schafer 1996); this can include sensory impairment, physical disability or specific learning difficulty. The reverse statistic is that approximately 2%–5% of children with disabilities may also be gifted (Johnson et al. 1997; Whitmore 1981; Yewchuk & Lupart 1993).

Children with learning disabilities are the most commonly studied group of gifted disabled children (Yewchuk & Lupart 1993). These children have some skills below the norm while other skills are within the gifted range. This can be reflected in IQ tests, where a pattern of high spatial scores and low sequential scores is evident (Brown 1984; Smith et al. 1977). A learning disability is thought to come about because of information-processing deficiencies (Baum et al. 1991; Cruickshank 1977), resulting in problems with expressing or communicating ideas in written or verbal form or impoverished perception, organisation, retention or comprehension of information (Gunderson et al. 1987; Whitmore & Maker 1985; Wingenbach 1998).

Their disabilities can hinder learning in the impaired channel (Hishinuma & Tadaki 1996), although affected gifted children will be highly capable in other conceptual areas. These difficulties will lead to failure at particular academic tasks and may result in ineffective learning strategies, including poor attention span, low self-esteem, disruptive behaviour and overactivity (Baum et al. 1991; Wingenbach 1998). Their wide spread of abilities can leave these children frustrated and confused, their parents exasperated, and their teachers feeling helpless (Fall & Nolan 1993).

Types of gifted learning disabled children

There are three types of gifted learning disabled children (Baum 1989; Baum et al. 1991; Ellston 1993; Gunderson et al. 1987; Rivera et al. 1995; Toll 1993). The first are *subtle gifted learning disabled* children, who are noticed for their high achievements while their learning disabilities go unrecognised. Their advanced abilities—such as retentive memory— allow them to compensate partially for their difficulties, and so their problems remain hidden. However, as they grow older, their disabilities lead to a growing discrepancy between their expected and actual performance, and so it appears that they are 'not trying hard enough' (Baum 1989; Baum et al. 1991; Toll 1993). This group of children tend to be recognised much later than less able children with specific learning difficulties (Montgomery 1996).

The second group—*recognised learning disabled*—comprises children who are identified as having learning disabilities but not as being gifted. They are noticed for what they *cannot* do (Baum 1989; Baum et al. 1991). Their disability depresses their intellectual performance and so their giftedness is not recognised (Toll 1993). Their special talents and interests are overlooked; moreover, they are labelled as being 'deficient' (Baum et al. 1991): there is something wrong with them which must be fixed before anything else can happen (Baum 1989). The result can be low self-esteem, plus low achievement and disruptive behaviour at school. Meanwhile, these children display their creative talents at home, when they are allowed to produce work in other than written form, or when they are taught non-traditionally (Baum et al. 1991; Ellston 1993).

The third group is the *hidden gifted learning disabled* children, whose dual exceptionalities are both hidden. They do not come to teachers' attention because their abilities mask their learning problems. Because they invest high levels of energy in compensating for their learning difficulties, they are able to achieve at age level. The results are that their overall abilities are thought to be average, while the energy drain can take its toll emotionally and on their concentration span. Their gifted abilities often surface when given creative projects to do, or when they are working in their area of greatest talent (Toll 1993).

While all three groups are educationally disadvantaged, the children most at risk are the third group—namely, the children whose gifts and disabilities both go unrecognised (Rivera et al. 1995).

Identification of gifted learning disabled children

Identification of dual exceptionalities is hampered by single assessment measures, stereotypical views about what gifted children are like, and a lack of information and training for professionals (Davis & Rimm 1998; Johnson et al. 1997; Moltzen 1996b; Winner 1996). Suitable educational provisions are obstructed by a lack of supportive technology, inadequate teacher training and inadequate funding (Johnson et al. 1997; Moltzen 1996b).

The box on p. 238 lists some specific characteristics that are often displayed by gifted children with learning disabilities. Some of these are similar to gifted children's characteristics, some equate to the traits of children with learning disabilities, and some are unique to children with both exceptionalities (Baum 1984; Vespi & Yewchuk 1992; Yewchuk & Lupart 1993). Baum (1984: 16) describes this blend:

> Like their learning disabled peers with average cognitive ability these learning disabled superior students often have weaknesses in areas involving memory and perception resulting in deficits in reading, writing or mathematics. However, these students may also display extraordinary talent in tasks involving abstract and creative thinking much like their peers who are gifted.

On the other hand, many of these characteristics are shared by under-achieving gifted children (Silverman 1989). This could be because what appears to be underachievement is actually due to unrecognised learning disabilities (Baum et al. 1995; Gallagher 1991a), or simply because underachievement and learning disabilities result in similar behaviours. It could also be because, faced with a child's chronic underachievement, we hasten to find a diagnosis for the problem and incorrectly label the child as learning disabled or inattentive (Rimm 1986; Tucker and Hafenstein 1997). It is thus difficult to determine whether a child *will not*, or *cannot* do the work (Silverman 1989).

The emotional and social difficulties of children who are gifted and also have disabilities are most apparent when their weaker areas are

SOME CHARACTERISTICS OF GIFTED CHILDREN WHO ALSO HAVE LEARNING DISABILITIES

If a child shows the majority of the following characteristics often or always, further assessment is indicated.

Intellectual strengths

- Has expertise in at least one specific area, such as musical, artistic or mechanical skills.
- Has an active imagination.
- Has an extensive vocabulary.
- Has exceptional comprehension.
- Excels at tasks requiring abstract thinking and problem solving.
- Has excellent visual memory.
- Is capable at puzzles and mazes.
- Has exceptional ability in geometry and science.
- Has a sophisticated sense of humour.
- Shows expertise in a particular topic.
- Is deeply committed to and highly creative in activities outside of school.
- Grasps concepts at once, rather than 'step by step'.

Academic difficulties

- Has poor handwriting.
- Spells poorly.
- Has difficulty with phonics.
- Cannot do simple tasks, but can complete more sophisticated activities.

- Has difficulty with computation but demonstrates higher-level mathematical reasoning.
- Does well in mathematics but poorly in language arts.
- Does well in language arts but poorly in mathematics.
- Does not do well under pressure (e.g. on timed tasks).
- Has problems completing tasks comprising a sequence of steps, but can take part in discussions that examine issues from a broad perspective.
- May have difficulty with rote memorisation.
- May appear inattentive.

Emotional signs

- Generalises minor academic failures to feelings of overall inadequacy.
- Has unrealistically high or low self-expectations.
- Feels academically inept.
- Is confused about his or her abilities.
- Has strong anxiety or fear of failure in academic tasks.
- Is sensitive to criticism of his or her work, even constructive criticism.
- Experiences intense frustration.
- Has low self-esteem.
- Reports feeling different from others.
- Has poor social skills with children and adults.

Behaviours

- Is disruptive in class.
- Is often off-task.
- Is disorganised, especially when unmotivated.
- Acts out without thinking about the consequences.
- Makes creative excuses to avoid difficult tasks.
- Is often aggressive.
- May be withdrawn.

Sources: Baum (1988); Baum & Owen (1988); Fall & Nolan (1993); Gunderson et al. (1987); Kitano (1986); Moltzen (1996b); Rivera et al. (1995); Silverman (1989); Vespi & Yewchuk (1992); Yewchuk & Lupart (1993).

actually below average (Kitano 1986) and their disability impairs their achievement in areas that they value highly (Whitmore & Maker 1985). Although frustration is common for all people with disabilities, gifted children who have disabilities are especially vulnerable because of their sensitivity, high self-expectations and strong desire for independence. These internal issues can be exacerbated by others' lack of awareness of the possibility of dual exceptionalities and subsequent inadequate educational programming (Whitmore & Maker 1985).

ATTENTION-DEFICIT HYPERACTIVITY DISORDER

Attention-deficit hyperactivity disorder (ADHD) is a relatively new term for a condition that was first identified almost 100 years ago (Anastopoulos & Barkley 1992). The syndrome is 'an extreme and sustained condition of restless, inattentive and impulsive behaviour' (Lambert 1990: 43). Today's label recognises that there are two manifestations of the attention-deficit disorders: ADHD, which comprises inattentiveness *and* hyperactivity; and ADD, which involves inattentiveness only.

The causes of ADD and ADHD are not known. Those who take a biological (as opposed to an environmental) view of the conditions contend that the behaviours are due to immaturity in the child's development—perhaps in how the frontal parts of the brain function. This area of the brain is responsible for planning. The cause of this neurological immaturity is not known, but as ADHD runs in families, genetic and environmental causes are both possible. Conditions of pregnancy appear not to cause ADHD, and the sometimes negative parenting pattern that was once blamed for these children's disruptive behaviour is now regarded as the result of having a child with the condition rather than its cause.

ADD and ADHD are usually thought to occur in around 3%–5% of children. When we combine this statistic with the rate of giftedness, which conservative estimates put at 3%–5% also, then the chances of children being both gifted and diagnosed as having ADD or ADHD are, at most, 1 in 400 (Mendaglio 1995a). Despite this statistic, the subject of a combination of ADHD and giftedness often comes up, partly because gifted children's high physical and verbal activity levels and inattention to routine activities are often misinterpreted as hyperactivity.

Signs of ADD and ADHD

Most clinicians use the DSM-IV criteria (American Psychiatric Association 1994) as a starting point for diagnosis (Blum & Mercugliano 1997). These criteria are reproduced in the box, opposite.

DIAGNOSTIC CRITERIA FOR ADD AND ADHD

To receive the diagnosis of ADD or ADHD, symptoms must begin prior to 7 years of age; continue for at least six months—longer in the early childhood age range; be present in at least two situations; result in significant impairment of the child's social or academic functioning; and not be the result of other conditions. The primary or diagnostic criteria as listed in the DSM-IV (American Psychiatric Association 1994: 83–5) comprise:

Inattentive symptoms

The child displays six or more of the following behaviours for at least six months to a degree that is maladaptive and inconsistent with his or her developmental level:

- often fails to give close attention to details or makes careless mistakes in school work, work, or other activities;
- often has difficulty sustaining attention in tasks or play activities;
- often does not seem to listen when spoken to directly;
- often does not follow through on instructions and fails to finish school work, chores, or duties in the workplace (not due to oppositional behaviour or failure to understand instructions);
- often has difficulty organising tasks and activities;
- often avoids, dislikes, or is reluctant to engage in tasks that require sustained mental effort (such as school work or homework);
- often loses things necessary for tasks or activities (e.g. toys, school assignments, pencils, books, tools);
- is often easily distracted by extraneous stimuli;
- is often forgetful in daily activities.

Hyperactivity

The following symptoms of hyperactivity-impulsivity have persisted for at least six months and to a degree that is maladaptive and inconsistent with developmental level:

- often fidgets with hands or feet or squirms in seat;
- often leaves seat in classroom or in other situations in which remaining seated is expected;

- often runs about or climbs excessively in situations in which it is inappropriate (in adolescents or adults, may be limited to subjective feelings of restlessness);
- often has difficulty playing or engaging in leisure activities quietly;
- is often 'on the go'; or often acts as if 'driven by a motor';
- often talks excessively.

Impulsivity

- often blurts out answers before questions have been completed;
- often has difficulty awaiting turn;
- often interrupts or intrudes on others (e.g. butts into conversations or games).

Individuals will be diagnosed with ADD when they display a range of inattentive behaviours; they might have the hyperactive-impulsive symptoms alone; or they will be determined to have ADHD when they display all three types of behaviours.

Source: American Psychiatric Association (1994). Reprinted with permission.

Unlike normally boisterous activity, ADHD activity levels are excessive, task-irrelevant, developmentally inappropriate, and pervasive across settings (Anastopoulos & Barkley 1992). The core behaviours occur in a variety of situations, but are most noticeable when the children are tired, expected to concentrate for long periods, and are in a group rather than one-to-one situations; when the activity is boring or repetitive and is highly structured; when movement is restricted; and when there is little supervision (Anastopoulos & Barkley 1992).

As well as the primary symptoms outlined in the box, children with ADHD often show secondary symptoms associated with the condition. These secondary problems are not included in the criteria for diagnosis but they can complicate management considerably. They include: behavioural problems; emotional difficulties; relationship difficulties with peers and at home; learning disabilities; and a higher than normal rate of health problems such as incoordination, sleep disturbances, middle ear and upper respiratory infections, asthma, and allergies (Anastopoulos & Barkley 1992). Given the similarities between these secondary features of ADD/ADHD and the signs of advanced development, it is no wonder the question of a dual diagnosis is often raised.

Assessment of ADD/ADHD

ADD and ADHD are difficult to diagnose accurately because of variations in children's constellation of symptoms, the severity of their symptoms, and because other conditions—including giftedness—have some characteristics in common with the attention-deficit disorders. Because affected children's behaviour will fluctuate across settings, an accurate diagnosis is possible only when information is gained from many sources, including parents, caregivers or teachers, and developmental and medical assessments. The aims of the latter are to rule out other possible conditions and to gain a history of the secondary problems that are associated with ADHD.

Distinguishing ADHD from giftedness

Many gifted children are restless, inattentive day-dreamers with high levels of physical or verbal activity (Mendaglio 1995a; Webb & Latimer 1997; Silverman 1998b). All these features are common both to ADHD and to giftedness (Mendaglio 1995a). Thus, for gifted children who are active, there is a danger that their positive manifestations of giftedness will be misinterpreted as personal defects, while the effects of an inappropriate environment are ignored (Baum et al. 1998).

In order to tease out the differences between children who are 'gifted but wriggly' (Silverman 1998b) and those with ADHD, you can take the following steps (Baum et al. 1998; Silverman 1998b; Webb & Latimer 1997).

- Examine the situations in which the children's behaviour becomes a problem. Children with ADHD will exhibit difficulties in many settings, while gifted children's behaviour will improve in enriched settings.
- Observe the children's attention span. Again, children with ADHD will have difficulties concentrating in most settings, while gifted children will be off-task mainly when the activity is well below their developmental level.
- Observe the children's learning *styles*. If they can pay attention during visual or active tasks but are inattentive to auditory input, perhaps they have spatial gifts and less well-developed verbal skills.
- Observe the children's activity levels. Children with ADHD have activity levels that are random or irrelevant to the task; gifted children's activity levels are generally focused and directed—even if they are not directed at the activities which you require them to be doing!

- Assess the quality of children's output. Children with ADHD produce variable performances, while gifted children produce consistently high performances when they like the teacher and are being challenged.
- Check adults' discipline styles. If adults have not taught children to moderate their impulses, perhaps the children simply need someone to insist that they do so. Children who are driven to achieve might not be willing to postpone their agendas and need firm direction to do so.

Nevertheless, we must still consider that a child might both be gifted *and* have ADHD, or is inattentive as a result of a learning disability. The potential for misdiagnosis is huge and must be guarded against by careful observation and multidisciplinary assessment (Silverman 1998b).

Treatment of ADHD

ADD and ADHD are complex conditions, whose accurate diagnosis and treatment are especially complicated in the early childhood years. Many studies have found that, despite relatively common side-effects (Levy 1993), medication alone provides similar or equal benefits to a combination of interventions (Anastopoulos & Barkley 1992; Fox & Rieder 1993; Goldstein 1995). However, this could be due to the incorrect targeting of alternative interventions. For example, behavioural interventions might be misguided when they try to impose external controls as a way of teaching children to control themselves internally; cognitive interventions have incorrectly focused on teaching children to self-instruct when they are already doing so (Berk & Landau 1993; Berk & Potts 1991; Diaz & Berk 1995).

These two traditional treatments—modification of children's outward behaviours and cognitive skills training—are still being developed for this group of children. Alongside them are the less orthodox homeopathic, naturopathic and chiropractic treatments, including dietary management (see Dengate 1997). Some preliminary findings suggest that, for example, some children's insulin levels might be so high as to deprive their frontal lobes of sufficient glucose (Blum & Mercugliano 1997). Evidence about the effectiveness of these alternatives is lacking as yet, although parents who choose to try them are judging that they cannot wait for the evidence to accumulate: they need to help their child *now*.

Limitations in our knowledge of ADD/ADHD

It is important to keep in mind that, unlike some diagnostic categories, the ADD/ADHD label is not prognostic: a child born with Down syndrome will always have Down syndrome, but the same cannot be said for children with attention deficits (see Hart et al. 1995). Neither is the label explanatory. This is evident in the circular nature of the diagnosis: 'Why does your child behave that way?' 'Because he has ADHD.' 'How do you know he has ADHD?' 'Because he behaves that way.' At this stage of our knowledge the label is simply descriptive: it is a shorthand way of describing the characteristic behaviours of this group of children. It neither explains nor predicts their behaviour, however.

In short, there are huge gaps in our knowledge of the attention-deficit disorders. Nevertheless, our relative ignorance is not a reason to blame children, their parents or their teachers for the condition. It is true that labelling children can allow adults to avoid responsibility for making children's environments more responsive to their needs (Mendaglio 1995a). But criticism or a lack of treatment will condemn children and their families to an array of primary and secondary difficulties that can severely lower their productivity and self-esteem.

Just as there are big gaps in our understanding of ADD and ADHD, there are even bigger gaps in our understanding of stimulant medication, the commonest form of treatment. Thus, for children with mild symptoms, drugs should not be the first treatment option, although the impact of severe symptoms on affected children and their families might justify administration of drugs. The decision to use medication will depend on the severity of the condition; whether other methods have been tried and have failed; the child's age; the child's and family's attitude to medication; and the ability of parents and caregivers or teachers to supervise a medication regimen adequately (Goldstein & Goldstein 1995).

Whatever combination of treatment programs is used, treatment needs to be designed specifically for individuals, to include a combination of approaches, and to be continued for extended periods of time.

RESPONDING TO THE NEEDS OF ATYPICAL CHILDREN

When a child does not conform to expectations, we often blame the child. This is the square-peg-in-the-round-hole dilemma: do you force an atypical child to fit in, or do you make the context more suitable for the child? The answer is 'both': thus, the measures recommended in this section pay attention to children's understanding of themselves as learners as well as external responses to their efforts and how these might be enhancing or reducing their motivation (Patrick 1990).

Identification of disguised giftedness

Identification of children with dual exceptionalities will be helped when we can overcome our stereotypes about how giftedness (and disabilities) is manifested (see chapter 4)—these stereotypes cause us to ignore those children whose language skills limit their verbal or written output, whose history of failure has impaired their motivation, and who have specific learning disabilities (Whitmore 1981; Yewchuk & Lupart 1993).

Thus, we need to reformulate our definition of giftedness in order to encompass non-traditional abilities (Frasier 1989, 1993, 1997; Harslett 1996). We will need to look for unconventional expressions of creativity and imagination as demonstrated by the following characteristics (Frasier 1993; Gibson 1998; Torrance 1998):

- ability to improvise with commonplace materials;
- communication skills that are rich in imagery;
- ability to apply knowledge to new situations;
- skills in group activities, including leadership;
- reasoning (logical thinking) abilities;
- persistence and originality in problem solving;
- insight;
- ability in visual or performing arts;
- emotional expressiveness;
- responsiveness to the feelings of others;
- passionate interests.

Multi-dimensional assessment. This broadening of our conception of ability will necessitate a change in identification procedures from uni-dimensional testing to multi-dimensional assessment (see chapter 5), in a range of settings (Butler-Por 1993; Kitano & Perez 1998; McKenzie 1986; Renzulli 1973; Robisheaux & Banbury 1994). As part of this information-gathering process, it can be useful to obtain formal assessments by child specialists with experience in disabilities *and* giftedness (Yewchuk & Lupart 1993).

Parents' reports. In addition to detailed assessments of children's skills in all developmental domains (Diaz 1998), comprehensive assessment will involve taking account of parents' reports, as parents are more likely to hear their child's concerns and have a longer and more detailed observation history of their child (Hishinuma & Tadaki 1996). Detailed assessment is important in building a partnership with parents, in case they feel that the school is persecuting their child or that the child is not trying hard enough (Fox 1984). A partnership with parents will convince children that their parents and teachers respect each other and have the same expectations for their achievements.

Children's self-reports. Assessment will also entail listening to the children's concerns or complaints and taking these seriously to plan more appropriate and motivating curricula.

Observation. Caregivers' or teachers' observations are valuable and need to give particular attention to those children whose performance varies significantly in different domains (Ellston 1993).

Emotional needs

Swesson (1994) states that gifted children who have learning difficulties often do not understand, and they do not understand why they do not understand, but they know that they are not stupid. The development of a healthy self-esteem is vital for children with dual exceptionalities. This means that these children will need support in the following ways (Butler-Por 1993; Clasen & Clasen 1995; Ellston 1993; Fall & Nolan 1993; Hishinuma 1993; Kitano 1986; Montgomery 1996; Swesson 1994; Vespi & Yewchuk 1992; Whitmore 1981; Whitmore & Maker 1985).

- Develop a warm relationship with underfunctioning children so that they know that you are interested in them as individuals. As Ellston (1993: 19) states: 'Gifted-learning disabled children need to know that they have value as people, not just for what they do, achieve or produce.'
- Help children to recognise that they are gifted and to understand the implications of this for them. They will need to accept both their talents and their weaknesses—that is, to develop some comfort with a realistic self-concept.
- Guide children to make their expectations more reasonable, as they can often set unrealistically high or too low standards for themselves. A cooperative rather than competitive setting will encourage these children not to shun any task where they will not be perfect.
- Give them experience of genuine success at meaningful tasks, so that their opinion of their abilities improves. These children need success, not more 'discipline': simply 'trying harder' is not the answer.
- Encourage them to be independent in age-appropriate ways.
- Assist them to find ways to express their frustration and confusion appropriately.
- Guide them to act less impulsively when under stress.

- Teach children how to value learning, through modelling, communicating interest in their efforts, and making learning a pleasure by incorporating their interests.

Social skills

Caregivers and teachers will need to facilitate positive social experiences for atypical children (Whitmore & Maker 1985) to give them confidence that other children will be open to their overtures of friendship (Vespi & Yewchuk 1992). Some children will need help to reflect on their social behaviour and its effects on the other children's willingness to play with them (Kitano 1986). Others need help in negotiating social situations, as they might blame other children for their feelings of isolation or can react aggressively to feeling out of place socially (Kitano 1986).

Developing accepting relationships with other children who value achievement is a significant factor in reversing underachievement for many children (Baum et al. 1995). Thus, it is important that we model peer support for excellence while, at the same time, are aware of how our comments can provoke peer rejection of bright children—for instance, by holding them up as a role model for others (Clasen & Clasen 1995).

Educational remediation

The curriculum for children with dual exceptionalities must tap into the vast reservoir of their interests. Rather than regarding their interests as irrelevant, using them as a vehicle for teaching allows children to learn in their preferred style, produce in their favourite mode, and concentrate on their areas of strength. This is fundamental to motivating them to learn, particularly as they will have experienced so much previous failure (Baum et al. 1994, 1995; Clements et al. 1994).

The second fundamental principle of working with these atypical children is that the educational program must focus primarily on their gifts rather than their deficits, even though remediation in their area of difficulty will be necessary (Baum et al. 1989; Ellston 1993; Wingenbach 1998). This focus on their strengths 'enables students to flourish, become excited about school, and begin to believe in themselves' (Ellston 1993: 19). Importantly, it respects them for their abilities rather than highlighting their deficiencies (Baum et al. 1989). Specifically, children with dual exceptionalities will need the educational measures outlined in the box, opposite.

EDUCATIONAL MEASURES FOR CHILDREN WITH DUAL EXCEPTIONALITIES

Attitudinal factors

- Provide a nurturing environment that not only recognises but also honours diversity and individual differences (Bernal 1989).
- Parents in particular should not tell or pressure children to achieve, but model high achievement so that their children will copy their example (Freeman 1993).
- Make no assumptions about children's strengths and limitations based on their school performance or disabling conditions. Create a delicate balance between making allowances for children's difficulties, while helping them to acquire basic skills, compensate for their difficulties, and continue to advance in their areas of talent.
- Encourage children to take safe risks and to learn that neither failure nor success is a threat.

Teacher variables

- Ensure that children have warm and accepting relationships with a teacher who acts as a facilitator rather than an instructor.
- Do not demand conformity but tolerate and encourage creativity.

Curriculum and teaching methods

- Encourage children to explore their world and promote age-appropriate independence.
- Identify the appropriate *level* of learning for each child, so that the work is neither too easy nor too hard and teacher expectations of children are appropriate (neither too high nor too low).
- Identify children's preferred learning *style*, and employ that teaching style as much as possible.
- Keep instructions brief and concise and deliver them both orally and visually. For children with learning difficulties, expect to have to repeat instructions more often than usual.
- When children have fallen behind others academically,

curriculum enrichment measures may fail to meet their needs unless they are given extra help in developing learning strategies and expanding their knowledge base (Borland & Wright 1994). Thus, remedial work will need to be provided in their area of difficulty.

- Remember that gifted children often learn concepts while neglecting the details; while not allowing them to avoid necessary detail, give them opportunities to explore global concepts as well (Roeper 1995a).

- Teach learning skills such as perseverance, organisation, research skills, goal setting, critical thinking, problem solving, and working independently.

- Recommend outside activities, such as Saturday clubs, where children can exercise their talents in a safe setting.

- Do not submerge children in activities where achievement is the goal, as doing so may provoke a perfectionist pattern.

- Give children control over their own learning: if they participate in an activity because of pressure from outside, then even success at the task will not improve their motivation.

- Acceleration is unlikely to be an effective measure for gifted children who have significant learning difficulties; therefore, provide enriching and challenging activities that circumvent their areas of difficulty and employ their strengths, so that there is not an exclusive focus on their weaknesses.

- Allow children to complete projects that call on their creative abilities and to present products in a medium (e.g. orally or with photographs) that avoids their problems with written expression. This might include using computers, scribes or dictaphone machines to circumvent handwriting and spelling difficulties.

- Ensure that they have sufficient time to generate these products, as accuracy is more important than speed.

- Apply basic skills in real-life, practical ways rather than investigating abstract ideas or engaging in repetitious learning.

- Encourage children to ask for educational modifications and to explain why they need these.

- Gifted children from minority cultures may feel especially sensitive to participating in activities that mark them out from members of their own cultural group (Evans 1993). This suggests the need to promote pluralism to allow children from minority cultures to preserve their own cultural heritage at the same time as acquiring the knowledge and skills that are necessary for success in the majority culture (Maker & Schiever 1989). The children might also need help to acquire skills for moving within and between cultures (Frasier 1997).

- Similarly, children from impoverished backgrounds who later attend middle-class schools (perhaps on scholarships) can find it difficult to fit into their new social stratum and may need support to maintain contact with both strata (Freeman 1993).
- Ensure that remedial services are coordinated, both within your own setting and between agencies (Johnson et al. 1997).

Sources: Baum (1984, 1988, 1989); Baum & Owen (1988); Baum et al. (1989, 1994, 1995); Butler-Por (1993); Clements et al. (1994); Davis & Rimm (1998); Dix & Schafer (1996); Fox (1984); Heacox (1991); Hishinuma (1993); Miller (1991); Moltzen (1996b); Montgomery (1996); Patrick (1990); Rimm (1986, 1987); Silverman (1989); Toll (1993); Wees (1993); Whitmore (1981, 1986); Whitmore & Maker (1985); Wingenbach (1998); Yewchuk & Lupart (1993).

Parents can be a valuable resource for helping children with dual exceptionalities (Johnson et al. 1997). In particular, when their child's disability has been recognised for some time, parents may already be familiar with the individual education plan model, and might feel comfortable about making active contributions to the educational plan for their child. At the same time, many parents will be confused by the puzzling array of their child's skills and may need support from teachers in their efforts to understand and encourage their child (Fall & Nolan 1993).

CONCLUSION

There is no prescription or formula that will suit all children with dual exceptionalities (Baum et al. 1995). Each disadvantaging condition has a myriad of causes, which can occur in different combinations and with different expressions for each child. However, Robinson observes that, whatever the reason for some children not being socialised into the subculture of academic success, all children who have advanced capabilities need to be socialised into a culture that is focused on accomplishment, whose values centre on (1996: 135):

- striving for conceptual understanding;
- a creative spirit and intellectual risk-taking;

- curiosity;
- a love of learning for its own sake;
- appreciation of deep thinking and skilful discourse;
- goal orientation and hard work, leading to expertise and the fulfilment of passions;
- extensive and deep knowledge;
- enjoyment of friends who share one's interests and capabilities.

A promising finding is that children whose gifts and disabilities are recognised and addressed in early childhood maintain their improved talents over time (Johnson et al. 1997). Baum and colleagues (1994, 1995) use the metaphor of a prism: when light enters the prism, it is split into beautiful colours and progresses in a new direction. Likewise, when children with dual exceptionalities are presented with a program that meets their emotional, social and educational needs, their performances both change direction and take on a new quality.

SUGGESTED FURTHER READING

The following texts provide clear overviews of many of the groups of gifted children whose special challenges are introduced in this chapter: Baum, S., Owen, S.V. and Dixon, J. 1991 *To be gifted and learning disabled: from identification to practical intervention strategies* Hawker Brownlow Education, Melbourne; Clark, B. 1997 *Growing up gifted* 5th edn, Merrill, Upper Saddle River, NJ; Colangelo, N. and Davis, G.A. (eds) 1997 *Handbook of gifted education* 2nd edn, Allyn & Bacon, Boston, MA; Davis, G.A. and Rimm, S.B. 1998 *Education of the gifted and talented* 4th edn, Allyn & Bacon, Boston, MA.

Chapter 7 ('Helping the underfunctioning able') in the following text provides a useful overview: Montgomery, D. 1996 *Educating the able* Cassell, London.

A practical approach to helping school-aged children who are underachieving is presented in: Heacox, D. 1991 *Up from under-achievement: how teachers, students and parents can work together to promote student success* Hawker Brownlow Education, Melbourne.

Two small texts providing excellent summaries of the challenges facing gifted girls are: Freeman, J. 1996 *Highly able girls and boys* Department for Education and Employment, London; and Smutny, J.F. 1998 *Gifted girls* Phi Delta Kappa Educational Foundation, Bloomington, IN.

DISCUSSION QUESTIONS

1. In your view, is it any easier these days for girls to be gifted than it was? If there has been a change, what accounts for it? Does anything else need to happen to encourage girls' achievements?

2. What can early childhood professionals do to prevent problems arising for gifted boys and girls?

3. What do the special needs of children from minority backgrounds, those living in poverty, or rural children imply for educational practice in the early childhood years?

4. What steps could you take to determine whether a child has dual exceptionalities—such as giftedness coupled with a learning disability or ADHD?

13

COUNSELLING GIFTED
YOUNG CHILDREN AND
THEIR FAMILIES

When we are willing to explore the social and emotional needs of the gifted from their viewpoint, we are most effective in leading them to thrive and survive the challenges that accompany high potential.

Galbraith (1985: 18, in Kunkel et al. 1992: 10)

KEY POINTS

- Counselling does not have to be a formal affair: it can comprise any natural conversation aimed at helping gifted young children to understand their abilities, develop relationships and manage stress.
- Parents have many concerns when they first encounter the possibility of their child's giftedness. They might lose confidence in their own ability to supply what the child needs, or worry about what giftedness means for the child's and family's adjustment. They sometimes experience difficulties in liaising with schools and in their contacts with parents of children whose development is proceeding at the average pace.

INTRODUCTION

The term *counselling* often conjures up images of a psychiatrist sitting in a comfortable armchair while the 'patient' reclines on a sofa and talks about his or her troubled past. However, I envisage counselling to be any interaction that is aimed at helping individuals 'to help themselves by making better choices and becoming better choosers' (Nelson-Jones

1988: 4). I see these helpful exchanges as occurring in naturalistic settings, and using natural activities (mainly play) as a venue for offering constructive comments to children who could be at risk of misunderstanding their experiences.

Although the traditional notion of counselling is a hierarchical one, with the counsellor in charge (Thompson & Rudolph 1996), I see helpful interactions between adults and gifted children as reciprocal exchanges, in which the adult listens to the child's ideas, as well as passing on information.

Finally, counselling is often thought to be problem-focused and a response to problems *after* they have arisen (Hickson 1992; Silverman 1993c). Instead, preventive counselling is far more effective and humane.

COUNSELLING GOALS FOR GIFTED CHILDREN AND THEIR FAMILIES

General counselling goals include enabling children to deal with sensitive issues; helping them to match their thoughts, feelings and behaviours; and helping them to adjust to their strengths and limitations (Geldard & Geldard 1997). It is particularly important to let gifted children know that 'they are not abnormal, they are not weird, and they are not alone' (Davis & Rimm 1998: 390). Therefore, the focus when supporting or counselling young gifted children and their families will be on (Hickson 1992):

- the development of healthy emotions and attitudes to themselves and others;
- self-knowledge, understanding and acceptance;
- training in communication and relationship skills;
- ways to manage stress;
- parent and teacher education.

By explaining to young gifted children their experience of being gifted (without using that label), we can validate their emotional and social experiences. It is possible to prevent later learning difficulties and underachievement that could arise from misunderstandings and discouragement (Kitano 1986).

COUNSELLING ISSUES FOR GIFTED CHILDREN

In general, counselling issues for gifted children centre on their sense of being different, on social concerns and educational issues. From an early age they are aware of being different from other children, and they need an explanation for these perceptions (Chitwood 1986; Delisle 1992).

Misunderstanding of giftedness

From a young age, gifted children need to understand giftedness and its significance for them (Davis & Rimm 1998). Your role can be to explain to children, other caregivers or teachers and parents what the label means, and to examine and clarify some of the stereotypes attached to the label (Manaster et al. 1994).

Dweck (1995, in Robinson 1996) explains that some children view giftedness from an 'entity' perspective, which states that the more gifted you are the less work you have to do. This view causes them to avoid investing energy in tasks requiring delayed gratification and to avoid activities in which they cannot become instant experts. Those children who regard giftedness from an 'incremental' perspective realise that ability develops from study and hard work. You will need to convince entity thinkers that putting in the work will both produce results and be more fun for themselves (Robinson 1996). At the same time it is important not to put pressure on gifted children to be at peak performance all the time (Delisle 1992).

Effects of labelling

Although children need an explanation for the feelings of being different from other children, this does not mean that they need to be assigned the label 'gifted'. Cornell (1989) found that when parents used the *gifted* label, their gifted children had lower self-esteem regarding their physical appearance and reported higher levels of anxiety. In addition, labelled children were less well-accepted by their classmates. These effects might not have resulted from being labelled but from the fact that those parents who avoided using the label—even though they knew their child was indeed gifted—were being more than ordinarily careful to emphasise their child's multi-dimensionality, rather than choosing to focus only on his or her areas of particular talent.

In a study by Manaster and colleagues (1994), three-quarters of the adolescents had been well aware that they were different, and identification or labelling merely confirmed that. The remaining quarter of their subjects doubted the accuracy of the label. Nevertheless, most accepted the label—even when they did not agree with it. Few had to struggle with coming to terms with their own giftedness as a result of being labelled, as the label merely explained and confirmed their experience.

Most gifted children see the label as helpful if it leads to improved educational opportunities; if identification is not followed up with special provisions, being labelled can be perceived as stressful (Hershey & Oliver 1988; Ring & Shaughnessy 1993). These studies exemplify the conclusions of Fisher (1981: 49):

> Labels can be useful when they stimulate achievement, enhance self-concept or become a force for allocating additional or scarce resources. Labelling becomes a problem when it is inappropriate, or when the person labelled is in disagreement with the labelers, or when the label becomes a fact rather than a description of certain characteristics . . . Labels can be helpful or harmful. They can be accurate or misleading . . . They can be negative or positive. They can be a burden or a welcome recognition.

Social issues

Gifted children often infer from labelling that being different is wrong and that, furthermore, it must be their fault (Robinson 1996). Pressure to be like one's peers accounts for the dip in social self-esteem commonly experienced during the middle high school years (Robinson 1996). Some of the social dilemmas of young gifted children include:

- pressure to conform—perhaps by hiding their talents (Davis & Rimm 1998);
- isolation from peers, with resulting loneliness (Kunkel et al. 1992);
- excessive competitiveness;
- lack of a true peer group;
- criticism and jealousy from age mates (Kunkel et al. 1992).

Although gifted children generally have positive views about giftedness and its contribution to their personal growth, they sense that many teachers, peers and siblings have a negative perception of giftedness (Colangelo 1997; Coleman & Cross 1988; Cross et al. 1991, 1992; Kerr et al. 1988; Swiatek 1995; Tidwell 1980; van Boxtel & Mönks 1992).

As well as having immediate social concerns, gifted children are often more concerned about broader social issues than their age mates, before they have the emotional maturity to cope (Clark & Hankins 1985; Delisle 1992; Robinson 1996). Their raised awareness means that they will need more reassurance and opportunity to talk about the social issues that are causing them concern (Clark & Hankins 1985).

Educational issues

The educational problems that gifted children and their families often need to overcome include: boredom (intellectual frustration) (Davis & Rimm 1998; Kunkel et al. 1992); poor study habits; refusal to do routine work; and underachievement.

It is important that gifted children learn that it is okay to be talented (Fraser 1996). They also need to learn how to be tactful when displaying their talents, while not allowing themselves to underachieve or hide their abilities just to feel less different from others or to make other people feel better. Educational counselling could encourage children in 'positive perfectionism', in which they are encouraged to set high standards for themselves, systematically work at meeting those standards, and take pleasure in their attainments (Robinson 1996).

SUGGESTIONS FOR SUPPORTING GIFTED CHILDREN

Children will need information explaining their giftedness so that they can generate an accurate understanding of their experience of being different from others.

Naturalistic counselling

Naturalistic counselling can occur between children and any adult whom they know well and trust. It will involve more than just talking, as otherwise young children will become distracted (Geldard & Geldard 1997). Some suggestions for activities during which you might offer some helpful ideas include:

- using a telephone in the home corner and holding a conversation with a child who is on the other play phone;
- using puppets to discuss indirectly topics that might be too sensitive to address more directly;
- engaging in cooperative play with children, discussing sensitive topics that arise spontaneously or which you weave into the play;
- taking part in their superhero play to help them resolve its issues;
- talking with children about their drawings and other artistic constructions—both the products and the process of achieving them;
- helping children to resolve differences between themselves without allocating blame for a disagreement;
- using story-telling and books to raise topics which the two of you can discuss. This can be highly effective with gifted children, especially avid readers (Honig 1986b; Silverman 1993c; Webb 1993). It can be less confronting for them to negotiate a social dilemma through a fictional character than in real life, while providing the same social learning and emotional release.

Talking with verbally gifted young children is aided by their ⸻anced language abilities, while intellectually gifted children are likely to be less egocentric than others and so can be especially receptive to helpful conversations.

When talking, it is tempting to pursue the content of what a child is telling you by asking who, what, why, where and when questions; instead it would be more useful to follow the feelings that the child is conveying (Thompson & Rudolph 1996). It is beyond the scope of this text to cover listening skills in detail, but many responses to children's statements convey judgments, inappropriately offer solutions, or try to distract children from their valid emotions (Gordon 1970, 1974). The adult usually intends to listen empathically, but these types of responses nevertheless block the communication.

Not all issues have to be spoken. Adults can 'listen with their eyes' (Porter 1997a, 1999) and observe what children's non-verbal behaviour is saying about their needs. Pugh and Selleck (1996: 126) observe that young children 'are more creative and advanced in their thinking than many adults give them credit for and the skilful adult . . . is able through observation and listening to gain real insight into children's preoccupations, thoughts and feelings'.

Gifted children will respond positively to creative problem solving and the opportunity to think independently (Culross 1995). At the same time, attempts to reward or otherwise manipulate them are likely to engender resistance, boredom or lack of interest (Culross 1995).

Explaining the assessment procedure

Young children will have some idea of what is happening during an assessment, and so need clear information about its purpose (Riley 1997). When I am about to administer an IQ or other developmental test, I explain to children that their parents need to know about how their brain learns and what interests them. I explain that some of the items will be familiar to them while others will be new. Some might seem hard, but that is because they are for older children, while others might seem too easy. They are not to worry about that, as that is part of what I need to know. I always have a parent present for an assessment of young children although, once the children are 8 or older, I ask the parents to check with the child that she or he feels comfortable with a parent being present. (Some older children in particular do not like to be watched.)

I find many advantages to having parents present: their attendance helps to reassure the child; it avoids teaching children to accompany a stranger; and it allows me to check with parents during the session about their child's emotional state, or whether I can safely encourage a child to persist at a task because he or she can normally do it. After the session, parents' attendance helps us to discuss the implications of the assessment, as they are aware of what I have observed and can give me feedback about whether their child's performance during the session was typical.

Explaining assessment findings

At the next session, which the child does not attend, I explain to parents what I have found out and receive their reports of their child's abilities. Subsequently, I often explain the findings to the children themselves. On the latter occasion I avoid the 'gifted' label. Instead, I begin by asking the children whether they have ever sat in a shopping centre watching everyone pass by. They might have noticed that even though every face is made up of the same ingredients—two eyes, a nose, mouth, chin—no two people look alike. So it is with brains. They all have a front part which is in charge of their thinking, a back part which works their bodies, and two halves, controlling language, music and visual thinking. (This description is simplified, of course.) Despite the fact that everyone's brain has the same parts or ingredients, all brains work differently.

Next, I describe to the children that their brain is a machine for learning. I explain that just as some children can run more quickly, so too can some children learn more quickly than others. Then I tell them that I have discovered that their brain is particularly good at learning: they can learn more quickly than usual. I mention that this is exciting because they can find lots of different things that interest them, but they still have to stay in charge of their brains. I talk about other machines that might interest them, such as motorbikes or cars. No matter how good their family car is—it might be a BMW—it needs someone to steer it; it cannot travel by itself. In the same way, no matter how good a brain is—no matter how quickly it learns—it needs someone to be in charge of it.

When children have been referred for behavioural or emotional difficulties that were thought to be associated with giftedness, I go on to explain to them that the second part of having a brain which learns quickly is that they sometimes feel things that aren't real. Their brains sometimes play tricks on them. As a result, they might criticise themselves too much, become too worried, or strive too hard to please. I suggest that, over time, they will need to find ways to notice when this is happening. I point out that I cannot help them to take charge of their feelings and neither can their parents, because it is not our brain. The children are the only ones who can figure out how to take charge of their own brains. We adults might be able to suggest ideas for taking charge, but only the children can carry them out.

Riley (1997) reports that this type of information about their gifts and talents—rather than making children self-satisfied or smug—merely confirms what they already know about themselves. It also replaces inaccurate explanations for the differences they have noticed with more accurate pictures of themselves. Rather than thinking that they feel different from others because there is something wrong with them, the children are able to understand the benefits and challenges of 'having brains that learn quickly'.

Stress management training

Gifted children can benefit from learning how to manage stress (Silverman 1993c). However (as mentioned in chapter 9), the actual coping methods children use are probably less important than the fact that they attempt to take charge of stressors (Rutter 1985). Rather than directly teaching particular coping methods, therefore, you could simply highlight the ones the children are already using, helping them to notice that they are doing so and to evaluate their effects.

Children with disguised gifts

Given the particular needs of educationally disadvantaged gifted children (see chapter 12), we need to help young people challenge sex- and cultural stereotypes and to understand their own capabilities, interests and values, in order to enhance their awareness of their options. Adults need to avoid overprotecting gifted children and refuse to cooperate with their urge to be popular at the expense of achieving their dreams (Kerr 1985; Silverman 1991).

Formal counselling for children

I do not envisage that teachers will engage in formal counselling with young gifted children. However, for those of you who are trained and employed in a counselling role, a brief description of an existential counselling approach might be useful. This approach is presented by LeVine and Kitano (1998), and looks at children who are having difficulties coming to terms with being gifted, evidenced by refusing to participate in educational activities or having emotional or behavioural difficulties.

Counselling begins with the realisation that gifted young children's experiences are often invalidated by the many people in their lives who deny their feelings and experiences of being 'out of step' with children of their own age. The first phase, then, involves teaching these children that what they feel is okay and that they can trust their perceptions.

Second, the children are helped to enjoy their deeper understandings and not to feel at fault when other people do not share these. Neither do they have to take responsibility for other people's problems.

In the third phase, the children are empowered to use their superb thinking skills to solve the problems that those same skills have provoked. The message here is that the children have the ability to solve their own problems.

Next, it is necessary for gifted children to accept that one cost of being gifted is a certain degree of alienation from others (LeVine & Kitano 1998). Conforming and being 'normal', or the same as everyone else, is not an option. Being different is okay (to a point, beyond which some conformity to reality can be encouraged).

As the children begin to take charge of their lives and make positive changes, the counsellor will help them to accept the anxiety and uncertainty that always accompanies doing something unfamiliar. At the same time, the children are helped to accept both the possibilities and limits on change (LeVine & Kitano 1998).

ISSUES FOR THE FAMILY

Parents of gifted children are often characterised as pushing their 'star' children to feed their own egos; teaching their children to act as if they are superior to others; bragging about their gifted children; comparing their children to others; and being overprotective at the same time as making their children into adults (Silverman 1997). The reality is, however, that most gifted children have parents who are also gifted and who have good problem-solving skills and healthy personal adjustments. These adult skills in turn feed the family's overall healthy interaction patterns (Chamrad & Robinson 1986; Silverman 1997).

Parents of gifted children experience many concerns relating to their children's advanced development (Hackney 1981; Keirouz 1990; Silverman 1997):

- recognition of giftedness;
- worry about their gifted children;
- diminished self-confidence;
- altered family relationships;
- behaviour management issues;
- issues created between the family and school;
- issues created between the family and community.

Recognition of giftedness

As discussed in chapter 5, not all parents are aware that their child is gifted, while others attempt to deny the possibility (Davis & Rimm 1998; Fisher 1981). Even those who are willing to consider the possibility are often concerned about what it could mean. They might have another family member who was gifted but unsuccessful or socially isolated, and fear that their child might turn out similarly (Damiani 1997). Therefore, parents might need information to offset their preconceptions about giftedness.

Worry about their gifted child

Parents' main concerns usually centre on their child's social and emotional needs (Dangel & Walker 1991). Parents who themselves were gifted as children can be especially sensitive to the challenges that might lie ahead for their own gifted child.

Many parents worry about introversion, which tends to characterise 50% of gifted children compared with around 25% of children with average development (Silverman 1997, 1998c). Parents are concerned when their children dwell on social issues before they have the *emotional* maturity to cope (Keirouz 1990), fearing that they might be deprived of their childhood (Mares & Byles 1994).

Parents often worry also about their children's *social* isolation, or choice of less able companions (Keirouz 1990), not realising that the latter can come about because children need a break from the pressure to achieve.

A common *educational* concern of parents is their gifted child's underachievement (Moon et al. 1997), especially from the middle school years onwards.

Impact on parents' confidence

As Hickson (1992: 94) states: 'Having a gifted child is not a uniformly positive experience for all families.' Nevertheless, there are few studies of the effects of gifted children on their parents' self-confidence; most of the literature is based on observations—often of parents who have been referred for counselling, and who could therefore be expected to have some worries. Anecdotal reports suggest that, on the whole, the more similar the gifted child is in ability to his or her parents, the less confusion, uncertainty and anxiety the parents feel (Colangelo & Dettman 1983; Keirouz 1990). Some parental reactions include the following.

- After identification of their child's giftedness, parents often have to come to terms with being gifted themselves (Silverman 1997).

- Parents often have to come to terms with their own unsatisfactory education (Damiani 1997). Negative experiences can cause them to have extra fears for their child, without acknowledging that their experiences occurred a generation ago and might not be relevant now (Damiani 1997).
- Because of the confusion surrounding the 'gifted' label, many parents will harbour misconceptions and stereotypical views about their gifted child's needs (Hickson 1992).
- Parents might mourn the loss of the 'normal' child, whose needs could be catered for routinely within the education system (Silverman 1997).
- Parents can feel inadequately prepared to meet their gifted child's needs (Colangelo & Dettman 1983; Fisher 1981; Silverman 1997). Because many parents do not see themselves as gifted, they feel guilty for not being able to provide their gifted child with the necessary intellectual stimulation or educational opportunities (Hackney 1981; Keirouz 1990).
- Parents often feel that others will see them as 'pushy' if they try to secure special services for their gifted child (Silverman 1997).
- It is confusing to parent a child with development at many stages simultaneously (Silverman 1997).
- If the parents themselves are not gifted and if obvious displays of talent make them feel inadequate, they might put pressure on their gifted child not to excel (Hickson 1992).

Family adjustment

Although a happy childhood is not essential to the realisation of gifted potential, it 'provides a smoother, and perhaps happier path' towards the gifted child's ultimate talented achievements (Snowden & Conway 1996: 98). Therefore, successful family adjustment can help gifted children, both emotionally and in their performances.

Some families are indifferent to their gifted child's special needs, while others become overinvolved in their child's life (Hickson 1992). Many parents believe they must put greater energy and resources into their gifted child (Colangelo & Brower 1987; Colangelo 1997; Fisher 1981; Hackney 1981). The result is that the family becomes organised around the gifted child's 'specialness', to the detriment of other aspects of the family's functioning (Colangelo 1997; Hackney 1981).

Some family difficulties might come about not because of a single gifted child but because all family members are more or less gifted, and more or less emotionally intense. This can mean that the gifted child's emotional outbursts spark off and are added to by reactions of other family members (Silverman 1997).

But while there are some short-term adjustments to be made once a child has been labelled as gifted, this soon settles and the family adjusts well in the long term (Colangelo & Brower 1987).

Sibling relationships

Labelling one child as gifted has the unfortunate implication that the siblings are 'non-gifted' and so must adjust to their new devalued status (Colangelo & Brower 1987).

The impact on sibling relationships is not as might be expected: siblings with average development report more positive feelings about family relationships than the gifted children themselves do (Chamrad et al. 1995; Colangelo & Brower 1987; Keirouz 1990). But the picture is mixed: younger siblings of a gifted child might resent having such a hard act to follow (Grenier 1985), while older siblings with average development might be embarrassed that a younger gifted brother or sister is surpassing them (Keirouz 1990). These tensions are felt less when there is a bigger age gap between the siblings, and when they have different interests and so are not directly competing (Cornell & Grossberg 1986; Grenier 1985; Keirouz 1990). Another factor that can help siblings' positive adjustment is having two or more siblings with average development in the family (Keirouz 1990).

Then there is the effect of the gifted label on the other siblings' feelings about themselves. Some studies show that the siblings who are not identified as gifted can experience low self-esteem, poor emotional adjustment, heightened anxiety and competitiveness as a result of having a brother or sister who has been labelled as gifted, particularly when parents treat the children differently as a result of their disparate labels (Cornell & Grossberg 1986; Keirouz 1990). How parents treat children strongly influences how they feel about themselves (Grenier 1985).

Despite these findings, Silverman (1997) points out that only 20% of siblings evidence adjustment difficulties, and that in many cases these are due to the failure to identify the siblings as gifted: non-labelled siblings' jealousy and resentment of the labelled child often abates when they too are correctly identified as being gifted.

Finally, children who are gifted verbally or are perceptive can use these skills to manipulate and manage their parents and siblings (Hackney 1981). One result can be that the children with average development might perceive that they have three parents, which is not likely to be kindly received (Chamrad et al. 1995).

Marital relationship

No impact of identification has been detected on the parents' marriage, other than when they disagree about the child's label or about how to meet his or her special needs (Cornell 1989; Hickson 1992). The parent who agrees that the child is gifted—usually the mother—is likely to be closer to the child than the one who disputes the label (Keirouz 1990).

Behavioural issues

A gifted child often receives higher status in the family than any other member, including the parents (Hackney 1981; Keirouz 1990). Sometimes, knowledge that their child is 'different' justifies in parents' minds being tolerant of a child's unusual behaviour or excessive demands (Fisher 1981; Keirouz 1990; Sapon-Shevin 1987). In turn, the parents' reduced authority and the gifted child's increased power can lead to family tensions and inappropriately lenient behaviour management.

On the other hand, some parents react in a very controlling way to their gifted child's non-conformity and resistance to authority (Damiani 1997). A resolution to this behaviour management dilemma is suggested in chapter 11.

Issues between the family and school

Some parents will use the gifted label to justify demanding extra provisions from the school (Fisher 1981; Hackney 1981). Most, however, merely want appropriate—not better—educational provisions for their gifted child, and experience a continual battle to find an educational environment that suits their child's needs (Fraser 1996). Fraser reports that many parents achieve special educational provisions only when they instigate them, and that they have to spend a great deal of energy 'just trying to ensure that their children are actually learning at school' (Fraser 1996: 452). Hall (1994) reports that, over time, many parents in her study had accepted that their gifted children's scholastic achievement would be spasmodic.

In the early childhood years, parents need information about schooling options (Silverman 1997), about the advisability of early school entry and grade acceleration, and about how to plan for the transition to school. In addition, some might need support to use their skills for maintaining a cooperative relationship with teachers and school principals.

Issues with other parents and the community

Some of parents' most difficult moments can occur when they are talking with other parents whose children have not been labelled as gifted

(Hall 1994). When exchanging stories about their children, parents of gifted children often feel that they have to hold back for fear of appearing to brag (Fisher 1981), while other parents can be unsympathetic to the notion that a gifted child could be experiencing any difficulties (Hall 1994).

To shield their gifted child from rejection or teasing, some parents of gifted children try to enrol their child in the 'best' schools, live in the 'best' suburbs, and vet their child's companions so that their child associates with other gifted children (Hackney 1981; Keirouz 1990). Others protect themselves from feeling isolated by rationalising that they are different from others 'in a better way' (Hackney 1981). Either reaction can be seen to be elitist and, as a result, is likely to alienate others (Hackney 1981).

Supporting the parents

It always impresses me that, despite an almost complete absence of training for them, so many parents have such an accurate grasp of normal development and so many intuitively know their children. Nevertheless, many feel out of their depth when, for whatever reason, their child does not fit the normal developmental pattern. The most important thing to do when talking with parents is to 'normalise being abnormal', keeping them in touch with the fact that the gifted label does not change their child but is only a shorthand way of listing the characteristics of which they were already well aware. In this way, they can remain in charge of decisions about their child and family and do not have to defer to 'expert' outsiders.

Explaining giftedness to parents

How identification is conducted makes a difference to how parents respond to their child's needs (Ring & Shaughnessy 1993; Sapon-Shevin 1987b). Parents' beliefs about giftedness can manifest themselves in either debilitating or productive interactions with a labelled child (Sapon-Shevin 1987b; Webb 1993). Parents' messages to their children about their competence are a more powerful influence on their self-perceptions than actual success or failure at tasks (Phillips 1987). The gifted label might cause parents to raise their expectations of their children's achievement (Fisher 1981), perhaps causing them to give negative feedback when children do not meet these inflated expectations. This can later lead to reduced achievement and emotional difficulties (Windecker-Nelson et al. 1997). Alternatively, when parents believe that gifted children are 'odd' and inevitably unhappy, they appear to blame normal upsets on their children's giftedness and believe that there is nothing they can do to help them, with the result that the children's behaviour becomes more disturbed (Freeman 1991, 1994, 1997).

As many parents are labouring under misconceptions and because labelling has so many ramifications, their knowledge and questions need to be a specific focus during assessment. Parents will need information and support in order to understand standardised assessment results and tests' limitations (Chitwood 1986; Keirouz 1990), and to acknowledge their child's profile of abilities (Moon et al. 1997). At the same time, we need to be aware that not all parents look to books to find information, and that accounts of giftedness in the mass media tend to highlight prodigies (Mares & Byles 1994). Thus, professionals need training not only in identification but in how to convey to parents in a balanced way the implications of the gifted label (Sapon-Shevin 1987b; Vialle & Konza 1997; Webb 1993).

Parents who in the past have had few dealings with gifted education might need extra support to make them comfortable with their child's identification (Colangelo 1985). In easing their possible disquiet, you will need to highlight your interest in advancing the child's special talents while preserving the family's values (Colangelo 1985).

Advocacy

One dilemma for parents can be how to advocate for special provisions for their gifted children without making the children out to be better than—rather than merely different from—other children, and how to avoid stigmatising those who are not labelled as 'gifted' (Sapon-Shevin 1987b). Parents are often accused of advocating a better education for their gifted child than other children receive (Robinson 1996): while they must be their child's advocate, they also need to help him or her build bridges to others (Roeper 1995b).

Parents may face teachers who are indifferent at best, or 'downright hostile' at worst, to the needs of gifted children (Fraser 1996: 453; McBride 1992). Parents themselves are often blamed for their child's adjustment difficulties, even when these are either the normal ups and downs that any children can experience or are typical problems for gifted children (Robinson 1996).

When they are facing a lukewarm reception, you can help parents as they plan their child's transition to school by acting as an advocate for them and their child. Even though parents do not need experts to take over for them, at times they may need formal support to advocate for their child's needs.

Involve parents in their child's education

When children doubt that their parents believe they are gifted, they tend to adjust less well than when they are confident of their parents' support (Robinson 1990). Although in the past there has been a fear of involving 'over-invested' parents in their children's education, it is now clear that the children need their parents' backing (Robinson 1990; Webb 1993). Despite the myths, most parents seek a balanced education for their gifted child: they do not wish to promote intellectual skills alone (Creel & Karnes 1988). Therefore, it can help to acquaint parents with ways they can promote their children's continued development. These include the following (Colangelo & Dettman 1983; Phillips 1987; Robinson 1993):

- foster a positive attitude to learning;
- encourage self-confidence in children by giving informative but not evaluative feedback—that is, acknowledgment but not praise—as evidence to children that they are competent;
- encourage risk-taking and creativity;
- encourage (but do not force) reading;
- reinforce the information that children gain through reading with real-life experiences.

At the same time, parents will need to keep in mind that 'there is an ebb and flow to development': their children will not be gifted in everything all the time (Colangelo & Dettman 1983: 25). They also need to avoid an exclusive focus on their gifted child and attend equally to other aspects of family life, such as looking after themselves as individuals, their marital relationship, and any other children.

Empowerment of parents

Your role will be to support the parents as the leaders in their family so that they remain confident of being able to act in their child's best interests. Parents will be empowered to assist their gifted child when they can:

- acknowledge that, like them, caregivers and teachers often feel alone in their efforts, hampered by a lack of proper training in the field of giftedness, misinformation and bureaucratic constraints on best practice (Chyriwsky & Kennard 1997; Hall 1994);
- trust their child to know what he or she needs (Hall 1994);
- trust their own instincts about their child;
- accumulate information about giftedness in general;
- avoid immersing the child in too many activities (Hall 1994);

- maintain an accepting home environment as a 'safety zone' for the gifted child (Prichard 1985);
- remember to look after themselves and meet their own needs (Roeper 1995b).

Parent support groups

The quality of parents' social supports has a measurable impact on children's cognitive and social development, either because of parents' increased confidence arising from their knowledge that they can rely on others if they have parenting concerns, or because a wide parental network exposes children to a range of adult and child contacts (Melson et al. 1993). Thus, parents of gifted children often benefit from attending groups with other parents of gifted children, where they can normalise what they are experiencing, gain information and receive emotional support (Moon et al. 1997; Webb 1993). This can help to reduce parents' isolation and allows them to learn more about their child's needs (Hall 1994).

CONCLUSION

In order to support gifted children and their families, adults need above all to be responsive to the signals that the children are sending about their educational, social and emotional needs. Harrison (1995: 45) states that: 'Knowledge of the characteristics of giftedness, as well as knowledge of the individual child, can help parents, families and . . . educators to interpret and respond appropriately to the child's behaviour.' Counselling support for children and their families can help gifted children to understand and cope with their differences from their age mates, and can prevent later underachievement and learning problems (Kitano 1986). It can empower parents to continue to act in their child's best interests without feeling in awe of their child or of educational specialists.

Looking ahead . . .

At later ages, if the school environment is not responsive to gifted children's particular needs, additional educational issues can arise. Delisle (1992: 39) states: 'It is an unfortunate reality that school and learning are not synonyms—or, at least, related—in the minds of some gifted children.' Nevertheless, although some children will feel frustrated that their educational needs cannot fully be met, their dissatisfaction will be defused somewhat if an understanding adult acknowledges that their concerns are valid (Delisle 1992).

Gifted children begin to consider their career options earlier than other children—often during primary (or elementary) school—and, because of their high accomplishments, often set themselves career goals that require lengthy academic preparation (Moon et al. 1997). This makes career guidance an important counselling need from the late primary school years onwards. It is important that career planning occur in conjunction with individualised educational planning, so that the children's educational program relates to their interests, abilities and ultimate career goals (Moon et al. 1997; Van Tassel-Baska 1993).

One career guidance issue relates to the notion of multi-potentiality— that is, that it can be difficult for gifted young people to select a career path when they are capable and interested in so many fields at once (Achter et al. 1997; Webb 1993). However, recent research shows that this even pattern of abilities appears because the tests used to assess gifted children are not difficult enough: their ceilings are too low (Achter et al. 1997). When the tests are made more demanding, most gifted young people demonstrate particular strengths which, in combination with their interests and value systems, will guide career choices.

SUGGESTED FURTHER READING

If you would like to pursue more detail on counselling gifted children and their families, I suggest Silverman, L.K. (ed.) 1993 *Counseling the gifted and talented* Love Publishing, Denver, CO.

My favourite title on listening and other communication skills is Bolton, R. 1987 *People skills* Simon & Schuster, Sydney.

You might find the following small handbook useful for parents who need an introduction to giftedness: Porter, L. 1997 *Young gifted children: meeting their needs* Australian Early Childhood Association, Watson, ACT. Another useful and more detailed publication for parents and one which is very readable is Knight, B.A. and Bailey, S. (eds) 1997 *Parents as lifelong teachers of the gifted* Hawker Brownlow Education, Melbourne. I also liked the chapters on parenting in Davis, G.A. and Rimm, S.B. 1998 *Education of the gifted and talented* 4th edn, Allyn & Bacon, Boston; and Roeper, A. 1995 'Parenting the gifted' in *Annemarie Roeper: selected writings and speeches* Free Spirit, Minneapolis, MN.

DISCUSSION QUESTIONS

1. What could you do to help a young gifted child to adjust emotionally, socially and academically in an early childhood setting?

2. How could you support parents as they investigate their child's possible advanced development, come to terms with identification, and adjust their expectations of their child and themselves?
3. Is there a role for you in advocating for the parents' and child's needs in the child's next educational setting?
4. What special measures do you think are necessary for supporting educationally disadvantaged gifted children and their parents?

14

FORMULATING A POLICY ON ADVANCED LEARNERS

It seems obvious to suggest that [centres] adopt a model [for serving gifted children] which best suits the training and experience of the teachers involved, the resources available and the specific needs of the children.

Wilson (1996: 63)

KEY POINTS

- Formal policies have many benefits in that they provide guidelines about what services a centre will offer and how they will be delivered, and set the tone of a program.
- Your document could detail your beliefs (philosophy) and understanding (theory) about giftedness, and your recommended practices. All must conform to the wider official policies to which you are subject.
- Your policy could also include issues such as your intention to work in partnership with parents, referral of children to specialists, educationally disadvantaged gifted children, planning the transition to school, and the evaluation of your program.

INTRODUCTION

In general, policies are guidelines about what services you will offer and how you will deliver these. Your centre will have many policies governing its operations: the purpose of this chapter is to describe what a policy for advanced—that is, gifted—learners could comprise.

The first step in developing a policy for meeting the needs of advanced learners is to acknowledge that gifted children do exist in every centre (Eyre 1997; Wilson 1996). Anticipated provisions for gifted children will need to be built on the provisions for all children: 'It is impossible for a school to be a good school for able pupils unless it is already a good school' (Eyre 1997: 100).

BENEFITS OF FORMAL POLICIES

Written policies have many benefits.

- Their procedures can guide action when a difference of opinion occurs among or between staff, families and management (Farmer 1995).
- Policies offer children, staff and parents safeguards and clear expectations of their roles, rights, and responsibilities.
- Written guidelines help to ensure that decisions about practice are consistent across time and fair to all stakeholders (Farmer 1995).
- The process of formulating policy gives staff and parents the opportunity to clarify their views (Stonehouse 1991).
- The process of formulation is an opportunity to involve parents and staff collaboratively (Stonehouse 1991).
- Policy development allows staff to plan how to act rather than having to make hasty decisions in response to a problem that has already happened.
- Written documentation helps with familiarising new staff and parents with the philosophy and workings of the centre.
- Written policies assist in evaluation and accountability (Farmer 1995; Stonehouse 1991).
- Policies help to heighten awareness of specific issues—in this case, the needs of children with advanced development (Freeman 1995c).
- A centre's policy for atypical children signals its commitment to attending to the needs of all children (Freeman 1995c).

COMPONENTS OF A POLICY

Your policy could comprise: a definition of giftedness; your mandate; your philosophical underpinnings; theory; and a set of procedures or strategies for enacting your policy, including a procedure for evaluating its effects (DECS 1990; Eyre 1997; Farmer 1995).

Definition

You will need to begin by proffering a definition of advanced learners. You could choose to use the word 'gifted' although you might find that you have to qualify it somewhat. Given the controversy about the term itself with its implication of privilege, I recommend avoiding it where possible and focusing your definition on advanced learning instead. This will allow you to list the domains in which your staff value advancement, which might, for instance, comprise Howard Gardner's 'multiple intelligences'.

Mandate

Your centre's policy needs to be framed within outside guidelines, such as federal or state legislation on meeting the needs of gifted children, or the policy of your governing body. While Eyre (1997) laments the lack of formal policies on able or gifted children in Britain, this deficiency is not universal (see Heller et al. 1993). Nevertheless, even when official policies have been set down, they are mostly open to interpretation (Wilson 1996): they offer broad-brush guidelines only, with the detail to be filled in by practitioners.

Philosophy

This section might begin with a brief statement about your commitment to valuing all children and their diversity. Next, you could state your beliefs about children and how they learn, your rationale for a focus on advanced learners (a separate policy will focus on children with learning difficulties), and your beliefs about the role of environmental stimulation in the development of children's skills.

Theory

Your theoretical base will need to be comprehensive—that is, it should help you to understand gifted children's needs and give you a sound body of information about appropriate curriculum measures to cater for these needs. When selecting a guiding theory, you will need to evaluate its assumptions and practices on the basis of whether they are consistent with your views about regular education and child development, and whether they are known to be effective and ethical.

Practice

Practice comprises your goals, how to achieve them, and specific procedures to support staff and children.

Direction (goals)

Your policy on advanced learners will need to state your educational goals for them. This direction statement will need to be clearly written and feasible, should incorporate both educational and social-emotional goals (Carter & Hamilton 1985), and will need to be congruent with your choice of either the national resources or special education rationales for gifted education. Your specific goals might be identical for all children (and could comprise aims such as those listed at the beginning of chapter 10). At the same time, you could acknowledge the particular characteristics that accompany advanced learning and which can affect gifted children's ability to profit from a regular program.

Procedures

Your document will describe which procedures are to be used and by whom, in order to enact the principles in your policy. These procedures describe how you intend to achieve your goals. This section will incorporate statements of your assessment methods—both proactive measures (e.g. parent interviews and structured observations) and reactive measures (e.g. referral for standardised testing).

Your specific curriculum differentiation measures will need to be described here as well. These must be clearly articulated (Piirto 1999) and represent a planned and integrated approach to the curriculum, rather than just offering busy or trivial activities to keep advanced children out of trouble. The measures chosen must be aimed at providing appropriate challenge for advanced learners (see chapter 10) in a range of domains because, as Wilson (1996: 70) observes, 'content and process are of equal importance and . . . the affective domain demands careful consideration' in any curriculum planning.

You might state how you plan to:

- cultivate all children's talents and abilities and enhance their confidence in themselves as learners;
- identify and develop children's specific aptitudes which emerge in response to the curriculum;
- differentiate the curriculum for those children whose learning is advanced generally;
- detect advanced development that is manifested in atypical ways (e.g. dual exceptionalities) or in non-traditional domains (e.g. creativity) (Braggett 1992).

Having arrived at some recommended practices, you might ask the following questions about them (adapted from Cowin et al. 1990; Sharp & Thompson 1994).

- Are your recommended practices realistic?
- Do they reflect actual practice or are they a 'wish list' (Eyre 1997)?
- Will the staff be willing to carry them out?
- Do you have the skills to do so?
- If not, how could you be equipped with the required skills?
- What additional resources (including materials and personnel) will be necessary to enact the recommendations? Are these available (Freeman 1995c; Wilson 1996)?
- What advantages do the recommended practices bring?
- What shortcomings do they have?
- Are the endorsed practices consistent with the centre's philosophy, aims and objectives, with the stated aims of the gifted policy, and with the policies of your governing authorities?

Partnership with parents

Your policy might express your faith in parents' judgments about their children's skills. Given the myth that 'all parents think their child is gifted' and the reality that many parents underestimate their children's skills (Chitwood 1986; Davis & Rimm 1998; Delisle 1992), it could be important for parents' self-confidence that you include a statement about your desire to work in partnership with them in meeting their child's exceptional needs, and your faith in their ability to support their gifted child.

Referral to consultants

It would be useful to include in the policy a statement about how the centre can use consultants, how and to whom to refer children and families, and in which circumstances children might be referred. Clear and uncomplicated procedures for making referrals will assist staff in gaining specialist help for children and their families.

Special issues

You might want to cover methods of identifying advanced development in non-traditional domains or in children who are experiencing poverty or other disadvantaging circumstances (e.g. dual exceptionalities). You could look at other 'high-risk' groups such as gifted girls (or boys) separately, as well as mentioning some methods for preventing children's underachievement.

Finally, you might want to describe how you plan to advocate for the needs of gifted children in their next educational setting and how to execute the transition to school, especially in cases of early entry.

277

Evaluation of the policy

In order to make improvements in your program, the document will need to include a method for ongoing (that is, formative) review and evaluation of the program's effectiveness (Borland 1997; Carter & Hamilton 1985). Given that programs for gifted children must fit their unique context and that, therefore, your goals will be individually tailored for your setting, your evaluation also will be specific to your centre (Carter & Hamilton 1985). During a formal evaluation, you could find it useful to ask the following questions, negative answers to which will provoke a change in practices (Borland 1997; Davis & Rimm 1998):

- Is your differentiated curriculum plan consistent with theory?
- Is your program being enacted as originally conceived? Which activities are being offered regularly? Which are neglected?
- Are the outcomes congruent with what you set out to accomplish— that is, your original goals?
- Are there other, important, unanticipated outcomes?
- Are there gifted children for whom the program is more or less successful than others? (For instance, you might want to take special note of the effects of the program on children from other cultures.)

In terms of outcomes, given that the children are young, much of your evaluation will be based on your own observations and parents' feedback. You might choose to focus on the children's levels of involvement with the curriculum (Bryant 1987); or you could design authentic outcome measures to assess and record improvements in the children's knowledge of significant information (content), learning skills (process), and attitude to learning (Gallagher 1998).

As well as assessing the outcomes of your gifted provisions, you will need to evaluate the effectiveness of inputs, such as the resources being used, the efficient use of teaching and planning time, and the involvement of parents (Davis & Rimm 1998).

Although evaluation can seem burdensome, it can be professionally fulfilling to be able to demonstrate to yourself—if to no one else—that what you are doing is effective. Reflecting on your practice can only enhance your confidence in what you do, which in turn will empower you to advocate for the children.

CONCLUSION

Although formulating policy is time-consuming, the process gives all participants the opportunity to clarify their values and to become clear about how to enact the specified procedures. It can serve an educational process for all those who are involved and can ensure that actions based on the policy receive wide-based support.

SUGGESTED FURTHER READING

For an overview of the policies in use in Australia, I recommend: Wilson, P. 1996 *Challenges and changes in policy and thinking in gifted education in Australia* Hawker Brownlow Education, Melbourne.

For an international perspective, you could consult: Heller, K.A., Mönks, F.J. and Passow, A.H. (eds) 1993 *International handbook of research and development of giftedness and talent* Pergamon, Oxford, UK.

DISCUSSION QUESTIONS

1. To what extent has the topic of gifted education arisen in your staff group as an issue to be included in the centre's policies?

2. How could you enlist the support of parents for this controversial area to be included in your centre's policy?

3. What resources are necessary for your workplace to institute a planned approach for meeting the needs of advanced learners?

4. If you were writing your centre's policy on gifted learners, what would it comprise?

Appendix I
CHECKLISTS

Characteristics of giftedness scale by Linda Kreger Silverman and Elizabeth Maxwell

Mark these characteristics in the following way to show how they pertain to the child:

One X if true
Two XX if very true
? if not sure
Add * if important to discuss further

1. Reasons well (good thinker) _____
2. Learns rapidly _____
3. Has an extensive vocabulary _____
4. Has an excellent memory _____
5. Has a long attention span (If interested, does the child stay with tasks for a long period?) _____
6. Sensitive (feeling hurt easily) _____
7. Shows compassion _____
8. Perfectionistic _____
9. Intense _____
10. Morally sensitive _____
11. Has strong curiosity _____
12. Perseverant in interests (If interested, does the child persevere at tasks?) _____
13. Has a high degree of energy _____
14. Prefers older companions or adults _____
15. Has a wide range of interests _____
16. Has a great sense of humour _____
17. Early or avid reader (If child is too young to read, is he or she intensely interested in books?) _____
18. Is concerned with justice, fairness _____
19. Judgment mature for age *at times* _____
20. Is a keen observer _____
21. Has a vivid imagination _____
22. Is highly creative _____
23. Tends to question authority _____
24. Has facility with numbers _____
25. Good at jigsaw puzzles _____

Source: Silverman and Maxwell (1996); reproduced with permission.

Things this young child has done

Child's name _____ Your name _____

School name _____ Your position _____

Child's birthday (day, month and year) __/__/__ Today's date: __/__/__

The following is a list of characteristics of gifted young children. The examples after each item are there to help you understand that item. A child may not show all of the examples given and he or she may exhibit the item characteristic in ways not listed. Indicate how much you think this child is like the item by using the scale to the right of each item (mark strongly agree **SA** to strongly disagree **SD**). Fill in one circle for each item. If you are unclear or haven't noticed how this child compares to an item, fill in the **Unsure or don't know** circle. Use the space below the item for examples concerning this child, add as many details as you can remember. The space is small, feel free to add extra pages of stories or examples to tell us more.

THIS CHILD:

1. **Has quick accurate recall of information** (*e.g. good short- and long-term memory; quick to provide facts, details or stories related to complex events; learns quickly and recalls accurately words to songs, poems, stories or conversations; points out connections between ideas and events*).

    An example:

⑪⑩⑨⑧⑦⑥⑤④③②①
SA   SD
◯ Unsure or don't know

2. **Shows intense curiosity and deeper knowledge than other children** (*e.g. asks questions incessantly once imagination has been aroused; pays close attention when learning; has an enthusiastic need to know and explore; remembers things in great detail*).

    An example:

⑪⑩⑨⑧⑦⑥⑤④③②①
SA   SD
◯ Unsure or don't know

3. Is empathetic, feels more deeply than do other children that age (*e.g. exhibits maturity usually associated with older children; shows unusual hurt or pain when he or she displeases someone; displays pride in advanced accomplishments; is sensitive to others' feelings and shows distress at other children's or adults' distress; will subjugate his or her needs to the needs of others; reads body language*).

⑪⑩⑨⑧⑦⑥⑤④③②①
SA   SD
○ Unsure or don't know

An example:

4. May not always display their advanced understanding in everyday situations (*e.g. becomes cranky or non-compliant when fatigued or stressed; playground behaviour may not reflect their verbal reasoning about the same situations; may be frustrated with their ability to meet their own high expectations*).

⑪⑩⑨⑧⑦⑥⑤④③②①
SA   SD
○ Unsure or don't know

An example:

5. Uses advanced vocabulary (*e.g. correctly uses vocabulary and phrasings adults would expect from older children; surprises adults and children with the big words or phrases they use; likes complex communication and conversations*).

⑪⑩⑨⑧⑦⑥⑤④③②①
SA   SD
○ Unsure or don't know

An example:

6. Reads, writes, or uses numbers in advanced ways (*e.g. reads earlier than most children or if learns to read at same time as most children does so very quickly; likes to read rapidly to get the gist of a story even though some words are skipped or mispronounced; interest in coping or using letters, words, or numbers; uses computational skills earlier than others*).

An example:

⑪ ⑩ ⑨ ⑧ ⑦ ⑥ ⑤ ④ ③ ② ①
SA   SD
◯ Unsure or don't know

7. Advanced play interests and behaviours (*e.g. exhibits play interests that resemble those of older children; likes to play board games designed for older children, teens or adults; more apt to be interested in cooperative play, complex play situations or sophisticated play activities*).

An example:

⑪ ⑩ ⑨ ⑧ ⑦ ⑥ ⑤ ④ ③ ② ①
SA   SD
◯ Unsure or don't know

8. Shows unusually intense interest and enjoyment when learning about new things (*e.g. spends long periods exploring interesting new things; listens for long periods to stories and conversations; retells events and stories in great detail; entertains self for long periods; shows unwavering attention, sometimes to the point of stubbornness; sits patiently when reading or listening to books*).

An example:

⑪ ⑩ ⑨ ⑧ ⑦ ⑥ ⑤ ④ ③ ② ①
SA   SD
◯ Unsure or don't know

9. Has an advanced sense of humour or sees incongruities as funny (*e.g. is humorous in speech, social interactions, art or story-telling; makes jokes, puns, plays on words; sees humour in situations, even ones against him or her and laughs at the situation*).

An example:

⑪ ⑩ ⑨ ⑧ ⑦ ⑥ ⑤ ④ ③ ② ①
SA   SD
◯ Unsure or don't know

284

10. Understands things well enough to teach others (*e.g. likes to play school with other children, dolls or stuffed animals; talks like an 'expert' or likes to discuss certain topics a lot; explains ideas to adults when she or he doesn't think the adult understands very well*).

An example:

⑪ ⑩ ⑨ ⑧ ⑦ ⑥ ⑤ ④ ③ ② ①
SA   SD
○ Unsure or don't know

11. Is comfortable around older children and adults (*e.g. craves attention from adults; likes to be with older children and adults; listens to or joins in adult conversations; often plays with and is accepted by older children*).

An example:

⑪ ⑩ ⑨ ⑧ ⑦ ⑥ ⑤ ④ ③ ② ①
SA   SD
○ Unsure or don't know

12. Shows leadership abilities (*e.g. has a verbal understanding of social situations; sought out by other children for play ideas; adapts his or her own words and expectations to needs or skill level of playmates; may be seen as bossy; uses verbal skills to deal with conflicts or to influence other children*).

An example:

⑪ ⑩ ⑨ ⑧ ⑦ ⑥ ⑤ ④ ③ ② ①
SA   SD
○ Unsure or don't know

13. Is resourceful and improvises well (*e.g. makes ingenious or functional things from LEGOs or other building toys; uses toys in unique or non-traditional ways; plays with or carries on conversations with imaginary friends; makes up believable endings to stories*).

An example:

⑪ ⑩ ⑨ ⑧ ⑦ ⑥ ⑤ ④ ③ ② ①
SA   SD
○ Unsure or don't know

14. **Shows logical and metacognitive skills in managing own learning** (*e.g. understands game rules quickly; learns from mistakes in playing games; sees errors or losses as learning experiences rather than failures; monitors difficulty of task to push self to more challenging levels*).

(11)(10)(9)(8)(7)(6)(5)(4)(3)(2)(1)
SA   SD
○ Unsure or don't know

An example:

15. **Uses imaginative methods to accomplish tasks** (*e.g. presents unique arguments in order to convince others to allow him or her to do or get things; finds imaginative ways to get out of doing things he or she doesn't want to do; curious with a high energy level that is goal directed*).

(11)(10)(9)(8)(7)(6)(5)(4)(3)(2)(1)
SA   SD
○ Unsure or don't know

An example:

Use the rest of this page to tell us anything you think is important about this child that we have not asked about. Please feel free to add any information you think might be useful in giving us a clearer picture of what the child is like. Be as specific as possible in describing the child's interests and accomplishments. If you can share some copies of this child's creative work, we would be delighted to have them.

Source: Copyright © 1994 Michael Sayler *Investigation of talented students* University of North Texas, Denton, TX.

Things my young child has done

Your child's name _____ Your name _____

Child's birthday (day, month and year) __/__/__ Today's date: __/__/__

The following is a list of descriptions of children. Decide how well each item describes your child. The examples after each item are there to help you understand that item. Your child may not show all of the examples given and he or she may exhibit the item characteristic in ways not listed. Indicate how much you think your child is like the item by using the scale to the right of each item (mark strongly agree **SA** to strongly disagree **SD**). Fill in one circle for each item. If you are unclear or haven't noticed how your child compares to an item, fill in the **Unsure or don't know** circle. Use the space below the item for examples concerning your child, add as many details as you can remember. The space is small, feel free to add extra pages of stories or examples to tell us more about your child.

MY CHILD:

1. **Has quick recall of information** (*e.g. remembers complex happenings and describes them long afterwards in clear details; learns notes and words to songs quickly; remembers landmarks and turns on the way to familiar places*).

⑪⑩⑨⑧⑦⑥⑤④③②①
SA   SD
◯ Unsure or don't know

A personal example:

2. **Intense curiosity leading to deeper knowledge than other children** (*e.g. insatiable need to know and explore; later on he or she collects things and then learns all he or she can about them; remembers things in great detail*).

⑪⑩⑨⑧⑦⑥⑤④③②①
SA   SD
◯ Unsure or don't know

A personal example:

3. Feels more deeply than do other children that age; is empathetic (*e.g. feels unusual hurt or pain when he or she displeases someone; shows pride in advanced accomplishments; sensitive to others' feelings and shows distress at other children's or adults' distress; will subjugate their needs to the needs of others; reads body language*).

A personal example:

(11)(10)(9)(8)(7)(6)(5)(4)(3)(2)(1)
SA   SD
○ Unsure or don't know

4. Uses advanced vocabulary (*e.g. correctly uses vocabulary adults would expect from older children; surprises adults with the big words they use; knows more words than other children; stops to ask about new words then remembers them and uses them correctly later*).

A personal example:

(11)(10)(9)(8)(7)(6)(5)(4)(3)(2)(1)
SA   SD
○ Unsure or don't know

5. Began to read, write or use numbers early (*e.g. early interest in the alphabet and or numbers; liked to imitate writing as a toddler; copied letters, words or numbers; learned to read or count early without formal instruction; developed computational skills earlier than others*).

A personal example and approximate age of child at the time:

(11)(10)(9)(8)(7)(6)(5)(4)(3)(2)(1)
SA   SD
○ Unsure or don't know

6. Understood phrases or brief sentences as an infant (*e.g. listened intently; understood and acted on short sentences: 'Give Mum a hug', 'Bring me the book and I will read to you' etc.*).

A personal example and approximate age of child at the time:

(11)(10)(9)(8)(7)(6)(5)(4)(3)(2)(1)
SA   SD
○ Unsure or don't know

7. **Began speaking in words and sentences earlier than other children** (*e.g. spoke first words before age one; went from saying individual words to speaking in sentences quickly or spoke first words later than age one but quickly moved to speaking in complete sentences; carried on conversations with adults as if they were peers*).

A personal example and age of child at the time:

⑪⑩⑨⑧⑦⑥⑤④③②①
SA   SD
○ Unsure or don't know

8. **Early motor development** (*e.g. very visually attentive during the first six months; watched people carefully; followed movements intently; walked early; fed himself or herself sooner than other children; active use of toys and puzzles*).

A personal example and age of child at the time:

⑪⑩⑨⑧⑦⑥⑤④③②①
SA   SD
○ Unsure or don't know

9. **Shows unusually intense interest and enjoyment when learning about new things** (*e.g. listens for long periods to stories and conversations; retells events and stories in great detail; entertains self for long periods; shows unwavering attention, sometimes to the point of stubbornness; sits patiently when reading or listening to books*).

A personal example:

⑪⑩⑨⑧⑦⑥⑤④③②①
SA   SD
○ Unsure or don't know

10. **Has an advanced sense of humour or sees incongruities as funny** (*e.g. is humorous in speech, social interactions, art or story-telling; makes jokes, puns, plays on words*).

A personal example and age of child at the time:

⑪⑩⑨⑧⑦⑥⑤④③②①
SA   SD
○ Unsure or don't know

11. Understands things well enough to teach others (*e.g. likes to play school with other children, dolls or stuffed animals; talks like an 'expert' or likes to discuss certain topics a lot; explains ideas to adults when she or he doesn't think the adult understands very well*).

A personal example:

⑪⑩⑨⑧⑦⑥⑤④③②①
SA   SD
○ Unsure or don't know

12. Is comfortable around older children and adults (*e.g. craves attention from adults; likes to be with older children and adults; listens to or joins in adult conversations; likes to play board games designed for teens or adults; often plays with and is accepted by older children*).

A personal example:

⑪⑩⑨⑧⑦⑥⑤④③②①
SA   SD
○ Unsure or don't know

13. Shows leadership abilities (*e.g. sought out by other children for play ideas; adapts his or her own words and expectations to needs or skill level of playmates; may be seen as bossy; uses verbal skills to deal with conflicts or to influence other children*).

A personal example:

⑪⑩⑨⑧⑦⑥⑤④③②①
SA   SD
○ Unsure or don't know

14. Is resourceful and improvises well (*e.g. finds unique or non-traditional ways to use toys; plays for long periods with imaginary friends; diligent in getting things they want regardless of where you've put them; makes up believable endings to stories*).

A personal example:

⑪⑩⑨⑧⑦⑥⑤④③②①
SA   SD
○ Unsure or don't know

15. **Uses imaginative methods to accomplish tasks** (e.g. presents unique arguments in order to convince others to allow him or her to do or get things; finds imaginative ways to get out of doing things he or she doesn't want to do; curious with a high energy level that is goal directed).

⑪⑩⑨⑧⑦⑥⑤④③②①
SA   SD

◯ Unsure or don't know

A personal example:

Use the rest of this page to tell us anything you think is important about your child that we have not asked about. Please feel free to add any information you think might be useful in giving us a clearer picture of what your child is like. Be as specific as possible in describing your child's interests and accomplishments. If you can share some copies of your child's creative work, we would be delighted to have them.

Source: Copyright © 1994, Michael Sayler *Investigation of talented students*, University of North Texas, Denton, TX.

Appendix II

IQ TESTS

WECHSLER PRESCHOOL AND PRIMARY SCALE OF INTELLIGENCE (WPPSI-R)

The WPPSI-R was published in 1989 (Wechsler 1989) as an update of the original WPPSI (Wechsler 1967). The first edition was designed for use with 4 to $6\frac{1}{2}$-year-olds; the revised version covers the age range from 3 to $7\frac{1}{4}$ years, although Kaufman (1990) states that the items are too hard for children aged just 3 and are unreliable for those aged 7. Thus, at the extremes of the age range it is less useful than in the middle.

The WPPSI-R was standardised on 100 US children in each age group, with the exception of the 7 to 7 years 3 months group, for which only 50 children contributed to the standardisation. The preliminary items that were proposed for inclusion in the WPPSI-R were tested on 500 children. Those items that did not discriminate between them or which were difficult to administer were subsequently deleted. The test was also reviewed by a panel, and items which they judged to have cultural bias were either altered or deleted. Sattler (1992a, 1992b) classifies its standardisation as excellent.

The revised version added colour to some verbal and performance materials, and Object Assembly (a puzzle test) was included, in favour of the unattractive Animal House subtest, which has now become a supplementary test only (now called Animal Pegs). The test is begun with a performance task, with verbal and performance subtests alternating thereafter. The box opposite describes the WPPSI-R subtests.

SUBTESTS COMPRISING THE WECHSLER
PRESCHOOL AND PRIMARY SCALE OF
INTELLIGENCE—REVISED EDITION (WPPSI-R)

In the following table, each subtest is numbered in the sequence in which it is administered.

Performance scale

1. Object Assembly: This subtest presents six formboards and puzzles which the child must complete within time limits, with bonus points for quick completion. The subtest mainly tests synthesis skills, particularly in the visual domain.

3. Geometric Design: In the first seven items, the child chooses from an array of four shapes one that matches the reference shape. In subsequent items, the child has to draw shapes copied from the stimulus booklet. The test requires, among other skills, visual discrimination and eye–hand coordination, plus an ability to alternate one's attention from the reference shape to one's own reproduction of it.

5. Block Design: The child is asked to reproduce designs using flat square blocks. In the initial items, the blocks are red on one side and white on the other. In later items, one side is red and the other side is cut diagonally into half red and half white. The subtest taps analysis skills, visual organisation and spatial ability.

7. Mazes: The child has to trace the route taken through increasingly complex mazes. The subtest requires attention to and memory for instructions, although children who are familiar with this type of activity might be able to do it without relying on instructions. The subtest taps visual–motor coordination and control, planning ability and perceptual organisation.

9. Picture Completion: The child must identify a missing part of a picture. This requires recognition of the pictured item and appreciation of its incompleteness. The subtest requires, therefore, reasoning, visual organisation, long-term visual memory and concentration.

11. Animal Pegs: This is a supplementary subtest whose results do not contribute to the calculation of the child's overall or performance IQs. It is a coding task in which the child must place different-coloured pegs under the picture of an animal. There are four animals, each with its own coloured peg. Memory, attention span, goal awareness, concentration, dexterity, sequencing and learning ability may all be involved.

Verbal scale

2. Information: The child has to answer a broad range of questions of facts. Success is said to depend on the child's natural abilities but also opportunities and experience. The test measures recall rather than reasoning as, just because children can recall facts, does not mean that they can apply their knowledge effectively.

4. Comprehension: This subtest asks children to explain social cause–effect relationships, for instance, by asking what should you do if you lose a friend's ball. It draws on the child's ability to use practical information and to generalise from experience. Success may reflect the child's linguistic skills, logical reasoning, knowledge of conventional standards of behaviour and cultural opportunities.

6. Arithmetic: This subtest contains 23 arithmetic and numerical items presented verbally, beginning with simple counting tasks and graduating to mental addition and subtraction. The child needs to be able to understand and remember verbal directions, concentrate on the salient parts of the question, carry out numerical operations and perform the later two-step arithmetic operations in sequence.

8. Vocabulary: This is a test for word knowledge. It assesses learning ability, richness of memory for language and concept formation. It is a good overall test of mental ability, even though it relies on environmental opportunities to acquire language.

10. Similarities: In the first part of this subtest, the child is asked which pictured object (from an array of four) belongs with a group of objects pictured at the top of the page of the stimulus book. In part two, the child has to complete a sentence, such as, 'You wear shoes and you also wear . . . ?'. In part three, the child has to say how two items are alike. Success is related to the child's cultural opportunities, language skills including vocabulary, ability to categorise objects, memory, and logical thinking.

12. Sentences: This subtest is optional and its score does not contribute to the calculation of the overall or verbal IQs. The child is asked to repeat increasingly long sentences after the examiner. It is a test of short-term auditory memory, attention, listening comprehension and auditory processing. A child will need the requisite language skills in order to succeed with the task.

Source: Sattler (1992a, 1992b).

Perhaps because of its modernisation, Sattler (1992a, 1992b) says that the WPPSI-R has a high interest level for most children; in dissent Kaufman (1990: 388) endorses my observation that, even with the changes to the new edition, the test is unattractive:

> . . . unfortunately for the examiners and the young children they test, the revised battery has fallen prey to the main weakness of its predecessor: It has failed to take into account the special needs and capabilities of the young preschool child.

Three main issues arise when assessing very young children. The first is raised by Kaufman (1990: 392), who contends that the test is not user-friendly because it does not take into account the examiners' needs 'when testing a group of children who are, almost by definition, impulsive, distractable, and active'. When children are distractable, the examiner has very little discretion to alter the format to suit the child (Brown 1984): the very rigour that makes standardised tests reliable also makes them inflexible.

Second, as with all the Wechsler scales, the child must fail a number of consecutive items before a subtest is discontinued (Mazes requires six failures), which Kaufman (1990: 390) judges to be 'cruel and unusual punishment to a child'. A string of failures can seriously disrupt children's motivation.

Third, the use of bonus points for speed on the Block Design and Object Assembly subtests can penalise reflective children or those with eye–hand coordination difficulties (Kaufman 1992, 1993). Accuracy of response more reliably distinguishes high- from average-achievers, with speed being less relevant (Reams et al. 1990). Children should be able to aim for maximum accuracy at the speed at which they are most comfortable for that task (Lajoie & Shore 1986; Sternberg 1982). Otherwise, constant requests to hurry can destroy rapport with them and put them under pressure.

If a child is nearing 6 years of age and is expected to have abilities in the average range or higher, because of the limitations of the WPPSI-R, it can be better to wait to administer the WISC-III (Wechsler Intelligence Scale for Children—third edition) instead. The WISC-III has better reliability than the WPPSI-R, it will be briefer for the young child and, if necessary, it allows for repeat testing on the same instrument later in the child's life.

WECHSLER INTELLIGENCE SCALE FOR CHILDREN—THIRD EDITION (WISC-III)

The WISC-III was published in 1991 (Wechsler 1991), replacing the WISC-R (Wechsler 1974). It is used for young people aged 6 years to

16 years 11 months. Of the items in the third edition, 27% are new. The WISC-III was standardised on a sample of 200 children in each age group (6–16 years) who were representative of the US 1988 census data (Kaufman 1993).

The WISC-III comprises ten subtests in the standard administration, with an elongated test comprising thirteen subtests, although the additional three subtest scores do not contribute to a calculation of the IQ score. Some testers administer a shortened version, using as few as four subtests, but confidence in these results has to be limited.

As with all Wechsler tests, raw scores for each of the subtests are converted to scaled scores using tables in the manual. Scaled scores have a mean (average) of 10 and a standard deviation of 3 points.

Interpretation of the Wechsler tests

The Wechsler tests are based on the assumption that there is one global ability that underlies our skill in all areas. Hence, they report an overall IQ, but results are also further divided into Performance and Verbal IQ scores. These scores, plus the pattern of subtest scores, can all be used by examiners to inform their interpretation of a child's results.

The first step after scoring each answer is to refer to tables in the manual to convert the child's scores on each subtest to what is termed a scaled score. This scaled score has an average of 10 and a standard deviation of 3 points. The next step is to total all of these scaled scores (from the compulsory subtests but omitting the results of the optional subtests) and then, using tables in the manual, converting these totals into Verbal IQs, Performance IQs and Full Scale IQs. These IQ scores have an average (mean) of 100 and a standard deviation of 15.

In addition to using these absolute scores, examiners are able to observe how the child goes about solving the tasks presented in the test. Kaufman (1979) lists some processing skills that can be investigated:

- eye–hand coordination skills;
- sequencing problems;
- recall or reasoning difficulties, in either verbal or performance tasks;
- ability to comprehend long versus short instructions;
- ability with long versus short answers;
- simultaneous or successive (sequential) processing difficulties;
- right-hemisphere or integrated brain functioning.

Score profiles and observations can also give additional clues to children's emotional wellbeing. If, for example, they attain a broad range of scores, the examiner may investigate low self-esteem as children often expect all their skills to be at the level of their highest, and are disappointed in themselves when this is not so.

The information thus gleaned from the overall test results, analysis of a child's pattern of scores and observations of the child during testing can be combined to suggest a direction for further inquiry and for the design of special programs.

The WISC-III also reports Index scores, which are calculated by totalling the scaled scores for each subtest contributing to that factor. The four factors are:

- Verbal Comprehension: comprising the Information, Similarities, Vocabulary and Comprehension subtests.
- Perceptual Organisation: including the Picture Completion, Picture Arrangement, Block Design and Object Assembly scaled scores. Sattler (1992a, 1992b) argues against including Picture Arrangement because it loads almost as heavily on verbal comprehension as on the perceptual organisation factor.
- Processing Speed: comprising Coding and the supplementary subtest, Symbol Search. (Coding's correlation with overall IQ is so low that Kaufman (1993) recommends substituting Symbol Search in the standard, 10-subtest administration.)
- Freedom from Distraction: comprising Arithmetic and the supplementary subtest, Digit Span. Sattler (1992a, 1992b), however, cites research evidence against the existence of this factor, while low scores on these subtests do not discriminate children with attention-deficit disorders, which would be expected if the factor were valid (Schwean & Saklofske 1998).

The one remaining subtest, Mazes, does not figure in any of these four factors, has a very low correlation with overall IQ and is contaminated by modern children's exposure to mazes in activity books and computer programs. So in a standard, 10-subtest administration, Mazes should be deleted and replaced with Symbol Search (Kaufman 1993, 1994).

STANFORD-BINET INTELLIGENCE SCALE—FOURTH EDITION (SB:FE)

This test covers the ages 2–23 years, although not all subtests are administered to people of all ages, with Vocabulary, Comprehension, Pattern Analysis, Quantitative, Bead Memory, and Memory for Sentences being the tests that are common to all ages.

Sattler (1988), one of the authors of the SB:FE, reports that items were reviewed by a panel of ethnic minority group members to evaluate them for biased content. The test was standardised in the US on a total of 5013 people in seventeen age groups, ranging from a minimum of 194 subjects (in the 18–23 age range) to 460 subjects (in the 5–6 age group). The sample was selected to be in line with 1980 US census data.

The SB:FE comprises fifteen separate subtests, whose results are analysed into four areas (Cohen et al. 1988). The subtests are described in the box below. Subtest scores have an average of 50 and a standard deviation of 8 points. These scores are also combined to yield a composite IQ score which has a mean of 100 and a standard deviation of 16. (The Wechsler tests have the same mean but a standard deviation of 15 points.)

The number of items in the SB:FE makes it a demanding test to learn to administer. This might account for its lesser popularity with US psychologists (Sparrow & Gurland 1998), compared with the straightforward structure of the Wechsler tests. Its complex structure also makes for a high error rate in administration, with up to two-thirds of administrators making errors on the pattern analysis subtest, for instance (Taylor 1997).

SUBTESTS OF THE STANFORD-BINET INTELLIGENCE SCALE—FOURTH EDITION (SB:FE)

The SB:FE comprises fifteen separate subtests whose results are analysed into four factors. The number of items administered in each subtest will depend on the child's age.

1. Verbal reasoning

- Vocabulary (46 items). This subtest asks children to name 14 pictured items and define 32 words that are presented orally or visually. It is used to determine the starting point or entry level for the other subtests.
- Comprehension (42 items). Items range in difficulty from identifying parts of the body to questions requiring social judgment. Items are presented orally or visually.
- Absurdities (32 items). The child must identify what is wrong or silly about a picture.
- Verbal relations (18 items). The child is given four words and has to identify what is similar about the first three and different about the fourth.

---

2. Abstract/visual reasoning

- Pattern analysis (36 items). Depending on the child's age, this subtest range from completion of formboards to reproducing complex designs with blocks.
- Copying (28 items). The young child copies designs with blocks; the older child copies them with pencil and paper.
- Matrices (26 items). The child must solve increasingly difficult matrices, selecting answers from a multiple-choice format.
- Paper folding and cutting (18 items). The child has to identify how a folded and cut piece of paper would look if it were unfolded. The child chooses from a multiple-choice menu.

3. Quantitative reasoning

- Quantitative (34 items). This involves counting and calculation.
- Number series (26 items). The child must supply the next number in a numerical sequence.
- Equation-building (18 items). The child must rearrange a scrambled arithmetic equation so that it makes sense.

4. Short-term memory

- Bead memory (42 items). The child studies a picture of a bead sequence for 5 seconds and must then reproduce it from memory by threading the beads in their correct order, shape and colours onto a stick.
- Memory for sentences (42 items). The child repeats a sentence after the examiner.
- Memory for digits (12 items). The child must listen to a series of digits and then repeat them in the same or reverse order.
- Memory for objects (14 items). The examiner shows the child familiar objects at the rate of one per second and the child has to recall the order in which they were presented.

(Note that, in comparison, the WISC-III has only one test of short-term memory, which is the Digit Span subtest.)

Sources: Cohen et al. (1988: 211); Taylor (1997).

Suitability of these tests for assessing gifted children

Because there are so few extremely gifted youngsters in the general population, all tests have built their norms on very small samples of children in the upper end of the ability range (Borland 1997). Of the 2200 children in the norming sample for the WISC-III, for instance, only 118 scored within the gifted range (Sparrow & Gurland 1998). This means that norms in the upper ability ranges are less reliable than in the middle range.

Despite these low numbers, categories of giftedness have been traditionally tied to particular IQ ranges. These are reproduced in table II.1. (Note that, in chapter 5, I endorsed Gagné's 1998 alternative classification system as it can be applied to domains other than the academic and it does not assume reliable assessment above the range of 160 IQ points.)

Table II.1 Levels of intellectual giftedness with their associated IQ scores

IQ range		Degree of giftedness	Proportion of population
Wechsler	Stanford-Binet		
125–129	127–131	Mild	1 in 20
130–144	132–147	Moderate	~1 in 50 (2.14%)
145–159	148–163	High	~1 in 1000 (0.13%)
160–179	164–179	Exceptional	1 in 10 000 (0.01%)
180+	180+	Profound	<1 in 1 000 000

Source: Gross (1993a).

WPPSI-R

Although the content of this test is suitable for younger ages, the process of sitting across an examination table from a strange adult is not typical of the tasks usually required of 3-year-olds. Particularly with gifted children, the WPPSI-R can take up to 90 minutes to administer, as bright children often complete all of the items in every subtest. Thus, because each subtest is of longer duration, gifted children need extraordinary concentration skills to complete the whole battery.

Nevertheless, when one needs an assessment of a young child's academic skills, the WPPSI-R is among the most recognised measures. It appears to be as good a predictor of abilities as its multi-dimensional competitors such as the Differential Ability Scales (DAS) (McNemar

1964). Also, the DAS is in less common use and so information from it is less easily interpreted by consumers of assessment information.

WISC-III

Although a very reliable test, the WISC-III does have a major limitation when assessing gifted children—namely, that the highest attainable full-scale IQ is 160. This means that the test can distinguish *between* gifted and average learners, but is poorer at discriminating *among* the gifted population (Burns et al. 1990; Davis & Rimm 1998; Kaufman 1992; Sparrow & Gurland 1998; Tolan 1998). This is technically called having a low ceiling and means that there are not enough difficult items on which children could demonstrate their full capacities. The result is that the WISC-III may underestimate the abilities of gifted children and adolescents.

Speed has a big impact on children's scores on the WISC-III: children over the age of 12 who are reflective or have mild coordination difficulties will actually earn below-average scores on Picture Arrangement, Block Design and Object Assembly despite perfect (but slow) execution of the tasks (Kaufman 1993).

Stanford-Binet Intelligence Scale (fourth edition)

Perhaps because of the low ceiling on the WISC-III, Gross (1993a, 1993c) comments that she prefers the SB:FE for assessing exceptionally gifted children. However, other authors do not agree: Davis and Rimm (1998) report that the SB:FE has an upper limit of 164 IQ points, which is equivalent to the WISC-III ceiling.

Given that the norms have been updated, it may now be harder to attain high scores on the SB:FE and WISC-III than it was on their earlier editions (Form LM and WISC-R) (Davis & Rimm 1998; Taylor 1997), although in more rigorous studies other researchers have found high agreement between the WISC-R and WISC-III scores (Sabatino et al. 1995). In terms of *overall* IQs, children tend to obtain similar scores on the SB:FE and WPPSI-R; while WPPSI-R *verbal* IQ scores tend to be five points lower than on the SB:FE (Taylor 1997).

Conclusion: IQ testing for gifted children

Whichever test is used, when children are achieving at very high levels, one or two answers on a subtest can make a big difference to their resulting scaled score on the subtest. In comparison, when children are achieving in the average range, an answer here or there can make less difference to a scaled score (Smutny et al. 1989). This makes the scores of children who are achieving at high levels more vulnerable to non-intellectual sources of contamination.

One of these sources of contamination is when bright children think that a simple question is a trick and so proffer an elaborate answer which, however, does not fulfil the scoring criteria (Silverman 1998a); another is when they are reluctant to get an answer wrong and so spend too long checking their work (Reams et al. 1990); or when they do not give an answer for fear that it might not be correct.

A final point to note is that gifted children show a greater spread of scores than children who achieve within normal limits (Sparrow & Gurland 1998). Overdiagnosis of learning difficulties can result from interpreting these fluctuations as atypical when in fact they are common to this group of children (Silverman 1998a).

STATISTICAL INTERPRETATION OF SCORES

If I received a score of 18 on a test, that number by itself would be meaningless. To interpret it, I would want to know whether that was 18 out of 20, or 18 out of 100! Next, I may want to know what the average score is, so that I can assess if my performance was adequate and, last, I might want to know the range of scores: is 18 one of the lowest, in the middle or near the upper end of the range? We have statistics for each of these purposes. When using these statistics to interpret an IQ score, their purpose is to determine how the child's assessed abilities compare with other children's.

Average (mean)

Calculating the average is a straightforward arithmetical procedure of totalling everyone's scores and dividing the total by the number of people assessed. When the ability being assessed has a normal distribution, half of the group achieve above the average and half below.

In the Wechsler scales, each subtest has an average of 10; in the SB:FE, each subtest has an average of 50; both tests have average Full Scale IQs of 100 points.

An average sounds like a sensible figure to use. However, there are times when it is inappropriate. The main occasion is when children have wide discrepancies among their abilities. In these instances, an averaged score might in fact not represent any of their skills. For example, if a child achieves at 50 months in two skill domains and 40 months in another two areas, the average score would be 45 months, even though none of his or her skills in fact fall at that level. To average children's scores in this way in effect subtracts their weaknesses from their strengths, thus denying both (Silverman 1998a).

When applying this awareness to the Wechsler tests, the usual practice is that when children have a more than 9-point difference between their Verbal and Performance scale scores, the two scores are not combined to yield a single IQ figure, as it could be misleading (Kaufman 1994).

Standard deviation

The standard deviation figure reflects the variability of a set of scores (Taylor 1997). I won't bore you with how it is arrived at arithmetically; all that is necessary to know is that the standard deviation tells us whether a particular child's score falls near to or a long way from the mean (average). If it is near the average, then the child is likely to be well provided for by a regular program; if the score deviates a long way from the mean, then this tells us that she or he might need some special educational provisions.

When a child's score is converted into a standard deviation, an average score obviously has a standard deviation value of zero, because the score does not depart at all from the average. Figure II.1 displays the IQ scores, standard deviations and Wechsler subtest scores and their corresponding categorical labels. It also gives proportions of the population who fall within each category. Using this diagram, you can convert any score into a category and establish how commonly that category occurs within the population.

Percentile ranks

A further type of standard score, in addition to the standard deviation, is the percentile rank (PR). This figure tells us that the child 'did as well as, or better than, x% of age mates'. However, a percentile ranking quickly becomes extreme: for instance, between zero and +1 standard deviations, the percentile ranks range from 50 to 84. This range of figures can make it seem as if a child who scores at a percentile ranking of 85 must be doing much better than one at 80, but the difference in their actual IQs might be only a point or two, which is easily accounted for by testing error or other situational factors. Therefore, I find the percentile rank misleading, especially to lay readers of assessment reports. Also, in the gifted field, once a child qualifies as being gifted, his or her score is at least above the 95th percentile, after which discriminations between each ranking become meaningless.

Figure II.1 Distribution of abilities within a population

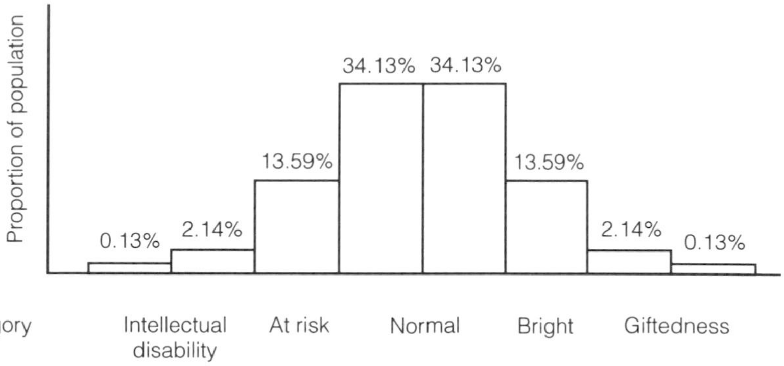

Category label	Intellectual disability	At risk	Normal		Bright	Giftedness		
Standard deviation	−4	−3	−2	−1	0	+1	+2	+3	+4
Wechsler subtest scores		1	4	7	10	13	16	19	
Wechsler full-scale IQ scores	40	55	70	85	100	115	130	145	160
Stanford-Binet IQ scores	36	52	68	84	100	116	132	148	164
Percentile ranks		0.1	2.2	16	50	84	97.7	99	

Source: Adapted from Sattler (1988: 17).

Conversion to mental age

When IQ tests were first devised, the IQ was calculated by dividing children's mental age by their chronological (actual) age and then multiplying that figure by 100:

$$IQ = \frac{\text{mental age}}{\text{actual age}} \times 100$$

When a child's mental age and actual age were the same, this yielded an average IQ of 100. This figure was called a ratio IQ. More recently, a different way of calculating IQs has superseded the ratio IQ. The new figure is called a deviation IQ and represents a comparison between the child's abilities and the normal abilities for that age. However, an IQ score can be fairly meaningless to a lay reader or to a teacher who is trying to gauge at which level a child is actually functioning. So, one way to make the IQ score easier to interpret and apply educationally is to convert the IQ to a mental age. This is done using the old ratio formula.

To give an example, if a 4-year-old child has obtained an IQ score of 140, her mental age is calculated by multiplying her chronological age by her IQ and dividing by 100 (or the equivalent is to multiply her age by her IQ%). Therefore, her mental age will be:

$$MA = CA \times IQ\%$$
$$= 48 \text{ months} \times 140\%$$
$$= 67 \text{ months (5 years 7 months)}$$

Technically, deviation IQs should not be converted in this way—that is, by using the old ratio formula. Nevertheless, putting a child's needs into more easily understood terms can help parents and teachers to anticipate what activities might be beneficial for the child, given his or her developmental level (Chamrad & Robinson 1986; Smutny et al. 1989). As with overall IQ scores, age equivalencies are insensitive to the fluctuations in the child's profiles and thus such calculations need to be interpreted cautiously and should be regarded as a rough estimate only.

BIBLIOGRAPHY

Ablard, K.E. 1997 'Self-perceptions and needs as a function of type of academic ability and gender' *Roeper Review* vol. 20, no. 2, pp. 110–16

Achter, J.A., Benbow, C.P. and Lubinski, D. 1997 'Rethinking multipotentiality among the intellectually gifted: a critical review and recommendations' *Gifted Child Quarterly* vol. 41, no. 1, pp. 5–13

Ackerman, C.M. 1997 'Identifying gifted adolescents using personality characteristics: Dabrowski's overexcitabilities' *Roeper Review* vol. 19, no. 4, pp. 229–36

Adderholdt-Elliot, M. 1992 *Perfectionism: what's bad about being too good* Hawker Brownlow Education, Melbourne

Adler, R., Rosenfeld, L. and Towne, N. 1995 *Interplay: the process of interpersonal communication* 6th edn, Harcourt Brace, Fort Worth, TX

Albert, R.S. and Runco, M.A. 1986 'The achievement of eminence: a model based on a longitudinal study of exceptionally gifted boys and their families' in *Conceptions of giftedness* eds R.J. Sternberg & J.E. Davidson, Cambridge University Press, Cambridge, UK

Alberto, P.A. and Troutman, A.C. 1999 *Applied behaviour analysis for teachers* 5th edn, Merrill, Upper Saddle River, NJ

Allan, S.D. 1991 'Ability-grouping research reviews: what do they say about grouping and the gifted?' *Educational Leadership* vol. 48, no. 6, pp. 60–5

Amabile, T.M. 1990 'Within you, without you: the social psychology of creativity, and beyond' in *Theories of creativity* eds M. Runco & R.S. Albert, Pitzer College, Claremont, CA

Amatea, E.S. 1989 *Brief strategic intervention for school behavior problems* Jossey-Bass, San Francisco, CA

Ambrose, D. 1998 'A model for clarification and expansion of conceptual foundations' *Gifted Child Quarterly* vol. 42, no. 2, pp. 77–86

American Psychiatric Association 1994 *Diagnostic and statistical manual of mental disorders* 4th edn, American Psychiatric Association, Washington, DC

Anastopoulos, A.D. and Barkley, R.A. 1992 'Attention deficit-hyperactivity disorder' in *Handbook of clinical child psychology* 2nd edn, eds C.E. Walker & M.C. Roberts, John Wiley and Sons, New York

Anderson, M. 1992 *Intelligence and development: a cognitive theory* Blackwell, London

BIBLIOGRAPHY

Anderson, R.H. 1985 'Viewpoint: teachers of gifted children' *Roeper Review* vol. 7, no. 3, pp. 137–9

Archambault, F.X. Jr, Westberg, K.L., Brown, S.W., Hallmark, B.W., Zhang, W. and Emmons, C.L. 1993 'Classroom practices used with gifted third and fourth grade students' *Journal for the Education of the Gifted* vol. 16, no. 2, pp. 103–19

Arthur, L., Beecher, B., Dockett, S., Farmer, S. and Death, E. 1996 *Programming and planning in early childhood settings* 2nd edn, Harcourt Brace, Sydney

Asher, S.R. and Gottman, J.M. (eds) 1981 *The development of children's friendships* Cambridge University Press, Cambridge, UK

Asher, S.R. and Parker, J.G. 1989 'Significance of peer relationship problems in childhood' in *Social competence in developmental perspective* eds B.H. Schneider, G. Attili, J. Nadel & R.P. Weissberg, Kluwer Academic Publishers, Dordrecht, Netherlands

Asher, S.R. and Renshaw, P.D. 1981 'Children without friends: social knowledge and social-skill training' in *The development of children's friendships* eds S.R. Asher & J.M. Gottman, Cambridge University Press, Cambridge, UK

Assouline, S.G. 1997 'Assessment of gifted children' in *Handbook of gifted education* 2nd edn, eds N. Colangelo & G.A. Davis, Allyn & Bacon, Boston, MA

Austin, A.B. and Draper, D.C. 1981 'Peer relationships of the academically gifted: a review' *Gifted Child Quarterly* vol. 25, no. 3, pp. 129–33

Bailey, D.B. and Harbin, G.L. 1980 'Nondiscriminatory evaluation' *Exceptional Children* vol. 46, no. 8, pp. 590–6

Bailey, D.B. and Leonard, J. 1977 'A model for adapting Bloom's taxonomy to a preschool curriculum for the gifted' *The Gifted Child Quarterly* vol. 21, no. 1, pp. 97–103

Bailey, D.B. and Wolery, M. 1984 *Teaching infants and preschoolers with handicaps* Merrill, Columbus, OH

Bailey, S. 1993 'Acceleration: an introduction' in *Gifted children need help?: a guide for parents and teachers* ed. D. Farmer, New South Wales Association for Gifted and Talented Children, Sydney

——1997 'Acceleration as an option for talented students' in *Parents as lifelong teachers of the gifted* eds B.A. Knight & S. Bailey, Hawker Brownlow Education, Melbourne

——1998 'Missionary zeal and surviving in the meantime' Eminent Australian address to the *7th National Conference of the Australian Association for the Education of the Gifted* June 1998, Hobart

Bailey, S., Knight, B.A. and Riley, D. 1995 *Developing children's talents: guidelines for schools* Hawker Brownlow Education, Melbourne

Baldwin, A.Y. 1993 'Teachers of the gifted' in *International handbook of research and development of giftedness and talent* eds K.A. Heller, F.J. Mönks & A.H. Passow, Pergamon Press, Oxford, UK

Balson, M. 1992 *Understanding classroom behaviour* 3rd edn, ACER, Melbourne

——1994 *Becoming better parents* 4th edn, ACER, Melbourne

Bandura, A. 1986 *Social foundations of thought and action* Prentice Hall, Englewood Cliffs, NJ

Barbour, N.B. 1992 'Early childhood gifted education: a collaborative perspective' *Journal for the Education of the Gifted* vol. 15, no. 2, pp. 145–62

Barbour, N.E. & Shaklee, B.D. 1998 'Gifted education meets Reggio Emilia: visions for curriculum in gifted education for young children' *Gifted Child Quarterly* vol. 42, no. 4, pp. 228–37

Barclay, K. and Benelli, C. 1994 'Are labels determining practice?: programming for preschool gifted children' *Childhood Education* vol. 70, no. 3, pp. 133–6

Baska, L.K. 1989 'Characteristics and needs of the gifted' in *Excellence in educating the gifted* eds J. Feldhusen, J. Van Tassel-Baska & K. Seeley, Love Publishing, Denver, CO

Baum, S. 1984 'Meeting the needs of learning disabled gifted students' *Roeper Review* vol. 7, no. 1, pp. 16–19

——1986 'The gifted preschooler: an awesome delight' *Gifted Child Today* vol. 9, no. 4, pp. 42–5

——1988 'An enrichment program for gifted learning disabled students' *Gifted Child Quarterly* vol. 32, no. 1, pp. 226–30

——1989 'Gifted but learning disabled: a puzzling paradox' *Preventing School Failure* vol. 34, no. 1, pp. 11–14

Baum, S. and Owen, S.V. 1988 'High ability/learning disabled students: how are they different' *Gifted Child Quarterly* vol. 32, no. 3, pp. 321–6

Baum, S., Emerick, L.J., Herman, G.N. and Dixon, J. 1989 'Identification, programs and enrichment strategies for gifted learning disabled youth' *Roeper Review* vol. 12, no. 1, pp. 48–53

Baum, S.M., Olenchak, F.R. and Owen, S.V. 1998 'Gifted students with attention deficits: fact and/or fiction?: or, can we see the forest for the trees?' *Gifted Child Quarterly* vol. 42, no. 2, pp. 96–104

Baum, S., Owen, S.V. and Dixon, J. 1991 *To be gifted and learning disabled: from identification to practical intervention strategies* Hawker Brownlow Education, Melbourne

Baum, S., Renzulli, J.S. and Hébert, T.P. 1994 'Reversing underachievement: stories of success' *Educational Leadership* vol. 52, no. 3, pp. 48–53

——1995 'Reversing underachievement: creative productivity as a systematic intervention' *Gifted Child Quarterly* vol. 39, no. 4, pp. 224–35

Baumrind, D. 1967 'Child care practices anteceding three patterns of preschool behavior' *Genetic Psychology Monographs* vol. 75, pp. 43–88.

Bay-Hinitz, A.K., Peterson, R.F., and Quilitch, R. 1994 'Cooperative games: a way to modify aggressive and cooperative behaviors in young children' *Journal of Applied Behavior Analysis* vol. 27, no. 3, pp. 435–46

Beck, A. 1976 *Cognitive therapy and the emotional disorders* International Universities Press, New York

Belcastro, F.P. 1987 'Elementary pull-out program for the intellectually gifted—boon or bane?' *Roeper Review* vol. 9, no. 4, pp. 208–12

Belgrad, S.F. 1998 'Creating the most enabling environment for young gifted children' in *The young gifted child: potential and promise, an anthology* ed. J.F. Smutny, Hampton Press, Cresskill, NJ

Ben Ari, R. and Rich, Y. 1992 'Meeting the educational needs of all students in the heterogeneous class' in *To be young and gifted* eds P.S. Klein & A.J. Tannenbaum, Ablex, Norwood, NJ

Benbow, C.P. 1991 'Meeting the needs of gifted students through use of acceleration' in *Handbook of special education: research and practice* eds M.C. Wang, M.C. Reynolds & H.J. Walberg, Pergamon Press, Oxford, UK

——1992 'Challenging the gifted: grouping and acceleration' *Gifted Child Quarterly* vol. 3, no. 2, p. 59

Benson, A.J. and Presbury, J.H. 1989 'The cognitive tradition in schools' in *Cognitive-behavioral psychology in the schools* eds J.N. Hughes & R.J. Hall, Guilford, New York

Bergan, J.R. and Feld, J.K. 1993 'Developmental assessment: new directions' *Young Children* vol. 48, no. 5, pp. 41–7

Berger, S.L. and McIntire, J. 1998 'Technology-based instruction for young gifted children' in *The young gifted child: potential and promise, an anthology* ed. J.F. Smutny, Hampton Press, Cresskill, NJ

Berk, L. 1997 *Child development* 4th edn, Allyn & Bacon, Boston, MA

Berk, L.E. and Landau, S. 1993 'Private speech of learning disabled and normally achieving children in classroom academic and laboratory contexts' *Child Development* vol. 64, no. 2, pp. 556–71

BIBLIOGRAPHY

Berk, L.E. and Potts, M.K. 1991 'Development and functional significance of private speech among attention-deficit hyperactivity disordered and normal boys' *Journal of Abnormal Child Psychology* vol. 19, no. 3, pp. 357–77

Bernal, E.M. 1989 '"Pluralism and power"—dare we reform education of the gifted along these lines?' in *Critical issues in gifted education: defensible programs for cultural and ethnic minorities* eds C.J. Maker & S.W. Schiever, Pro-Ed, Austin, TX

Bevan-Brown, J. 1996 'Special abilities: a Māori perspective' in *Gifted and talented: New Zealand perspectives* eds D. McAlpine & R. Moltzen, ERDC Press, Palmerston North

Birch, J.W. 1984 'Is any identification procedure necessary?' *Gifted Child Quarterly* vol. 28, no. 4, pp. 157–61

Birch, L.L., Johnson, S.L. and Fischer, J.A. 1995 'Children's eating: the development of food-acceptance patterns' *Young Children* vol. 50, no. 2, pp. 71–8

Bland, L.C., Sowa, C.J. and Callahan, C.M. 1994 'Overview of resilience in gifted children' *Roeper Review* vol. 17, no. 2, pp. 77–80

Blum, N.J. and Mercugliano, M. 1997 'Attention-deficit/hyperactivity disorder' in *Children with disabilities* 4th edn, ed. M.L. Batshaw, MacLennan and Petty, Sydney

Bogie, C.E. and Buckhalt, J.A. 1987 'Reactions to failure and success among gifted, average, and EMR students' *Gifted Child Quarterly* vol. 31, no. 2, pp. 70–2

Bolton, R. 1987 *People skills* Simon and Schuster, Sydney

Borkowski, J.G. and Peck, V.A. 1986 'Causes and consequences of metamemory in gifted children' in *Conceptions of giftedness* eds R.J. Sternberg & J.E. Davidson, Cambridge University Press, Cambridge, UK

Borland, J.H. 1978 'Teacher identification of the gifted: a new look' *Journal for the Education of the Gifted* vol. 2, no. 1, pp. 22–32

——1986a 'IQ tests: throwing out the bathwater, saving the baby' *Roeper Review* vol. 8, no. 3, pp. 163–7

——1986b 'A note on the existence of certain divergent-production abilities' *Journal for the Education of the Gifted* vol. 9, no. 4, pp. 239–51

——1990 'Postpositivist inquiry: implications of the "new philosophy of science" for the field of education of the gifted' *Gifted Child Quarterly* vol. 34, no. 4, pp. 161–7

——1996a 'Playing favorites: gifted education and the disruption of community' Roeper Review vol. 18, no. 4, pp. 309–11

——1996b 'Gifted education and the threat of irrelevance' *Journal for the Education of the Gifted* vol. 19, no. 2, pp. 129–47

——1997 'Evaluating gifted programs' in *Handbook of gifted education* 2nd edn, eds N. Colangelo & G.A. Davis, Allyn & Bacon, Boston, MA

Borland, J.H. and Wright, L. 1994 'Identifying young, potentially gifted economically disadvantaged students' *Gifted Child Quarterly* vol. 38, no. 4, pp. 164–71

Bouchard, L.L. 1991 'Mixed age groupings for gifted students' *Gifted Child Today* vol. 14, no. 5, pp. 30–5

Bowles, S. and Gintis, H. 1976 *Schooling in capitalist America* Routledge and Kegan Paul, London

Braggett, E.J. 1992 *Pathways for accelerated learners* Hawker Brownlow Education, Melbourne

——1993 'Acceleration: what, why, how and when?' in *Gifted children need help?: a guide for parents and teachers* ed. D. Farmer, New South Wales Association for Gifted and Talented Children, Sydney

——1994 *Developing programs for gifted students* Hawker Brownlow Education, Melbourne

——1997 'A developmental concept of giftedness: implications for the regular classroom' *Gifted Education International* vol. 12, no. 2, pp. 64–71

——1998a 'Gifted and talented children' in *Educating children with special needs* 3rd edn, eds A. Ashman & J. Elkins, Prentice Hall, Sydney

——1998b 'The regular classroom teacher: the weak link?' Keynote address to the

7th National Conference of the Australian Association for the Education of the Gifted June 1998, Hobart

Braggett, E.J., Day, A. and Minchin, M. 1997 *Differentiated programs for primary schools* Hawker Brownlow Education, Melbourne

Brody, L.E. and Benbow, C.P. 1986 'Social and emotional adjustment of adolescents extremely talented in verbal or mathematical reasoning' *Journal of Youth and Adolescence* vol. 15, no. 6, pp. 1–18

——1987 'Accelerative strategies: how effective are they for the gifted?' *Gifted Child Quarterly* vol. 31, no. 3, pp. 105–10

Bromfield, R. 1994 'Fast talkers: verbally precocious youth present challenges for parents and teachers' *Gifted Child Today* vol. 17, no. 2, pp. 32–3

Brooks, P.R. 1998 'Targeting potentially talented and gifted minority students for academic achievement' in *The young gifted child: potential and promise, an anthology* ed. J.F. Smutny, Hampton Press, Cresskill, NJ

Brounstein, P.J., Holahan, W. and Dreyden, J. 1991 'Change in self-concept and attributional styles among academically gifted adolescents' *Journal of Applied Social Psychology* vol. 21, no. 3, pp. 198–218

Brown, B. 1986 'We can help children to be self-reliant' *Children Today* Jan-Feb, pp. 26–8

Brown, S.W. 1984 'The use of WISC-R subtest scatter in the identification of intellectually gifted handicapped children: an inappropriate task?' *Roeper Review* vol. 7, no. 1, pp. 20–3

Bryant, M.A. 1987 'Meeting the needs of gifted first grade children in a heterogeneous classroom' *Roeper Review* vol. 9, no. 4, pp. 214–16

Buescher, T.M. 1985 'A framework for understanding the social and emotional development of gifted and talented adolescents' *Roeper Review* vol. 8, no. 1, pp. 10–15

Bullock, J.R. 1993 'Lonely children' *Young Children* vol. 48, no. 6, pp. 53–7

Burns, J.M., Mathews, F.N. and Mason, A. 1990 'Essential steps in screening and identifying preschool gifted children' *Gifted Child Quarterly* vol. 34, no. 3, pp. 102–7

Burns, R.B. 1982 *Self-concept development and education* Holt, Rhinehart & Winston, London

Burton-Szabo, S. 1996 'Gifted classes for gifted students?: absolutely' *Gifted Child Today* vol. 19, no. 1, pp. 12–15; 50

Butler-Por, N. 1993 'Underachieving gifted students' in *International handbook of research and development of giftedness and talent* eds K.A. Heller, F.J. Mönks & A.H. Passow, Pergamon Press, Oxford, UK

Butterworth, D. 1991 'The challenge of day care: liberation or constraint?' *Australian Journal of Early Childhood* vol. 16, no. 2, pp. 20–3

Cahan, S. and Gejman, A. 1993 'Constancy of IQ scores among gifted children' *Roeper Review* vol. 15, no. 3, pp. 140–3

Callahan, C.M. 1991 'An update on gifted females' *Journal for the Education of the Gifted* vol. 14, no. 2, pp. 284–311

——1996 'A critical self-study of gifted education: healthy practice, necessary evil, or sedition?' *Journal for the Education of the Gifted* vol. 19, no. 2, pp. 148–63

Callahan, C.M., Cunningham, C.M. and Plucker, J.A. 1994 'Foundations for the future: the socio-emotional development of gifted, adolescent women' *Roeper Review* vol. 17, no. 2, pp. 99–105

Cameron, J. and Pierce, W.D. 1994 'Reinforcement, reward, and intrinsic motivation: a meta-analysis' *Review of Educational Research* vol. 64, no. 3, pp. 363–423

——1996 'The debate about rewards and intrinsic motivation: protests and accusations do not alter the results' *Review of Educational Research* vol. 66, no. 1, pp. 39–51

Carey, M. 1994 'New fashioned apartheid?' *Education Links* no. 47, pp. 18–22

Carr, M., Alexander, J. and Schwanenflugel, P. 1995 'Where gifted children do and do not excel on metacognitive tasks' *Roeper Review* vol. 18, no. 3, pp. 212–17

Carr, M. and Borkowski, J.G. 1987 'Metamemory in gifted children' *Gifted Child Quarterly* vol. 31, no. 1, pp. 40–4

Carter, K.R. 1986 'Evaluating the consequences of participating in a gifted pullout program' *Journal for the Education of the Gifted* vol. 9, no. 4, pp. 265–75

Carter, K.R. and Hamilton, W. 1985 'Formative evaluation of gifted programs: a process and a model' *Gifted Child Quarterly* vol. 29, no. 1, pp. 5–11

Casey, J.P. and Quisenberry, N.L. 1976 'A review of the research related to giftedness in early childhood education' in *Gifted children: looking to their future* eds J. Gibson & P. Chennells, Latimer, London

Cathcart, R. 1996 'Educational provisions: an overview' in *Gifted and talented: New Zealand perspectives* eds D. McAlpine & R. Moltzen, ERDC Press, Palmerston North

Chamrad, D.L. and Robinson, N.M. 1986 'Parenting the intellectually gifted preschool child' *Topics in Early Childhood Special Education* vol. 6, no. 1, pp. 74–87

Chamrad, D.L., Robinson, N.M. and Janos, P.M. 1995 'Consequences of having a gifted sibling: myths and realities' *Gifted Child Quarterly* vol. 39, no. 3, pp. 135–45

Chapman, J.W., Lambourne, R. and Silva, P.A. 1990 'Some antecedents of academic self-concept: a longitudinal study' *British Journal of Educational Psychology* vol. 60, part 1, pp. 142–52

Chapman, J.W. and McAlpine, D.D. 1988 'Students' perceptions of ability' *Gifted Child Quarterly* vol. 32, no. 1, pp. 222–5

Chan, L.K.S. 1988 'The perceived competence of intellectually talented students' *Gifted Child Quarterly* vol. 32, no. 3, pp. 310–14

——1996 'Motivational orientations and metacognitive abilities of intellectually gifted students' *Gifted Child Quarterly* vol. 40, no. 4, pp. 184–94

Charles, C.M. 1996 *Building classroom discipline: from models to practice* 5th edn, Longman, New York

Cheng, P-W. 1993 'Metacognition and giftedness: the state of the relationship' *Gifted Child Quarterly* vol. 37, no. 3, pp. 105–12

Chitwood, D.G. 1986 'Guiding parents seeking testing' *Roeper Review* vol. 8, no. 3, pp. 177–9

——1992 'Recognizing giftedness in early childhood settings' in *Alike and different: exploring our humanity with young children* (rev. edn) ed. A. Neugebauer, National Association for the Education of Young Children, Washington, DC

Christie, W. 1995 'Let their minds stretch: flexibility of options for gifted learners: a practitioner's perspective' *Gifted and Talented International* vol. 10, no. 2, pp. 61–6

Chyriwsky, M. & Kennard, R. 1997 'Attitudes to able children: a survey of mathematics teachers in English secondary schools' *High Ability Studies* vol. 8, no. 1, pp. 47–59

Ciha, T.E., Harris, R., Hoffman, C. and Potter, M.W. 1974 'Parents as identifiers of giftedness, ignored but accurate' *Gifted Child Quarterly* vol. 18, no. 3, pp. 191–5

Clarizio, H.F. and Mehrens, W.A. 1985 'Psychometric limitations of Guilford's structure-of-intellect model for identification and programming for the gifted' *Gifted Child Quarterly* vol. 29, no. 3, pp. 113–20

Clark, B. 1997 *Growing up gifted* 5th edn, Merrill, Upper Saddle River, NJ

Clark, W.H. and Hankins, N.E. 1985 'Giftedness and conflict' *Roeper Review* vol. 8, no. 1, pp. 50–3

Clasen, D.R. and Clasen, R.E. 1995 'Underachievement of highly able students and peer society' *Gifted and Talented International* vol. 10, no. 2, pp. 67–76

Clements, C., Lundell, F. and Hishinuma, E.S. 1994 'Serving the gifted dyslexic and gifted at risk' *Gifted Child Today* vol. 17, no. 4, pp. 12–14; 16–17; 36–7

Cohen, L.M. 1987 'Thirteen tips for teaching gifted students' *Teaching Exceptional Children* vol. 20, no. 1, pp. 34–8

——1989 'Understanding the interests and themes of the very young gifted child' *Gifted Child Today* vol. 12, no. 4, pp. 6–9

——1998 'Facilitating the interest themes of young bright children' in *The young gifted child: potential and promise, an anthology* ed. J.F. Smutny, Hampton Press, Cresskill, NJ

Cohen, R., Duncan, M. and Cohen, S. L. 1994 'Classroom peer relations of children participating in a pull-out enrichment program' *Gifted Child Quarterly* vol. 38, no. 1, pp. 33–7

Cohen, R.J., Montague, P., Nathanson, L.S. and Swerdlik, M.E. 1988 *Psychological testing: an introduction to tests and measurement* Mayfield, Mountain View, CA

Colangelo, N. 1985 'Counseling needs of culturally diverse gifted students' *Roeper Review* vol. 8, no. 1, pp. 33–5

——1997 'Counselling gifted students: issues and practices' in *Handbook of gifted education* 2nd edn, eds N. Colangelo & G.A. Davis, Allyn & Bacon, Boston

Colangelo, N. and Brower, P. 1987 'Labelling gifted youngsters: long-term impact on families' *Gifted Child Quarterly* vol. 31, no. 2, pp. 75–8

Colangelo, N. and Davis, G.A. 1997 'Introduction and overview' *Handbook of gifted education* 2nd edn, eds N. Colangelo & G.A. Davis, Allyn & Bacon, Boston, MA

Colangelo, N. and Dettman, D.F. 1983 'A review of research on parents and families of gifted children' *Exceptional Children* vol. 50, no. 1, pp. 20–7

Coleman, J.M. and Fults, B.A. 1982 'Self-concept and the gifted classroom: the role of social comparison' *Gifted Child Quarterly* vol. 26, no. 3, pp. 116–20

Coleman, L.J. 1994 'Portfolio assessment: a key to identifying hidden talents and empowering teachers of young children' *Gifted Child Quarterly* vol. 38, no. 2, pp. 65–9

——1995 'The power of specialized educational environments in the development of giftedness: the need for research on social context' *Gifted Child Quarterly* vol. 39, no. 3, pp. 171–6

Coleman, L.J. and Cross, T.L. 1988 'Is being gifted a social handicap?' *Journal for the Education of the Gifted* vol. 11, no. 4, pp. 41–56

Coleman, L.J., Sanders, M.D. and Cross, T.L. 1997 'Perennial debates and tacit assumptions in the education of gifted children' *Gifted Child Quarterly* vol. 41, no. 3, pp. 105–11

Compas, B.E. 1987 'Coping with stress during childhood and adolescence' *Psychological Bulletin* vol. 101, no. 3, pp. 393–403

Cook, R.E., Tessier, A. and Klein, M.D. 1996 *Adapting early childhood curricula for children in inclusive settings* 4th edn, Merrill, Englewood Cliffs, NJ

Cooper, C.R. 1990 'Ten mandates for gifted education in the 1990s: let's resolve the issues and move on' in *The challenges of excellence: a vision splendid: selected papers from the 8th World Conference on Gifted and Talented children* eds S. Bailey, E. Braggett & M. Robinson Australian Association for the Education of the Gifted and Talented, Wagga Wagga, NSW

Cooper, C.S. and McEvoy, M.A. 1996 'Group friendship activities: an easy way to develop the social skills of young children' *Teaching Exceptional Children* vol. 28, no. 3, pp. 67–9

Corey, G. 1996 *Theory and practice of counseling and psychotherapy* 5th edn, Brooks/Cole, Monterey, CA

Cornell, D.G. 1989 'Child adjustment and parent use of the term "gifted"' *Gifted Child Quarterly* vol. 33, no. 2, pp. 59–64

Cornell, D.G., Delcourt, M.A.B., Bland, L.C., Goldberg, M.D. and Oram, G. 1994 'Low incidence of behavior problems among elementary school students in gifted programs' *Journal for the Education of the Gifted* vol. 18, no. 1, pp. 4–19

Cornell, D.G. and Grossberg, I.N. 1986 'Siblings of children in gifted programs' *Journal for the Education of the Gifted* vol. 9, no. 4, pp. 253–64

——1987 'Family environment and personality adjustment in gifted program children' *Gifted Child Quarterly* vol. 31, no. 2, pp. 59–64

Corrigan, S.Z. 1994 'For the sake of the children' *Gifted Child Today* vol. 17, no. 2, pp. 22–3; 30; 41

Cowin, M., Freeman, L., Farmer, A., James, M., Drent, A. and Arthur, R. 1990 *Positive school discipline: a practical guide to developing policy* rev. edn Narbethong Publications, Boronia, VIC

Cramond, B. and Martin, C.E. 1987 'Inservice and preservice teachers' attitudes toward the academically brilliant' *Gifted Child Quarterly* vol. 31, no. 1, pp. 15–19

Craven, R.G. and Marsh, H.W. 1997 'Threats to gifted and talented students' self-concepts in the big pond: research results and educational implications' *The Australasian Journal of Gifted Education* vol. 6, no. 2, pp. 7–17

Creel, C.S. and Karnes, F.A. 1988 'Parental expectancies and young gifted children' *Roeper Review* vol. 11, no. 1, pp. 48–50

Cropley, A. 1997 'Creativity: a bundle of paradoxes' *Gifted and Talented International* vol. 12, no. 1, pp. 8–14

Cropper, C. 1998 'Is competition an effective classroom tool for the gifted student?' *Gifted Child Today* vol. 21, no. 3, pp. 28–31

Cross, T.L., Coleman, L.J. and Stewart, R.A. 1992 'The social cognition of gifted adolescents: an exploration of the stigma of giftedness paradigm' *Roeper Review* vol. 16, no. 1, pp. 37–40

Cross, T.L., Coleman, L.J. and Terhaar-Yonkers, M. 1991 'The social cognition of gifted adolescents in schools: managing the stigma of giftedness' *Journal for the Education of the Gifted* vol. 15, no. 1, pp. 44–55

Cruickshank, W.M. 1977 'Myths and realities in learning disabilities' *Journal of Learning Disabilities* vol. 10, no. 1, pp. 51–8

Csikszentmihályi, M. 1991 'Commentary' *Human Development* vol. 34, pp. 32–4

Csikszentmihályi, M. and Robinson, R.E. 1986 'Culture, time and the development of talent' in *Conceptions of giftedness* eds R.J. Sternberg & J.E. Davidson, Cambridge University Press, Cambridge, UK

Culross, R.R. 1995 'Counselling the gifted: taking an active role in the achievement of highly able students' *Gifted Child Today* vol. 18, no. 1, pp. 36–7; 40–1

Curry, N.E. and Johnson, C.N. 1990 *Beyond self-esteem: developing a genuine sense of human value* National Association for the Education of Young Children, Washington, DC

Czeschlik, T. and Rost, D.H. 1994 'Socio-emotional adjustment in elementary school boys and girls: does giftedness make a difference?' *Roeper Review* vol. 16, no. 4, pp. 294–7

Damiani, V.B. 1997 'Young gifted children in research and practice: the need for early childhood programs' *Gifted Child Today* vol. 20, no. 3, pp. 18–23

Dangel, H.L. and Walker, J.J. 1991 'An assessment of the needs of parents of gifted students for parent education programs' *Roeper Review* vol. 14, no. 1, pp. 40–1

Dauber, S.L. and Benbow, C.P. 1990 'Aspects of personality and peer relations of extremely talented adolescents' *Gifted Child Quarterly* vol. 34, no. 1, pp. 10–14

Davis, G.A. and Rimm, S.B. 1998 *Education of the gifted and talented* 4th edn, Allyn & Bacon, Boston, MA

de Shazer, S. and Molnar, A. 1984 'Four useful interventions in brief family therapy' *Journal of Marital and Family Therapy* vol. 10, no. 3, pp. 297–304

de Shazer, S., Berg, I.K., Lipchik, E., Nunnally, E., Molnar, A., Gingerich, W. and Weiner-Davis, M. 1986 'Brief therapy: focused solution development' *Family Process* vol. 25, no. 2, pp. 207–22

Delisle, J.R. 1992 *Guiding the social and emotional development of gifted youth* Longman, New York

——1994a 'The top ten statements that should never again be made by advocates of gifted children' *Gifted Child Today* vol. 17, no. 2, pp. 34–5; 42

——1994b 'Dealing with the stereotype of underachievement' *Gifted Child Today* vol. 17, no. 6, pp. 20–1

——1994c 'The inclusion movement is here—good . . . it's about time' *Gifted Child Today* vol. 17, no. 4, pp. 30–1

——1998 'Gifted girls: who's limiting whom?' *Gifted Child Today* vol. 21, no. 4, pp. 20–1

Dengate, S. 1997 'Dietary management of attention deficit disorder' *Australian Journal of Early Childhood* vol. 22, no. 4, pp. 29–33

Denton, C. & Postlethwaite, K. 1984 'A study of the effectiveness of teacher-based identification of pupils with high ability in the secondary school' *Gifted Education International* vol. 2, no. 2, pp. 100–6

Department of Education and Children's Services (DECS) 1990 *Guidelines for policy development* Department of Education and Children's Services, Adelaide

——1996 *Foundation areas of learning* Department of Education and Children's Services, Adelaide

Derevensky, J. and Coleman, E.B. 1989 'Gifted children's fears' *Gifted Child Quarterly* vol. 33, no. 2, pp. 65–8

Diaz, E.I. 1998 'Perceived factors influencing the academic underachievement of talented students of Puerto Rican descent' *Gifted Child Quarterly* vol. 42, no. 2, pp. 105–22

Diaz, R.M. and Berk, L.E. 1995 'A Vygotskian critique of self-instructional training' *Development and Psychopathology* vol. 7, no. 2, pp. 369–92

Dickey, J.P. and Henderson, P. 1989 'What young children say about stress and coping in school' *Health Education* Feb/March, pp. 14–17

Diezman, C.M. and Watters, J.J. 1997 'Bright but bored: optimising the environment for gifted children' *Australian Journal of Early Childhood* vol. 22, no. 2, pp. 17–21

Dinkmeyer, D. and McKay, G. 1989 *Systematic training for effective parenting* 3rd edn, American Guidance Service, Minneapolis, MN

Dinkmeyer, D., McKay, G. and Dinkmeyer, D. 1980 *Systematic training for effective teaching* American Guidance Service, Minneapolis, MN

Dix, J. and Schafer, S. 1996 'From paradox to performance: practical strategies for identifying and teaching GT/LD students' *Gifted Child Today* vol. 19, no. 1, pp. 22–4; 28–9

Dobson, K.S. and Pusch, D. 1993 'Towards a definition of the conceptual and empirical boundaries of cognitive therapy' *Australian Psychologist* vol. 28, no. 3, pp. 137–44

Dowdall, C.B. and Colangelo, N. 1982 'Underachieving gifted students: review and implications' *Gifted Child Quarterly* vol. 26, no. 4, pp. 179–84

Doyle, W. 1986 'Classroom organization and management' in *Handbook of research on teaching* 3rd edn, ed. M.C. Wittrock, Macmillan, New York

Durrant, M. 1995 *Creative strategies for school problems* Eastwood Family Therapy Centre, Sydney

Dyck, M.J. 1993 'New directions in cognitive-behaviour therapy' *Australian Psychologist* vol. 28, no. 3, pp. 133–6

Eales, C. and de Paoli, W. 1991 'Early entry and advanced placement of talented students in primary and secondary schools' *Gifted Education International* vol. 7, no. 3, pp. 140–4

Ebert, E.S. 1994 'The cognitive spiral: creative thinking and cognitive processing' *Journal of Creative Behaviour* vol. 28, no. 4, pp. 275–90

Eisenberger, R. and Armeli, S. 1997 'Can salient reward increase creative performance without reducing intrinsic creative interest?' *Journal of Personality and Social Psychology* vol. 72, no. 3, pp. 652–63

Elkind, D. 1988 'Acceleration' *Young Children* vol. 43, no. 4, p. 2

Ellston, T. 1993 'Gifted and learning disabled: a paradox?' *Gifted Child Today* vol. 16, no. 1, pp. 17–19

BIBLIOGRAPHY

Elmore, R.F. and Zenus, V. 1994 'Enhancing social-emotional development of middle school gifted students' *Roeper Review* vol. 16, no. 3, pp. 182–5

Emerick, L.J. 1992 'Academic underachievement among the gifted: students' perceptions of factors that reverse the pattern' *Gifted Child Quarterly* vol. 36, no. 3, pp. 140–6

Evans, K. 1993 'Multicultural counseling' in *Counseling the gifted and talented* ed. L.K. Silverman, Love Publishing, Denver, CO

Eyre, D. 1997 *Able children in ordinary schools* David Fulton, London

Eysenck, H.J. 1986 'The biological basis of intelligence' in *Giftedness: a continuing worldwide challenge* eds K.K. Urban, H. Wagner & W. Wieczerkowski, Trillium Press, New York

Fall, J. and Nolan, L. 1993 'A paradox of exceptionalities' *Gifted Child Today* vol. 16, no. 1, pp. 46–9

Fallen, N. and Umansky, W. 1985 *Young children with special needs* 2nd edn, Merrill, Columbus, OH

Farmer, S. 1995 *Policy development in early childhood services* Community Child Care Cooperative Ltd, Sydney

Fatouros, C. 1986 'Early identification of gifted children is crucial . . . but how should we go about it?' *Gifted Education International* vol. 4, no. 1, pp. 24–8

Feiring, C., Louis, B., Ukeje, I., Lewis, M. and Leong, P. 1997 'Early identification of gifted minority kindergarten students in Newark, NJ' *Gifted Child Quarterly* vol. 41, no. 3, pp. 76–82

Feldhusen, J.F. 1985 'The teacher of gifted students' *Gifted Education International* vol. 3, no. 2, pp. 87–93

——1986 'A conception of giftedness' in *Conceptions of giftedness* eds R.J. Sternberg & J.E. Davidson, Cambridge University Press, Cambridge, UK

——1989 'Synthesis of research on gifted youths' *Educational Leadership* vol. 46, no. 6, pp. 6–11

——1992 'Early admission and grade advancement for young gifted learners' *Gifted Child Today* vol. 15, no. 2, pp. 45–9

——1996 'Talent as an alternative conception of giftedness' *Gifted Education International* vol. 11, no. 3, pp. 124–7

——1997 'Educating teachers for work with talented youth' in *Handbook of gifted education* 2nd edn, eds N. Colangelo & G.A. Davis, Allyn & Bacon, Boston, MA

Feldhusen, J.F. and Baska, L.K. 1989 'Identification and assessment of the gifted' in *Excellence in educating the gifted* eds J. Feldhusen, J. Van Tassel-Baska & K. Seeley, Love Publishing, Denver, CO

Feldhusen, J.F. and Hoover, S.M. 1984 'The gifted at risk in a place called school' *Gifted Child Quarterly* vol. 28, no. 1, pp. 9–11

——1986 'A conception of giftedness: intelligence, self concept and motivation' *Roeper Review* vol. 8, no. 3, pp. 140–3

Feldhusen, J.F. and Kroll, M.D. 1991 'Boredom or challenge for the academically talented in school' *Gifted Education International* vol. 7, no. 2, pp. 80–1

Feldhusen, J.F. and Moon, S.M. 1992 'Grouping gifted students: issues and concerns' *Gifted Child Quarterly* vol. 36, no. 2, pp. 63–7

Feldhusen, J.F. and Nimlos-Hippen, A.L. 1992 'An exploratory study of self concepts and depression among the gifted' *Gifted Education International* vol. 8, no. 3, pp. 136–8

Feldhusen, J.F., Sayler, M.F., Nielson, M.E. and Kolloff, P.B. 1990 'Self-concepts of gifted children in enrichment programs' *Journal for the Education of the Gifted* vol. 13, no. 4, pp. 380–7

Feldhusen, J.F., Van Winkle, L., and Ehle, D.A. 1996 'Is it acceleration or simply appropriate instruction for precocious youth?' *Teaching Exceptional Children* vol. 28, no. 3, pp. 48–51

Feldman, D.H. 1984 'A follow-up of subjects scoring above 180 IQ in Terman's "Genetic studies of genius" ' *Exceptional Children* vol. 50, no. 6, pp. 518–23

——1993 'Child prodigies: a distinctive form of giftedness' *Gifted Child Quarterly* vol. 37, no. 4, pp. 188–93

Feldman, D.H. and Benjamin, A.C. 1986 'Giftedness as a developmentalist sees it' in *Conceptions of giftedness* eds R.J. Sternberg & J.E. Davidson, Cambridge University Press, Cambridge, UK

Fiedler, E.D., Lange, R.E. and Winebrenner, S. 1993 'In search of reality: unraveling the myths about tracking, ability grouping and the gifted' *Roeper Review* vol. 16, no. 1, pp. 4–7

Field, T. 1991 'Quality infant day-care and grade school behavior and performance' *Child Development* vol. 62, no. 4, pp. 863–70

Fields, M.V. and Boesser, C. 1998 *Constructive guidance and discipline: preschool and primary education* 2nd edn, Merrill, Upper Saddle River, NJ

Finch, M. and Hops, H. 1983 'Remediation of social withdrawal in young children: considerations for the practitioner' in *Social skills training for children and youth* ed. C.W. LeCroy, Haworth Press, New York

Fine, M.J. and Pitts, R. 1980 'Intervention with underachieving gifted children: rationale and strategies' *Gifted Child Quarterly* vol. 24, no. 2 pp. 51–5

Fisch, R., Weakland, J.H. and Segal, L. 1982 *The tactics of change: doing therapy briefly* Jossey-Bass, San Francisco, CA

Fisher, E. 1981 'The effect of labelling on gifted children and their families' *Roeper Review* vol. 3, no. 3, pp. 49–51

Fitzgerald, J. and Keown, R. 1996 'Gifted and talented females' in *Gifted and talented: New Zealand perspectives* eds D. McAlpine & R. Moltzen, ERDC Press, Palmerston North

Fontana, D. 1985 *Classroom control* British Psychological Press and Methuen, London

Ford, D.Y., Russo, C.J. and Harris, J.J. III 1993 'The quest for equity in gifted education' *Gifted Child Today* vol. 16, no. 6, pp. 8–11

Ford, M.A. 1989 'Students' perceptions of affective issues impacting the social emotional development and school performance of gifted/talented youngsters' *Roeper Review* vol. 11, no. 3, pp. 131–4

Fowler, W., Ogston, K., Roberts-Fiati, G. and Swenson, A. 1995 'Patterns of giftedness and high competence in high school students educationally enriched during infancy: variation across educational racial/ethnic backgrounds' *Gifted and Talented International* vol. 10, no. 1, pp. 31–6

Fox, A.M. and Rieder, M.J. 1993 'Risks and benefits of drugs used in the management of the hyperactive child' *Drug Safety* vol. 9, no. 1, pp. 38–50

Fox, L.H. 1984 'The learning-disabled gifted child' *Learning Disabilities* vol. 8, no. 10, pp. 117–28

Fraser, N. 1996 'Parenting' in *Gifted and talented: New Zealand perspectives* eds D. McAlpine & R. Moltzen, ERDC Press, Palmerston North

Frasier, M.M. 1989 'Poor and minority students can be gifted too!' *Educational Leadership* vol. 46, no. 6, pp. 16–18

——1993 'Issues, problems and programs in nurturing the disadvantaged and culturally different talented' in *International handbook of research and development of giftedness and talent* eds K.A. Heller, F.J. Mönks & A.H. Passow, Pergamon Press, Oxford, UK

——1997 'Gifted minority students: reframing approaches to their identification and education' in *Handbook of gifted education* 2nd edn, eds N. Colangelo & G.A. Davis, Allyn & Bacon, Boston, MA

Freeman, J. 1983 'Emotional problems of the gifted child' *Journal of Child Psychology and Psychiatry and Related Disciplines* vol. 24, no. 3, pp. 481–5

——1991 *Gifted children growing up* Cassell, London

——1993 'Parents and families in nurturing giftedness and talent' in *International handbook of research and development of giftedness and talent* eds K.A. Heller, F.J. Mönks & A.H. Passow, Pergamon Press, Oxford, UK

——1994 'Some emotional aspects of being gifted' *Journal for the Education of the Gifted* vol. 17, no. 2, pp. 180–97

——1995a 'Review of current thinking on the development of talent' *Actualizing talent: a lifelong challenge* eds J. Freeman, P. Span & H. Wagner, Cassell, London

——1995b 'Annotation: recent studies of giftedness in children' *Journal of Child Psychology and Psychiatry* vol. 36, no. 4, pp. 531–47

——1995c 'Toward a policy for actualizing talent' in *Actualizing talent: a lifelong challenge* eds J. Freeman, P. Span & H. Wagner, Cassell, London

——1996 *Highly able girls and boys* Department for Education and Employment, London

——1997 'The emotional development of the highly able' *European Journal of Psychology of Education* vol. 12, no. 4, pp. 479–93

——1998a *Educating the very able: current international research* Office for Standards in Education, London

——1998b 'Mentoring gifted pupils' in *Mentoring and tutoring by students* ed. S. Goodlad, Sterling, London

Frosh, S. 1983 'Children and teachers in schools' in *Developments in social skills training* eds S. Spence & G. Shepherd, Academic Press, London

Fuchs-Beauchamp, K.D., Karnes, M.B. and Johnson, L.J. 1993 'Creativity and intelligence in preschoolers' *Gifted Child Quarterly* vol. 37, no. 3, pp. 113–17

Furman, R.A. 1995 'Helping children cope with stress and deal with feelings' *Young Children* vol. 50, no. 2, pp. 33–41

Gagné, F. 1991 'Toward a differentiated model of giftedness and talent' in *Handbook of gifted education* eds N. Colangelo & G.A. Davis, Allyn & Bacon, Boston, MA

——1994 'Are teachers really poor talent detectors?: comments on Pegnato and Birch's (1959) study of the effectiveness and efficiency of various identification techniques' *Gifted Child Quarterly* vol. 38, no. 3, pp. 124–6

——1995 'From giftedness to talent: A developmental model and its impact on the language of the field' *Roeper Review* vol. 18, no. 2, pp. 103–11

——1997 'Critique of Morelock's (1996) definitions of giftedness and talent' *Roeper Review* vol. 20, no. 2, pp. 76–85

——1998 'A proposal for subcategories within gifted or talented populations' *Gifted Child Quarterly* vol. 42, no. 2, pp. 87–95

Galbraith, J. 1985 'The eight great gripes of gifted kids: responding to special needs' *Roeper Review* vol. 8, no. 1, pp. 15–18

Gallagher, J.J. 1988 'National agenda for educating gifted students: statement of priorities' *Exceptional Children* vol. 55, no. 2, pp. 107–14

——1991a 'Personal patterns of underachievement' *Journal for the Education of the Gifted* vol. 14, no. 3, pp. 221–33

——1991b 'Educational reform, values, and gifted students' *Gifted Child Quarterly* vol. 35, no. 1, pp. 12–19

——1996 'A critique of critiques of gifted education' *Journal for the Education of the Gifted* vol. 19, no. 2, pp. 234–49

——1997 'Issues in the education of gifted students' in *Handbook of gifted education* 2nd edn, eds N. Colangelo & G.A. Davis, Allyn & Bacon, Boston, MA

——1998 'Accountability for gifted students' *Phi Delta Kappan* vol. 79, no. 10, pp. 739–42

Gallagher, J.J. and Gallagher, S.A. 1994 *Teaching the gifted child* 4th edn, Allyn & Bacon, Boston, MA

Gallagher, J., Harradine, C.C. and Coleman, M.R. 1997 'Challenge or boredom?: gifted students' views on their schooling' *Roeper Review* vol. 19, no. 3, pp. 132–6

Gallagher, J.J. and Moss, J.W. 1963 'New concepts of intelligence and their effect on exceptional children' *Exceptional Children* Sept, pp. 1–5

Gallucci, N.T. 1988 'Emotional adjustment of gifted children' *Gifted Child Quarterly* vol. 32, no. 2, pp. 273–6

Gamoran, A. 1992 'Is ability grouping equitable?' *Educational Leadership* vol. 50, no. 2, pp. 11–17

Gardner, H. 1983 *Frames of mind: the theory of multiple intelligences* Basic Books, New York

——1995 'Reflections on multiple intelligences: myths and messages' *Phi Delta Kappan* vol. 77, no. 3, pp. 200–9

Gartrell, D. 1994 *A guidance approach to discipline* Delmar, New York

Geake, J. 1997 'Thinking as evolution in the brain: implications for giftedness' *The Australasian Journal of Gifted Education* vol. 6, no. 1, pp. 27–33

Gear, G.H. 1976 'Accuracy of teacher judgement in identifying intellectually gifted children: a review of the literature' *Gifted Child Quarterly* vol. 20, no. 4, pp. 478–90

——1978 'Effects of training in teachers' accuracy in identifying gifted children' *Gifted Child Quarterly* vol. 22, no. 1, pp. 90–7

Gelbrich, J.A. 1998 'Identifying the gifted infant' in *The young gifted child: potential and promise, an anthology* ed. J.F. Smutny, Hampton Press, Cresskill, NJ

Geldard, K. and Geldard, D. 1997 *Counselling children: a practical introduction* Sage, London

Gibson, K. 1997 'Identification issues' in *Parents as lifelong teachers of the gifted* eds B.A. Knight & S. Bailey, Hawker Brownlow Education, Melbourne

——1998 'A promising approach for identifying gifted Aboriginal students in Australia' *Gifted Education International* vol. 13, no. 1, pp. 73–88

Gillman, J. and Hansen, H. 1987 'Gifted education in Minnesota kindergartens' *Roeper Review* vol. 9, no. 4, pp. 212–14

Ginott, H. 1972 *Teacher and child* Macmillan, New York

Glasser, W. 1977 'Ten steps to good discipline' *Today's Education* vol. 66, pp. 61–3

——1986 *Control theory in the classroom* Harper & Row, New York

——1992 *The quality school* 2nd edn, Harper & Row, New York

Goldstein, M. and Goldstein, S. 1995 'Medications and behavior in the classroom' in *Understanding and managing children's classroom behavior* ed. S. Goldstein, John Wiley & Sons, New York

Goldstein, S. 1995 'Attention deficit hyperactivity disorder' in *Understanding and managing children's classroom behavior* ed. S. Goldstein, John Wiley & Sons, New York

Goodman, S.H., Brumley, H.E., Schwartz, K.R. and Purcell, D.W. 1993 'Gender and age in the relation between stress and children's school adjustment' *Journal of Early Adolescence* vol. 13, no. 3, pp. 329–45

Gordon, T. 1970 *Parent effectiveness training* Plume, New York

——1974 *Teacher effectiveness training* Peter H. Wyden, New York

——1991 *Teaching children self-discipline at home and at school* Random House, Sydney

Gould, S.J. 1981 *The mismeasure of man* W.W. Norton, New York

Greenberg, P. 1992a 'Why not academic preschool? (part 2): autocracy or democracy in the classroom?' *Young Children* vol. 47, no. 3, pp. 54–64

——1992b 'Ideas that work with young children: how to institute some simple democratic practices pertaining to respect, rights, roots and responsibilities in any classroom (without losing your leadership position)' *Young Children* vol. 47, no. 5, pp. 10–17

Grenier, M.E. 1985 'Gifted children and other siblings' *Gifted Child Quarterly* vol. 29, no. 4, pp. 164–7

Grigorenko, E.L. and Sternberg, R.J. 1997 'Styles of thinking, abilities and academic performance' *Exceptional Children* vol. 63, no. 3, pp. 295–312

Grinder, R.E. 1985 'The gifted in our midst: by their divine deeds, neuroses, and mental test scores we have known them' in *The gifted and talented: developmental perspectives* eds F.D. Horowitz & M. O'Brien, American Psychological Association, Washington, DC

Gross, M.U.M. 1992 'The use of radical acceleration in cases of extreme intellectual precocity' *Gifted Child Quarterly* vol. 36, no. 2, pp. 91–9

——1993a *Exceptionally gifted children* Routledge, London

——1993b 'The use of radical acceleration in cases of extreme intellectual precocity' in *Gifted children need help?: a guide for parents and teachers* ed. D. Farmer, New South Wales Association for Gifted and Talented Children, Sydney

——1993c 'Nurturing the talents of exceptionally gifted individuals' in *International handbook of research and development of giftedness and talent* eds K.A. Heller, F.J. Mönks & A.H. Passow, Pergamon Press, Oxford, UK

——1996 'The pursuit of excellence or the search for intimacy: the forced-choice dilemma for gifted youth' in *Gifted children: the challenge continues: a guide for parents and teachers* eds A. Jacob & G. Barnsley, New South Wales Association for Gifted and Talented Children, Sydney

——1997 'How ability grouping turns big fish into little fish—or does it?: of optical illusions and optimal environments' *The Australasian Journal of Gifted Education* vol. 6, no. 2, pp. 18–30

——1998 'Fishing for the facts: a response to Craven and Marsh (1998)' *The Australasian Journal of Gifted Education* vol. 7, no. 1, pp. 16–28

Gross, M.U.M. and Start, K.B. 1990 ' "Not waving, but drowning": the exceptionally gifted child in Australia' in *The challenges of excellence: a vision splendid: selected papers from the 8th World Conference on Gifted and Talented Children* eds S. Bailey, E. Braggett & M. Robinson, Australian Association for the Education of the Gifted and Talented, Wagga Wagga, NSW

Grossberg, I.N. and Cornell, D.G. 1988 'Relationship between personality adjustment and high intelligence: Terman versus Hollingworth' *Exceptional Children* vol. 55, no. 3, pp. 266–72

Gruber, H.E. 1986 'The self-construction of the extraordinary' in *Conceptions of giftedness* eds R.J. Sternberg & J.E. Davidson, Cambridge University Press, Cambridge, UK

Guilford, A.M., Scheuerle, J. and Shonburn, S. 1981 'Aspects of language development in the gifted' *Gifted Child Quarterly* vol. 25, no. 4, pp. 159–63

Guilford, J.P. 1959 'Three faces of intellect' *American Psychologist* vol. 14, no. 8, pp. 469–79

Gunderson, C.W., Maesch, C. and Rees, J.W. 1987 'The gifted/learning disabled student' *Gifted Child Quarterly* vol. 31, no. 4, pp. 158–60

Guskin, S.L., Peng, C.J. and Majd-Jabbari, M. 1988 'Teachers' perceptions of giftedness' *Gifted Child Quarterly* vol. 32, no. 1, pp. 216–21

Gust, K. 1997 'Is the literature on social and emotional needs empirically based?' *Gifted Child Today* vol. 20, no. 3, pp. 12–13

Hackney, H. 1981 'The gifted child, the family, and the school' *Gifted Child Quarterly* vol. 25, no. 2, pp. 51–4

Hadaway, N. and Marek-Schroer, M.F. 1992 'Multidimensional assessment of the gifted minority student' *Roeper Review* vol. 15, no. 2, pp. 73–7

Haensly, P.A. and Reynolds, C.R. 1989 'Creativity and intelligence' in *Handbook of creativity* eds J.A. Glover, R.R. Ronning & C.R. Reynolds, Plenum Press, New York

Haensly, P.A., Reynolds, C.R. and Nash, W.R. 1986 'Giftedness: coalescence, context, conflict, and commitment' in *Conceptions of giftedness* eds R.J. Sternberg & J.E. Davidson, Cambridge University Press, Cambridge, UK

Haladyna, T., Haas, N. and Allison, J. 1998 'Continuing tensions in standardized testing' *Childhood Education* vol. 74, no. 5, pp. 262–73

Hall, E.G. 1993 'Educating preschool gifted children' *Gifted Child Today* vol. 16, no. 3, pp. 24–7

Hall, J.M. 1994 'Schooling concerns of gifted children' *Gifted* August, 1994, pp. 7–10

Hallinan, M.T. 1990 'The effects of ability grouping in secondary schools: a response to Slavin's best-evidence synthesis' *Review of Educational Research* vol. 60, no. 3, pp. 501–4

Hannah, C.L. and Shore, B.M. 1995 'Metacognition and high intellectual ability: insights from the study of learning-disabled gifted students' *Gifted Child Quarterly* vol. 39, no. 2, pp. 95–109

Hanninen, G.E. 1998 'Designing a preschool program for the gifted and talented' in *The young gifted child: potential and promise, an anthology* ed. J.F. Smutny, Hampton Press, Cresskill, NJ

Hansen, J.B. and Feldhusen, J.F. 1994 'Comparison of trained and untrained teachers of gifted students' *Gifted Child Quarterly* vol. 38, no. 3, pp. 115–21

Hansen, J.B. and Linden, K.W. 1990 'Selecting instruments for identifying gifted and talented students' *Roeper Review* vol. 13, no. 1, pp. 10–15

Hany, E.A. 1993 'How teachers identify gifted students: feature processing or concept based classification' *European Journal for High Ability* vol. 4, pp. 196–211

Harrison, C. 1995 *Giftedness in early childhood* KU Children's Services, Sydney

Harrison, C. and Tegel, K. 1999 'Play and the gifted child' in *Child's play: revisiting play in early childhood settings* ed. E. Dau, MacLennan & Petty, Sydney

Harrison, J. 1996 *Understanding children: towards responsive relationships* 2nd edn, ACER, Melbourne

Harslett, M. 1996 'The concept of giftedness from an aboriginal cultural perspective' *Gifted Education International* vol. 11, no. 2, pp. 100–6

Hart, E.L., Lahey, B.B., Loeber, R., Applegate, B. and Frick, P.J. 1995 'Developmental change in attention-deficit hyperactivity in boys: a four-year longitudinal study' *Journal of Abnormal Child Psychology* vol. 23, no. 6, pp. 729–49

Hartup, W.W. 1979 'Peer relations and social competence' in *Social competence in children* eds M.W. Kent & J.E. Rolf, University Press of New England, Hanover, NH

Hastorf, A.H. 1997 'Lewis Terman's longitudinal study of the intellectually gifted: early research, recent investigations and the future' *Gifted and Talented International* vol. 12, no. 1, pp. 3–7

Hatch, T.C. and Gardner, H. 1986 'From testing intelligence to assessing competences: a pluralistic view of intellect' *Roeper Review* vol. 8, no. 3, pp. 147–50

Hay, I. 1993 'Motivation, self-perception and gifted students' *Gifted Education International* vol. 9, no. 1, pp. 16–21

Heacox, D. 1991 *Up from under-achievement: how teachers, students and parents can work together to promote student success* Hawker Brownlow Education, Melbourne

Hebert, E.A. 1992 'Portfolios invite reflection—from students and staff' *Educational Leadership* vol. 49, no. 8, pp. 58–61

Hébert, T.P. 1996 'Portraits of resilience: the urban life experience of gifted Latino young men' *Roeper Review* vol. 19, no. 2, pp. 82–90

Heinbokel, A. 1997 'Acceleration through grade skipping in Germany' *High Ability Studies* vol. 8, no. 1, pp. 61–77

Heller, K.A., Mönks, F.J. and Passow, A.H. (eds) 1993 *International handbook of research and development of giftedness and talent* Pergamon Press, Oxford, UK

Henriques, M.E. 1997 'Increasing literacy among kindergartners through cross-age training' *Young Children* vol. 52, no. 4, pp. 42–7

Hensel, N.H. 1990 'Developing leadership and prosocial behaviours in young gifted children' in *The challenges of excellence: a vision splendid: selected papers from the 8th World Conference on Gifted and Talented Children* eds S. Bailey, E. Braggett & M. Robinson, Australian Association for the Education of the Gifted and Talented, Wagga Wagga, NSW

——1991 'Social leadership skills in young children' *Roeper Review* vol. 14, no. 1, pp. 4–6

BIBLIOGRAPHY

Herbert, M. 1987 *Behavioural treatment of children with problems: a practice manual* 2nd edn, Academic Press, London

Herman, J.L. and Winters, L. 1994 'Portfolio research: a slim collection' *Educational Leadership* vol. 52, no. 2, pp. 48–55

Hershey, M. and Oliver, E. 1988 'The effects of the label gifted on students identified for special programs' *Roeper Review* vol. 11, no. 1, pp. 33–4

Hertzog, N.B. 1998 'Open-ended activities: differentiation through learner responses' *Gifted Child Quarterly* vol. 42, no. 4, pp. 212–27

Hess, L.L. 1994 'Life, liberty and the pursuit of perfection' *Gifted Child Today* vol. 17, no. 3, pp. 28–31

Hickson, J. 1992 'A framework for guidance and counseling of the gifted in a school setting' *Gifted Education International* vol. 8, no. 2, pp. 93–103

Hill, S. 1992 *Games that work: cooperative games and activities for the primary school classroom* Eleanor Curtin, Melbourne

Hill, S. and Hill, T. 1990 *The collaborative classroom: a guide to cooperative learning* Eleanor Curtin, Melbourne

Hill, S. and Reed, K. 1989 'Promoting social competence at preschool: the implementation of a cooperative games programme' *Australian Journal of Early Childhood* vol. 14, no. 4, pp. 25–31

Hinshaw, S.P. and Erhardt, D. 1991 'Attention-deficit hyperactivity disorder' in *Child and adolescent therapy: cognitive-behavioral procedures* ed. P.C. Kendall, Guilford, New York

Hishinuma, E.S. 1993 'Counseling gifted/at risk and gifted/dyslexic youngsters' *Gifted Child Today* vol. 16, no. 1, pp. 30–3

——1996 'Motivating the gifted underachiever: implementing reward menus and behavioral contracts within an integrated approach' *Gifted Child Today* vol. 19, no. 4, pp. 30–6; 43–8

Hishinuma, E. and Tadaki, S. 1996 'Addressing diversity of the gifted/at risk: characteristics for identification' *Gifted Child Today* vol. 19, no. 5, pp. 20–5; 28–9; 45; 50

Hitz, R. and Driscoll, A. 1988 'Praise or encouragement? New insights into praise: implications for early childhood teachers' *Young Children* vol. 43, no. 5, pp. 6–13

Hoge, R.D. and McSheffrey, R. 1991 'An investigation of self-concept in gifted children' *Exceptional Children* vol. 57, no. 3, pp. 238–45

Hoge, R.D. and Renzulli, J.S. 1993 'Exploring the link between giftedness and self-concept' *Review of Educational Research* vol. 63, no. 4, pp. 449–65

Holahan, C.K. 1996 'Lifetime achievement among the Terman gifted women' *Gifted and Talented International* vol. 11, no. 2, pp. 65–71

Holden, B. 1996 'Educational provisions: early childhood' in *Gifted and talented: New Zealand perspectives* eds D. McAlpine & R. Moltzen, ERDC Press, Palmerston North

Honig, A.S. 1986a 'Stress and coping in children (Part 1)' *Young Children* vol. 41, no. 4, pp. 50–63

——1986b 'Stress and coping in children (Part 2)' *Young Children* vol. 41, no. 5, pp. 47–59

Hooper, S.R. and Edmondson, R. 1998 'Assessment of young children: standards, stages and approaches' in *Young children with special needs* 3rd edn, eds W. Umansky & S.R. Hooper, Merrill, Upper Saddle River, NJ

Hops, H. and Lewin, L. 1984 'Peer sociometric forms' in *Child behavioral assessments* eds T.H. Ollendick & M. Hersen, Pergamon Press, New York

Horowitz, F.D. 1987 'A developmental view of giftedness' *Gifted Child Quarterly* vol. 31, no. 4, pp. 165–8

——1992 'A developmental view on the early identification of the gifted' in *To be young and gifted* eds P.S. Klein & A.J. Tannenbaum, Ablex, Norwood, NJ

Howard-Hamilton, M. and Franks, B.A. 1995 'Gifted adolescents: psychological behaviors, values and developmental implications' *Roeper Review* vol. 17, no. 3, pp. 186–91

Humphrey, J.H. and Humphrey, J.N. 1985 *Controlling stress in children* Charles C. Thomas, Chicago, IL

Hunsaker, S.L. 1994 'Creativity as a characteristic of giftedness: teachers see it, then they don't' *Roeper Review* vol. 17, no. 1, pp. 11–15

Hunsaker, S.L., Finley, V.S. and Frank, E.L. 1997 'An analysis of teacher nominations and student performance in gifted programs' *Gifted Child Quarterly* vol. 41, no. 2, pp. 19–24

Irvine, D. 1987 'What research doesn't show about gifted dropouts' *Educational Leadership* vol. 44, no. 6, pp. 79–80

——1991 'Gifted education without a state mandate: the importance of vigorous advocacy' *Gifted Child Quarterly* vol. 35, no. 4, pp. 196–9

Jackson, N.E. 1992 'Precocious reading of English: origins, structure, and predictive significance' in *To be young and gifted* eds P.S. Klein & A.J. Tannenbaum, Ablex, Norwood, NJ

Jackson, N.E. and Butterfield, E.C. 1986 'A conception of giftedness designed to promote research' in *Conceptions of giftedness* eds R.J. Sternberg & J.E. Davidson, Cambridge University Press, Cambridge, UK

Jacobs, H.H. and Borland, J.H. 1986 'The interdisciplinary concept model: theory and practice' *Gifted Child Quarterly* vol. 30, no. 4, pp. 159–63

Jacobs, J.C. 1971 'Effectiveness of teacher and parent identification of gifted children as a function of school level' *Psychology in the Schools* vol. 8, no. 2, pp. 140–2

Jacobs, J.E. and Weisz, V. 1992 'Gender stereotypes: implications for gifted education' *Roeper Review* vol. 16, no. 3, pp. 152–5

James, J.E. 1993 'Cognitive-behavioural theory: an alternative conception' *Australian Psychologist* vol. 28, no. 3, pp. 151–5

Janos, P.M. 1987 'A fifty-year follow-up of Terman's youngest college students and IQ-matched agemates' *Gifted Child Quarterly* vol. 31, no. 2, pp. 55–8

Janos, P.M., Marwood, K.A. and Robinson, N.M. 1985 'Friendship patterns in highly intelligent children' *Roeper Review* vol. 8, no. 1, pp. 46–53

Janos, P.M. and Robinson, N.M. 1985 'Psychosocial development in intellectually gifted children' in *The gifted and talented: developmental perspectives* eds F.D. Horowitz & M. O'Brien, American Psychological Association, Washington, DC

Jarrell, R.H. and Borland, J.H. 1990 'The research base for Renzulli's three-ring conception of giftedness' *Journal for the Education of the Gifted* vol. 13, no. 4, pp. 288–308

Jausovec, N. 1997 'Differences in EEG alpha activity between gifted and non-identified individuals: insights into problem solving' *Gifted Child Quarterly* vol. 41, no. 1, pp. 26–31

Jenkins-Friedman, R. 1982 'Myth: cosmetic use of multiple selection criteria!' *Gifted Child Quarterly* vol. 26, no. 1, pp. 24–6

Jenkins-Friedman, R. and Murphy, D.L. 1988 'The Mary Poppins effect: relationships between gifted students' self-concept and adjustment' *Roeper Review* vol. 11, no. 1, pp. 26–30

Johnsen, S., Ryser, G. and Dougherty, E. 1993 'The validity of product portfolios in the identification of gifted students' *Gifted International* vol. 8, no. 1, pp. 43–7

Johnson, D.W. and Johnson, R.T. 1991 *Learning together and alone* 3rd edn, Allyn & Bacon, Boston, MA

Johnson, D.W., Johnson, R.T. and Holubec, E.J. 1990 *Circles of learning: cooperation in the classroom* 3rd edn, Interaction Books, Minneapolis, MN

Johnson, L.J., Karnes, M.B. and Carr, V.W. 1997 'Providing services to children with gifts and disabilities: a critical need' in *Handbook of gifted education* 2nd edn, eds N. Colangelo & G.A. Davis, Allyn & Bacon, Boston, MA

Jones, K. and Day, J.D. 1996 'Cognitive similarities between academically and socially gifted students' *Roeper Review* vol. 18, no. 4, pp. 270–3

Jones, V.F. and Jones, L.S. 1995 *Comprehensive classroom management: creating positive learning environments for all students* 4th edn, Allyn & Bacon, Boston, MA

Joyce, B.R. 1991 'Common misconceptions about cooperative learning and gifted students: a response to Allan' *Educational Leadership* vol. 48, no. 6, pp. 72–4

Kammer, P.P. 1986 'Attribution for academic successes and failures of students participating and not participating in programs for the gifted' *Journal for the Education of the Gifted* vol. 9, no. 2, pp. 123–31

Kanevsky, L. 1992 'The learning game' in *To be young and gifted* eds P.S. Klein & A.J. Tannenbaum, Ablex, Norwood, NJ

——1994 'A comparative study of children's learning in the zone of proximal development' *European Journal for High Ability* vol. 5, pp. 163–75

Karnes, M.B. and Johnson, L.J. 1991 'The preschool/primary gifted child' *Journal for the Education of the Gifted* vol. 14, no. 3, pp. 267–83

Karnes, F.A. and Wherry, J.N. 1981 'Self-concepts of gifted students as measured by the Piers-Harris children's self-concept scale' *Psychological Reports* vol. 49, no. 1, pp. 903–6

Karnes, M.B., Shwedel, A.M. and Kemp, P.B. 1985 'Preschool: programming for the young gifted child: maximising the potential of the young gifted child' *Roeper Review* vol. 7, no. 4, pp. 204–9

Katz, L.G. 1988 'What should children be doing?' *Rattler* Spring 1988, pp. 4–6

——1995 *Talks with teachers of young children* Ablex, Norwood, NJ

Katz, L.G., Evangelou, D. and Hartman, J.A. 1990 *The case for mixed-age grouping in early education* National Association for the Education of Young Children, Washington, DC

Kaufman, A.S. 1990 'The WPPSI-R: you can't judge a test by its colors' *Journal of School Psychology* vol. 28, pp. 387–94

——1992 'Evaluation of the WISC-III and WPPSI-R for gifted children' *Roeper Review* vol. 14, no. 3, pp. 154–8

——1993 'King WISC the third assumes the throne' *Journal of School Psychology* vol. 31, pp. 345–54

——1994 *Intelligent testing with the WISC-III* John Wiley & Sons, New York

Kaufman, A.S. and Harrison, P.L. 1986 'Intelligence tests and gifted assessment: what are the positives?' *Roeper Review* vol. 8, no. 3, pp. 154–9

Keirouz, K.S. 1990 'Concerns of parents of gifted children: a research review' *Gifted Child Quarterly* vol. 34, no. 2, pp. 56–63

Kelly, A. 1988 'Gender differences in teacher–pupil interactions: a meta-analytic view' *Research in Education* vol. 39, pp. 1–23

Kelly, K.R. and Moon, S.M. 1998 'Personal and social talents' *Phi Delta Kappan* vol. 79, no. 10, pp. 743–6

Kelly, R. & Colangelo, N. 1984 'Academic and social self-concepts of gifted, general, and special students' *Exceptional Children* vol. 50, no. 6, pp. 551–4

Kendall, P. (ed.) 1991 *Child and adolescent therapy: cognitive-behavioral procedures* Guilford, New York

Kerr, B.A. 1985 'Smart girls, gifted women: special guidance concerns' *Roeper Review* vol. 8, no. 1, pp. 30–3

——1996 *Smart girls two: a new psychology of girls, women and giftedness* Hawker Brownlow Education, Melbourne

——1997 'Developing talents in girls and young women' in *Handbook of gifted education* 2nd edn, eds N. Colangelo & G.A. Davis, Allyn & Bacon, Boston

Kerr, B., Colangelo, N. and Gaeth, J. 1988 'Gifted adolescents' attitudes towards their giftedness' *Gifted Child Quarterly* vol. 32, no. 2, pp. 245–7

Kerr, M. and Nelson, M. 1998 *Strategies for managing behaviour problems in the classroom* 3rd edn, Merrill, Columbus, OH

Kerry, T. & Kerry, C. 1997 'Teaching the more able: primary and secondary practice compared' *Education Today* vol. 47, no. 3, pp. 11–16

Khatena, J. 1992 *Gifted: challenge and response for education* F.E. Peacock, Chicago, IL

Kingore, B. 1995 'Portfolios for young children' *Understanding Our Gifted* vol. 7, no. 3, pp. 1; 10–13

Kitano, M. 1982 'Young gifted children: strategies for preschool teachers' *Young Children* vol. 37, no. 4, pp. 14–24

——1985 'Ethnography of a preschool for the gifted: what gifted young children actually do' *Gifted Child Quarterly* vol. 29, no. 2, pp. 67–71

——1986 'Counseling gifted preschoolers' *Gifted Child Today* vol. 9, no. 4, pp. 20–5

——1990a 'A developmental model for identifying and serving young gifted children' *Early Child Development and Care* vol. 63, pp. 19–31

——1990b 'Intellectual abilities and psychological intensities in young children: implications for the gifted' *Roeper Review* vol. 13, no. 1, pp. 5–10

Kitano, M. and Perez, R.I. 1998 'Developing the potential of young gifted children from low-income and culturally and linguistically diverse backgrounds' in *The young gifted child: potential and promise, an anthology* ed. J.F. Smutny, Hampton Press, Cresskill, NJ

Klein, A.G. and Zehms, D. 1996 'Self-concept and gifted girls: a cross sectional study of intellectually gifted females in grades 3, 5, 8' *Roeper Review* vol. 19, no. 1, pp. 30–4

Klein, P.S. 1992 'Mediating the cognitive, social, and aesthetic development of precocious young children' in *To be young and gifted* eds P.S. Klein & A.J. Tannenbaum, Ablex, Norwood, NJ

Kline, B.E. and Meckstroth, E.A. 1985 'Understanding and encouraging the exceptionally gifted' *Roeper Review* vol. 8, no. 1, pp. 24–30

Kline, B.E. and Short, E.B. 1990 'Gender differences: a research review of social and emotional considerations' in *The challenges of excellence: a vision splendid: selected papers from the 8th World Conference on Gifted and Talented children* eds S. Bailey, E. Braggett & M. Robinson, Australian Association for the Education of the Gifted and Talented, Wagga Wagga, NSW

——1991 'Changes in emotional resilience: gifted adolescent females' *Roeper Review* vol. 13, no. 3, pp. 118–21

Kline, P. 1991 *Intelligence: the psychometric view* Routledge, London

Knight, B.A. 1995 'The influence of locus of control on gifted and talented students' *Gifted Education International* vol. 11, no. 1, pp. 31–3

Knight, B.A. and Bailey, S. (eds) 1997 *Parents as lifelong teachers of the gifted* Hawker Brownlow Education, Melbourne

Knight, B.A., Knight, C. and Brown, T. 1997 'Using computers to develop children's talents' in *Parents as lifelong teachers of the gifted* eds B.A. Knight & S. Bailey, Hawker Brownlow Education, Melbourne

Knight, T. 1991 'Democratic schooling: basis for a school code of behaviour' in *Classroom discipline* eds M.N. Lovegrove & R. Lewis, Longman Cheshire, Melbourne

Knopper, D. 1998 'Social/emotional considerations in young gifted children' in *The young gifted child: potential and promise, an anthology* ed. J.F. Smutny, Hampton Press, Cresskill, NJ

Kohler, F.W. and Strain, P.S. 1993 'The early childhood social skills program' *Teaching Exceptional Children* vol. 25, no. 2, pp. 41–2

Kohn, A. 1996 'By all available means: Cameron and Pierce's defense of extrinsic motivators' *Review of Educational Research* vol. 66, no. 1, pp. 1–4

Kolloff, P.B. and Moore, A.D. 1989 'Effects of summer programs on the self-concepts of gifted children' *Journal for the Education of the Gifted* vol. 12, no. 4, pp. 268–76

Kontos, S. and Wilcox-Herzog, A. 1997 'Teachers' interactions with children: why are they so important?' *Young Children* vol. 52, no. 2, pp. 4–12

Konza, D. 1997 'Developing an affective curriculum: programming for the social/emotional needs of gifted students' *The Australasian Journal of Gifted Education* vol. 6, no. 1, pp. 5–10

Krechevsky, M., Hoerr, T. and Gardner, H. 1995 'Complementary energies: implementing MI theory from the laboratory and from the field' in *Creating new educational communities* eds J. Oakes & K.H. Quartz, National Society for the Study of Education, Chicago, IL

Kulik, J.A. and Kulik, C-L.C. 1982 'Research synthesis on ability grouping' *Educational Leadership* vol. 39, no. 8, pp. 619–21

——1984 'Synthesis of research on effects of accelerated instruction' *Educational Leadership* vol. 42, no. 2, pp. 84–9

——1992 'Meta-analytic findings on grouping programs' *Gifted Child Quarterly* vol. 36, no. 2, pp. 73–7

——1997 'Ability grouping' in *Handbook of gifted education* 2nd edn, eds N. Colangelo & G.A. Davis, Allyn & Bacon, Boston, MA

Kunkel, M.A., Chapa, B., Patterson, G. and Walling, D.D. 1992 'Experience of giftedness: "Eight great gripes" six years later' *Roeper Review* vol. 15, no. 1, pp. 10–14

——1995 'The experience of giftedness: a concept map' *Gifted Child Quarterly* vol. 39, no. 3, pp. 126–34

Ladd, G.W. and Mize, J. 1983 'Social skills training and assessment with children: a cognitive-social learning approach' in *Social skills training for children and youth* ed. C.W. LeCroy, Haworth Press, New York

Lajoie, S.P. and Shore, B.M. 1981 'Three myths?: the over-representation of the gifted among dropouts, delinquents and suicides' *Gifted Child Quarterly* vol. 25, no. 3, pp. 138–43

——1986 'Intelligence: the speed and accuracy tradeoff in high aptitude individuals' *Journal for the Education of the Gifted* vol. 9, no. 2, pp. 85–104

Lambert, B. 1990 'Hyperactivity: a review of research' *Australian Journal of Early Childhood* vol. 15, no. 2, pp. 43–8

Landau, E.. Weissler, K. and Golod, G. 1996 'Motivation and giftedness' *Gifted Education International* vol. 11, no. 3, pp. 139–42

Lando, B.Z. and Schneider, B.H. 1997 'Intellectual contributions and mutual support among developmentally advanced children in homogeneous and heterogeneous work/discussion groups' *Gifted Child Quarterly* vol. 41, no. 2, pp. 44–57

Langrehr, J. 1995 *Becoming a better thinker* North Brighton, VIC

Laycock, F. 1979 *Gifted children* Scott, Foresman & Co., Glenview, IL

Lea-Wood, S.S. and Clunies-Ross, G. 1995 'Self-esteem of gifted adolescent girls in Australian schools' *Roeper Review* vol. 17, no. 3, pp. 195–7

Lee, C. 1993 'Cognitive theory and therapy: distinguishing psychology from ideology' *Australian Psychologist* vol. 28, no. 3, pp. 156–60

Lehman, E.B. and Erdwins, C.J. 1981 'The social and emotional adjustment of young, intellectually-gifted children' *Gifted Child Quarterly* vol. 25, no. 3, pp. 134–7

Lepping, M.R., Keavney, M. and Drake, M. 1996 'Intrinsic motivation and extrinsic rewards: a commentary on Cameron and Pierce's meta-analysis' *Review of Educational Research* vol. 66, no. 1, pp. 5–32

Leroux, J.A. 1988 'Voices from the classroom: academic and social self-concepts of gifted adolescents' *Journal for the Education of the Gifted* vol. 11, no. 3, pp. 3–18

LeVine, E.S. and Kitano, M.K. 1998 'Helping young gifted children reclaim their strengths' in *The young gifted child: potential and promise, an anthology* ed. J.F. Smutny, Hampton Press, Cresskill, NJ

LeVine, E.S. and Tucker, S. 1986 'Emotional needs of gifted children: a preliminary, phenomenological view' *The Creative Child and Adult Quarterly* vol. 11, no. 3, pp. 156–65

Levy, F. 1993 'Side effects of stimulant use' *Journal of Paediatric Child Health* vol. 29, pp. 250–4

Lewis, M. and Louis, B. 1991 'Young gifted children' in *Handbook of gifted education* eds N. Colangelo & G.A. Davis, Allyn & Bacon, Boston, MA

Lewis, R.B., Kitano, M.K. and Lynch, E.W. 1992 'Psychological intensities in gifted adults' *Roeper Review* vol. 15, no. 1, pp. 25–31

Li, A.K.F. and Adamson, G. 1992 'Gifted secondary students' preferred learning style: cooperative, competitive, or individualistic?' *Journal for the Education of the Gifted* vol. 16, no. 1, pp. 46–54

Lloyd, L. 1997 'Multi-age classes: an option for all students?' *The Australasian Journal of Gifted Education* vol. 6, no. 1, pp. 11–20

Loeb, R.C. and Jay, G. 1987 'Self-concept in gifted children: differential impact in boys and girls' *Gifted Child Quarterly* vol. 31, no. 1, pp. 9–14

Louis, B. and Lewis, M. 1992 'Parental beliefs about giftedness in young children and their relation to actual ability level' *Gifted Child Quarterly* vol. 36, no. 1, pp. 27–31

Lovecky, D.V. 1992 'Exploring social and emotional aspects of giftedness in children' *Roeper Review* vol. 15, no. 1, pp. 18–25

——1993 'The quest for meaning: counseling issues with gifted children and adolescents' in *Counseling the gifted and talented* ed. L.K. Silverman, Love Publishing, Denver, CO

——1994a 'Exceptionally gifted children: different minds' *Roeper Review* vol. 17, no. 2, pp. 116–20

——1994b 'The moral gifted child in a violent world' *Understanding our gifted* vol. 6, no. 3, p. 3

Lowrie, T. 1998 'Developing metacognitive thinking in young children: a case study' *Gifted Education International* vol. 13, no. 1, pp. 23–7

Lubinski, D., Benbow, C.P. and Sanders, C.E. 1993 'Reconceptualizing gender differences in achievement among the gifted' in *International handbook of research and development of giftedness and talent* eds K.A. Heller, F.J. Mönks & A.H. Passow, Pergamon Press, Oxford, UK

Luftig, R.L. and Nichols, M.L. 1990 'Assessing the social status of gifted students by their age peers' *Gifted Child Quarterly* vol. 34, no. 3, pp. 111–15

——1991 'An assessment of the social status and perceived personality and school traits of gifted students by non-gifted peers' *Roeper Review* vol. 13, no. 3, pp. 148–53

Lupowski, A.E. 1984 'Gifted students in rural schools do not *have* to move to the city' *Roeper Review* vol. 7, no. 1, pp. 13–16

Luthar, S.S. and Zigler, E. 1991 'Vulnerability and competence: a review of the research on resilience in childhood' *American Journal of Orthopsychiatry* vol. 6, pp. 6–22

Luthar, S.S., Zigler, E. and Goldstein, D. 1992 'Psychosocial adjustment among intellectually gifted adolescents: the role of cognitivedevelopmental and experiential factors' *Journal of Child Psychology and Psychiatry and Related Disciplines* vol. 33, no. 1, pp. 361–73

Lynd-Stevenson, R.M. and Herne, C.M. in press 'Perfectionism and depressive affect: the pros and cons of being a perfectionist' *Personality and Individual Differences*

McAlpine, D. 1996 'Who are the gifted and talented?: concepts and definitions' in *Gifted and talented: New Zealand perspectives* eds D. McAlpine & R. Moltzen, ERDC Press, Palmerston North

McBride, N. 1992 'Early identification of the gifted and talented students: where do teachers stand?' *Gifted Education International* vol. 8, no. 1, pp. 19–22

McCaslin, M. and Good, T.L. 1992 'Compliant cognition: the misalliance of management and instructional goals in current school reform' *Educational Researcher* vol. 21, no. 3, pp. 4–17

McClelland, R., Yewchuk, C. and Mulcahy, R. 1991 'Locus of control in underachieving and achieving gifted students' *Journal for the Education of the Gifted* vol. 14, no. 4, pp. 380–92

McCluskey, K.W., Baker, P.A. and Massey, K.J. 1996 'A twenty-four year longitudinal look at early entrance to kindergarten' *Gifted and Talented International* vol. 11, no. 2, pp. 72–5

McCord, J. 1993 'Conduct disorder and antisocial behaviour: some thoughts about processes' *Development and Psychopathology* vol. 5, pp. 321–9

McCormick, L. and Schiefelbusch, R. 1984 *Early language intervention: an introduction* Merrill, Columbus, OH

McKenzie, J.A. 1986 'The influence of identification practices, race and SES on the identification of gifted students' *Gifted Child Quarterly* vol. 30, no. 2, pp. 93–5

McLoughlin, J.A. and Lewis, R.B. 1994 *Assessing special students* 4th edn, Merrill, New York

McNemar, Q. 1964 'Lost: our intelligence? Why?' *American Psychologist* vol. 19, no. 12, pp. 871–82

Maddux, C.D., Scheiber, L.M. and Bass, J.E. 1982 'Self-concept and social distance in gifted children' *Gifted Child Quarterly* vol. 26, no. 2, pp. 77–81

Maker, C.J. 1996 'Identification of gifted minority students: a national problem, needed changes and a promising solution' *Gifted Child Quarterly* vol. 40, no. 1, pp. 41–50

Maker, C.J. and Nielson, A.B. 1995 *Teaching models in education of the gifted* 2nd edn, Pro-Ed, Austin, TX

Maker, C.J. and Schiever, S.W. 1989 'Purpose and organization of the volume' in *Critical issues in gifted education: defensible programs for cultural and ethnic minorities* eds C.J. Maker & S.W. Schiever, Pro-Ed, Austin, TX

Manaster, G.J. and Powell, P.M. 1988 'A framework for understanding gifted adolescents' psychological maladjustment' *Roeper Review* vol. 6, no. 1, pp 70–3

Manaster, G.J., Chan, J.C., Watt, C. and Wiehe, J. 1994 'Gifted adolescents' attitudes toward their giftedness: a partial replication' *Gifted Child Quarterly* vol. 38, no. 4, pp. 176–8

Manning, B.H., Glasner, S.E. and Smith, E.R. 1996 'The self-regulated learning aspect of metacognition: a component of gifted education' *Roeper Review* vol. 18, no. 3, pp. 217–23

Mares, L. 1991 *Young gifted children* Hawker Brownlow Education, Melbourne

——1997 'Personality characteristics and achievement: how parents can help' in *Parents as lifelong teachers of the gifted* eds B.A. Knight & S. Bailey, Hawker Brownlow Education, Melbourne

Mares, L. and Byles, J. 1994 *One step ahead: early admission of, and school provisions for, gifted infants* Hawker Brownlow Education, Melbourne

Marsh, H.W. and Craven, R.G. 1998 'The big fish little pond effect, optimal illusions, and misinterpretations: a response to Gross (1997)' *The Australasian Journal of Gifted Education* vol. 7, no. 1, pp. 6–15

Marsh, H.W., Chessor, D., Craven, R. and Roche, L. 1995 'The effects of gifted and talented programs on academic self-concept: the big fish strikes again' *American Educational Research Journal* vol. 32, no. 2, pp. 285–319

Martinsen, Ø. 1997 'The construct of cognitive style and its implications for creativity' *High Ability Studies* vol 8, no. 2, pp. 135–58

Mason, D.A. and Burns, R.B. 1996 ' "Simply no worse and simply no better" may simply be wrong: a critique of Veenman's conclusion about multigrade classes' *Review of Educational Research* vol. 66, no. 3, pp. 307–22

Masten, W.G. 1985 'Identification of gifted minority students: past research, future directions' *Roeper Review* vol. 8, no. 2, pp. 83–5

Matthews, D. 1988 'Gardner's multiple intelligence theory: an evaluation of relevant research literature and a consideration of its application to gifted education' *Roeper Review* vol. 11, no. 2, pp. 100–4

Matthews, M. 1992 'Gifted students talk about cooperative learning' *Educational Leadership* vol. 50, no. 2, pp. 48–50

Matthews, M.R. 1980 *The Marxist theory of schooling* Harvester Press, Sussex

Meador, K. 1996 'Meeting the needs of young gifted students' *Childhood Education* vol. 72, no. 5, pp. 6–9

Meininger, L. 1998 'Curriculum for the young gifted child' in *The young gifted child: potential and promise, an anthology* ed. J.F. Smutny, Hampton Press, Cresskill, NJ

Melson, G.F., Ladd, G.W. and Hsu, H-C. 1993 'Maternal support networks, maternal cognitions, and young children's social and cognitive development' *Child Development* vol. 64, no. 5, pp. 1401–17

Mendaglio, S. 1994 'Gifted sensitivity to criticism' *Gifted Child Today* vol. 17, no. 3, pp. 24–5

——1995a 'Children who are gifted/ADHD' *Gifted Child Today* vol. 18, no. 4, pp. 37–40

——1995b 'Sensitivity among gifted persons: a multi-faceted perspective' *Roeper Review* vol. 17, no. 3, pp. 169–73

Milburn, D. 1981 'A study of multi-age or family-grouped classrooms' *Phi Delta Kappan* vol. 62, no. 7, pp. 513–14

Miller, M. 1991 'Self-assessment as a specific strategy for teaching the gifted learning disabled' *Journal for the Education of the Gifted* vol. 14, no. 2, pp. 178–88

Miller, N.B., Silverman, L.K. and Falk, R.F. 1994 'Emotional development, intellectual ability, and gender' *Journal for the Education of the Gifted* vol. 18, no. 1, pp. 20–38

Mize, J. 1995 'Coaching preschool children in social skills: a cognitive-social learning curriculum' in *Teaching social skills to children* 3rd edn, eds G. Cartledge & J.F. Milburn, Pergamon Press, New York

Molnar, A. and Lindquist, B. 1989 *Changing problem behaviour in schools* Jossey-Bass, San Francisco, CA

Moltzen, R. 1996a 'Characteristics of gifted children' in *Gifted and talented: New Zealand perspectives* eds D. McAlpine & R. Moltzen, ERDC Press, Palmerston North

——1996b 'Underachievement' in *Gifted and talented: New Zealand perspectives* eds D. McAlpine & R. Moltzen, ERDC Press, Palmerston North

——1998 'Maximising the potential of the gifted child in the regular classroom: a professional development issue' *Gifted Education International* vol. 13, no. 1, pp. 36–45

Montgomery, D. 1996 *Educating the able* Cassell, London

Moon, S.M., Kelly, K.R. and Feldhusen, J.F. 1997 'Specialized counseling services for gifted youth and their families: a needs assessment' *Gifted Child Quarterly* vol. 41, no. 1, pp. 16–25

Moore, L.C. and Sawyers, J.K. 1987 'The stability of original thinking in young children' *Gifted Child Quarterly* vol. 31, no. 3, pp. 126–9

Morelock, M.J. 1996 'Perspectives of giftedness: on the nature of giftedness and talent: imposing order on chaos' *Roeper Review* vol. 19, no. 1, pp. 4–12

Morelock, M.J. and Morrison, K. 1996 *Gifted children have talents too: multi-dimensional programmes for the gifted in early childhood* Hawker Brownlow Education, Melbourne

Morgan, H. 1996 'An analysis of Gardner's theory of multiple intelligences' *Roeper Review* vol. 18, no. 4, pp. 263–9

Moss, E. 1990 'Social interaction and metacognitive development in gifted preschoolers' *Gifted Child Quarterly* vol. 34, no. 1, pp. 16–20

——1992 'Early interactions and metacognitive development of gifted preschoolers' in *To be young and gifted* eds P.S. Klein & A.J. Tannenbaum, Ablex, Norwood, NJ

Mosteller, F., Light, R.J. and Sachs, J.A. 1996 'Sustained inquiry in education: lessons from skill grouping and class size' *Harvard Educational Review* vol. 66, no. 4, pp. 797–842
Mulcahy, R., Wilgosh, L. and Peat, D. 1991 'The relationship between affect and achievement for gifted, average, and learning disabled students' *Gifted Education International* vol. 7, no. 3, pp. 123–5

Nail, J.M. and Evans, J.G. 1997 'The emotional adjustment of gifted adolescents: a view of global functioning' *Roeper Review* vol. 20, no. 1, pp. 18–21
National Association for the Education of Young Children (NAEYC) 1984 'Criteria for high quality early childhood programs' *Position paper from the National Academy of Early Childhood Programs* pp. 3–13
——1988 'NAEYC position statement on standardized testing of young children 3 through 8 years of age' *Young Children* vol. 43, no. 3, pp. 42–7
National Childcare Accreditation Council 1993 *Putting children first: quality improvement and accreditation system handbook* National Childcare Accreditation Council, Sydney
Nelson-Jones, R. 1988 *Practical counselling and helping skills* Holt, Rinehart and Winston, New York
Nevo, B. 1994 'Definitions, ideologies, and hypotheses in gifted education' *Gifted Child Quarterly* vol. 38, no. 4, pp. 184–6
Nidiffer, L.G. and Moon, S.M. 1994 'Serving the gifted dyslexic and gifted at risk: using differentiated-integrated curricula and enrichment' *Our Gifted Children* vol. 2, no. 8, pp. 39–43
Niebrzydowski, L. 1997 'Influences which promote high-level attainment in children of pre-school age' *High Ability Studies* vol. 8, no. 2, pp. 179–88

Olszewski-Kubilius, P., Kulieke, M.J. and Krasny, N. 1988 'Personality dimensions of gifted adolescents: a review of the empirical literature' *Gifted Child Quarterly* vol. 32, no. 4, pp. 347–52
Olszewski, P., Kulieke, M.J. and Willis, G. 1987 'Changes in the self-perceptions of gifted students who participate in rigorous academic programs' *Journal for the Education of the Gifted* vol. 10, no. 4, pp. 287–303
Oram, G.D., Cornell, D.G. and Rutemiller, L.A. 1995 'Relations between academic aptitude and psychosocial adjustment in gifted program students' *Gifted Child Quarterly* vol. 39, no. 4, pp. 236–44
Orange, C. 1997 'Gifted students and perfectionism' *Roeper Review* vol. 20, no. 1, pp. 39–41
Orlick, T. 1982 *The second cooperative sports and games book* Pantheon, New York

Parke, B.N. and Ness, P.S. 1988 'Curricular decision-making for the education of young gifted children' *Gifted Child Quarterly* vol. 32, no. 1, pp. 196–9
Parker, W. 1996 'Psychological adjustment in mathematically gifted students' *Gifted Child Quarterly* vol. 40, no. 3, pp. 154–61
Parker, W. and Adkins, K.K. 1995 'Perfectionism and the gifted' *Roeper Review* vol. 17, no. 3, pp. 173–6
Parker, W. and Mills, C.J. 1996 'The incidence of perfectionism in gifted students' *Gifted Child Quarterly* vol. 40, no. 4, pp. 194–9
Passow, A.H. and Frasier, M.M. 1996 'Toward improving identification of talent potential among minority and disadvantaged students' *Roeper Review* vol. 18, no. 3, pp. 198–202
Patrick, C.L. 1990 'Motivating the gifted under-achiever: unleashing potential' in *The challenges of excellence: a vision splendid: selected papers from the 8th World Conference on Gifted and Talented Children* eds S. Bailey, E. Braggett & M. Robinson, Australian Association for the Education of the Gifted and Talented, Wagga Wagga, NSW
Patton, M.M. and Kokoski, T.M. 1996 'How good is your early childhood science,

mathematics, and technology program?: strategies for extending your curriculum' *Young Children* vol. 51, no. 5, pp. 38–44

Paulson, F.L., Paulson, P.R. and Meyer, C.A. 1991 'What makes a portfolio a portfolio?' *Educational Leadership* vol. 48, no. 5, pp. 60–3

Paulus, P. 1984 'Acceleration: more than grade skipping' *Roeper Review* vol. 7, no. 2, pp. 98–100

Paulus, P.B. and Paulus, L.E. 1997 'Implications of research on group brainstorming for gifted education' *Roeper Review* vol. 19, no. 4, pp. 225–9

Pavan, B.N. 1992 'The benefits of nongraded schools' *Educational Leadership* vol. 50, no. 2, pp. 22–5

Pendarvis, E. and Howley, A. 1996 'Playing fair: the possibilities of gifted education' *Journal for the Education of the Gifted* vol. 19, no. 2, pp. 215–33

Perleth, C., Lehwald, G. and Browder, C.S. 1993 'Indicators of high ability in young children' in *International handbook of research and development of giftedness and talent* eds K.A. Heller, F.J. Mönks & A.H. Passow, Pergamon Press, Oxford, UK

Perry, D. and Bussey, K. 1984 *Social development* Prentice Hall, Englewood Cliffs, NJ

Peterson, J. 1993 'Peeling off the elitist label: smart politics' *Gifted Child Today* vol. 16, no. 2, pp. 31–3

Phillips, D.A. 1984 'The illusion of incompetence among academically competent children' *Child Development* vol. 55, no. 6, pp. 2000–16

——1987 'Socialization of perceived academic competence among highly competent children' *Child Development* vol. 58, no. 5, pp. 1308–20

Phillips, D.A. and Howes, C. 1987 'Indicators of quality child care: review of research' in *Quality in child care: what does research tell us?* ed. D. Phillips, National Association for the Education of Young Children, Washington, DC

Piechowski, M.M. 1997 'Emotional giftedness: the measure of interpersonal intelligence' in *Handbook of gifted education* 2nd edn, eds N. Colangelo & G.A. Davis, Allyn & Bacon, Boston, MA

Piirto, J. 1998 *Talented children and adults* 2nd edn, Merrill, Upper Saddle River, NJ

Plomin, R. 1997 'Genetics and intelligence' in *Handbook of gifted education* 2nd edn, eds N. Colangelo & G.A. Davis, Allyn & Bacon, Boston MA

Plucker, J.A., Callahan, C.M. and Tomchin, E.M. 1996 'Wherefore art thou, multiple intelligences?: alternative assessments for identifying talent in ethnically diverse and low income students' *Gifted Child Quarterly* vol. 40, no. 2, pp. 81–92

Plucker, J.A. and McIntire, J. 1996 'Academic survivability in high-potential, middle school students' *Gifted Child Quarterly* vol. 40, no. 1, pp. 7–14

Pohl, M. 1997 *Teaching thinking skills in the primary years: a whole school approach* Hawker Brownlow Education, Melbourne

Pope, A.W., McHale, S.M. and Craighead, E.W. 1988 *Self-esteem enhancement with children and adolescents* Pergamon Press, New York

Porath, M. 1996 'Affective and motivational considerations in the assessment of gifted learners' *Roeper Review* vol. 19, no. 1, pp. 13–17

Porteous, M.A. 1979 'A survey of the problems of normal 15-year-olds' *Journal of Adolescence* vol. 2, no. 4, pp. 307–23

Porter, L. 1996 *Student behaviour: theory and practice for teachers* Allen & Unwin, Sydney

——1997a *Children are people too: a parent's guide to young children's behaviour* 2nd edn, Porter, Adelaide

——1997b *Young gifted children: meeting their needs* Australian Early Childhood Association, Watson, ACT

——1997c 'A proposed model describing the realisation of gifted potential' *The Australasian Journal of Gifted Education* vol. 6, no. 2, pp. 33–43

——1997d 'Selected perspectives on ADD and ADHD' *Australian Journal of Early Childhood* vol. 22, no. 4, pp. 7–14

——1999 Young children's behaviour: practical approaches for caregivers and teachers MacLennan & Petty, Sydney

Prichard, B. 1985 'Parenting gifted children—the fun, the frustration' Gifted Child Today no. 41, pp. 10–13

Proctor, T.B., Black, K.N. and Feldhusen, J.F. 1986 'Early admission of selected children to elementary school: a review of the research literature' Journal of Educational Research vol. 80, no. 2, pp. 70–6

Proctor, T.B., Feldhusen, J.F. and Black, K.N. 1988 'Guidelines for early admission to elementary school' Psychology in the Schools vol. 25, no. 1, pp. 41–3

Pugach, M. 1988 'Special education as a constraint on teacher education reform' Journal of Teacher Education vol. 49, no. 3, pp. 52–9

Pugh, G. and Selleck, D.R. 1996 'Listening to and communicating with young children' in The voice of the child: a handbook for professionals eds R. Davie, G. Upton & V. Varma, Falmer Press, London

Purcell, J.H. 1993 'The effects of the elimination of gifted and talented programs on participating students and their parents' Gifted Child Quarterly vol. 37, no. 4, pp. 177–87

Putallaz, M. and Wasserman, A. 1990 'Children's entry behavior' in Peer rejection in childhood eds S.R. Asher & J.D. Coie, Cambridge University Press, Cambridge, UK

Pyryt, M.C. 1996 'IQ: easy to bash, hard to replace' Roeper Review vol. 18, no. 4, pp. 255–8

Pyryt, M.C. and Mendaglio, S. 1994 'The multidimensional self-concept: a comparison of gifted and average-ability adolescents' Journal for the Education of the Gifted vol. 17, no. 3, pp. 299–305

Rabinowitz, M. and Glaser, R. 1985 'Cognitive structure and process in highly competent performance' in The gifted and talented: developmental perspectives eds F.D. Horowitz & M. O'Brien, American Psychological Association, Washington, DC

Ramos-Ford, V. and Gardner, H. 1991 'Giftedness from a multiple intelligences perspective' in Handbook of gifted education eds N. Colangelo & G.A. Davis, Allyn & Bacon, Boston, MA

——1997 'Giftedness from a multiple intelligences perspective' in Handbook of gifted education 2nd edn, eds N. Colangelo & G.A. Davis, Allyn & Bacon, Boston, MA

Ramsay, S.G. and Richards, H.C. 1997 'Cooperative learning environments: effects on academic attitudes of gifted students' Gifted Child Quarterly vol. 41, no. 4, pp. 160–8

Randall, V. 1997 'Gifted girls: what challenges do they face: a summary of the research' Gifted Child Today vol. 20, no. 4, pp. 42–4; 46–9

Readdick, C.A. 1993 'Solitary pursuits: supporting children's privacy needs in early childhood settings' Young Children vol. 49, no. 1, pp. 60–4

Reams, R., Chamrad, D. and Robinson, N.M. 1990 'The race is not necessarily to the swift: validity of WISC-R bonus points for speed' Gifted Child Quarterly vol. 34, no. 3, pp. 108–10

Redding, R.E. 1990 'Learning preferences and skill patterns among underachieving gifted adolescents' Gifted Child Quarterly vol. 34, no. 2, pp. 72–5

Reis, S.M. 1987 'We can't change what we don't recognize: understanding the special needs of gifted females' Gifted Child Quarterly vol. 31, no. 2, pp. 83–9

Reis, S.M. and Callahan, C.M. 1989 'Gifted females: they've come a long way—or have they?' Journal for the Education of the Gifted vol. 12, no. 2, pp. 99–117

Reis, S.M. and Purcell, J.H. 1993 'An analysis of content elimination and strategies used by elementary classroom teachers in the curriculum compacting process' Journal for the Education of the Gifted vol. 16, no. 2, pp. 147–70

Reis, S.M. and Renzulli, J.S. 1982 'A case for a broadened conception of giftedness' Phi Delta Kappan vol. 63, no. 9, pp. 619–20

——1992 'Using curriculum compacting to challenge the above-average' *Educational Leadership* vol. 50, no. 2, pp. 51–7

Reis, S.M. and Westberg, K.L. 1994 'The impact of staff development on teachers' ability to modify curriculum for gifted and talented students' *Gifted Child Quarterly* vol. 38, no. 3, pp. 127–35

Reis, S.M., Westberg, K.L., Kulikowich, J.M. and Purcell, J.H. 1998 'Curriculum compacting and achievement test scores: what does the research say?' *Gifted Child Quarterly* vol. 42, no. 2, pp. 123–9

Renzulli, J.S. 1973 'Talent potential in minority group students' *Exceptional Children* vol. 39, no. 6, pp. 437–44

——1982 'Dear Mr. and Mrs. Copernicus: we regret to inform you . . .' *Gifted Child Quarterly* vol. 26, no. 1, pp. 11–14

——1986 'The three-ring conception of giftedness: a developmental model for creative productivity' in *Conceptions of giftedness* eds R.J. Sternberg & J.E. Davidson, Cambridge University Press, Cambridge, UK

——1988 'The multiple menu model for developing differentiated curriculum for the gifted and talented' *Gifted Child Quarterly* vol. 32, no. 3, pp. 298–309

Renzulli, J.S. and Delcourt, M.A.B. 1986 'The legacy and logic of research on the identification of gifted persons' *Gifted Child Quarterly* vol. 30, no. 1, pp. 20–3

Renzulli, J.S. and Reis, S.M. 1997 'The school-wide enrichment model: new directions for developing high-end learning' in *Handbook of gifted education* 2nd edn, eds N. Colangelo & G.A. Davis, Allyn & Bacon, Boston, MA

Richert, E.S. 1987 'Rampant problems and promising practices in the identification of disadvantaged gifted students' *Gifted Child Quarterly* vol. 31, no. 4, pp. 149–54

——1997 'Excellence with equity in identification and programming' in *Handbook of gifted education* 2nd edn, eds N. Colangelo & G.A. Davis, Allyn & Bacon, Boston, MA

Riggs, G.G. 1998 'Parents of gifted children: sheep in wolves' clothing?' in *The young gifted child: potential and promise, an anthology* ed. J.F. Smutny, Hampton Press, Cresskill, NJ

Riley, T.L. 1997 'Talking about "being gifted" with your child' *Tall Poppies* August, 1997, pp. 10–12

Rimm, S.B. 1984 'The characteristics approach: identification and beyond' *Gifted Child Quarterly* vol. 28, no. 4, pp. 181–7

——1986 *Underachievement syndrome: causes and cures* Apple Publishing, Watertown, WI

——1987 'Why do bright children underachieve' *Gifted Child Today* vol. 10, no. 6, pp. 30–6

——1997 'Underachievement syndrome: a national epidemic' in *Handbook of gifted education* 2nd edn, eds N. Colangelo & G.A. Davis, Allyn & Bacon, Boston, MA

Rimm, S.B. and Lovance, K.J. 1992a 'How acceleration may prevent underachievement syndrome' *Gifted Child Today* vol. 15, no. 2, pp. 9–14

——1992b 'The use of subject and grade skipping for the prevention and reversal of underachievement' *Gifted Child Quarterly* vol. 36, no. 2, pp. 100–5

Ring, B. and Shaughnessy, M.F. 1993 'The gifted label, gifted children and the aftermath' *Gifted Education International* vol. 9, no. 1, pp. 33–5

Risemberg, R. and Zimmerman, B.J. 1992 'Self-regulated learning in gifted students' *Roeper Review* vol. 15, no. 2, pp. 98–101

Rist, R.C. 1970 'Student social class and teacher expectations: the self-fulfilling prophecy in ghetto education' *Harvard Educational Review* vol. 40, no. 3, pp. 411–51

Rivera, D.B., Murdock, J. and Sexton, D. 1995 'Serving the gifted/learning disabled' *Gifted Child Today* vol. 18, no. 6, pp. 34–7

Robinson, A. 1990a 'Cooperation or exploitation?: the argument against cooperative learning for talented students' *Journal for the Education of the Gifted* vol. 14, no. 1, pp. 9–27

——1990b 'Does that describe me? Adolescents' acceptance of the gifted label' *Journal for the Education of the Gifted* vol. 13, no. 3, pp. 245–55

——1997 'Cooperative learning for talented students: emergent issues and implications' in *Handbook of gifted education* 2nd edn, eds N. Colangelo & G.A. Davis, Allyn & Bacon, Boston, MA

Robinson, N.M. 1987 'The early development of precocity' *Gifted Child Quarterly* vol. 31, no. 4, pp. 161–4

——1993 'Identifying and nurturing gifted, very young children' in *International handbook of research and development of giftedness and talent* eds K.A. Heller, F.J. Mönks & A.H. Passow, Pergamon Press, Oxford, UK

——1996 'Counseling agendas for gifted young people: a commentary' *Journal for the Education of the Gifted* vol. 20, no. 2, pp. 128–37

Robinson, N.M. and Chamrad, D.L. 1986 'Appropriate uses of intelligence tests with gifted children' *Roeper Review* vol. 8, no. 3, pp. 160–3

Robinson, N.M. and Noble, K.D. 1991 'Social-emotional development and adjustment of gifted children' in *Handbook of special education: research and practice* eds M.C. Wang, M.C. Reynolds & H.J. Walberg, Pergamon Press, Oxford, UK

Robinson, N.M. and Robinson, H. 1992 'The use of standardized tests with young gifted children' in *To be young and gifted* eds P.S. Klein & A.J. Tannenbaum, Ablex, Norwood, NJ

Robisheaux, J.A. and Banbury, M.M. 1994 'Students who don't fit the mold: identifying and educating gifted ESL students' *Gifted Child Today* vol. 17, no. 5, pp. 28; 31

Rodd, J. 1996 *Understanding young children's behaviour* Allen & Unwin, Sydney

Roedell, W.C., Jackson, N.E. and Robinson, H.B. 1980 *Gifted young children* Teachers College, Columbia University, New York

Roeper, A. 1995a 'How to help the underachieving gifted child' in *Annemarie Roeper: selected writings and speeches* Free Spirit, Minneapolis, MN

——1995b 'Parenting the gifted' in *Annemarie Roeper: selected writings and speeches* Free Spirit, Minneapolis, MN

——1977 'The young gifted child' *The Gifted Child Quarterly* vol. 21, no. 3, pp. 388–96

Rogers, C. 1951 *Client-centred therapy* Constable, London

——1978 *On personal power* Constable, London

Rogers, C.R. and Freiberg, H. 1994 *Freedom to learn* 3rd edn, Merrill, Columbus, OH

Rogers, K.B. and Kimpston, R.D. 1992 'Acceleration: what we do vs. what we do not know' *Educational Leadership* vol. 50, no. 2, pp. 58–61

Rogers, K.B. and Span, P. 1993 'Ability grouping with gifted and talented students: research and guidelines' in *International handbook of research and development of giftedness and talent* eds K.A. Heller, F.J. Mönks & A.H. Passow, Pergamon Press, Oxford, UK

Rogers, W. 1991 'Decisive discipline' in *Classroom discipline* eds M.N. Lovegrove & R. Lewis, Longman Cheshire, Melbourne

——1994 *Behaviour recovery* ACER, Melbourne

Rose, S.R. 1983 'Promoting social competence in children: a classroom approach to social and cognitive skill training' in *Social skills training for children and youth* ed. C.W. LeCroy, Haworth Press, New York

Rost, D.H. and Czeschlik, T. 1994 'The psycho-social adjustment of gifted children in middle childhood' *European Journal of the Psychology of Education* vol. 9, no. 1, pp. 15–25

Rothman, G.R. 1992 'Moral reasoning, moral behavior, and moral giftedness: A developmental perspective' in *To be young and gifted* eds P.S. Klein & A.J. Tannenbaum, Ablex, Norwood, NJ

Rowe, H. 1990 'Testing and evaluation of persons with handicap' in *The exceptional child* ed. S. Butler, Harcourt Brace Jovanovich, Sydney

——1991 'Introduction: paradigm and context' in *Intelligence: reconceptualization and measurement* ed. H. Rowe, Lawrence Erlbaum Associates, Hillsdale, NJ

Rubin, Z. 1980 *Children's friendships* Harvard University Press, Boston, MA

Runco, M.A. 1993 'Divergent thinking, creativity, and giftedness' *Gifted Child Quarterly* vol. 37, no. 1, pp. 16–22

——1997 'Is every child gifted?' *Roeper Review* vol. 19, no. 4, pp. 220–4

Rutter, M. 1985 'Resilience in the face of adversity: protective factors and resistance to psychiatric disorder' *British Journal of Psychiatry* vol. 147, pp. 598–611

——1990 'Psychosocial resilience and protective mechanisms' in *Risk and protective factors in the development of psychopathology* eds J. Rolf, A.S. Masten, D. Cicchetti, K.H. Nuechterlein & S. Weintraub, Cambridge University Press, New York

Ryan, N.M. 1989 'Stress-coping strategies identified from school age children's perspective' *Research in Nursing and Health* vol. 12, pp. 109–22

Ryan, R.M. and Deci, E.L. 1996 'When paradigms clash: comments on Cameron and Pierce's claim that rewards do not undermine intrinsic motivation' *Review of Educational Research* vol. 66, no. 1, pp. 33–8

Sabatino, D.A., Spangler, R.S. and Vance, H.B. 1995 'The relationship between the Wechsler Intelligence Scale for Children—Revised and the Wechsler Intelligence Scale for Children—III scales and subtests with gifted children' *Psychology in the Schools* vol. 32, no. 1, pp. 18–23

Sandel, A., McCallister, C. and Nash, W.R. 1993 'Child search and screening activities for preschool gifted children' *Roeper Review* vol. 16, no. 2, pp. 98–102

Sapon-Shevin, M. 1986 'Teaching cooperation' in *Teaching social skills to children: innovative approaches* 2nd edn, eds G. Cartledge & J.F. Milburn, Pergamon Press, New York

——1987a 'Giftedness as a social construct' *Teachers College Record* vol. 89, no. 1, pp. 39–53

——1987b 'Explaining giftedness to parents: why it matters what professionals say' *Roeper Review* vol. 9, no. 3, pp. 180–4

——1990 'Gifted education and the deskilling of classroom teachers' *Journal of Teacher Education* vol. 41, no. 1, pp. 39–48

——1994 *Playing favorites: gifted education and the disruption of community* State University of New York, Albany, NY

——1996a 'Beyond gifted education: building a shared agenda for school reform' *Journal for the Education of the Gifted* vol. 19, no. 2, pp. 194–214

——1996b 'Including all children and their gifts within regular classrooms' in *Controversial issues confronting special education: divergent perspectives* 2nd edn, eds W. Stainback & S. Stainback, Allyn & Bacon, Boston, MA

Satir, V. 1976 *Making contact* Celestial Arts, Millbrae, CA

Sattler, J.M. 1988 *Assessment of children* 3rd edn, Jerome M. Sattler, San Diego, CA

——1992a *Assessment of children: WISC-III and WPPSI-R supplement* Jerome M. Sattler, San Diego, CA

——1992b *Assessment of children* rev. 3rd edn, Jerome M. Sattler, San Diego, CA

Sawyer, R.N. 1988 'In defense of academic rigor' *Journal for the Education of the Gifted* vol. 11, no. 2, pp. 5–19

Sayler, M.F. and Brookshire, W.K. 1993 'Social, emotional, and behavioral adjustment of accelerated students, students in gifted classes, and regular students in eighth grade' *Gifted Child Quarterly* vol. 37, no. 4, pp. 150–4

Schauer, G.H. 1976 'Emotional disturbance and giftedness' *Gifted Child Quarterly* vol. 20, no. 4, pp. 470–8

Schetky, D.H. 1981 'A psychiatrist looks at giftedness: the social and emotional development of the gifted child' *Gifted Child Today* vol. 18, pp. 2–4

Schiever, S.W. and Maker, C.J. 1997 'Enrichment and acceleration: an overview and new directions' in *Handbook of gifted education* 2nd edn, eds N. Colangelo & G.A. Davis, Allyn & Bacon, Boston, MA

Schleblanova, H. 1996 'A longitudinal study of intellectual and creative development in gifted primary school children' *High Ability Studies* vol. 7, no. 1, pp. 51–4

Schlichter, C.L. 1981 'The multiple talent approach in mainstream and gifted programs' *Exceptional Children* vol. 48, no. 2, pp. 144–50

Schneider, B.H. 1989 'Between developmental wisdom and children's social skills training' in *Social competence in developmental perspective* eds B.H. Schneider, G. Attili, J. Nadel & R.P. Weissberg, Kluwer Academic Publishers, Dordrecht, Netherlands

Schneider, B.H., Clegg, M.R., Byrne, B.M., Ledingham, J.E. and Crombie, G. 1989 'Social relations of gifted children as a function of age and school program' *Journal of Educational Psychology* vol. 81, no. 1, pp. 48–56

Scholwinski, E. and Reynolds, C.R. 1985 'Dimensions of anxiety among high IQ children' *Gifted Child Quarterly* vol. 29, no. 3, pp. 125–30

Schraw, G. and Graham, T. 1997 'Helping gifted students develop metacognitive awareness' *Roeper Review* vol. 20, no. 1, pp. 4–8

Schunk, D.H. 1987 'Peer models and children's behavioral change' *Review of Educational Research* vol. 57, no. 2, pp. 149–74

Schwanenflugel, P.J., Stevens, T.P.M. and Carr, M. 1997 'Metacognitive knowledge of gifted children and nonidentified children in early elementary school' *Gifted Child Quarterly* vol. 41, no. 2, pp. 25–35

Schwean, V.L. and Saklofske, D.H. 1998 'WISC-III assessment of children with attention deficit/hyperactivity disorder' in *WISC-III clinical use and interpretation: scientist–practitioner perspectives* eds A. Prifitera and D. Saklofske, Academic Press, San Diego, CA

Scott, M.S., Deuel, L.S., Jean-Francois, B. and Urbano, R.C. 1996 'Identifying cognitive gifted ethnic minority children' *Gifted Child Quarterly* vol. 40, no. 3, pp. 147–53

Sears, R.R. 1977 'Sources of life satisfactions of the Terman gifted men' *American Psychologist* vol. 32, pp. 119–28

Seeley, K. 1993 'Gifted students at risk' in *Counseling the gifted and talented* ed. L.K. Silverman, Love Publishing, Denver, CO

Seely, A.E. 1996 *Portfolio assessment* Hawker Brownlow Education, Melbourne

Sekowski, A. 1995 'Self-esteem and achievements of gifted students' *Gifted Education International* vol. 10, no. 2, pp. 65–70

Seligman, M.E.P. 1975 *Helplessness: on depression, development and death* W.H. Freeman and Co., San Francisco, CA

——1995 *The optimistic child* Random House, Sydney

Shaklee, B.D. 1992 'Identification of young gifted students' *Journal for the Education of the Gifted* vol. 15, no. 2, pp. 134–44

——1998 'Educationally dynamic environments for young gifted children' in *The young gifted child: potential and promise, an anthology* ed. J.F. Smutny, Hampton Press, Cresskill, NJ

Shaklee, B.D. and Viechnicki, K.J. 1995 'A qualitative approach to portfolios: the early assessment for exceptional potential model' *Journal for the Education of the Gifted* vol. 18, no. 2, pp. 156–70

Sharp, S. and Thompson, D. 1994 'The role of whole-school policies in tackling bullying behaviour in schools' in *School bullying: insights and perspectives* eds P.K. Smith & S. Sharp, Routledge, London

Shore, B.M. and Delcourt, M.A.B. 1996 'Effective curricular and program practices in gifted education and the interface with general education' *Journal for the Education of the Gifted* vol. 20, no. 2, pp. 138–54

Shore, B.M. and Dover, A.C. 1987 'Metacognition, intelligence and giftedness' *Gifted Child Quarterly* vol. 31, no. 1, pp. 37–9

Shore, B.M. and Kanevsky, L.S. 1993 'Thinking processes: being and becoming gifted' in

International handbook of research and development of giftedness and talent eds K.A. Heller, F.J. Mönks & A.H. Passow, Pergamon Press, Oxford, UK

Silverman, L.K. 1989a 'Invisible gifts, invisible handicaps' *Roeper Review* vol. 12, no. 1, pp. 37–42

——1989b 'Personality plus: perfectionism' *Understanding our gifted* January, vol. 30, p. 11

——1991 'Helping gifted girls reach their potential' *Roeper Review* vol. 13, no. 3, pp. 122–3

——1993a 'The gifted individual' in *Counseling the gifted and talented* ed. L.K. Silverman, Love Publishing, Denver, CO

——1993b 'A developmental model for counseling the gifted' in *Counseling the gifted and talented* ed. L.K. Silverman, Love Publishing, Denver, CO

——1993c 'Techniques for preventive counseling' in *Counseling the gifted and talented* ed. L.K. Silverman, Love Publishing, Denver, CO

——1994a 'Perfectionism' *Gifted and Talented Children's Association Newsletter* no. 96, p. 8

——1994b 'The moral sensitivity of gifted children and the evolution of society' *Roeper Review* vol. 17, no. 2, pp. 110–16

——1997 'Family counseling' in *Handbook of gifted education* 2nd edn, eds N. Colangelo & G.A. Davis, Allyn & Bacon, Boston

——1998a 'Using test results to support clinical judgment' *Gifted Education Press Quarterly* vol. 12, no. 1, pp. 2–5

——1998b 'Through the lens of giftedness' *Roeper Review* vol. 20, no. 3, pp. 204–10

——1998c 'Personality and learning styles of gifted children' in *Excellence in educating gifted and talented learners* 3rd edn, ed. J. Van Tassel Baska, Love Publishing, Denver, CO

Silverman, L.K., Chitwood, D.G. and Waters, J.L. 1986 'Young gifted children: can parents identify giftedness?' *Topics in Early Childhood Special Education* vol 6, no. 1, pp. 23–38

Silverman, L.K. and Maxwell, E. 1996 *Characteristics of giftedness scale* Gifted Development Centre, Denver, CO

Silverman, W.K., La Greca, A.M. and Wasserstein, S. 1995 'What do children worry about? Worries and their relation to anxiety' *Child Development* vol. 66, pp. 671–86

Sisk, D.A. 1998 'The importance of early identification of gifted children and appropriate educational intervention' in *The young gifted child: potential and promise, an anthology* ed. J.F. Smutny, Hampton Press, Cresskill, NJ

Slater, A. 1995 'Individual difference in infancy and later IQ' *Journal of Child Psychology and Psychiatry and Related Disciplines* vol. 36, no. 1, pp. 69–112

Slavin, R.E. 1987a 'Ability grouping and student achievement in elementary schools: a best-evidence synthesis' *Review of Educational Research* vol. 57, no. 3, pp. 293–336

——1987b 'Cooperative learning and the cooperative school' *Educational Leadership* vol. 45, no. 3, pp. 7–13

——1990a 'Achievement effects of ability grouping in secondary schools: a best-evidence synthesis' *Review of Educational Research* vol. 60, no. 3, pp. 471–99

——1990b 'Response to Robinson: cooperative learning and the gifted: who benefits?' *Journal for the Education of the Gifted* vol. 14, no. 1, pp. 28–9

——1991 'Are cooperative learning and "untracking" harmful to the gifted?: response to Allan' *Educational Leadership* vol. 48, no. 6, pp. 68–71

——1992 'The nongraded elementary school: great potential, but keep it simple' *Educational Leadership* vol. 50, no. 2, p. 24

Slee P.T. 1991 'What stresses Australian children?' *Children Australia* vol. 16, no. 3, pp. 12–14

——1993 'Children, stressful life events and school adjustment: an Australian study' *Educational Psychology* vol. 23, no. 1, pp. 3–10

Smerechansky-Metzger, J.A. 1995 'The quest for multiple intelligences: using MI theory to create exciting teaching and learning experiences' *Gifted Child Quarterly* vol. 18, no. 3, pp. 12–15

Smith, D. 1995 'Social giftedness—its characteristics and identification' *Gifted Education International* vol. 11, no. 1, pp. 24–30

Smith, M.D., Coleman, M., Dokecki, P.R. and Davis, E.E. 1977 'Recategorized WISC-R scores of learning disabled children' *Journal of Learning Disabilities* vol. 10, no. 7, pp. 48–54

Smutny, J.F. 1998 *Gifted girls* Phi Delta Kappa Educational Foundation, Bloomington, IN

Smutny, J.F., Veenker, K. and Veenker, S. 1989 *Your gifted child: how to recognize and develop the special talents in your child from birth to age seven* Ballantine, New York

Smutny, J.F., Walker, S.Y. and Meckstroth, E.A. 1997 *Teaching young gifted children in the regular classroom: identifying, nurturing, and challenging ages 4–9* Free Spirit Publishing, Minneapolis, MN

Snowden, P.L. 1994 'Activities for young gifted children: using the CIBER method' *Gifted Child Today* vol. 17, no. 3, pp. 14–19

——1995 'Educating young gifted children' *Gifted Child Today* vol. 18, no. 6, pp. 16–25; 41

Snowden, P.L. and Conway, K.D. 1996 'A comparison of self-reported parenting behaviors and attitudes of parents of academically precocious and nonprecocious preschool children' *Roeper Review* vol. 19, no. 2, pp. 97–101

Southern, W.T., Jones, E.D., and Fiscus, E.D. 1989 'Practitioner objections to the academic acceleration of gifted children' *Gifted Child Quarterly* vol. 33, no. 1, pp. 29–35

Southern, W.T., Jones, E.D. and Stanley, J.C. 1993 'Accelertion and enrichment: the context and development of program options' in *International handbook of research and development of giftedness and talent* eds K.A. Heller, F.J. Mönks & A.H. Passow, Pergamon Press, Oxford, UK

Sowa, C.J. and May, K.M. 1997 'Expanding Lazarus and Folkman's paradigm to the social and emotional adjustment of gifted children and adolescents (SEAM)' *Gifted Child Quarterly* vol. 41, no. 2, pp. 36–43

Sowa, C.J., McIntire, J., May, K.M. and Bland, L. 1994 'Social and emotional adjustment themes across gifted children' *Roeper Review* vol. 17, no. 2, pp. 95–8

Spangler, R.S. and Sabatino, D.A. 1995 'Temporal stability of gifted children's intelligence' *Roeper Review* vol. 17, no. 3, pp. 207–10

Sparrow, S.S. and Gurland, S.T. 1998 'Assessment of gifted children with the WISC-III' in *WISC-III clinical use and interpretation: scientist–practitioner perspectives* eds A. Prifitera and D. Saklofske, Academic Press, San Diego, CA

Spearman, C. 1927 *The abilities of man* Macmillan, New York

Spicker, H.H. and Southern, W.T. 1998 'Early childhood giftedness among the rural poor' in *The young gifted child: potential and promise, an anthology* ed. J.F. Smutny, Hampton Press, Cresskill, NJ

Spicker, H.H., Southern, W.T. and Davis, B.I. 1987 'The rural gifted child' *Gifted Child Quarterly* vol. 31, no. 4, pp. 155–7

Spirito, A., Stark, L.J., Grace, N., and Stamoulis, D. 1991 'Common problems and coping strategies reported in childhood and early adolescence' *Journal of Youth and Adolescence* vol. 20, no. 5, pp. 531–44

Stanley, J.C. 1976 'Use of tests to discover talent' in *Intellectual talent: research and development* ed. D.P. Keating, The Johns Hopkins University Press, Baltimore, MD

Starko, A.J. 1986 'Meeting the needs of the gifted throughout the school day: techniques for curriculum compacting' *Roeper Review* vol. 9, no. 1, pp. 27–33

Stedtnitz, U. 1995 'Psychosocial dimensions of talent: some major issues' in *Actualizing talent: a lifelong challenge* eds J. Freeman, P. Span & H. Wagner, Cassell, London

Stephens, T.M. 1988 'Eliminating special education: is this the solution?' *Journal of Teacher Education* vol. 49, no. 3, pp. 60–4

Sternberg, R.J. 1982 'Lies we live by: misapplication of tests in identifying the gifted' *Gifted Child Quarterly* vol. 26, no. 4, pp. 157–61

——1986a 'A triarchic theory of intellectual giftedness' in *Conceptions of giftedness* eds R.J. Sternberg & J.E. Davidson, Cambridge University Press, Cambridge, UK

——1986b 'Identifying the gifted through IQ: why a little bit of knowledge is a dangerous thing' *Roeper Review* vol. 8, no. 3, pp. 143–7

——1988 'A three-facet model of creativity' in *The nature of creativity: contemporary psychological perspectives* ed. R.J. Sternberg, Cambridge University Press, Cambridge, UK

——1996 'Neither elitism nor egalitarianism: gifted education as a third force in American education' *Roeper Review* vol. 18, no. 4, pp. 261–3

——1997 'A triarchic view of giftedness: theory and practice' in *Handbook of gifted education* 2nd edn, eds N. Colangelo & G.A. Davis, Allyn & Bacon, Boston, MA

Sternberg, R.J. and Clinkenbeard, P.R. 1995 'The triarchic model applied to identifying, teaching, and assessing gifted children' *Roeper Review* vol. 17, no. 4, pp. 255–60

Sternberg, R.J. and Davidson, J.E. (eds) 1986 *Conceptions of giftedness* Cambridge University Press, Cambridge, UK

Sternberg, R.J., Ferrari, M., Clinkenbeard, P. and Grigorenki, E.L. 1996 'Identification, instruction, and assessment of gifted children: a construct validation of a triarchic model' *Gifted Child Quarterly* vol. 40, no. 3, pp. 129–37

Sternberg, R.J. and Grigorenko, E.L. 1993 'Thinking styles and the gifted' *Roeper Review* vol. 16, no. 2, pp. 122–30

Sternberg, R.J. and Lubart, T.I. 1991 'An investment theory of creativity and its development' *Human Development* vol. 34, pp. 1–31

——1992 'Creative giftedness in children' in *To be young and gifted* eds P.S. Klein & A.J. Tannenbaum, Ablex, Norwood, NJ

Sternberg, R.J. and Zhang, L. 1995 'What do we mean by giftedness?: a pentagonal implicit theory' *Gifted Child Quarterly* vol. 39, no. 2, pp. 88–94

Stewart, E.D. 1981 'Learning styles among gifted/talented students: instructional technique preferences' *Exceptional Children* vol. 48, no. 2, pp. 134–8

Stonehouse, A. 1988 'Characteristics of toddlers' in *Trusting toddlers: programming for one to three year olds in child care centres* ed. A. Stonehouse, Australian Early Childhood Association, Watson, ACT

——1991 *Opening the doors: child care in a multi-cultural society* Australian Early Childhood Association, Watson, ACT

——1994 *Not just nice ladies: a book of readings on early childhood care and education* Pademelon, Sydney

Storfer, M. 1990 *Intelligence and giftedness: the contributions of heredity and early environment* Jossey-Bass, San Francisco, CA

Strike, K.A. 1983 'Fairness and ability grouping' *Educational Theory* vol. 33, nos 3 & 4, pp. 125–34

Subotnik, R.F., Karp, D.E. and Morgan, E.R. 1989 'High IQ children at midlife: an investigation into the generalizability of Terman's genetic studies of genius' *Roeper Review* vol. 11, no. 3, pp. 139–44

Swadener, E.B. 1990 'Children and families "at risk": etiology, critique, and alternative paradigms' *Educational Foundations* vol. 4. no. 4, pp. 17–39

Swesson, K. 1994 'Helping the gifted/learning disabled: understanding the special needs of the "twice exceptional"' *Gifted Child Today* vol. 17, no. 5, pp. 24–6

Swetnam, L., Peterson, C.R. and Clark, H.B. 1983 'Social skills development in young children: preventive and therapeutic approaches' in *Social skills training for children and youth* ed. C.W. LeCroy, Haworth Press, New York

Swiatek, M.A. 1995 'An empirical investigation of the social coping strategies used by gifted adolescents' *Gifted Child Quarterly* vol. 39, no. 3, pp. 154–61

BIBLIOGRAPHY

——1998 'Helping gifted adolescents cope with social stigma' *Gifted Child Today* vol. 21, no. 3, pp. 42–6

Swiatek, M.A. and Benbow, C.P. 1991 'Ten-year longitudinal follow-up of ability-matched accelerated and unaccelerated gifted students' *Journal of Educational Psychology* vol. 83, no. 4, pp. 528–38

Sylva, K. 1994 'School influences of children's development' *Journal of Child Psychology and Psychiatry and Related Disciplines* vol. 35, no. 1, pp. 135–70

Tannenbaum, A.J. 1983 *Gifted children: psychological and educational perspectives* Macmillan, New York

——1986 'Giftedness: a psychosocial approach' in *Conceptions of giftedness* eds R.J. Sternberg & J.E. Davidson, Cambridge University Press, Cambridge, UK

——1991 'The meaning and making of giftedness' in *Handbook of gifted education* eds N. Colangelo & G.A. Davis, Allyn & Bacon, Boston, MA

——1992 'Early signs of giftedness: research and commentary' in *To be young and gifted* eds P.S. Klein & A.J. Tannenbaum, Ablex, Norwood, NJ

——1997 'The meaning and making of giftedness' in *Handbook of gifted education* 2nd edn, eds N. Colangelo & G.A. Davis, Allyn & Bacon, Boston, MA

Tanner, C.K. and Decotis, J.D. 1995 'The effects of continuous-progress nongraded primary school programs on student performance and attitudes toward learning' *Journal of Research and Development in Education* vol. 28, no. 3, pp. 135–43

Taplin, M. and White, M. 1998 'Parents' and teachers' perception of gifted provision' *The Australasian Journal of Gifted Education* vol. 7, no. 1, pp. 42–9

Tardif, T.Z. and Sternberg, R.J. 1988 'What do we know about creativity?' in *The nature of creativity* ed. R.J. Sternberg, Cambridge University Press, Cambridge, UK

Taylor, C.W. 1978 'How many types of giftedness can your programme tolerate?' *Journal of Creative Behaviour* vol. 12, no. 1, pp. 39–51

Taylor, R.L. 1997 *Assessment of exceptional students* 4th edn, Allyn & Bacon, Boston, MA

Taylor, S. 1996 'Social and emotional development' *Gifted and talented: New Zealand perspectives* eds D. McAlpine & R. Moltzen, ERDC Press, Palmerston North

Terman, L.M. 1919 *The measurement of intelligence* George G. Harrap and Co., London

Terman, L.M., Oden, M.H., Bayley, N., Marshall, H., McNemar, Q. and Sullivan, E.B. 1947 *The gifted child grows up* Stanford University Press, Stanford, CA

Theilheimer, R. 1993 'Something for everyone: benefits of mixed-age grouping for children, parents, and teachers' *Young Children* vol. 48, no. 5, pp. 82–7

Thompson, C.L. and Rudolph, L.B. 1996 *Counselling children* 4th edn, Brooks/Cole, Pacific Grove, CA

Thurstone, L.L. 1938 'Primary mental abilities' *Psychometric Monograph No. 1* University of Chicago Press, Chicago, IL

Tidwell, R. 1980 'A psycho-educational profile of 1,593 gifted high school students' *Gifted Child Quarterly* vol. 24, no. 2, pp. 63–8

Tolan, S.S. 1998 'Beginning brilliance' in *The young gifted child: potential and promise, an anthology* ed. J.F. Smutny, Hampton Press, Cresskill, NJ

Toll, M.F. 1993 'Gifted learning disabled: a kaleidoscope of needs' *Gifted Child Today* vol. 16, no. 1, pp. 34–5

Tomlinson, C.A. 1996 'Good teaching for one and all: does gifted education have an instructional identity?' *Journal for the Education of the Gifted* vol. 20, no. 2, pp. 155–74

Tong, J. and Yewchuk, C. 1996 'Self-concept and sex-role orientation in gifted high school students' *Gifted Child Quarterly* vol. 40, no. 1, pp. 15–23

Torrance, E.P. 1998 'Economically disadvantaged children' in *The young gifted child: potential and promise, an anthology* ed. J.F. Smutny, Hampton Press, Cresskill, NJ

Townsend, M.A.R. 1996 'Enrichment and acceleration: lateral and vertical perspectives in provisions for gifted and talented children' in *Gifted and talented: New Zealand perspectives* eds D. McAlpine & R. Moltzen, ERDC Press, Palmerston North

Treffinger, D.J. and Feldhusen, J.F. 1996 'Talent recognition and development: successor to gifted education' *Journal for the Education of the Gifted* vol. 19, no. 2, pp. 181–93

Treffinger, D.J. and Renzulli, J.S. 1986 'Giftedness as potential for creative productivity: transcending IQ scores' *Roeper Review* vol. 8, no. 3, pp. 150–4

Tremblay, R.E., Masse, B., Perron, D., LeBlanc, M., Schwartzman, A.E. and Ledingham, J.E. 1992 'Early disruptive behavior, poor school achievement, delinquent behavior, and delinquent personality: longitudinal analyses' *Journal of Consulting and Clinical Psychology* vol. 60, no. 1, pp. 64–72

Tucker, B. and Hafenstein N.L. 1997 'Psychological intensities in young gifted children' *Gifted Child Quarterly* vol. 41, no. 3, pp. 66–75

Tyler-Wood, T. and Carri, L. 1993 'Verbal measures of cognitive ability: the gifted low SES student's albatross' *Roeper Review* vol. 16, no. 2, pp. 102–5

Vallerand, R.J., Gagné, F., Senécal, C. and Pelletier, L.G. 1994 'A comparison of the school intrinsic motivation and perceived competence of gifted and regular students' *Gifted Child Quarterly* vol. 38, no. 4, pp. 172–5

van Boxtel, H.W. and Mönks, F.J. 1992 'General, social, and academic self-concepts of gifted adolescents' *Journal of Youth and Adolescence* vol. 21, no. 2, pp. 169–86

Van Tassel-Baska, J. 1992 'Educational decision making on acceleration and grouping' *Gifted Child Quarterly* vol. 36, no. 2, pp. 68–72

——1993 'Academic counseling for the gifted' in *Counseling the gifted and talented* ed. L.K. Silverman, Love Publishing, Denver, CO

——1994 *Comprehensive curriculum for gifted learners* 2nd edn, Allyn & Bacon, Boston, MA

——1995 'The development of talent through curriculum' *Roeper Review* vol. 18, no. 2, pp. 98–102

——1997 'What matters in curriculum for gifted learners: reflections on theory, research and practice' in *Handbook of gifted education* 2nd edn, eds N. Colangelo & G.A. Davis, Allyn & Bacon, Boston, MA

Van Tassel-Baska, J., Olszewski-Kubilius, P. and Kulieke, M. 1994 'Study of self-concept and social support in advantaged and disadvantaged seventh and eighth grade gifted students' *Roeper Review* vol. 16, no. 3, pp. 186–91

Vaughn, V.L., Feldhusen, J.F. and Asher, J.W. 1991 'Meta-analyses and review of research on pull-out programs in gifted education' *Gifted Child Quarterly* vol. 35, no. 2, pp. 92–8

Veenman, S. 1995 'Cognitive and noncognitive effects of multigrade and multi-age classes: a best-evidence synthesis' *Review of Educational Research* vol. 65, no. 4, pp. 319–81

——1996 'Effects of multigrade and multi-age classes reconsidered' *Review of Educational Research* vol. 66, no. 3, pp. 323–40

Vespi, L. and Yewchuk, C. 1992 'A phenomenological study of the social-emotional characteristics of gifted learning disabled children' *Journal for the Education of the Gifted* vol. 16, no. 1, pp. 55–72

Vestal, J.C. 1993 'Parental advocacy for the gifted' *Gifted Child Today* vol. 16, no. 2, pp. 8–13

Vialle, W. 1997 'Giftedness from a multiple intelligence perspective' in *Parents as lifelong teachers of the gifted* eds B.A. Knight & S. Bailey, Hawker Brownlow Education, Melbourne

——1998 'Acceleration: a coat of many colours' paper presented to the *7th National Conference of the Australian Association for the Education of the Gifted* June 1998, Hobart

Vialle, W. and Konza, D. 1997 'Testing times: problems arising from misdiagnosis' *Gifted Education International* vol. 12, no. 1, pp. 4–8

Walberg, H.J., Tsai, S-L, Weinstein, T., Gabriel, C.L., Rasher, S.P., Rosecrans, T., Rovai, E., Ide, J., Trujillo, M. and Vukosavich, P. 1981 'Childhood traits and environmental conditions of highly eminent adults' *Gifted Child Quarterly* vol. 25, no. 3, pp. 103–7

Walker, L.S. and Greene, J.W. 1986 'The social context of adolescent self-esteem' *Journal of Youth and Adolescence* vol. 15, no. 4, pp. 315–22

Walker, R. and Barlow, K. 1994 'Gifted and talented advocacy and the school' *Education Links* no. 47, pp. 23–6

Wallace, B. 1983 'Meeting the needs of exceptionally able children' *Gifted Education International* vol. 2, no. 1, pp. 4–7

——1986a 'Curriculum enrichment then curriculum extension: differentiated educational development in the context of equal opportunities for all children' *Gifted Education International* vol. 4, no. 1, pp. 4–9

——1986b 'Creativity: some definitions: the creative personality; the creative process; the creative classroom' *Gifted Education International* vol. 4, no. 2, pp. 68–73

Walters, J. and Gardner, H. 1986 'The crystallizing experience: discovering an intellectual gift' in *Conceptions of giftedness* eds R.J. Sternberg & J.E. Davidson, Cambridge University Press, Cambridge, UK

Wang, M.C. and Reynolds, M.C. 1985 'Avoiding the "catch 22" in special education reform' *Exceptional Children* vol. 51, no. 6, pp. 497–502

Ward, C.D. 1996 'Adult intervention: appropriate strategies for enriching the quality of children's play' *Young Children* vol. 51, no. 3, pp. 20–5

Webb, J.T. 1993 'Nurturing social-emotional development of gifted children' in *International handbook of research and development of giftedness and talent* eds K.A. Heller, F.J. Mönks & A.H. Passow, Pergamon Press, Oxford, UK

Webb, J.T. and Latimer, D. 1997 'ADHD and children who are gifted' *Gifted* April 1997, pp. 21–2

Webb, J.T., Meckstroth, E.A. and Tolan, S.S. 1991 *Guiding the gifted child: a practical source for parents and teachers* Hawker Brownlow Education, Melbourne

Wechsler, D. 1958 *The measurement and appraisal of adult intelligence* 4th edn, Williams & Wilkins, Baltimore, MD

——1967 *Manual for the Wechsler Preschool and Primary Scale of Intelligence* The Psychological Corporation, San Antonio, CA

——1974 *Manual for the Wechsler Intelligence Scale for Children—Revised* The Psychological Corporation, San Antonio, CA

——1989 *Manual for the Wechsler Preschool and Primary Scale of Intelligence—Revised* (WPPSI-R) The Psychological Corporation, San Antonio, CA

——1991 *Manual for the Wechsler Intelligence Scale for Children—Third Edition* The Psychological Corporation, San Antonio, CA

Wees, J. 1993 'Gifted/learning disabled: yes, they exist and here are some successful ways to teach them' *Gifted International* vol. 8, no. 1, pp. 48–51

Weill, M.P. 1987 'Gifted/learning disabled students: their potential may be buried treasure' *The Clearing House* vol. 60, no. 8, pp. 341–3

Weinreb, M.L. 1997 'Be a resiliency mentor: you may be a lifesaver for a high-risk child' *Young Children* vol. 52, no. 2, pp. 14–20

Wendel, R. and Heiser, S. 1989 'Effective instructional characteristics of teachers of junior high school gifted students' *Roeper Review* vol. 11, no. 3, pp. 151–3

Westberg, K.L., Archambault, F.X. Jr and Brown, S.W. 1997 'A survey of classroom practices with third and fourth grade students in the United States' *Gifted Education International* vol. 12, no. 1, pp. 29–33

Westberg, K.L., Archambault, F.X. Jr, Dobyns, S.M. and Salvin, T.J. 1993 'The classroom practices observation study' *Journal for the Education of the Gifted* vol. 16, no. 2, pp. 120–46

Westby, E. 1997 'Do teachers value creativity?' *Gifted and Talented International* vol. 12, no. 1, pp. 15–17

White, C.S. 1985 'Alternatives for assessing the presence of advanced intellectual abilities in young children' *Roeper Review* vol. 8, no. 2, pp. 73–5

White, K.R. 1982 'The relation between socioeconomic status and academic achievement' *Psychological Bulletin* vol. 91, no. 3, pp. 461–81

Whitmore, J.R. 1980 *Giftedness, conflict, and underachievement* Allyn & Bacon, Boston, MA

——1981 'Gifted children with handicapping conditions: a new frontier' *Exceptional Children* vol. 48, no. 2, pp. 106–14

——1986 'Understanding a lack of motivation to excel' *Gifted Child Quarterly* vol. 30, no. 2, pp. 66–9

Whitmore, J.R. and Maker, C.J. 1985 *Intellectual giftedness in disabled persons* Pro-ed, Austin, TX

Willard-Holt, C. 1994 'Strategies for individualising instruction in regular classrooms' *Roeper Review* vol. 17, no. 1, pp. 43–5

Wilson, P. 1996 *Challenges and changes in policy and thinking in gifted education in Australia* Hawker Brownlow Education, Melbourne

Windecker-Nelson, E., Melson, G.F. and Moon, S.M. 1997 'Intellectually gifted pre-schoolers' perceived competence: relations to maternal attitudes, concerns, and support' *Gifted Child Quarterly* vol. 41, no. 4, pp. 133–44

Wingenbach, N. 1998 'The gifted-learning-disabled child: in need of an integrative education' in *The young gifted child: potential and promise, an anthology* ed. J.F. Smutny, Hampton Press, Cresskill, NJ

Winner, E. 1996 *Gifted children: myths and realities* Basic Books, New York

Wolery, M., Bailey, D.B. and Sugai, G.M. 1988 *Effective teaching: principles and procedures of applied behavior analysis with exceptional students* Allyn & Bacon, Boston, MA

Wolfle, J. 1989 'The gifted preschooler: developmentally different, but still 3 or 4 years old' *Young Children* vol. 44, no. 3, pp. 41–8

——1990 'Gifted preschoolers within the classroom' *Early Child Development and Care* vol. 63, pp. 83–93

——1991 'Underachieving gifted males: are we missing the boat?' *Roeper Review* vol. 13, no. 4, pp. 181–4

Worthen, B.R. and Spandel, V. 1991 'Putting the standardized test debate in perspective' *Educational Leadership* vol. 48, no. 5, pp. 65–9

Wragg, J. 1989 *Talk sense to yourself: a program for children and adolescents* ACER, Melbourne

Wright, L. and Borland, J.H. 1993 'Using early childhood developmental portfolios in the identification and education of young, economically disadvantaged, potentially gifted students' *Roeper Review* vol. 15, no. 4, pp. 205–10

Wright, L. and Coulianos, C. 1991 'A model program for precocious children: Hollingworth preschool' *Gifted Child Today* vol. 14, no. 5, pp. 24–9

Wright, P.B. and Leroux, J.A. 1997 'The self-concept of gifted adolescents in a congregated program' *Gifted Child Quarterly* vol. 41, no. 3, pp. 83–94

Yarborough, B.H. and Johnson, R.A. 1983 'Identifying the gifted: a theory-practice gap' *Gifted Child Quarterly* vol. 27, no. 3, pp. 135–8

Yewchuk, C.R. 1995a 'The "mad genius" controversy: implications for gifted education' *Journal for the Education of the Gifted* vol. 19, no. 1, pp. 3–29

——1995b 'Eminence and emotional stability: historical and contemporary views' *Gifted and Talented International* vol. 10, no. 2, pp. 52–5

BIBLIOGRAPHY

Yewchuk, C.R. and Lupart, J.L. 1993 'Gifted handicapped: a desultory duality' in *International handbook of research and development of giftedness and talent* eds K.A. Heller, F.J. Mönks & A.H. Passow, Pergamon Press, Oxford, UK

Yong, F.L. 1994 'Self-concepts, locus of control, and Machiavellianism of ethnically diverse middle school students who are gifted' *Roeper Review* vol. 16, no. 3, pp. 192–4

Young, M.E. 1992 *Counseling methods and techniques: an eclectic approach* Merrill, New York

Zentall, S.S. 1989 'Self-control training with hyperactive and impulsive children' in *Cognitive-behavioral psychology in the schools* eds J.N. Hughes & R.J. Hall, Guilford, New York

Zimmerman, M.A. and Arunkumar, R. 1994 'Resiliency research: implications for schools and policy' *Social Policy Report* vol. 8, no. 4, pp. 1–17

Zorman, R. 1997 'Eureka: the cross-cultural model for identification of hidden talent through enrichment' *Roeper Review* vol. 20, no. 1, pp. 54–61

INDEX